KT-421-981

SUPERMAN

PAST AND FUTURE

SUPERMAN CREATED BY
JERRY SIEGEL
AND JOE SHUSTER

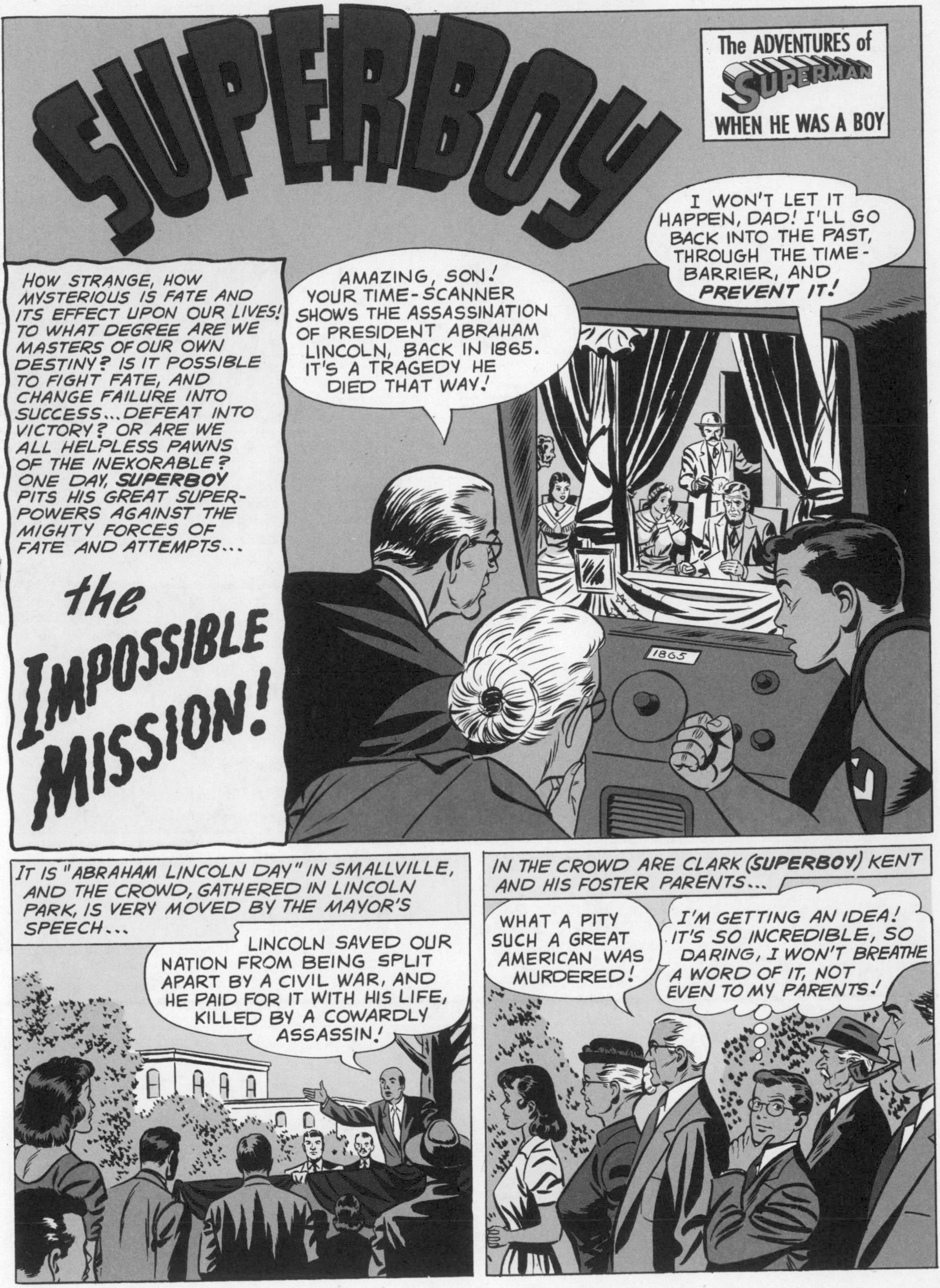
SUPERBOY
The ADVENTURES of SUPERMAN WHEN HE WAS A BOY
HOW STRANGE, HOW MYSTERIOUS IS FATE AND ITS EFFECT UPON OUR LIVES! TO WHAT DEGREE ARE WE MASTERS OF OUR OWN DESTINY? IS IT POSSIBLE TO FIGHT FATE, AND CHANGE FAILURE INTO SUCCESS...DEFEAT INTO VICTORY? OR ARE WE ALL HELPLESS PAWNS OF THE INEXORABLE? ONE DAY, SUPERBOY PITS HIS GREAT SUPER-POWERS AGAINST THE MIGHTY FORCES OF FATE AND ATTEMPTS...
the IMPOSSIBLE MISSION!
AMAZING, SON! YOUR TIME-SCANNER SHOWS THE ASSASSINATION OF PRESIDENT ABRAHAM LINCOLN, BACK IN 1865. IT'S A TRAGEDY HE DIED THAT WAY!
I WON'T LET IT HAPPEN, DAD! I'LL GO BACK INTO THE PAST, THROUGH THE TIME-BARRIER, AND PREVENT IT!
1865
IT IS "ABRAHAM LINCOLN DAY" IN SMALLVILLE, AND THE CROWD, GATHERED IN LINCOLN PARK, IS VERY MOVED BY THE MAYOR'S SPEECH...
LINCOLN SAVED OUR NATION FROM BEING SPLIT APART BY A CIVIL WAR, AND HE PAID FOR IT WITH HIS LIFE, KILLED BY A COWARDLY ASSASSIN!
IN THE CROWD ARE CLARK (SUPERBOY) KENT AND HIS FOSTER PARENTS...
WHAT A PITY SUCH A GREAT AMERICAN WAS MURDERED!
I'M GETTING AN IDEA! IT'S SO INCREDIBLE, SO DARING, I WON'T BREATHE A WORD OF IT, NOT EVEN TO MY PARENTS!

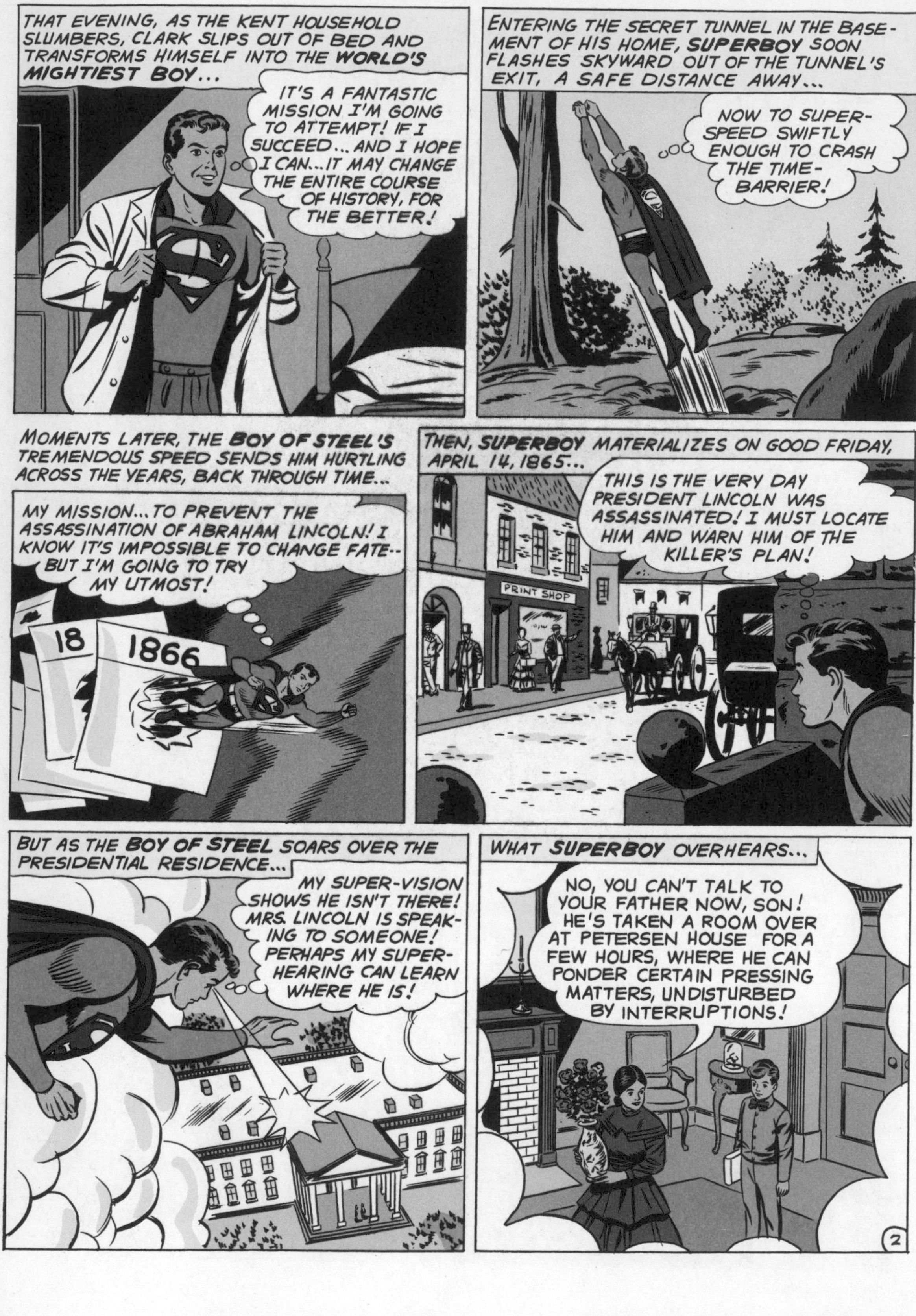

THAT EVENING, AS THE KENT HOUSEHOLD SLUMBERS, CLARK SLIPS OUT OF BED AND TRANSFORMS HIMSELF INTO THE WORLD'S MIGHTIEST BOY...
IT'S A FANTASTIC MISSION I'M GOING TO ATTEMPT! IF I SUCCEED... AND I HOPE I CAN... IT MAY CHANGE THE ENTIRE COURSE OF HISTORY, FOR THE BETTER!
ENTERING THE SECRET TUNNEL IN THE BASEMENT OF HIS HOME, SUPERBOY SOON FLASHES SKYWARD OUT OF THE TUNNEL'S EXIT, A SAFE DISTANCE AWAY...
NOW TO SUPER-SPEED SWIFTLY ENOUGH TO CRASH THE TIME-BARRIER!
MOMENTS LATER, THE BOY OF STEEL'S TREMENDOUS SPEED SENDS HIM HURTLING ACROSS THE YEARS, BACK THROUGH TIME...
MY MISSION... TO PREVENT THE ASSASSINATION OF ABRAHAM LINCOLN! I KNOW IT'S IMPOSSIBLE TO CHANGE FATE-- BUT I'M GOING TO TRY MY UTMOST!
18
1866
THEN, SUPERBOY MATERIALIZES ON GOOD FRIDAY, APRIL 14, 1865...
THIS IS THE VERY DAY PRESIDENT LINCOLN WAS ASSASSINATED! I MUST LOCATE HIM AND WARN HIM OF THE KILLER'S PLAN!
PRINT SHOP
BUT AS THE BOY OF STEEL SOARS OVER THE PRESIDENTIAL RESIDENCE...
MY SUPER-VISION SHOWS HE ISN'T THERE! MRS. LINCOLN IS SPEAKING TO SOMEONE! PERHAPS MY SUPER-HEARING CAN LEARN WHERE HE IS!
WHAT SUPERBOY OVERHEARS...
NO, YOU CAN'T TALK TO YOUR FATHER NOW, SON! HE'S TAKEN A ROOM OVER AT PETERSEN HOUSE FOR A FEW HOURS, WHERE HE CAN PONDER CERTAIN PRESSING MATTERS, UNDISTURBED BY INTERRUPTIONS!
2

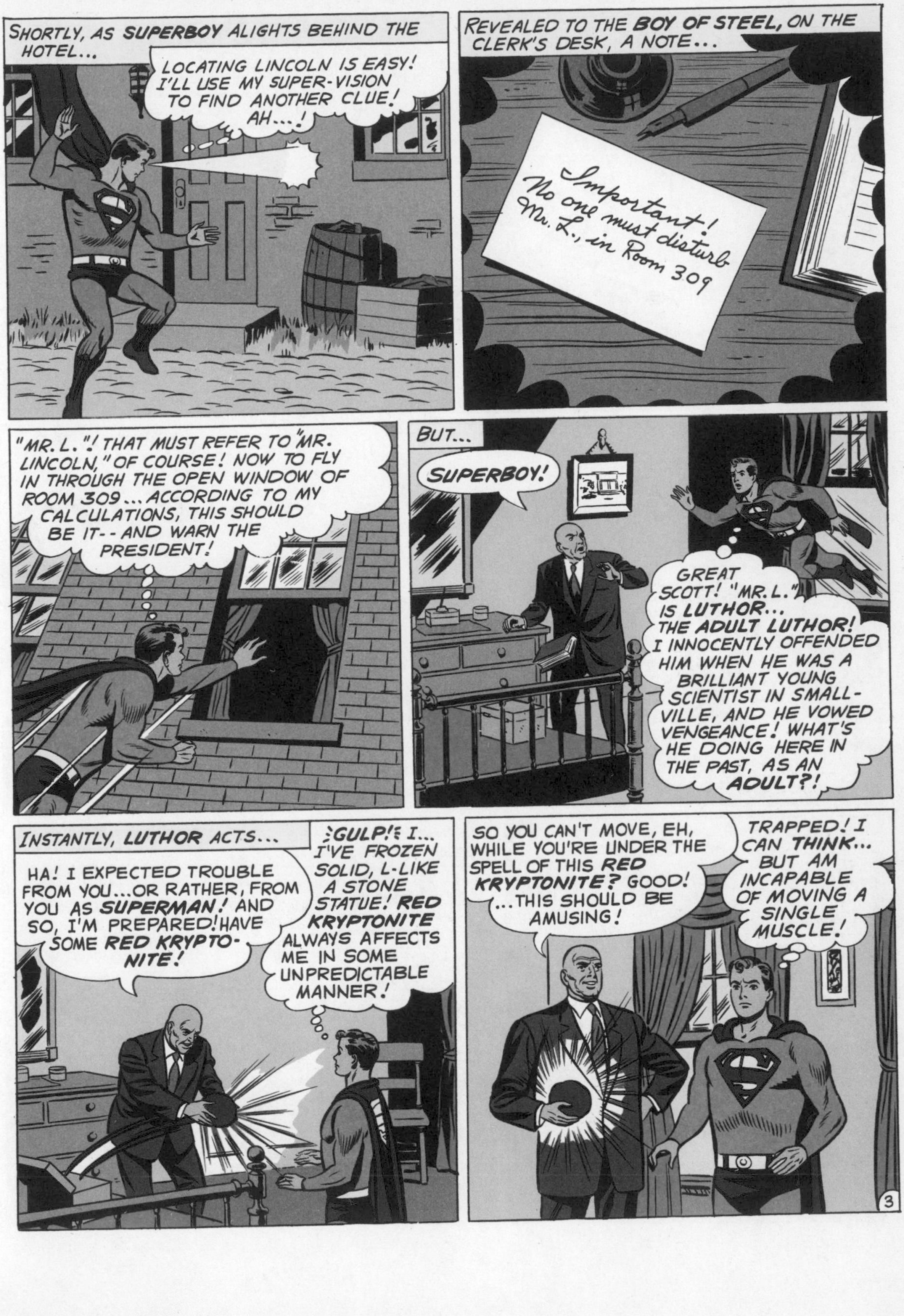

SHORTLY, AS SUPERBOY ALIGHTS BEHIND THE HOTEL...
LOCATING LINCOLN IS EASY! I'LL USE MY SUPER-VISION TO FIND ANOTHER CLUE! AH...!
REVEALED TO THE BOY OF STEEL, ON THE CLERK'S DESK, A NOTE...
Important! No one must disturb Mr. L., in Room 309
"MR. L."! THAT MUST REFER TO "MR. LINCOLN," OF COURSE! NOW TO FLY IN THROUGH THE OPEN WINDOW OF ROOM 309... ACCORDING TO MY CALCULATIONS, THIS SHOULD BE IT--AND WARN THE PRESIDENT!
BUT...
SUPERBOY!
GREAT SCOTT! "MR. L." IS LUTHOR... THE ADULT LUTHOR! I INNOCENTLY OFFENDED HIM WHEN HE WAS A BRILLIANT YOUNG SCIENTIST IN SMALL-VILLE, AND HE VOWED VENGEANCE! WHAT'S HE DOING HERE IN THE PAST, AS AN ADULT?!
INSTANTLY, LUTHOR ACTS...
HA! I EXPECTED TROUBLE FROM YOU...OR RATHER, FROM YOU AS SUPERMAN! AND SO, I'M PREPARED! HAVE SOME RED KRYPTO-NITE!
GULP! I... I'VE FROZEN SOLID, L-LIKE A STONE STATUE! RED KRYPTONITE ALWAYS AFFECTS ME IN SOME UNPREDICTABLE MANNER!
SO YOU CAN'T MOVE, EH, WHILE YOU'RE UNDER THE SPELL OF THIS RED KRYPTONITE? GOOD! ...THIS SHOULD BE AMUSING!
TRAPPED! I CAN THINK... BUT AM INCAPABLE OF MOVING A SINGLE MUSCLE!
3

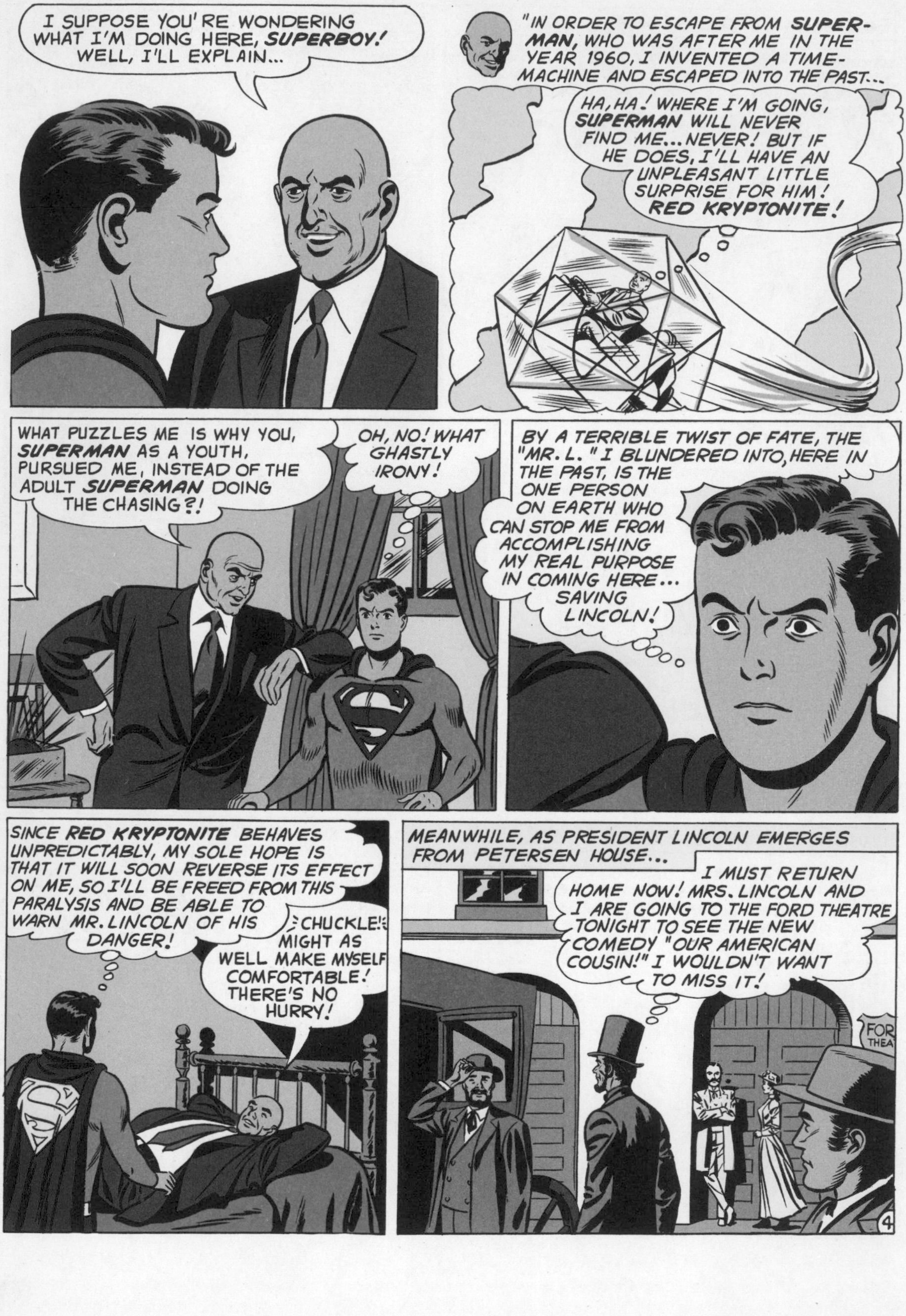
I SUPPOSE YOU'RE WONDERING WHAT I'M DOING HERE, SUPERBOY! WELL, I'LL EXPLAIN...
"IN ORDER TO ESCAPE FROM SUPERMAN, WHO WAS AFTER ME IN THE YEAR 1960, I INVENTED A TIME-MACHINE AND ESCAPED INTO THE PAST...
HA, HA! WHERE I'M GOING, SUPERMAN WILL NEVER FIND ME... NEVER! BUT IF HE DOES, I'LL HAVE AN UNPLEASANT LITTLE SURPRISE FOR HIM! RED KRYPTONITE!
WHAT PUZZLES ME IS WHY YOU, SUPERMAN AS A YOUTH, PURSUED ME, INSTEAD OF THE ADULT SUPERMAN DOING THE CHASING?!
OH, NO! WHAT GHASTLY IRONY!
BY A TERRIBLE TWIST OF FATE, THE "MR. L." I BLUNDERED INTO, HERE IN THE PAST, IS THE ONE PERSON ON EARTH WHO CAN STOP ME FROM ACCOMPLISHING MY REAL PURPOSE IN COMING HERE... SAVING LINCOLN!
SINCE RED KRYPTONITE BEHAVES UNPREDICTABLY, MY SOLE HOPE IS THAT IT WILL SOON REVERSE ITS EFFECT ON ME, SO I'LL BE FREED FROM THIS PARALYSIS AND BE ABLE TO WARN MR. LINCOLN OF HIS DANGER!
CHUCKLE! MIGHT AS WELL MAKE MYSELF COMFORTABLE! THERE'S NO HURRY!
MEANWHILE, AS PRESIDENT LINCOLN EMERGES FROM PETERSEN HOUSE...
I MUST RETURN HOME NOW! MRS. LINCOLN AND I ARE GOING TO THE FORD THEATRE TONIGHT TO SEE THE NEW COMEDY "OUR AMERICAN COUSIN!" I WOULDN'T WANT TO MISS IT!
FOR
THEA
4

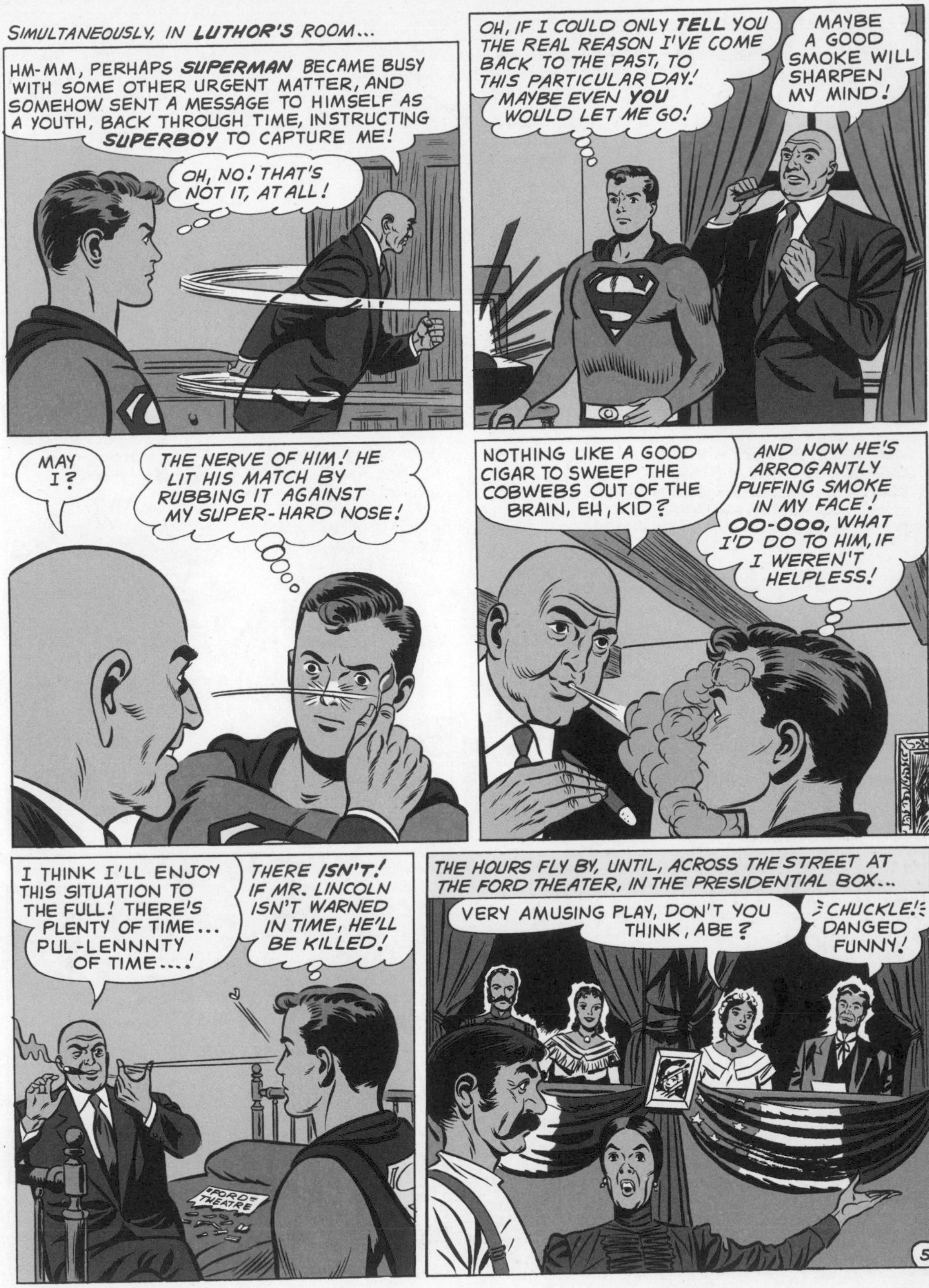
SIMULTANEOUSLY, IN LUTHOR'S ROOM...
HM-MM, PERHAPS SUPERMAN BECAME BUSY WITH SOME OTHER URGENT MATTER, AND SOMEHOW SENT A MESSAGE TO HIMSELF AS A YOUTH, BACK THROUGH TIME, INSTRUCTING SUPERBOY TO CAPTURE ME!
OH, NO! THAT'S NOT IT, AT ALL!
OH, IF I COULD ONLY TELL YOU THE REAL REASON I'VE COME BACK TO THE PAST, TO THIS PARTICULAR DAY! MAYBE EVEN YOU WOULD LET ME GO!
MAYBE A GOOD SMOKE WILL SHARPEN MY MIND!
MAY I?
THE NERVE OF HIM! HE LIT HIS MATCH BY RUBBING IT AGAINST MY SUPER-HARD NOSE!
NOTHING LIKE A GOOD CIGAR TO SWEEP THE COBWEBS OUT OF THE BRAIN, EH, KID?
AND NOW HE'S ARROGANTLY PUFFING SMOKE IN MY FACE! OO-OOO, WHAT I'D DO TO HIM, IF I WEREN'T HELPLESS!
I THINK I'LL ENJOY THIS SITUATION TO THE FULL! THERE'S PLENTY OF TIME... PUL-LENNNTY OF TIME...!
THERE ISN'T! IF MR. LINCOLN ISN'T WARNED IN TIME, HE'LL BE KILLED!
FORD THEATRE
THE HOURS FLY BY, UNTIL, ACROSS THE STREET AT THE FORD THEATER, IN THE PRESIDENTIAL BOX...
VERY AMUSING PLAY, DON'T YOU THINK, ABE?
CHUCKLE! DANGED FUNNY!
5

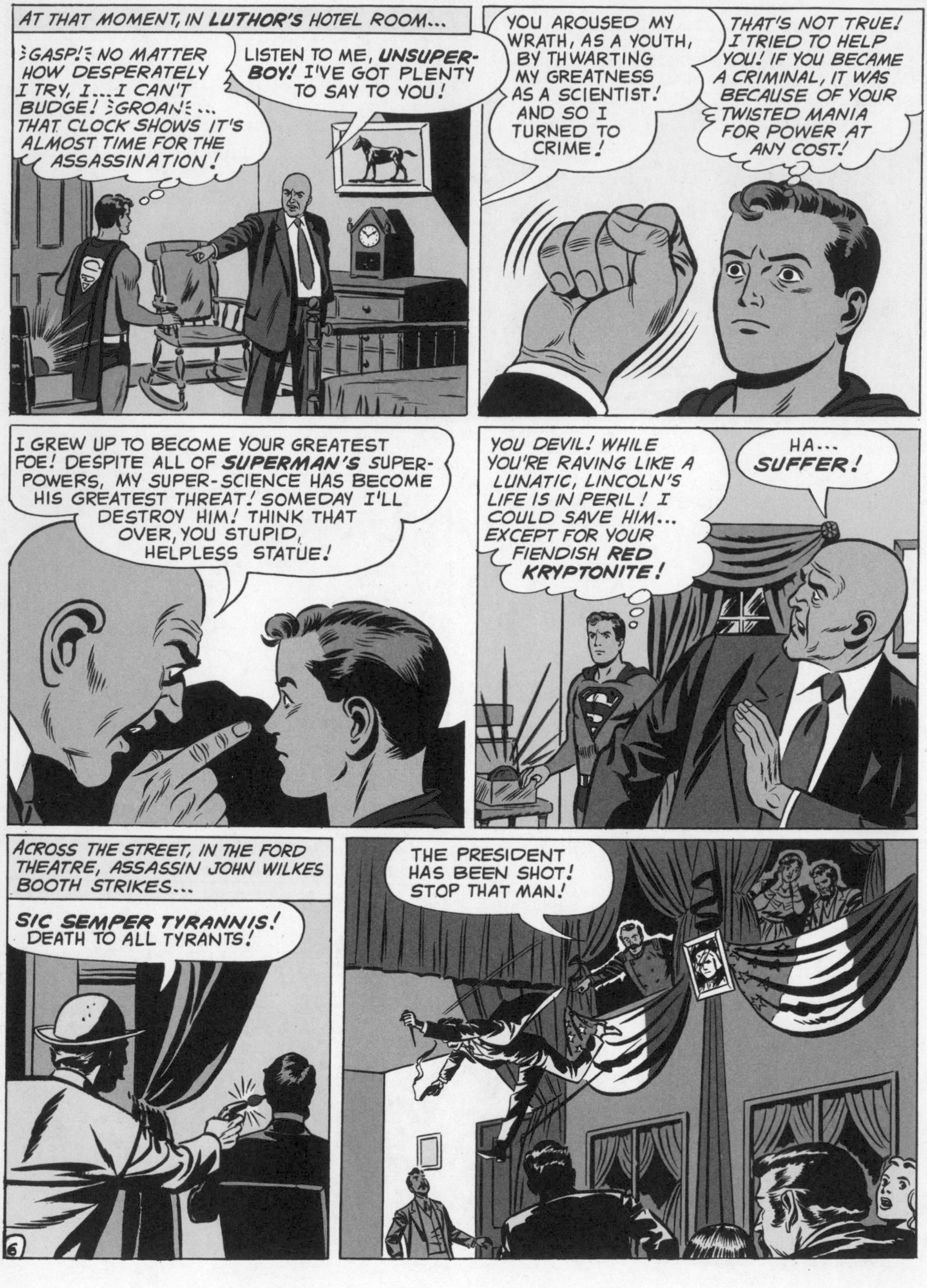
AT THAT MOMENT, IN LUTHOR'S HOTEL ROOM...
GASP! NO MATTER HOW DESPERATELY I TRY, I...I CAN'T BUDGE! GROAN! ... THAT CLOCK SHOWS IT'S ALMOST TIME FOR THE ASSASSINATION!
LISTEN TO ME, UNSUPER-BOY! I'VE GOT PLENTY TO SAY TO YOU!
YOU AROUSED MY WRATH, AS A YOUTH, BY THWARTING MY GREATNESS AS A SCIENTIST! AND SO I TURNED TO CRIME!
THAT'S NOT TRUE! I TRIED TO HELP YOU! IF YOU BECAME A CRIMINAL, IT WAS BECAUSE OF YOUR TWISTED MANIA FOR POWER AT ANY COST!
I GREW UP TO BECOME YOUR GREATEST FOE! DESPITE ALL OF SUPERMAN'S SUPER-POWERS, MY SUPER-SCIENCE HAS BECOME HIS GREATEST THREAT! SOMEDAY I'LL DESTROY HIM! THINK THAT OVER, YOU STUPID, HELPLESS STATUE!
YOU DEVIL! WHILE YOU'RE RAVING LIKE A LUNATIC, LINCOLN'S LIFE IS IN PERIL! I COULD SAVE HIM... EXCEPT FOR YOUR FIENDISH RED KRYPTONITE!
HA... SUFFER!
ACROSS THE STREET, IN THE FORD THEATRE, ASSASSIN JOHN WILKES BOOTH STRIKES...
SIC SEMPER TYRANNIS! DEATH TO ALL TYRANTS!
6
THE PRESIDENT HAS BEEN SHOT! STOP THAT MAN!

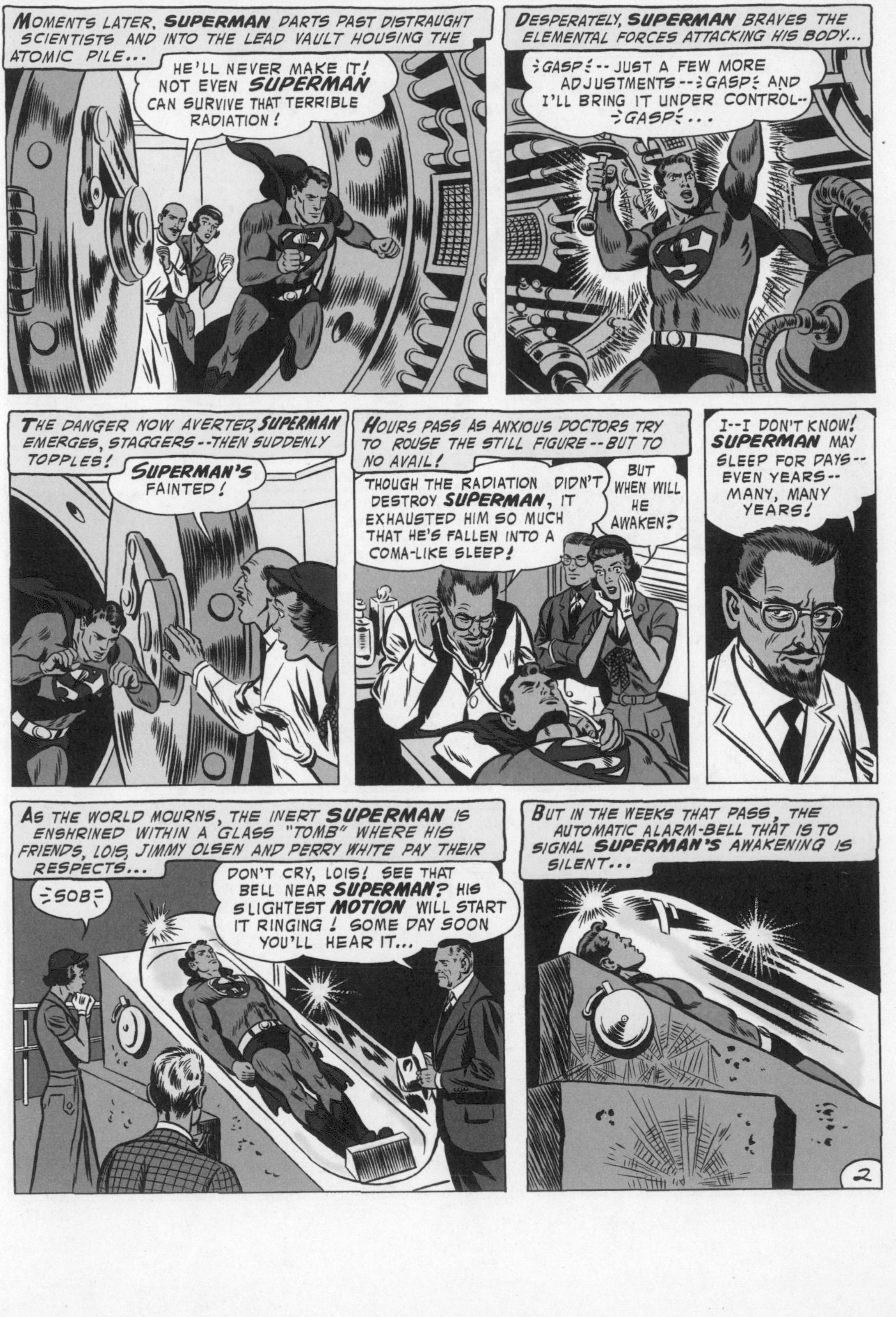
MOMENTS LATER, SUPERMAN DARTS PAST DISTRAUGHT SCIENTISTS AND INTO THE LEAD VAULT HOUSING THE ATOMIC PILE...
HE'LL NEVER MAKE IT! NOT EVEN SUPERMAN CAN SURVIVE THAT TERRIBLE RADIATION!
DESPERATELY, SUPERMAN BRAVES THE ELEMENTAL FORCES ATTACKING HIS BODY...
GASP -- JUST A FEW MORE ADJUSTMENTS -- GASP AND I'LL BRING IT UNDER CONTROL-- GASP...
THE DANGER NOW AVERTED, SUPERMAN EMERGES, STAGGERS--THEN SUDDENLY TOPPLES!
SUPERMAN'S FAINTED!
HOURS PASS AS ANXIOUS DOCTORS TRY TO ROUSE THE STILL FIGURE -- BUT TO NO AVAIL!
THOUGH THE RADIATION DIDN'T DESTROY SUPERMAN, IT EXHAUSTED HIM SO MUCH THAT HE'S FALLEN INTO A COMA-LIKE SLEEP!
BUT WHEN WILL HE AWAKEN?
I--I DON'T KNOW! SUPERMAN MAY SLEEP FOR DAYS -- EVEN YEARS -- MANY, MANY YEARS!
AS THE WORLD MOURNS, THE INERT SUPERMAN IS ENSHRINED WITHIN A GLASS "TOMB" WHERE HIS FRIENDS, LOIS, JIMMY OLSEN AND PERRY WHITE PAY THEIR RESPECTS...
SOB
DON'T CRY, LOIS! SEE THAT BELL NEAR SUPERMAN? HIS SLIGHTEST MOTION WILL START IT RINGING! SOME DAY SOON YOU'LL HEAR IT...
BUT IN THE WEEKS THAT PASS, THE AUTOMATIC ALARM-BELL THAT IS TO SIGNAL SUPERMAN'S AWAKENING IS SILENT...
2

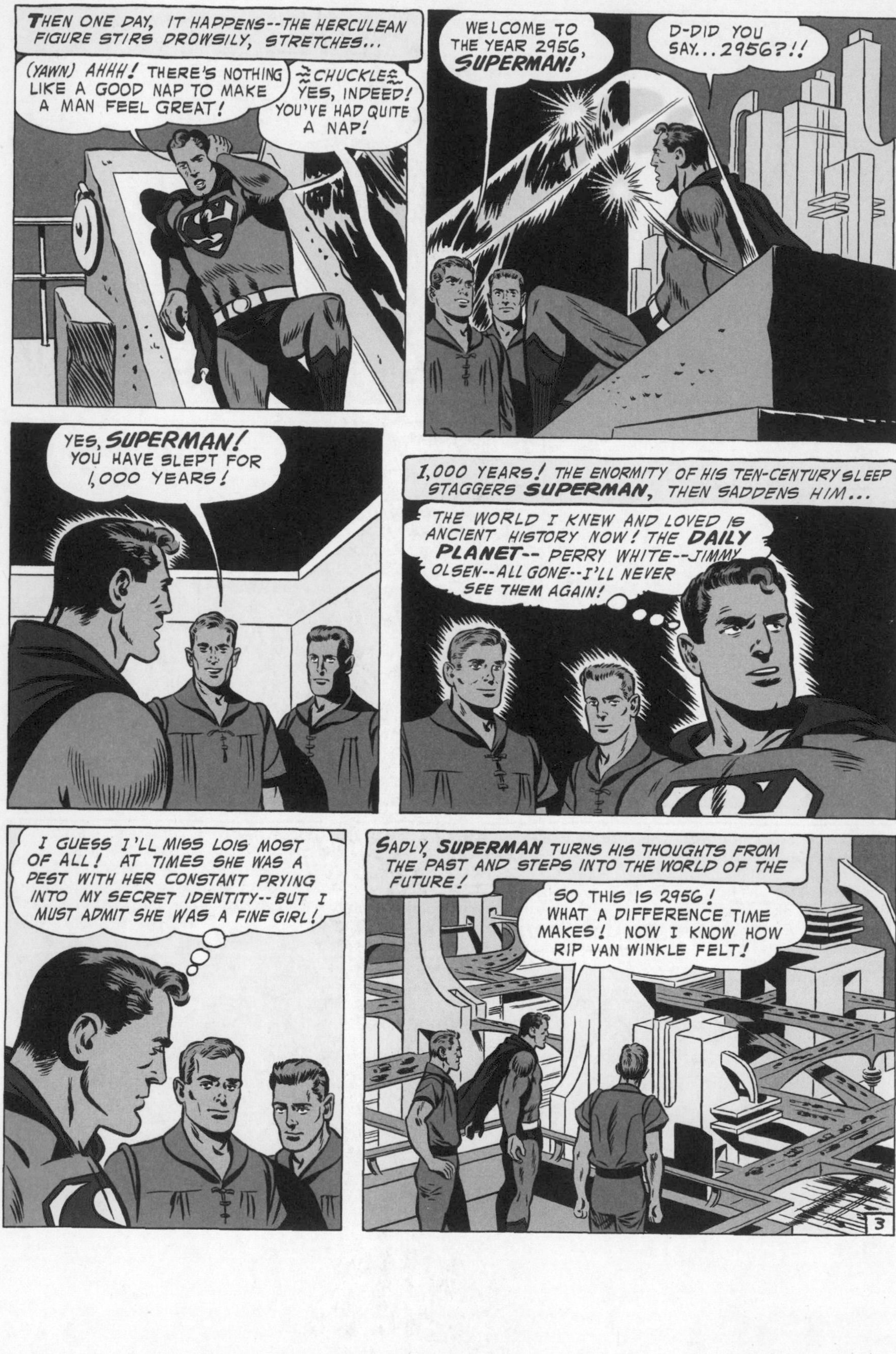
THEN ONE DAY, IT HAPPENS--THE HERCULEAN FIGURE STIRS DROWSILY, STRETCHES...
(YAWN) AHHH! THERE'S NOTHING LIKE A GOOD NAP TO MAKE A MAN FEEL GREAT!
CHUCKLE YES, INDEED! YOU'VE HAD QUITE A NAP!
WELCOME TO THE YEAR 2956, SUPERMAN!
D-DID YOU SAY...2956?!!
YES, SUPERMAN! YOU HAVE SLEPT FOR 1,000 YEARS!
1,000 YEARS! THE ENORMITY OF HIS TEN-CENTURY SLEEP STAGGERS SUPERMAN, THEN SADDENS HIM...
THE WORLD I KNEW AND LOVED IS ANCIENT HISTORY NOW! THE DAILY PLANET-- PERRY WHITE--JIMMY OLSEN--ALL GONE--I'LL NEVER SEE THEM AGAIN!
I GUESS I'LL MISS LOIS MOST OF ALL! AT TIMES SHE WAS A PEST WITH HER CONSTANT PRYING INTO MY SECRET IDENTITY-- BUT I MUST ADMIT SHE WAS A FINE GIRL!
SADLY, SUPERMAN TURNS HIS THOUGHTS FROM THE PAST AND STEPS INTO THE WORLD OF THE FUTURE!
SO THIS IS 2956! WHAT A DIFFERENCE TIME MAKES! NOW I KNOW HOW RIP VAN WINKLE FELT!
3

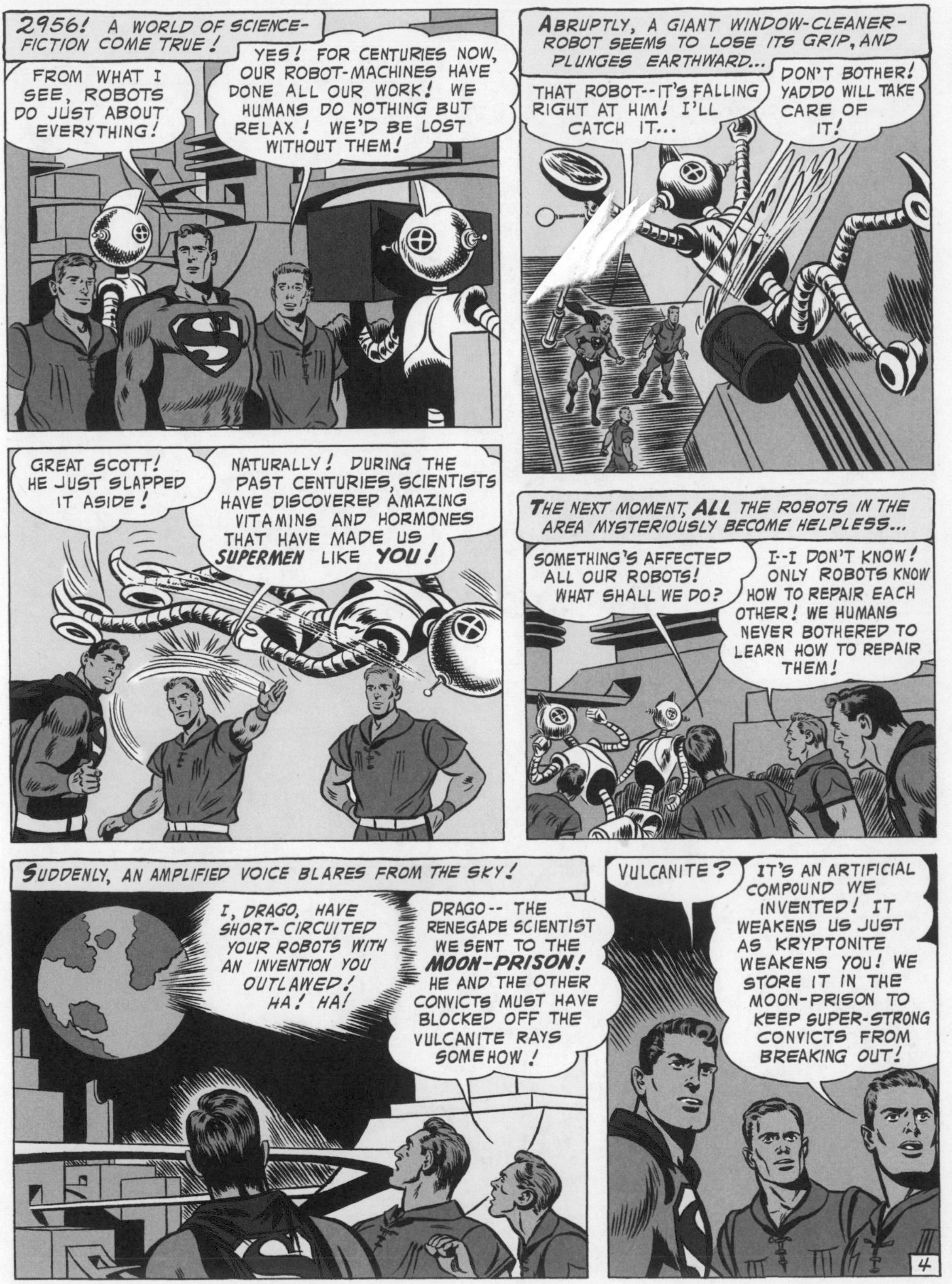
2956! A WORLD OF SCIENCE-FICTION COME TRUE!
FROM WHAT I SEE, ROBOTS DO JUST ABOUT EVERYTHING!
YES! FOR CENTURIES NOW, OUR ROBOT-MACHINES HAVE DONE ALL OUR WORK! WE HUMANS DO NOTHING BUT RELAX! WE'D BE LOST WITHOUT THEM!
ABRUPTLY, A GIANT WINDOW-CLEANER-ROBOT SEEMS TO LOSE ITS GRIP, AND PLUNGES EARTHWARD...
THAT ROBOT--IT'S FALLING RIGHT AT HIM! I'LL CATCH IT...
DON'T BOTHER! YADDO WILL TAKE CARE OF IT!
GREAT SCOTT! HE JUST SLAPPED IT ASIDE!
NATURALLY! DURING THE PAST CENTURIES, SCIENTISTS HAVE DISCOVERED AMAZING VITAMINS AND HORMONES THAT HAVE MADE US SUPERMEN LIKE YOU!
THE NEXT MOMENT, ALL THE ROBOTS IN THE AREA MYSTERIOUSLY BECOME HELPLESS...
SOMETHING'S AFFECTED ALL OUR ROBOTS! WHAT SHALL WE DO?
I--I DON'T KNOW! ONLY ROBOTS KNOW HOW TO REPAIR EACH OTHER! WE HUMANS NEVER BOTHERED TO LEARN HOW TO REPAIR THEM!
SUDDENLY, AN AMPLIFIED VOICE BLARES FROM THE SKY!
I, DRAGO, HAVE SHORT-CIRCUITED YOUR ROBOTS WITH AN INVENTION YOU OUTLAWED! HA! HA!
DRAGO-- THE RENEGADE SCIENTIST WE SENT TO THE MOON-PRISON! HE AND THE OTHER CONVICTS MUST HAVE BLOCKED OFF THE VULCANITE RAYS SOMEHOW!
VULCANITE?
IT'S AN ARTIFICIAL COMPOUND WE INVENTED! IT WEAKENS US JUST AS KRYPTONITE WEAKENS YOU! WE STORE IT IN THE MOON-PRISON TO KEEP SUPER-STRONG CONVICTS FROM BREAKING OUT!
4

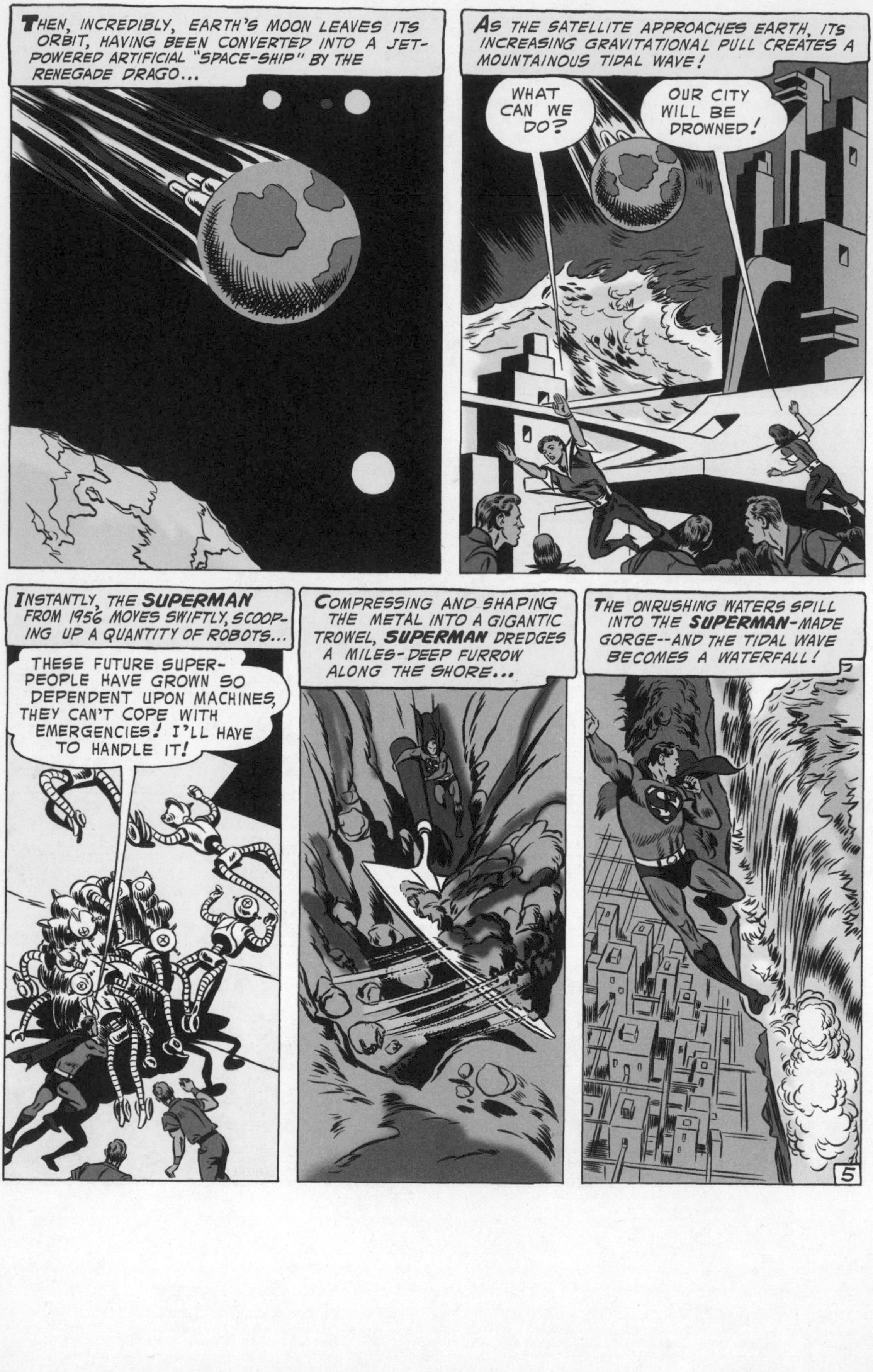
THEN, INCREDIBLY, EARTH'S MOON LEAVES ITS ORBIT, HAVING BEEN CONVERTED INTO A JET-POWERED ARTIFICIAL "SPACE-SHIP" BY THE RENEGADE DRAGO...
AS THE SATELLITE APPROACHES EARTH, ITS INCREASING GRAVITATIONAL PULL CREATES A MOUNTAINOUS TIDAL WAVE!
WHAT CAN WE DO?
OUR CITY WILL BE DROWNED!
INSTANTLY, THE SUPERMAN FROM 1956 MOVES SWIFTLY, SCOOPING UP A QUANTITY OF ROBOTS...
THESE FUTURE SUPER-PEOPLE HAVE GROWN SO DEPENDENT UPON MACHINES, THEY CAN'T COPE WITH EMERGENCIES! I'LL HAVE TO HANDLE IT!
COMPRESSING AND SHAPING THE METAL INTO A GIGANTIC TROWEL, SUPERMAN DREDGES A MILES-DEEP FURROW ALONG THE SHORE...
THE ONRUSHING WATERS SPILL INTO THE SUPERMAN-MADE GORGE--AND THE TIDAL WAVE BECOMES A WATERFALL!
5

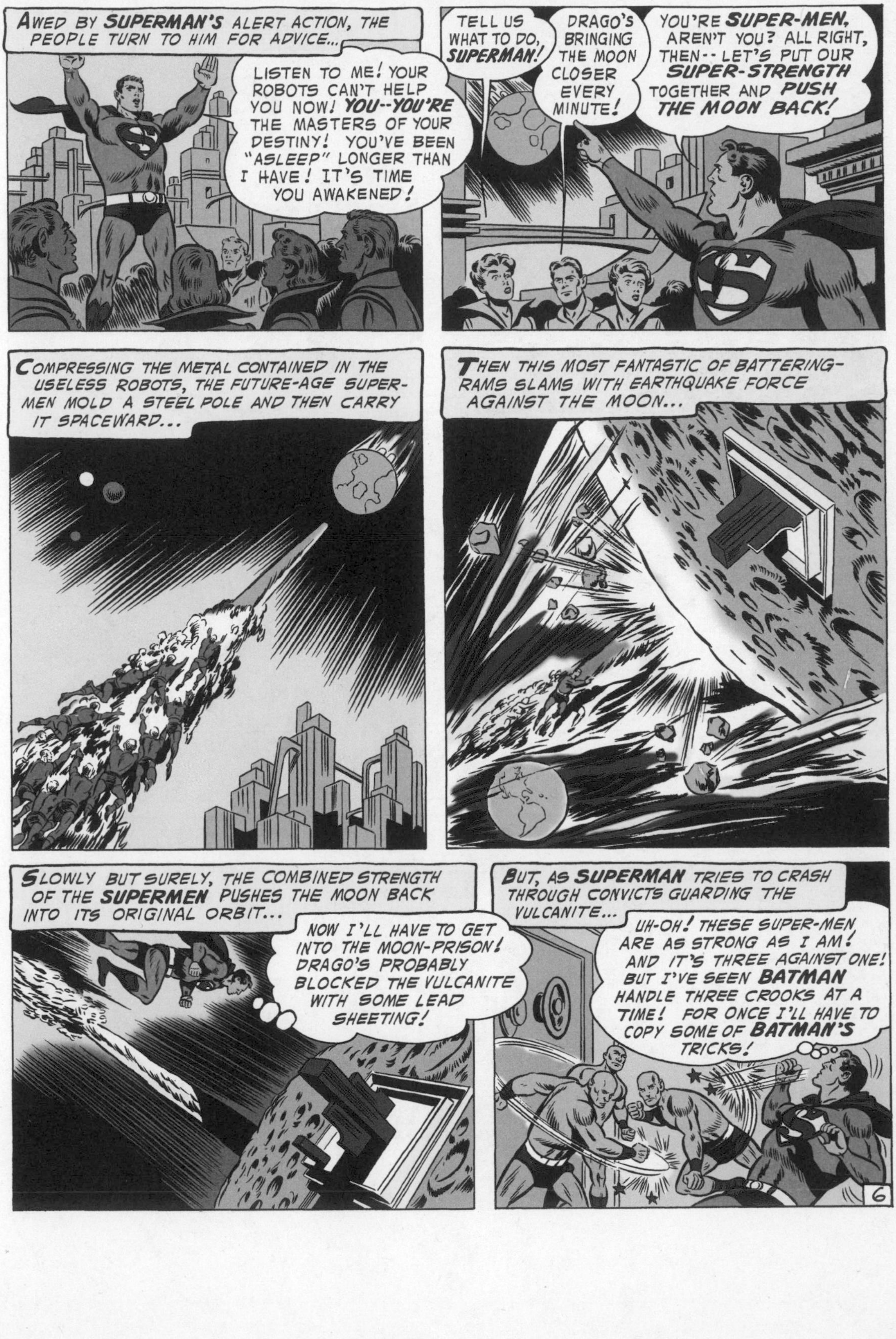
AWED BY SUPERMAN'S ALERT ACTION, THE PEOPLE TURN TO HIM FOR ADVICE...
LISTEN TO ME! YOUR ROBOTS CAN'T HELP YOU NOW! YOU--YOU'RE THE MASTERS OF YOUR DESTINY! YOU'VE BEEN "ASLEEP" LONGER THAN I HAVE! IT'S TIME YOU AWAKENED!
TELL US WHAT TO DO, SUPERMAN!
DRAGO'S BRINGING THE MOON CLOSER EVERY MINUTE!
YOU'RE SUPER-MEN, AREN'T YOU? ALL RIGHT, THEN--LET'S PUT OUR SUPER-STRENGTH TOGETHER AND PUSH THE MOON BACK!
COMPRESSING THE METAL CONTAINED IN THE USELESS ROBOTS, THE FUTURE-AGE SUPER-MEN MOLD A STEEL POLE AND THEN CARRY IT SPACEWARD...
THEN THIS MOST FANTASTIC OF BATTERING-RAMS SLAMS WITH EARTHQUAKE FORCE AGAINST THE MOON...
SLOWLY BUT SURELY, THE COMBINED STRENGTH OF THE SUPERMEN PUSHES THE MOON BACK INTO ITS ORIGINAL ORBIT...
NOW I'LL HAVE TO GET INTO THE MOON-PRISON! DRAGO'S PROBABLY BLOCKED THE VULCANITE WITH SOME LEAD SHEETING!
BUT, AS SUPERMAN TRIES TO CRASH THROUGH CONVICTS GUARDING THE VULCANITE...
UH-OH! THESE SUPER-MEN ARE AS STRONG AS I AM! AND IT'S THREE AGAINST ONE! BUT I'VE SEEN BATMAN HANDLE THREE CROOKS AT A TIME! FOR ONCE I'LL HAVE TO COPY SOME OF BATMAN'S TRICKS!
6

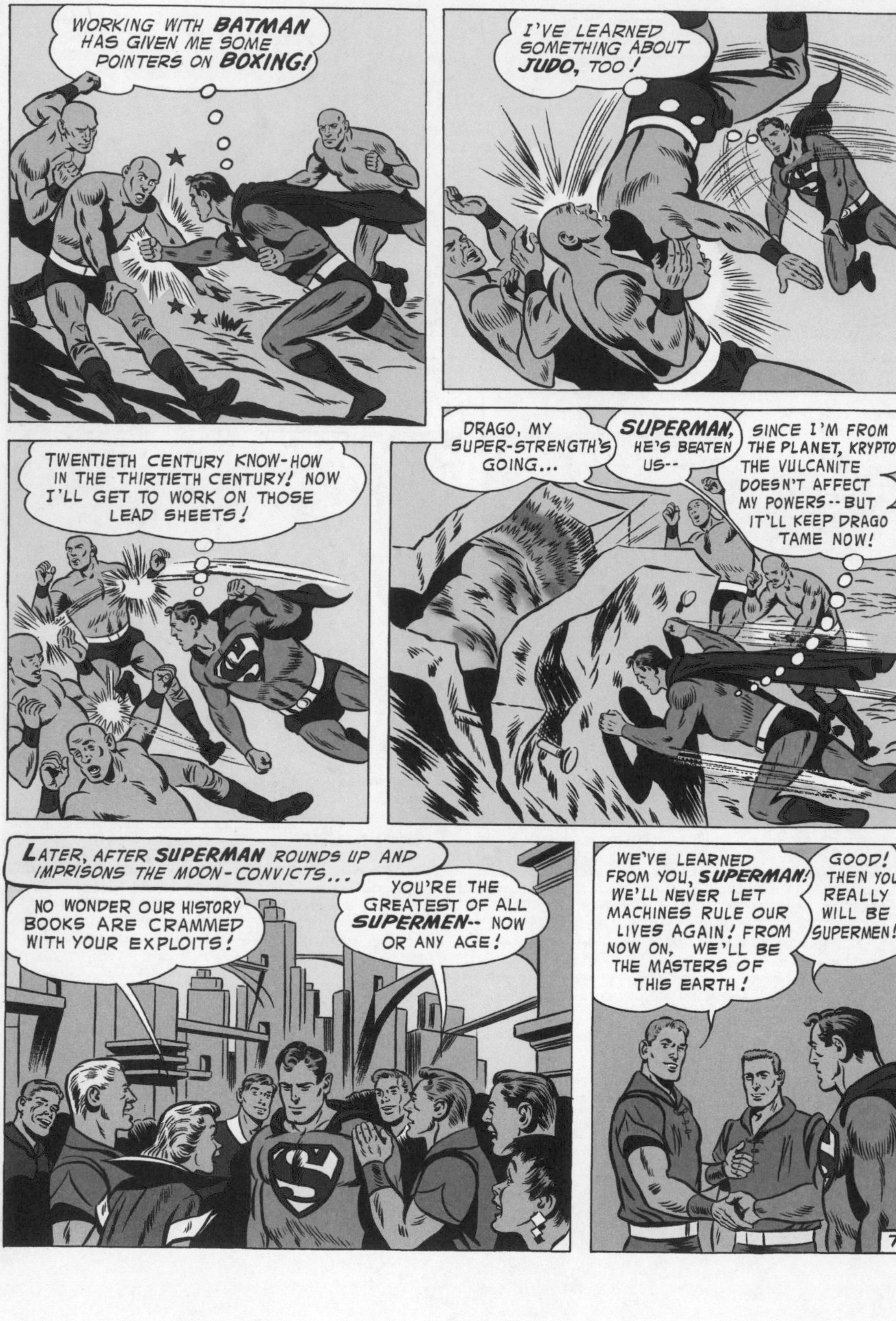
WORKING WITH BATMAN HAS GIVEN ME SOME POINTERS ON BOXING!
I'VE LEARNED SOMETHING ABOUT JUDO, TOO!
TWENTIETH CENTURY KNOW-HOW IN THE THIRTIETH CENTURY! NOW I'LL GET TO WORK ON THOSE LEAD SHEETS!
DRAGO, MY SUPER-STRENGTH'S GOING...
SUPERMAN, HE'S BEATEN US--
SINCE I'M FROM THE PLANET, KRYPTON, THE VULCANITE DOESN'T AFFECT MY POWERS--BUT IT'LL KEEP DRAGO TAME NOW!
LATER, AFTER SUPERMAN ROUNDS UP AND IMPRISONS THE MOON-CONVICTS...
NO WONDER OUR HISTORY BOOKS ARE CRAMMED WITH YOUR EXPLOITS!
YOU'RE THE GREATEST OF ALL SUPERMEN-- NOW OR ANY AGE!
WE'VE LEARNED FROM YOU, SUPERMAN! WE'LL NEVER LET MACHINES RULE OUR LIVES AGAIN! FROM NOW ON, WE'LL BE THE MASTERS OF THIS EARTH!
GOOD! THEN YOU REALLY WILL BE SUPERMEN!
7

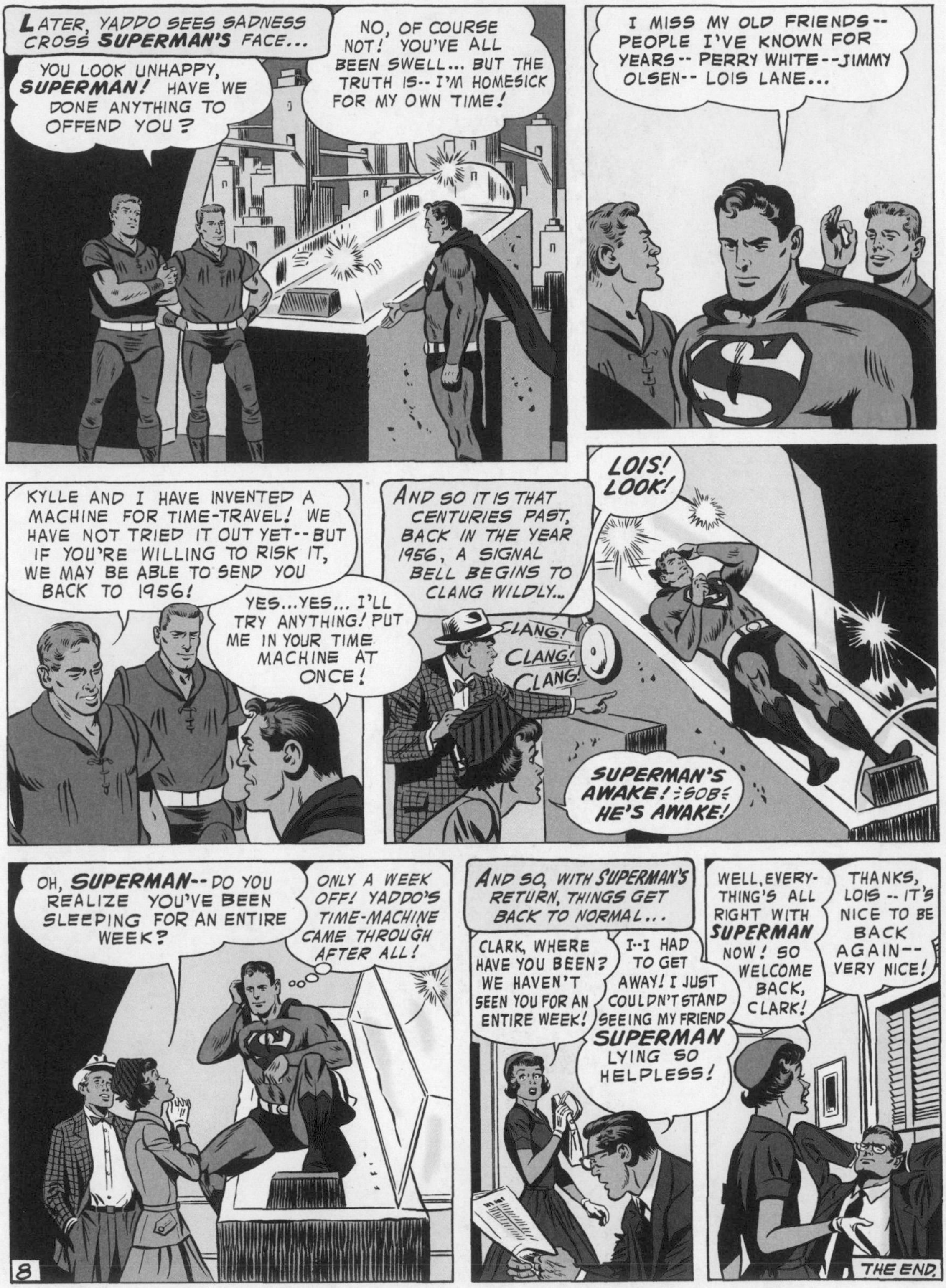
LATER, YADDO SEES SADNESS CROSS SUPERMAN'S FACE...
YOU LOOK UNHAPPY, SUPERMAN! HAVE WE DONE ANYTHING TO OFFEND YOU?
NO, OF COURSE NOT! YOU'VE ALL BEEN SWELL... BUT THE TRUTH IS-- I'M HOMESICK FOR MY OWN TIME!
I MISS MY OLD FRIENDS-- PEOPLE I'VE KNOWN FOR YEARS-- PERRY WHITE--JIMMY OLSEN-- LOIS LANE...
KYLLE AND I HAVE INVENTED A MACHINE FOR TIME-TRAVEL! WE HAVE NOT TRIED IT OUT YET--BUT IF YOU'RE WILLING TO RISK IT, WE MAY BE ABLE TO SEND YOU BACK TO 1956!
YES...YES... I'LL TRY ANYTHING! PUT ME IN YOUR TIME MACHINE AT ONCE!
AND SO IT IS THAT CENTURIES PAST, BACK IN THE YEAR 1956, A SIGNAL BELL BEGINS TO CLANG WILDLY...
CLANG! CLANG! CLANG!
LOIS! LOOK!
SUPERMAN'S AWAKE! SOB HE'S AWAKE!
OH, SUPERMAN-- DO YOU REALIZE YOU'VE BEEN SLEEPING FOR AN ENTIRE WEEK?
ONLY A WEEK OFF! YADDO'S TIME-MACHINE CAME THROUGH AFTER ALL!
8
AND SO, WITH SUPERMAN'S RETURN, THINGS GET BACK TO NORMAL...
CLARK, WHERE HAVE YOU BEEN? WE HAVEN'T SEEN YOU FOR AN ENTIRE WEEK!
I--I HAD TO GET AWAY! I JUST COULDN'T STAND SEEING MY FRIEND SUPERMAN LYING SO HELPLESS!
WELL, EVERYTHING'S ALL RIGHT WITH SUPERMAN NOW! SO WELCOME BACK, CLARK!
THANKS, LOIS -- IT'S NICE TO BE BACK AGAIN-- VERY NICE!
THE END.

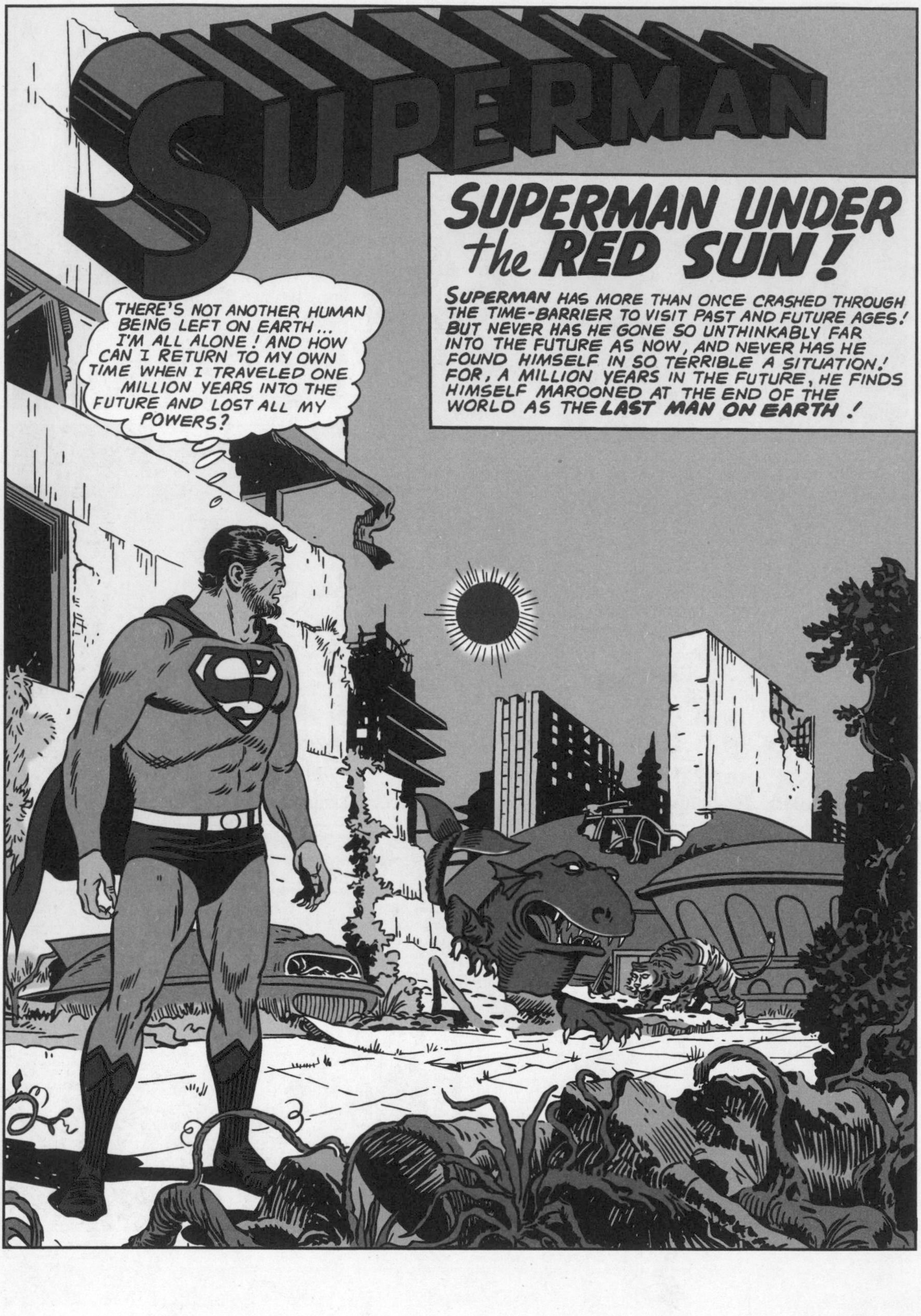
SUPERMAN
SUPERMAN UNDER the RED SUN!
SUPERMAN HAS MORE THAN ONCE CRASHED THROUGH THE TIME-BARRIER TO VISIT PAST AND FUTURE AGES! BUT NEVER HAS HE GONE SO UNTHINKABLY FAR INTO THE FUTURE AS NOW, AND NEVER HAS HE FOUND HIMSELF IN SO TERRIBLE A SITUATION! FOR, A MILLION YEARS IN THE FUTURE, HE FINDS HIMSELF MAROONED AT THE END OF THE WORLD AS THE LAST MAN ON EARTH!
THERE'S NOT ANOTHER HUMAN BEING LEFT ON EARTH... I'M ALL ALONE! AND HOW CAN I RETURN TO MY OWN TIME WHEN I TRAVELED ONE MILLION YEARS INTO THE FUTURE AND LOST ALL MY POWERS?

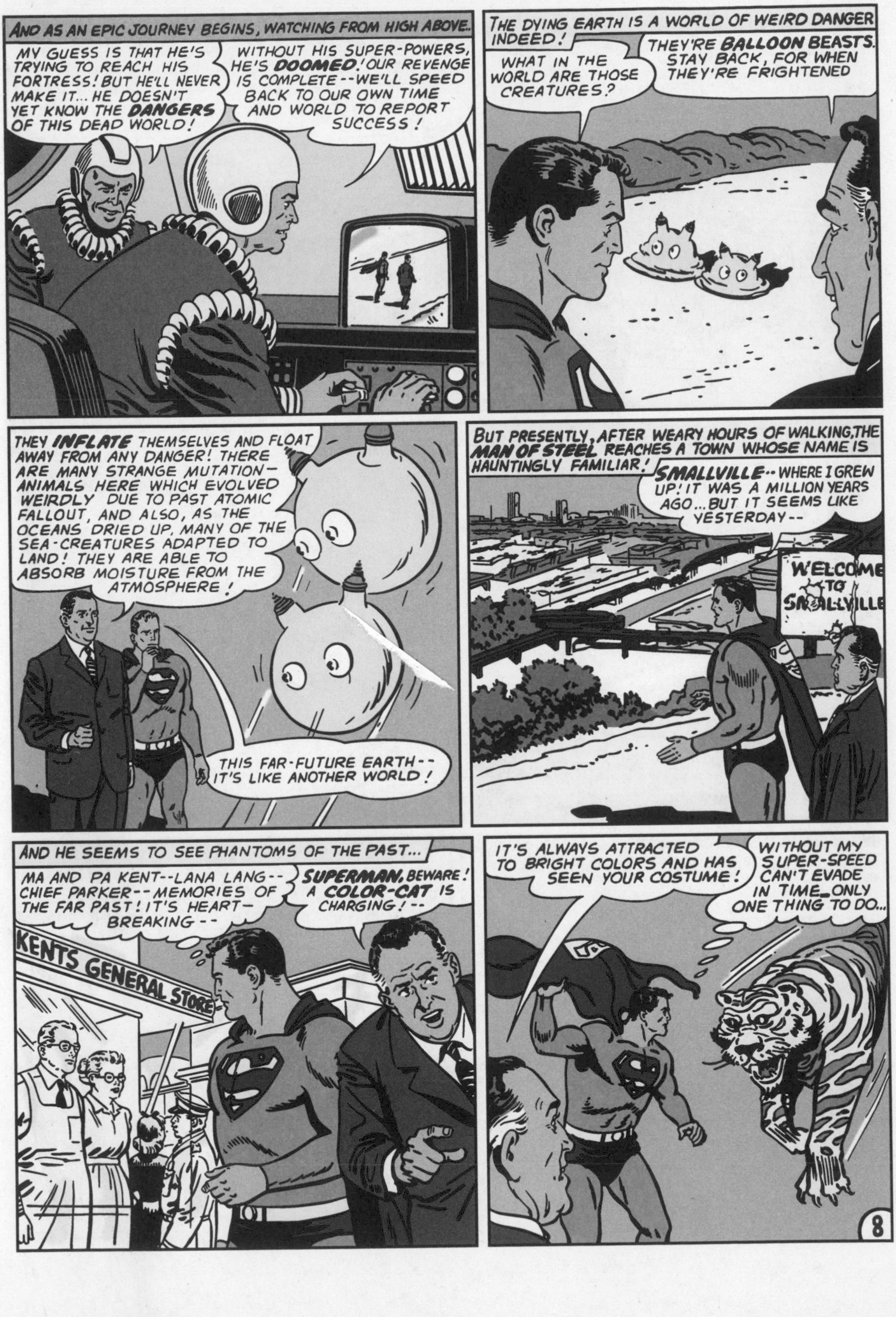
AND AS AN EPIC JOURNEY BEGINS, WATCHING FROM HIGH ABOVE..
MY GUESS IS THAT HE'S TRYING TO REACH HIS FORTRESS! BUT HE'LL NEVER MAKE IT... HE DOESN'T YET KNOW THE DANGERS OF THIS DEAD WORLD!
WITHOUT HIS SUPER-POWERS, HE'S DOOMED! OUR REVENGE IS COMPLETE--WE'LL SPEED BACK TO OUR OWN TIME AND WORLD TO REPORT SUCCESS!
THE DYING EARTH IS A WORLD OF WEIRD DANGER INDEED!
WHAT IN THE WORLD ARE THOSE CREATURES?
THEY'RE BALLOON BEASTS. STAY BACK, FOR WHEN THEY'RE FRIGHTENED
THEY INFLATE THEMSELVES AND FLOAT AWAY FROM ANY DANGER! THERE ARE MANY STRANGE MUTATION-ANIMALS HERE WHICH EVOLVED WEIRDLY DUE TO PAST ATOMIC FALLOUT, AND ALSO, AS THE OCEANS DRIED UP, MANY OF THE SEA-CREATURES ADAPTED TO LAND! THEY ARE ABLE TO ABSORB MOISTURE FROM THE ATMOSPHERE!
THIS FAR-FUTURE EARTH--IT'S LIKE ANOTHER WORLD!
BUT PRESENTLY, AFTER WEARY HOURS OF WALKING, THE MAN OF STEEL REACHES A TOWN WHOSE NAME IS HAUNTINGLY FAMILIAR!
SMALLVILLE--WHERE I GREW UP! IT WAS A MILLION YEARS AGO... BUT IT SEEMS LIKE YESTERDAY--
WELCOME TO SMALLVILLE
AND HE SEEMS TO SEE PHANTOMS OF THE PAST...
MA AND PA KENT--LANA LANG--CHIEF PARKER--MEMORIES OF THE FAR PAST! IT'S HEART-BREAKING--
SUPERMAN, BEWARE! A COLOR-CAT IS CHARGING!--
KENTS GENERAL STORE
IT'S ALWAYS ATTRACTED TO BRIGHT COLORS AND HAS SEEN YOUR COSTUME!
WITHOUT MY SUPER-SPEED CAN'T EVADE IN TIME_ONLY ONE THING TO DO...
8

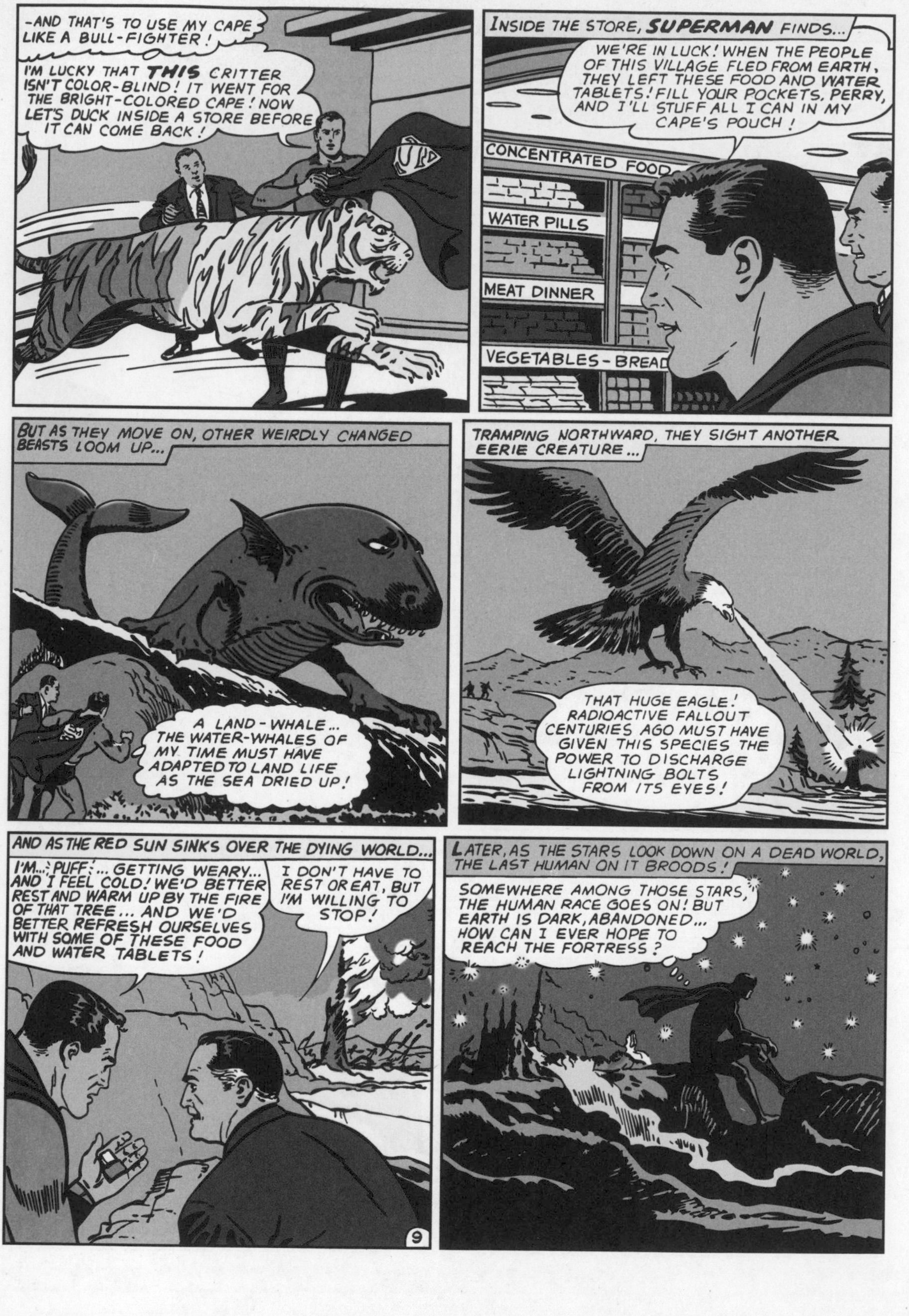

-AND THAT'S TO USE MY CAPE LIKE A BULL-FIGHTER!
I'M LUCKY THAT THIS CRITTER ISN'T COLOR-BLIND! IT WENT FOR THE BRIGHT-COLORED CAPE! NOW LET'S DUCK INSIDE A STORE BEFORE IT CAN COME BACK!
INSIDE THE STORE, SUPERMAN FINDS...
WE'RE IN LUCK! WHEN THE PEOPLE OF THIS VILLAGE FLED FROM EARTH, THEY LEFT THESE FOOD AND WATER TABLETS! FILL YOUR POCKETS, PERRY, AND I'LL STUFF ALL I CAN IN MY CAPE'S POUCH!
CONCENTRATED FOOD
WATER PILLS
MEAT DINNER
VEGETABLES-BREAD
BUT AS THEY MOVE ON, OTHER WEIRDLY CHANGED BEASTS LOOM UP...
A LAND-WHALE... THE WATER-WHALES OF MY TIME MUST HAVE ADAPTED TO LAND LIFE AS THE SEA DRIED UP!
TRAMPING NORTHWARD, THEY SIGHT ANOTHER EERIE CREATURE...
THAT HUGE EAGLE! RADIOACTIVE FALLOUT CENTURIES AGO MUST HAVE GIVEN THIS SPECIES THE POWER TO DISCHARGE LIGHTNING BOLTS FROM ITS EYES!
AND AS THE RED SUN SINKS OVER THE DYING WORLD...
I'M... PUFF!... GETTING WEARY... AND I FEEL COLD! WE'D BETTER REST AND WARM UP BY THE FIRE OF THAT TREE... AND WE'D BETTER REFRESH OURSELVES WITH SOME OF THESE FOOD AND WATER TABLETS!
I DON'T HAVE TO REST OR EAT, BUT I'M WILLING TO STOP!
9
LATER, AS THE STARS LOOK DOWN ON A DEAD WORLD, THE LAST HUMAN ON IT BROODS!
SOMEWHERE AMONG THOSE STARS, THE HUMAN RACE GOES ON! BUT EARTH IS DARK, ABANDONED... HOW CAN I EVER HOPE TO REACH THE FORTRESS?

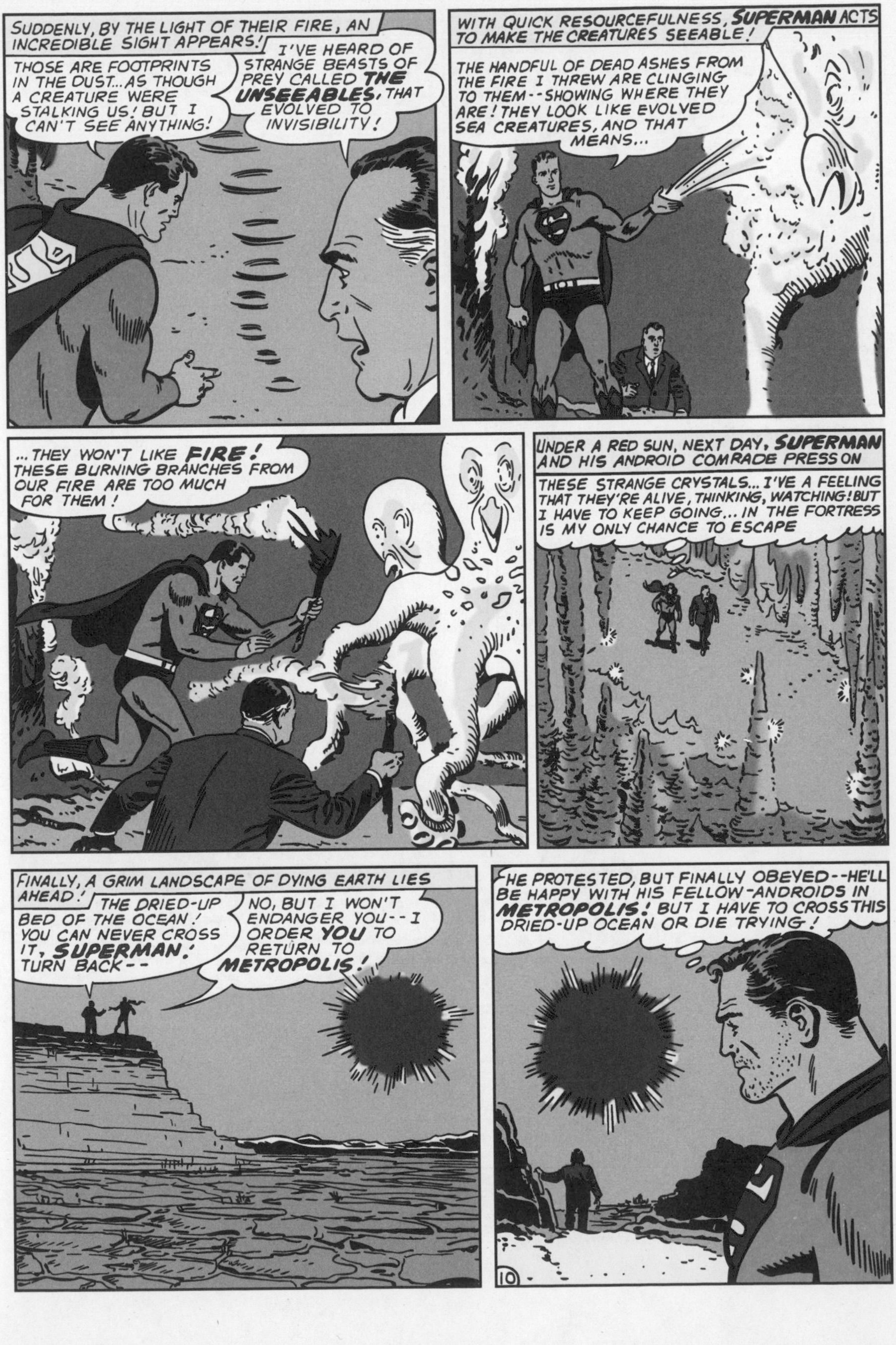

SUDDENLY, BY THE LIGHT OF THEIR FIRE, AN INCREDIBLE SIGHT APPEARS!
THOSE ARE FOOTPRINTS IN THE DUST...AS THOUGH A CREATURE WERE STALKING US! BUT I CAN'T SEE ANYTHING!
I'VE HEARD OF STRANGE BEASTS OF PREY CALLED THE UNSEEABLES, THAT EVOLVED TO INVISIBILITY!
WITH QUICK RESOURCEFULNESS, SUPERMAN ACTS TO MAKE THE CREATURES SEEABLE!
THE HANDFUL OF DEAD ASHES FROM THE FIRE I THREW ARE CLINGING TO THEM--SHOWING WHERE THEY ARE! THEY LOOK LIKE EVOLVED SEA CREATURES, AND THAT MEANS...
...THEY WON'T LIKE FIRE! THESE BURNING BRANCHES FROM OUR FIRE ARE TOO MUCH FOR THEM!
UNDER A RED SUN, NEXT DAY, SUPERMAN AND HIS ANDROID COMRADE PRESS ON
THESE STRANGE CRYSTALS... I'VE A FEELING THAT THEY'RE ALIVE, THINKING, WATCHING! BUT I HAVE TO KEEP GOING... IN THE FORTRESS IS MY ONLY CHANCE TO ESCAPE
FINALLY, A GRIM LANDSCAPE OF DYING EARTH LIES AHEAD!
THE DRIED-UP BED OF THE OCEAN! YOU CAN NEVER CROSS IT, SUPERMAN! TURN BACK--
NO, BUT I WON'T ENDANGER YOU--I ORDER YOU TO RETURN TO METROPOLIS!
HE PROTESTED, BUT FINALLY OBEYED--HE'LL BE HAPPY WITH HIS FELLOW-ANDROIDS IN METROPOLIS! BUT I HAVE TO CROSS THIS DRIED-UP OCEAN OR DIE TRYING!
10

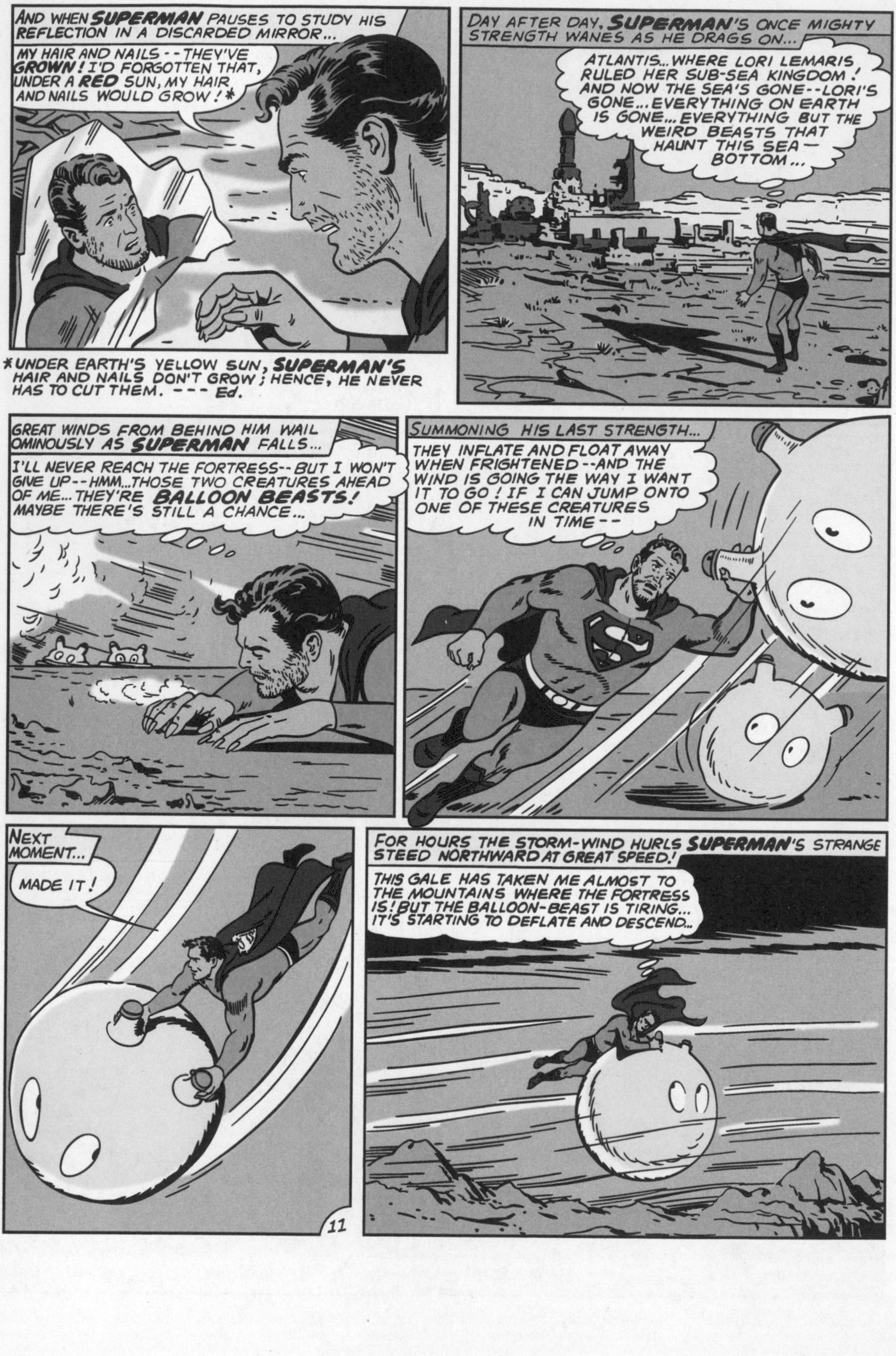
AND WHEN SUPERMAN PAUSES TO STUDY HIS REFLECTION IN A DISCARDED MIRROR...
MY HAIR AND NAILS--THEY'VE GROWN! I'D FORGOTTEN THAT, UNDER A RED SUN, MY HAIR AND NAILS WOULD GROW!*
*UNDER EARTH'S YELLOW SUN, SUPERMAN'S HAIR AND NAILS DON'T GROW; HENCE, HE NEVER HAS TO CUT THEM. --- Ed.
DAY AFTER DAY, SUPERMAN'S ONCE MIGHTY STRENGTH WANES AS HE DRAGS ON...
ATLANTIS... WHERE LORI LEMARIS RULED HER SUB-SEA KINGDOM! AND NOW THE SEA'S GONE--LORI'S GONE... EVERYTHING ON EARTH IS GONE... EVERYTHING BUT THE WEIRD BEASTS THAT HAUNT THIS SEA-BOTTOM...
GREAT WINDS FROM BEHIND HIM WAIL OMINOUSLY AS SUPERMAN FALLS...
I'LL NEVER REACH THE FORTRESS--BUT I WON'T GIVE UP--HMM...THOSE TWO CREATURES AHEAD OF ME... THEY'RE BALLOON BEASTS! MAYBE THERE'S STILL A CHANCE...
SUMMONING HIS LAST STRENGTH...
THEY INFLATE AND FLOAT AWAY WHEN FRIGHTENED--AND THE WIND IS GOING THE WAY I WANT IT TO GO! IF I CAN JUMP ONTO ONE OF THESE CREATURES IN TIME--
NEXT MOMENT...
MADE IT!
11
FOR HOURS THE STORM-WIND HURLS SUPERMAN'S STRANGE STEED NORTHWARD AT GREAT SPEED!
THIS GALE HAS TAKEN ME ALMOST TO THE MOUNTAINS WHERE THE FORTRESS IS! BUT THE BALLOON-BEAST IS TIRING... IT'S STARTING TO DEFLATE AND DESCEND...

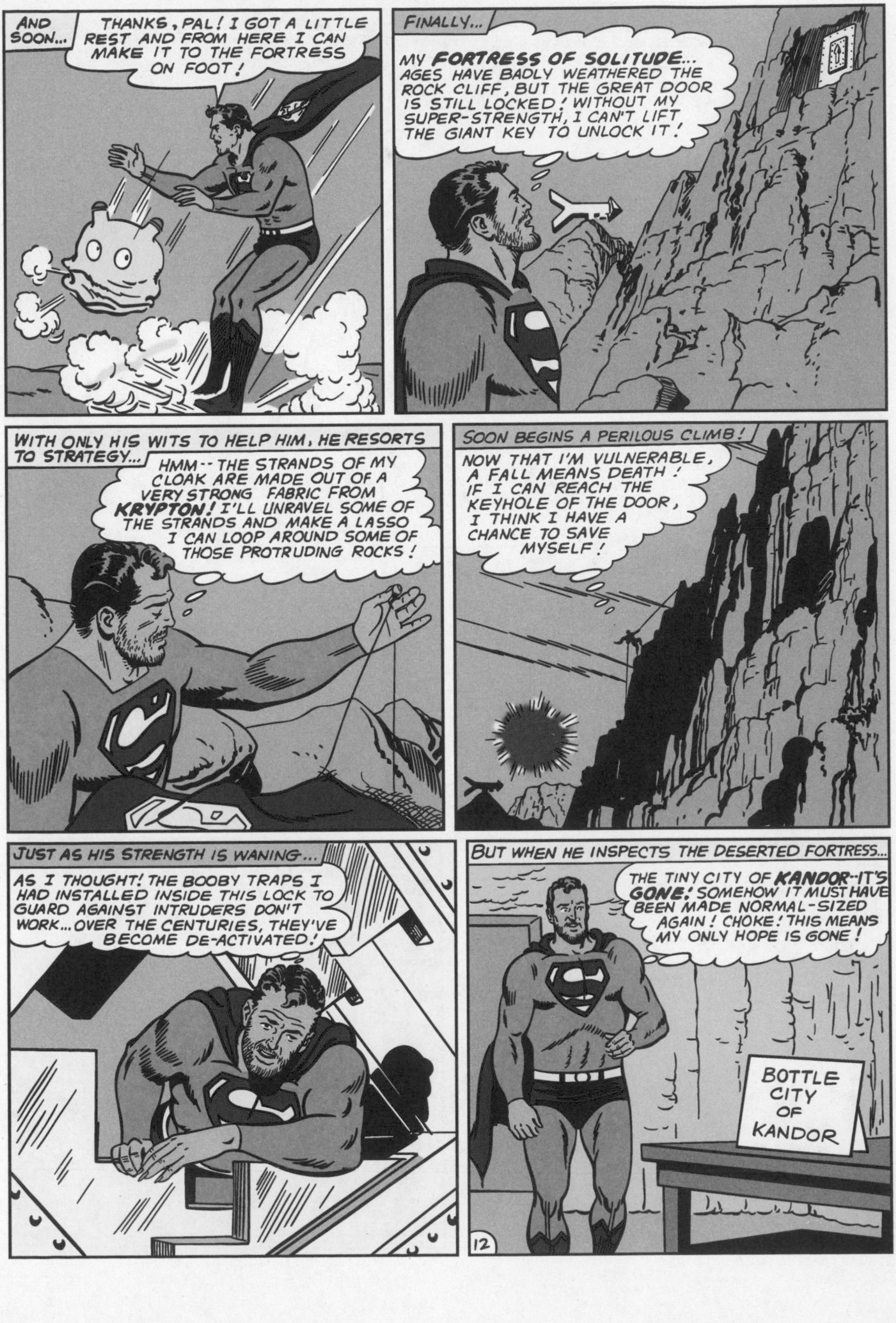
AND SOON...
THANKS, PAL! I GOT A LITTLE REST AND FROM HERE I CAN MAKE IT TO THE FORTRESS ON FOOT!
FINALLY...
MY FORTRESS OF SOLITUDE... AGES HAVE BADLY WEATHERED THE ROCK CLIFF, BUT THE GREAT DOOR IS STILL LOCKED! WITHOUT MY SUPER-STRENGTH, I CAN'T LIFT THE GIANT KEY TO UNLOCK IT!
WITH ONLY HIS WITS TO HELP HIM, HE RESORTS TO STRATEGY...
HMM-- THE STRANDS OF MY CLOAK ARE MADE OUT OF A VERY STRONG FABRIC FROM KRYPTON! I'LL UNRAVEL SOME OF THE STRANDS AND MAKE A LASSO I CAN LOOP AROUND SOME OF THOSE PROTRUDING ROCKS!
SOON BEGINS A PERILOUS CLIMB!
NOW THAT I'M VULNERABLE, A FALL MEANS DEATH! IF I CAN REACH THE KEYHOLE OF THE DOOR, I THINK I HAVE A CHANCE TO SAVE MYSELF!
JUST AS HIS STRENGTH IS WANING...
AS I THOUGHT! THE BOOBY TRAPS I HAD INSTALLED INSIDE THIS LOCK TO GUARD AGAINST INTRUDERS DON'T WORK... OVER THE CENTURIES, THEY'VE BECOME DE-ACTIVATED!
BUT WHEN HE INSPECTS THE DESERTED FORTRESS...
THE TINY CITY OF KANDOR--IT'S GONE! SOMEHOW IT MUST HAVE BEEN MADE NORMAL-SIZED AGAIN! CHOKE! THIS MEANS MY ONLY HOPE IS GONE!
BOTTLE CITY OF KANDOR
12

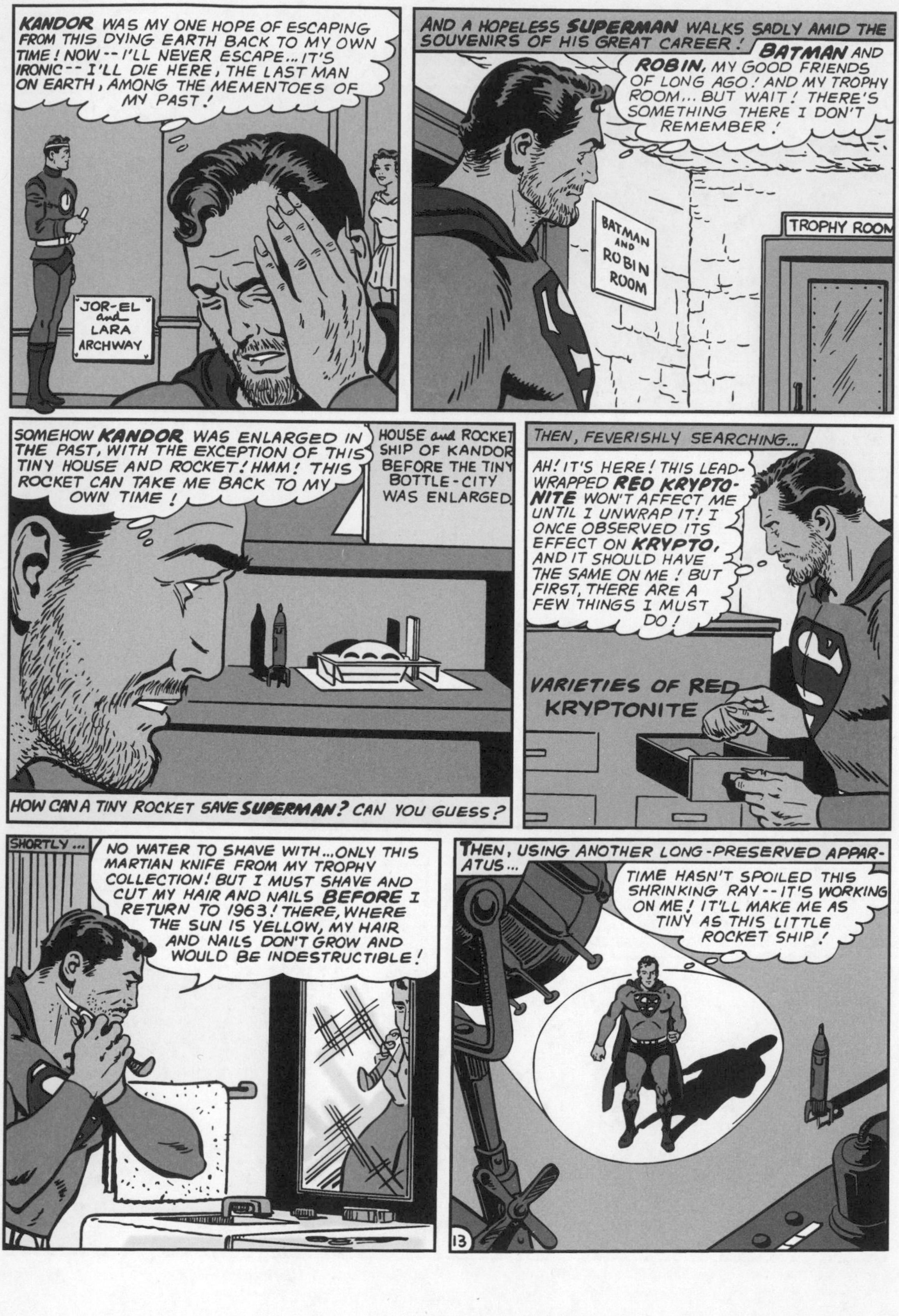
KANDOR WAS MY ONE HOPE OF ESCAPING FROM THIS DYING EARTH BACK TO MY OWN TIME! NOW -- I'LL NEVER ESCAPE... IT'S IRONIC -- I'LL DIE HERE, THE LAST MAN ON EARTH, AMONG THE MEMENTOES OF MY PAST!
JOR-EL and LARA ARCHWAY
AND A HOPELESS SUPERMAN WALKS SADLY AMID THE SOUVENIRS OF HIS GREAT CAREER!
BATMAN AND ROBIN, MY GOOD FRIENDS OF LONG AGO! AND MY TROPHY ROOM... BUT WAIT! THERE'S SOMETHING THERE I DON'T REMEMBER!
BATMAN AND ROBIN ROOM
TROPHY ROOM
SOMEHOW KANDOR WAS ENLARGED IN THE PAST, WITH THE EXCEPTION OF THIS TINY HOUSE AND ROCKET! HMM! THIS ROCKET CAN TAKE ME BACK TO MY OWN TIME!
HOUSE and ROCKET SHIP OF KANDOR BEFORE THE TINY BOTTLE-CITY WAS ENLARGED
HOW CAN A TINY ROCKET SAVE SUPERMAN? CAN YOU GUESS?
THEN, FEVERISHLY SEARCHING...
AH! IT'S HERE! THIS LEAD-WRAPPED RED KRYPTONITE WON'T AFFECT ME UNTIL I UNWRAP IT! I ONCE OBSERVED ITS EFFECT ON KRYPTO, AND IT SHOULD HAVE THE SAME ON ME! BUT FIRST, THERE ARE A FEW THINGS I MUST DO!
VARIETIES OF RED KRYPTONITE
SHORTLY...
NO WATER TO SHAVE WITH... ONLY THIS MARTIAN KNIFE FROM MY TROPHY COLLECTION! BUT I MUST SHAVE AND CUT MY HAIR AND NAILS BEFORE I RETURN TO 1963! THERE, WHERE THE SUN IS YELLOW, MY HAIR AND NAILS DON'T GROW AND WOULD BE INDESTRUCTIBLE!
THEN, USING ANOTHER LONG-PRESERVED APPARATUS...
TIME HASN'T SPOILED THIS SHRINKING RAY -- IT'S WORKING ON ME! IT'LL MAKE ME AS TINY AS THIS LITTLE ROCKET SHIP!
13

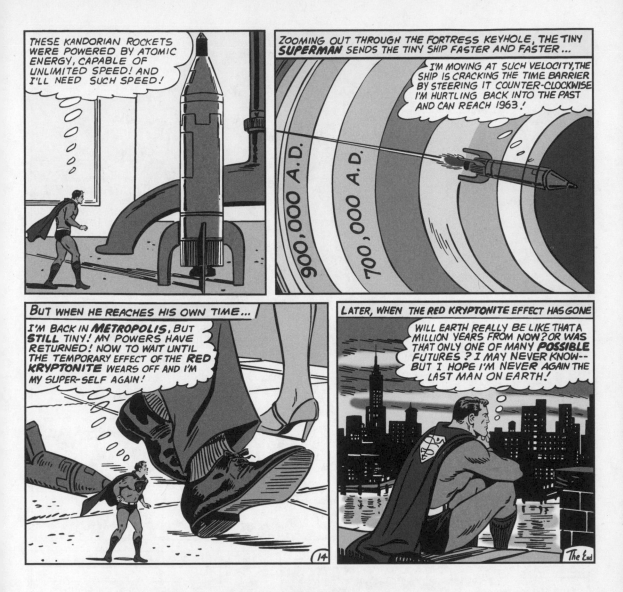

These Kandorian rockets were powered by atomic energy, capable of unlimited speed! And I'll need such speed!

Zooming out through the fortress keyhole, the tiny SUPERMAN sends the tiny ship faster and faster...

I'm moving at such velocity, the ship is cracking the time barrier by steering it counter-clockwise I'm hurtling back into the past and can reach 1963!

900,000 A.D.

700,000 A.D.

But when he reaches his own time...

I'm back in METROPOLIS, but STILL tiny! My powers have returned! Now to wait until the temporary effect of the RED KRYPTONITE wears off and I'm my super-self again!

Later, when the RED KRYPTONITE effect has gone

Will Earth really be like that a million years from now? Or was that only one of many POSSIBLE futures? I may never know-- but I hope I'm never again the last man on Earth!

The End

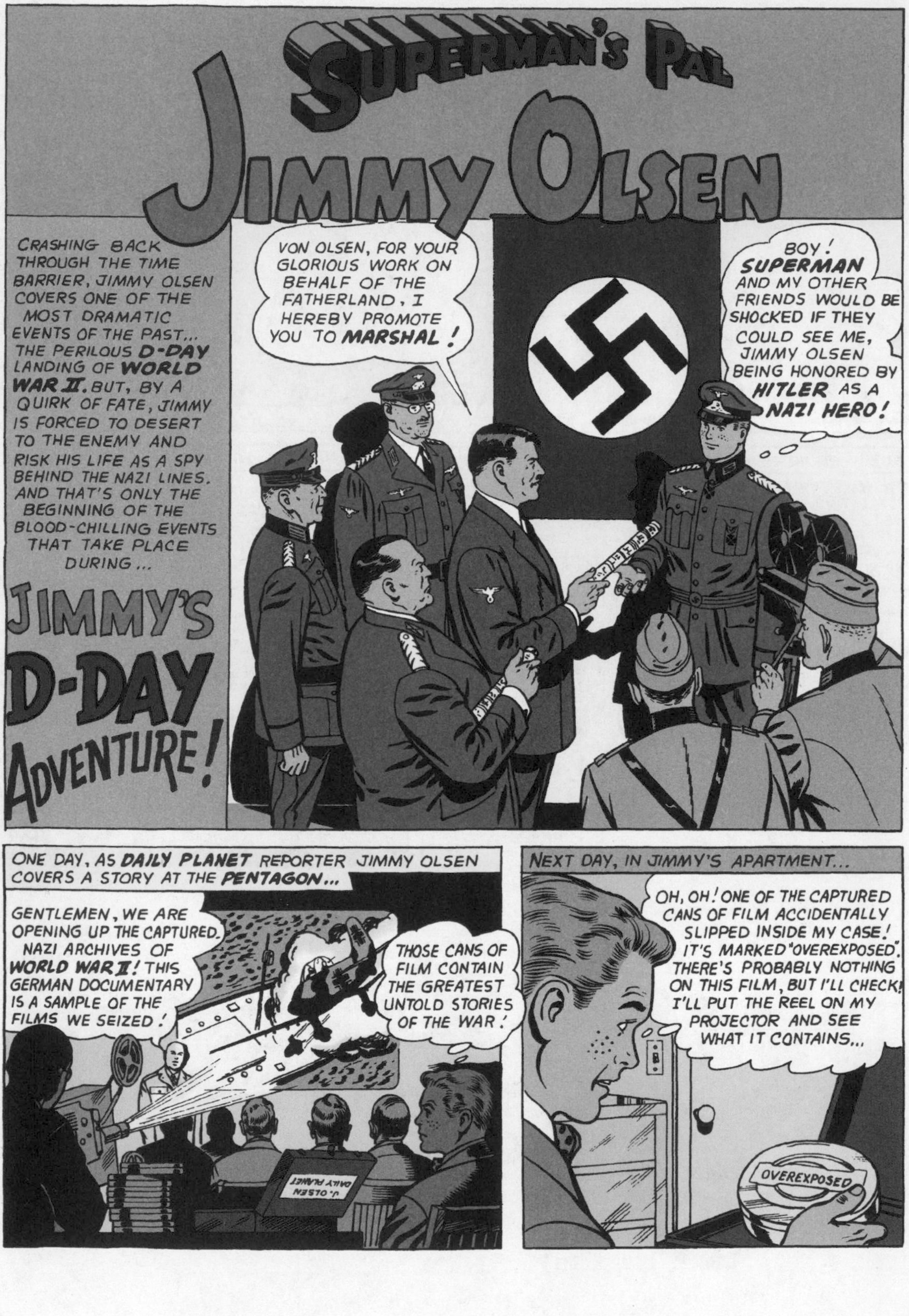
SUPERMAN'S PAL
JIMMY OLSEN
CRASHING BACK THROUGH THE TIME BARRIER, JIMMY OLSEN COVERS ONE OF THE MOST DRAMATIC EVENTS OF THE PAST... THE PERILOUS D-DAY LANDING OF WORLD WAR II. BUT, BY A QUIRK OF FATE, JIMMY IS FORCED TO DESERT TO THE ENEMY AND RISK HIS LIFE AS A SPY BEHIND THE NAZI LINES. AND THAT'S ONLY THE BEGINNING OF THE BLOOD-CHILLING EVENTS THAT TAKE PLACE DURING...
JIMMY'S D-DAY ADVENTURE!
VON OLSEN, FOR YOUR GLORIOUS WORK ON BEHALF OF THE FATHERLAND, I HEREBY PROMOTE YOU TO MARSHAL!
BOY! SUPERMAN AND MY OTHER FRIENDS WOULD BE SHOCKED IF THEY COULD SEE ME, JIMMY OLSEN BEING HONORED BY HITLER AS A NAZI HERO!
ONE DAY, AS DAILY PLANET REPORTER JIMMY OLSEN COVERS A STORY AT THE PENTAGON...
GENTLEMEN, WE ARE OPENING UP THE CAPTURED NAZI ARCHIVES OF WORLD WAR II! THIS GERMAN DOCUMENTARY IS A SAMPLE OF THE FILMS WE SEIZED!
THOSE CANS OF FILM CONTAIN THE GREATEST UNTOLD STORIES OF THE WAR!
J. OLSEN DAILY PLANET
NEXT DAY, IN JIMMY'S APARTMENT...
OH, OH! ONE OF THE CAPTURED CANS OF FILM ACCIDENTALLY SLIPPED INSIDE MY CASE! IT'S MARKED "OVEREXPOSED". THERE'S PROBABLY NOTHING ON THIS FILM, BUT I'LL CHECK! I'LL PUT THE REEL ON MY PROJECTOR AND SEE WHAT IT CONTAINS...
OVEREXPOSED

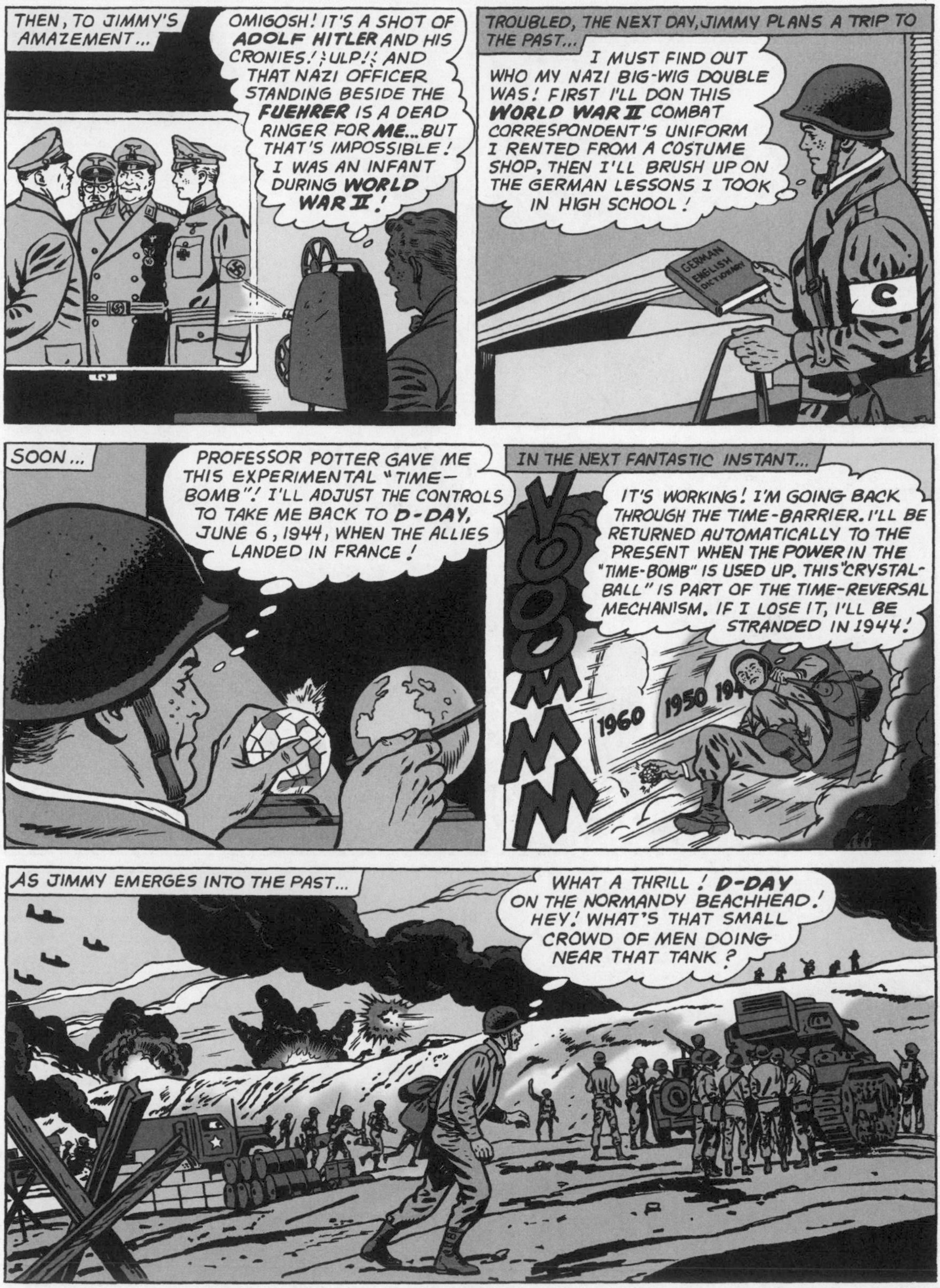
THEN, TO JIMMY'S AMAZEMENT...
OMIGOSH! IT'S A SHOT OF ADOLF HITLER AND HIS CRONIES! ULP! AND THAT NAZI OFFICER STANDING BESIDE THE FUEHRER IS A DEAD RINGER FOR ME...BUT THAT'S IMPOSSIBLE! I WAS AN INFANT DURING WORLD WAR II!
TROUBLED, THE NEXT DAY, JIMMY PLANS A TRIP TO THE PAST...
I MUST FIND OUT WHO MY NAZI BIG-WIG DOUBLE WAS! FIRST I'LL DON THIS WORLD WAR II COMBAT CORRESPONDENT'S UNIFORM I RENTED FROM A COSTUME SHOP, THEN I'LL BRUSH UP ON THE GERMAN LESSONS I TOOK IN HIGH SCHOOL!
GERMAN ENGLISH DICTIONARY
C
SOON...
PROFESSOR POTTER GAVE ME THIS EXPERIMENTAL "TIME-BOMB"! I'LL ADJUST THE CONTROLS TO TAKE ME BACK TO D-DAY, JUNE 6, 1944, WHEN THE ALLIES LANDED IN FRANCE!
IN THE NEXT FANTASTIC INSTANT...
VOOOMMMM
IT'S WORKING! I'M GOING BACK THROUGH THE TIME-BARRIER. I'LL BE RETURNED AUTOMATICALLY TO THE PRESENT WHEN THE POWER IN THE "TIME-BOMB" IS USED UP. THIS "CRYSTAL-BALL" IS PART OF THE TIME-REVERSAL MECHANISM. IF I LOSE IT, I'LL BE STRANDED IN 1944!
1960
1950
AS JIMMY EMERGES INTO THE PAST...
WHAT A THRILL! D-DAY ON THE NORMANDY BEACHHEAD! HEY! WHAT'S THAT SMALL CROWD OF MEN DOING NEAR THAT TANK?

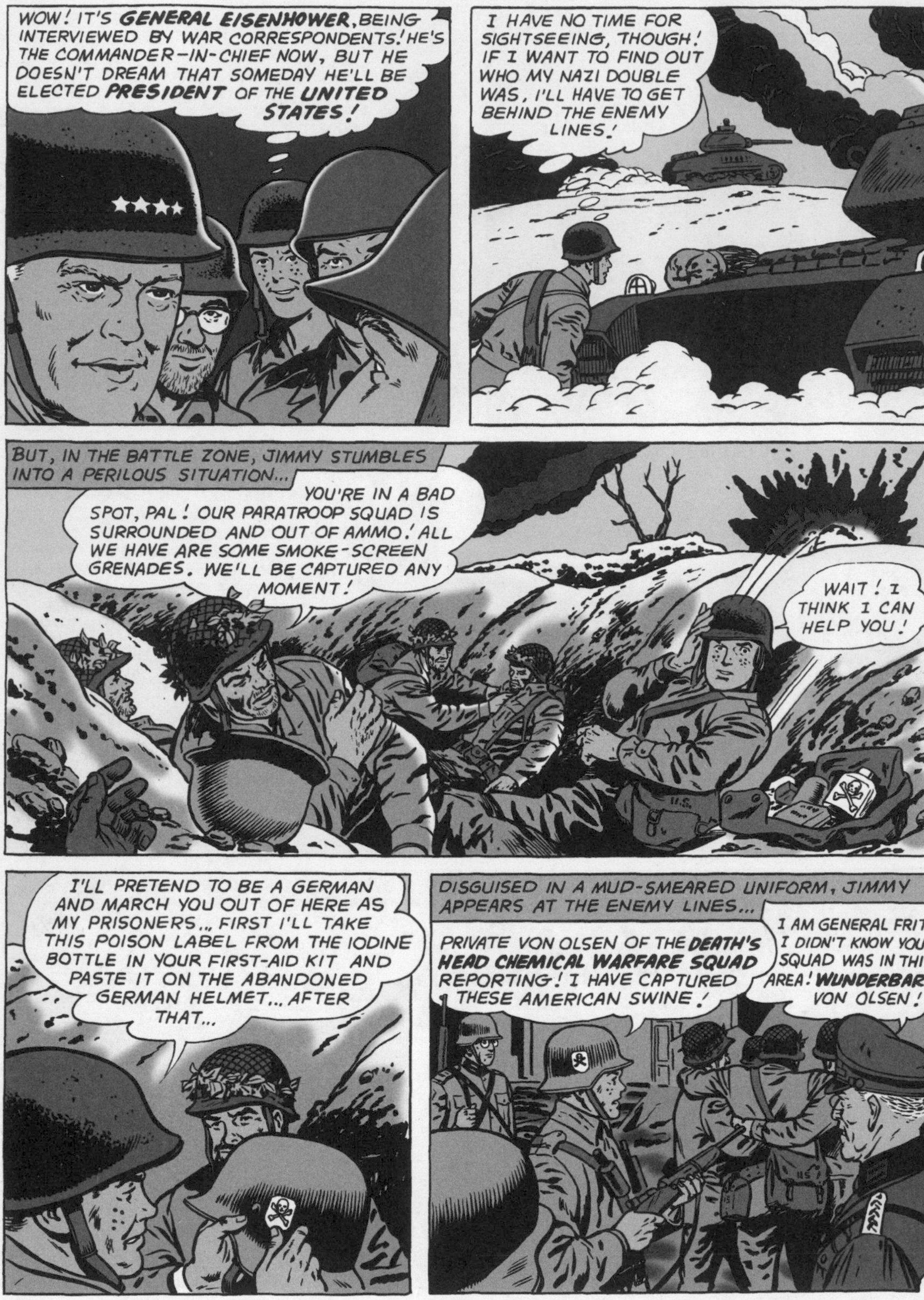
WOW! IT'S GENERAL EISENHOWER, BEING INTERVIEWED BY WAR CORRESPONDENTS! HE'S THE COMMANDER-IN-CHIEF NOW, BUT HE DOESN'T DREAM THAT SOMEDAY HE'LL BE ELECTED PRESIDENT OF THE UNITED STATES!
I HAVE NO TIME FOR SIGHTSEEING, THOUGH! IF I WANT TO FIND OUT WHO MY NAZI DOUBLE WAS, I'LL HAVE TO GET BEHIND THE ENEMY LINES!
BUT, IN THE BATTLE ZONE, JIMMY STUMBLES INTO A PERILOUS SITUATION...
YOU'RE IN A BAD SPOT, PAL! OUR PARATROOP SQUAD IS SURROUNDED AND OUT OF AMMO! ALL WE HAVE ARE SOME SMOKE-SCREEN GRENADES. WE'LL BE CAPTURED ANY MOMENT!
WAIT! I THINK I CAN HELP YOU!
I'LL PRETEND TO BE A GERMAN AND MARCH YOU OUT OF HERE AS MY PRISONERS... FIRST I'LL TAKE THIS POISON LABEL FROM THE IODINE BOTTLE IN YOUR FIRST-AID KIT AND PASTE IT ON THE ABANDONED GERMAN HELMET... AFTER THAT...
DISGUISED IN A MUD-SMEARED UNIFORM, JIMMY APPEARS AT THE ENEMY LINES...
PRIVATE VON OLSEN OF THE DEATH'S HEAD CHEMICAL WARFARE SQUAD REPORTING! I HAVE CAPTURED THESE AMERICAN SWINE!
I AM GENERAL FRITZ. I DIDN'T KNOW YOUR SQUAD WAS IN THIS AREA! WUNDERBAR, VON OLSEN!
3

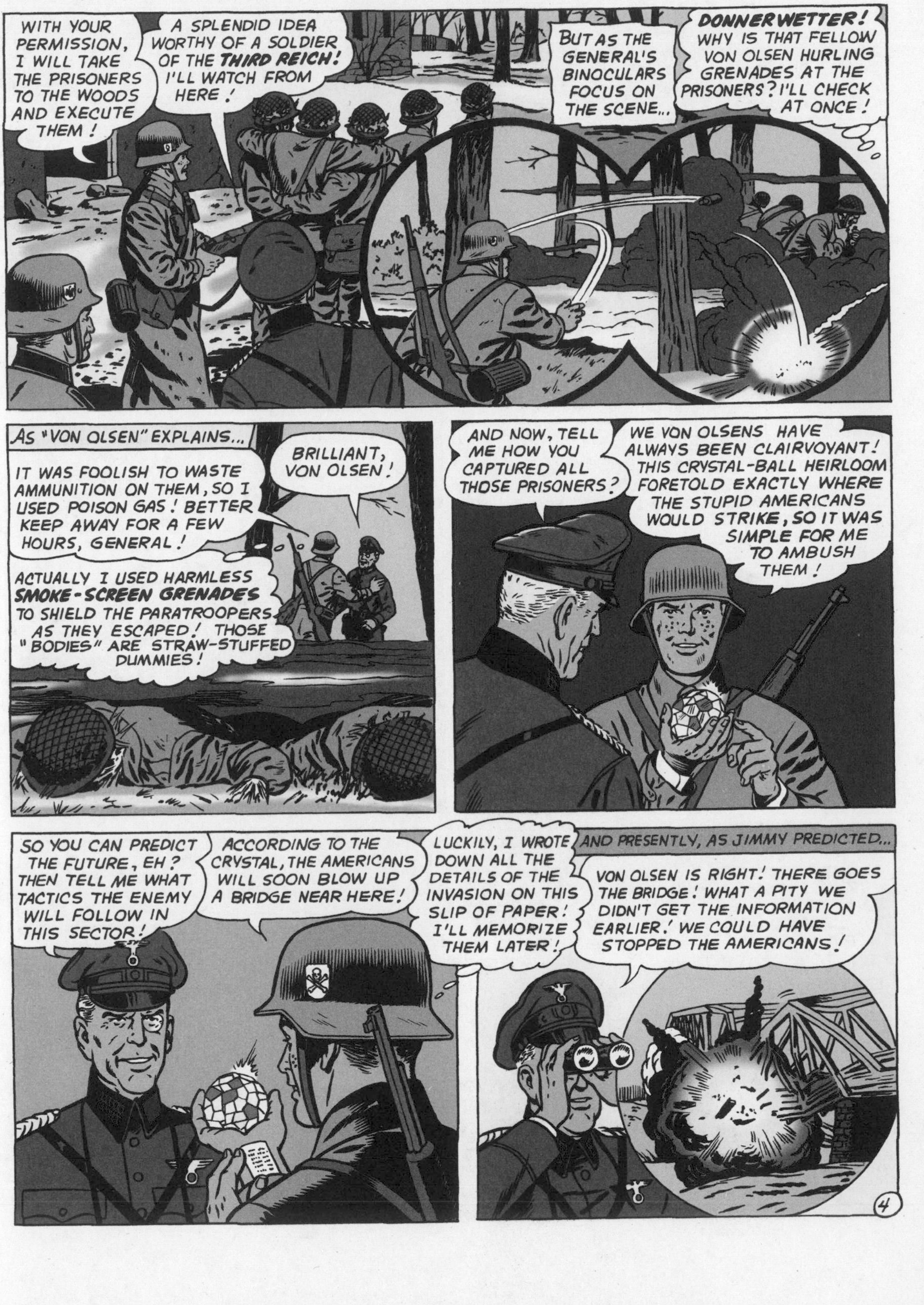
WITH YOUR PERMISSION, I WILL TAKE THE PRISONERS TO THE WOODS AND EXECUTE THEM!
A SPLENDID IDEA WORTHY OF A SOLDIER OF THE **THIRD REICH**! I'LL WATCH FROM HERE!
BUT AS THE GENERAL'S BINOCULARS FOCUS ON THE SCENE...
DONNERWETTER! WHY IS THAT FELLOW VON OLSEN HURLING GRENADES AT THE PRISONERS? I'LL CHECK AT ONCE!
AS "VON OLSEN" EXPLAINS...
IT WAS FOOLISH TO WASTE AMMUNITION ON THEM, SO I USED POISON GAS! BETTER KEEP AWAY FOR A FEW HOURS, GENERAL!
BRILLIANT, VON OLSEN!
ACTUALLY I USED HARMLESS **SMOKE-SCREEN GRENADES** TO SHIELD THE PARATROOPERS AS THEY ESCAPED! THOSE "BODIES" ARE STRAW-STUFFED DUMMIES!
AND NOW, TELL ME HOW YOU CAPTURED ALL THOSE PRISONERS?
WE VON OLSENS HAVE ALWAYS BEEN CLAIRVOYANT! THIS CRYSTAL-BALL HEIRLOOM FORETOLD EXACTLY WHERE THE STUPID AMERICANS WOULD STRIKE, SO IT WAS SIMPLE FOR ME TO AMBUSH THEM!
SO YOU CAN PREDICT THE FUTURE, EH? THEN TELL ME WHAT TACTICS THE ENEMY WILL FOLLOW IN THIS SECTOR!
ACCORDING TO THE CRYSTAL, THE AMERICANS WILL SOON BLOW UP A BRIDGE NEAR HERE!
LUCKILY, I WROTE DOWN ALL THE DETAILS OF THE INVASION ON THIS SLIP OF PAPER! I'LL MEMORIZE THEM LATER!
AND PRESENTLY, AS JIMMY PREDICTED...
VON OLSEN IS RIGHT! THERE GOES THE BRIDGE! WHAT A PITY WE DIDN'T GET THE INFORMATION EARLIER! WE COULD HAVE STOPPED THE AMERICANS!
4

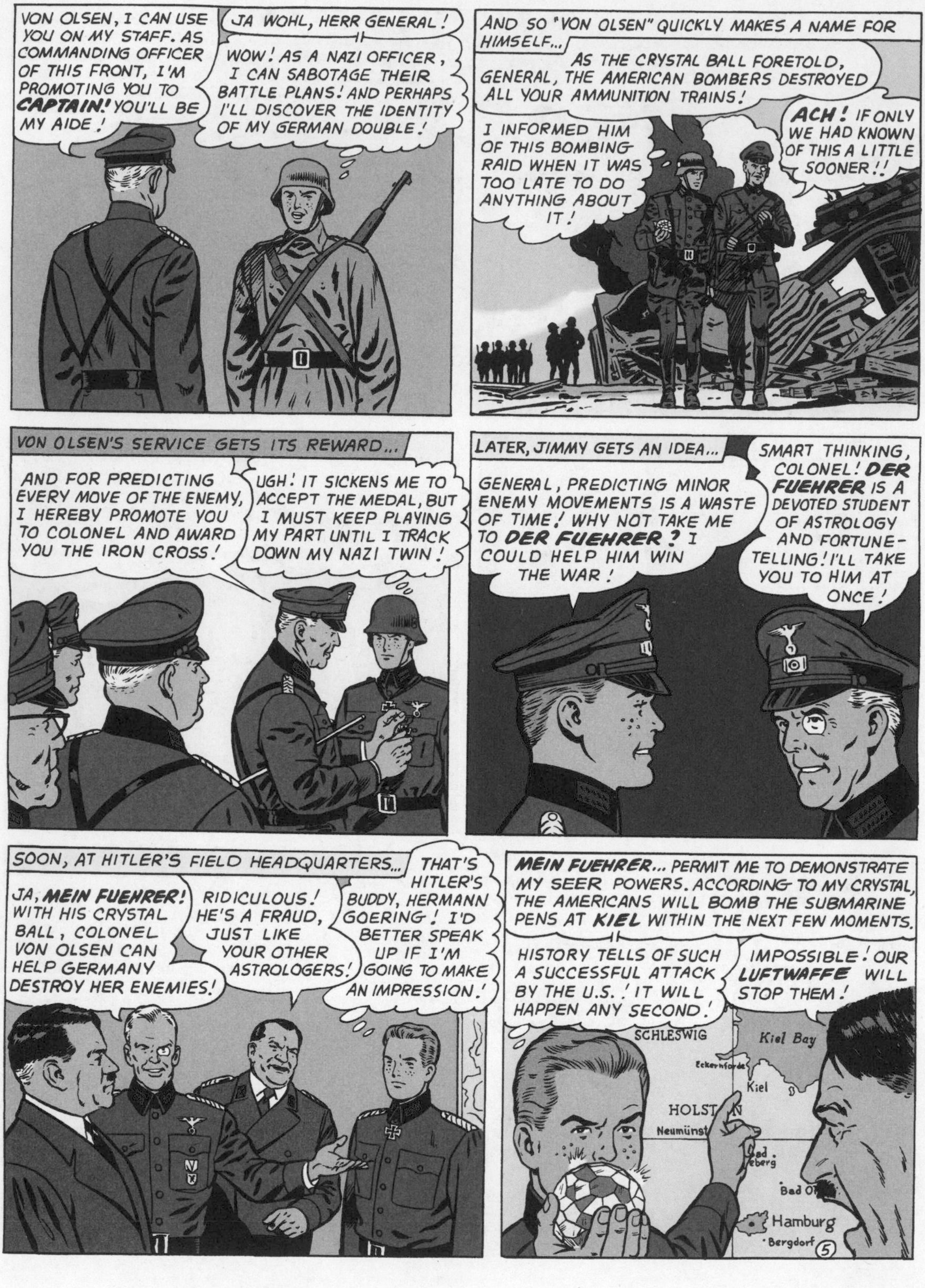
VON OLSEN, I CAN USE YOU ON MY STAFF. AS COMMANDING OFFICER OF THIS FRONT, I'M PROMOTING YOU TO CAPTAIN! YOU'LL BE MY AIDE!
JA WOHL, HERR GENERAL!
WOW! AS A NAZI OFFICER, I CAN SABOTAGE THEIR BATTLE PLANS! AND PERHAPS I'LL DISCOVER THE IDENTITY OF MY GERMAN DOUBLE!
AND SO "VON OLSEN" QUICKLY MAKES A NAME FOR HIMSELF...
AS THE CRYSTAL BALL FORETOLD, GENERAL, THE AMERICAN BOMBERS DESTROYED ALL YOUR AMMUNITION TRAINS!
I INFORMED HIM OF THIS BOMBING RAID WHEN IT WAS TOO LATE TO DO ANYTHING ABOUT IT!
ACH! IF ONLY WE HAD KNOWN OF THIS A LITTLE SOONER!!
VON OLSEN'S SERVICE GETS ITS REWARD...
AND FOR PREDICTING EVERY MOVE OF THE ENEMY, I HEREBY PROMOTE YOU TO COLONEL AND AWARD YOU THE IRON CROSS!
UGH! IT SICKENS ME TO ACCEPT THE MEDAL, BUT I MUST KEEP PLAYING MY PART UNTIL I TRACK DOWN MY NAZI TWIN!
LATER, JIMMY GETS AN IDEA...
GENERAL, PREDICTING MINOR ENEMY MOVEMENTS IS A WASTE OF TIME! WHY NOT TAKE ME TO DER FUEHRER? I COULD HELP HIM WIN THE WAR!
SMART THINKING, COLONEL! DER FUEHRER IS A DEVOTED STUDENT OF ASTROLOGY AND FORTUNE-TELLING! I'LL TAKE YOU TO HIM AT ONCE!
SOON, AT HITLER'S FIELD HEADQUARTERS...
JA, MEIN FUEHRER! WITH HIS CRYSTAL BALL, COLONEL VON OLSEN CAN HELP GERMANY DESTROY HER ENEMIES!
RIDICULOUS! HE'S A FRAUD, JUST LIKE YOUR OTHER ASTROLOGERS!
THAT'S HITLER'S BUDDY, HERMANN GOERING! I'D BETTER SPEAK UP IF I'M GOING TO MAKE AN IMPRESSION!
MEIN FUEHRER... PERMIT ME TO DEMONSTRATE MY SEER POWERS. ACCORDING TO MY CRYSTAL, THE AMERICANS WILL BOMB THE SUBMARINE PENS AT KIEL WITHIN THE NEXT FEW MOMENTS.
HISTORY TELLS OF SUCH A SUCCESSFUL ATTACK BY THE U.S.! IT WILL HAPPEN ANY SECOND!
IMPOSSIBLE! OUR LUFTWAFFE WILL STOP THEM!
SCHLESWIG
Kiel Bay
Kiel
HOLST
Hamburg
Bergdorf
5

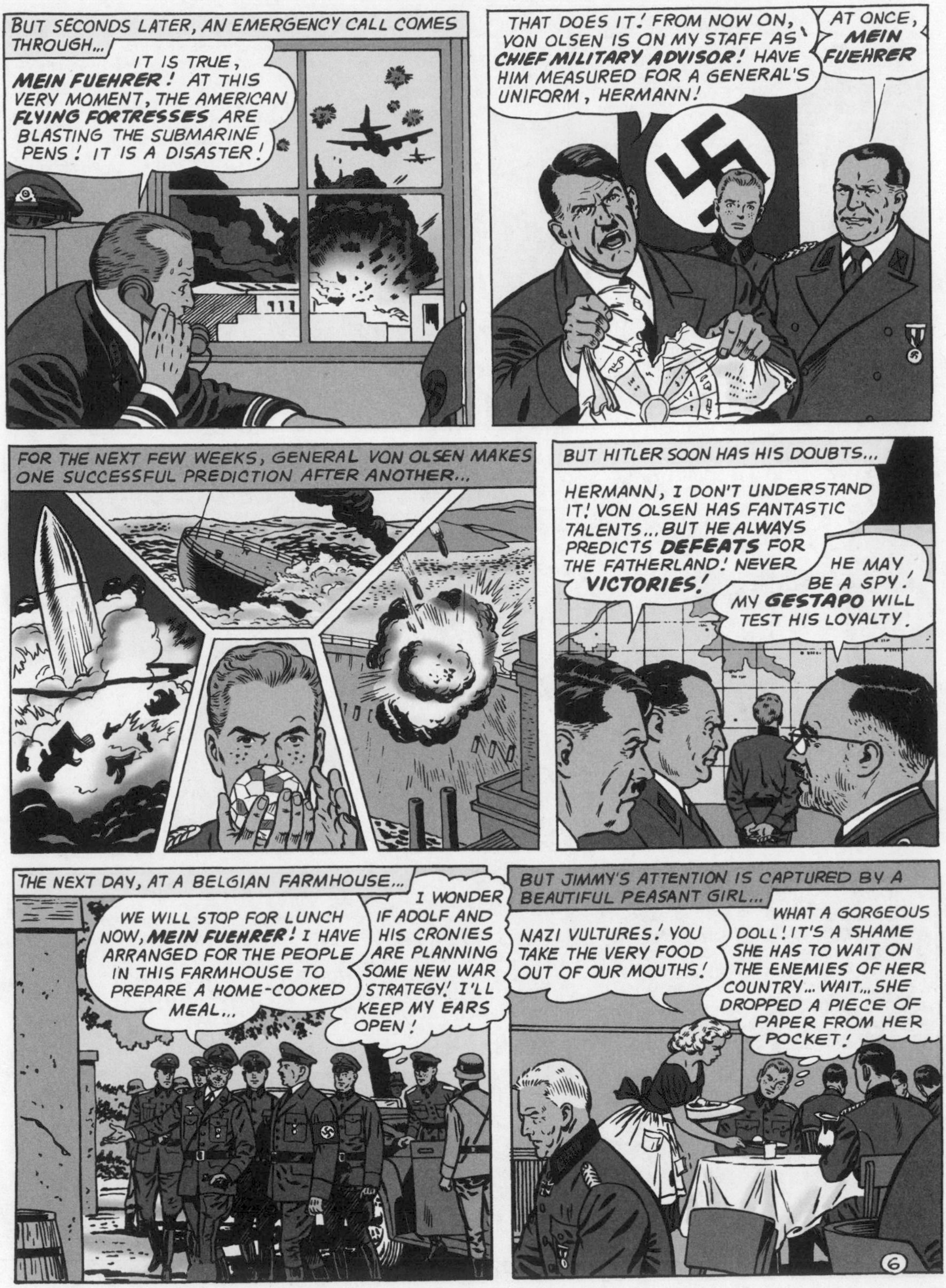

BUT SECONDS LATER, AN EMERGENCY CALL COMES THROUGH...
IT IS TRUE, MEIN FUEHRER! AT THIS VERY MOMENT, THE AMERICAN FLYING FORTRESSES ARE BLASTING THE SUBMARINE PENS! IT IS A DISASTER!
THAT DOES IT! FROM NOW ON, VON OLSEN IS ON MY STAFF AS CHIEF MILITARY ADVISOR! HAVE HIM MEASURED FOR A GENERAL'S UNIFORM, HERMANN!
AT ONCE, MEIN FUEHRER
FOR THE NEXT FEW WEEKS, GENERAL VON OLSEN MAKES ONE SUCCESSFUL PREDICTION AFTER ANOTHER...
BUT HITLER SOON HAS HIS DOUBTS...
HERMANN, I DON'T UNDERSTAND IT! VON OLSEN HAS FANTASTIC TALENTS... BUT HE ALWAYS PREDICTS DEFEATS FOR THE FATHERLAND! NEVER VICTORIES!
HE MAY BE A SPY! MY GESTAPO WILL TEST HIS LOYALTY.
THE NEXT DAY, AT A BELGIAN FARMHOUSE...
WE WILL STOP FOR LUNCH NOW, MEIN FUEHRER! I HAVE ARRANGED FOR THE PEOPLE IN THIS FARMHOUSE TO PREPARE A HOME-COOKED MEAL...
I WONDER IF ADOLF AND HIS CRONIES ARE PLANNING SOME NEW WAR STRATEGY! I'LL KEEP MY EARS OPEN!
BUT JIMMY'S ATTENTION IS CAPTURED BY A BEAUTIFUL PEASANT GIRL...
NAZI VULTURES! YOU TAKE THE VERY FOOD OUT OF OUR MOUTHS!
WHAT A GORGEOUS DOLL! IT'S A SHAME SHE HAS TO WAIT ON THE ENEMIES OF HER COUNTRY... WAIT... SHE DROPPED A PIECE OF PAPER FROM HER POCKET!
6

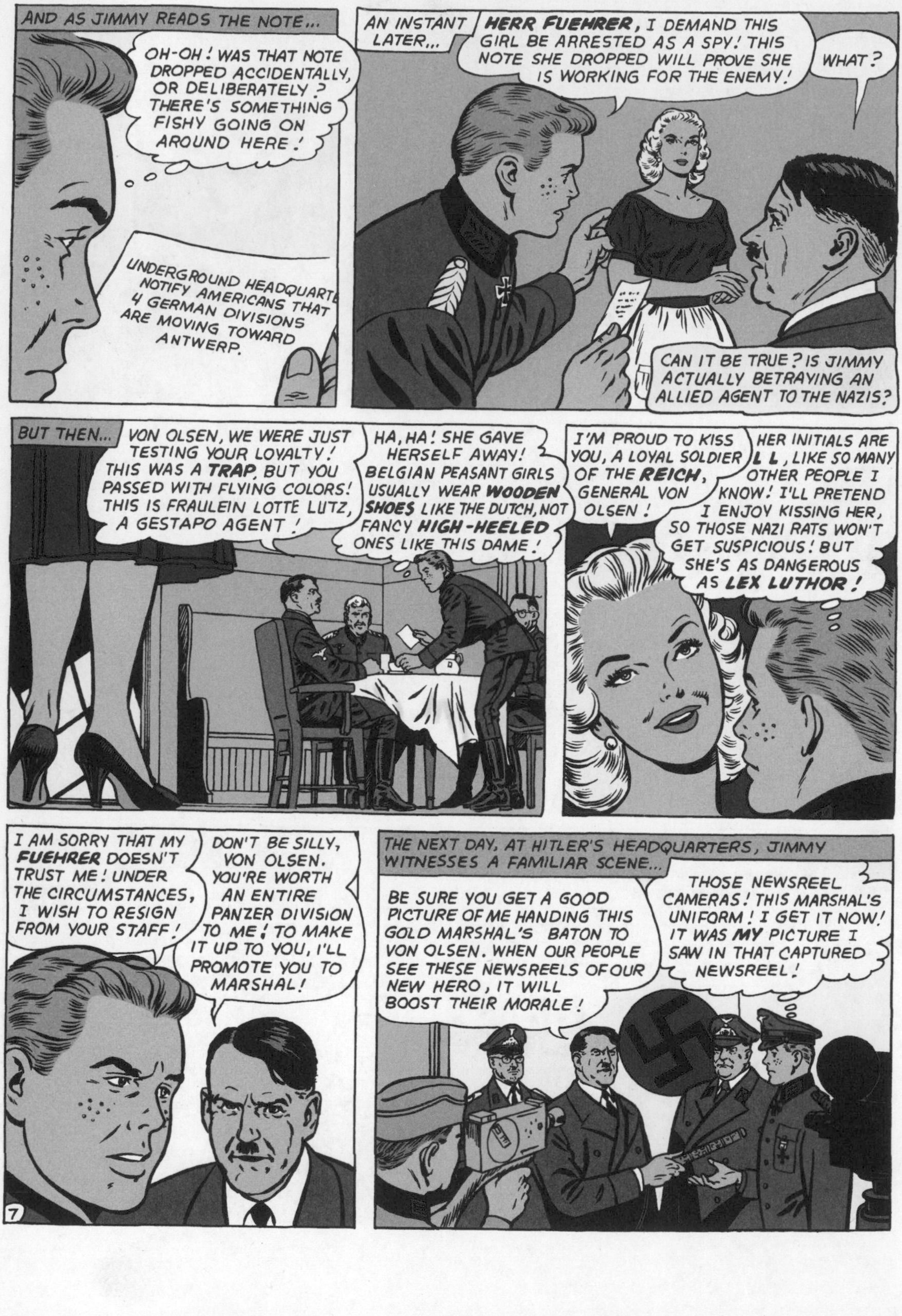
AND AS JIMMY READS THE NOTE...
OH-OH! WAS THAT NOTE DROPPED ACCIDENTALLY, OR DELIBERATELY? THERE'S SOMETHING FISHY GOING ON AROUND HERE!
UNDERGROUND HEADQUARTE NOTIFY AMERICANS THAT 4 GERMAN DIVISIONS ARE MOVING TOWARD ANTWERP.
AN INSTANT LATER...
HERR FUEHRER, I DEMAND THIS GIRL BE ARRESTED AS A SPY! THIS NOTE SHE DROPPED WILL PROVE SHE IS WORKING FOR THE ENEMY!
WHAT?
CAN IT BE TRUE? IS JIMMY ACTUALLY BETRAYING AN ALLIED AGENT TO THE NAZIS?
BUT THEN...
VON OLSEN, WE WERE JUST TESTING YOUR LOYALTY! THIS WAS A TRAP, BUT YOU PASSED WITH FLYING COLORS! THIS IS FRAULEIN LOTTE LUTZ, A GESTAPO AGENT!
HA, HA! SHE GAVE HERSELF AWAY! BELGIAN PEASANT GIRLS USUALLY WEAR WOODEN SHOES LIKE THE DUTCH, NOT FANCY HIGH-HEELED ONES LIKE THIS DAME!
I'M PROUD TO KISS YOU, A LOYAL SOLDIER OF THE REICH, GENERAL VON OLSEN!
HER INITIALS ARE L L, LIKE SO MANY OTHER PEOPLE I KNOW! I'LL PRETEND I ENJOY KISSING HER, SO THOSE NAZI RATS WON'T GET SUSPICIOUS! BUT SHE'S AS DANGEROUS AS LEX LUTHOR!
I AM SORRY THAT MY FUEHRER DOESN'T TRUST ME! UNDER THE CIRCUMSTANCES, I WISH TO RESIGN FROM YOUR STAFF!
DON'T BE SILLY, VON OLSEN. YOU'RE WORTH AN ENTIRE PANZER DIVISION TO ME! TO MAKE IT UP TO YOU, I'LL PROMOTE YOU TO MARSHAL!
7
THE NEXT DAY, AT HITLER'S HEADQUARTERS, JIMMY WITNESSES A FAMILIAR SCENE...
BE SURE YOU GET A GOOD PICTURE OF ME HANDING THIS GOLD MARSHAL'S BATON TO VON OLSEN. WHEN OUR PEOPLE SEE THESE NEWSREELS OF OUR NEW HERO, IT WILL BOOST THEIR MORALE!
THOSE NEWSREEL CAMERAS! THIS MARSHAL'S UNIFORM! I GET IT NOW! IT WAS MY PICTURE I SAW IN THAT CAPTURED NEWSREEL!

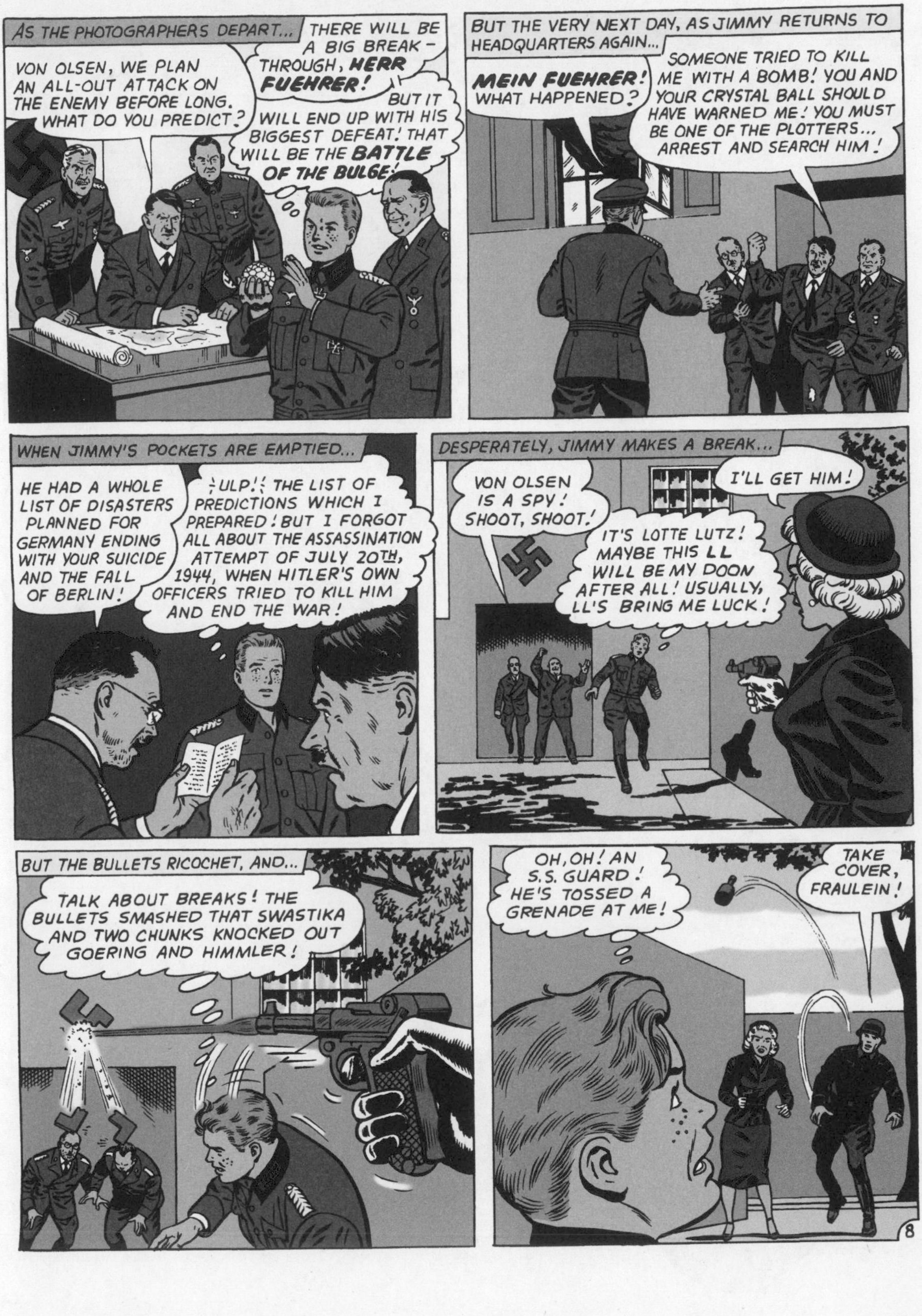

AS THE PHOTOGRAPHERS DEPART...
VON OLSEN, WE PLAN AN ALL-OUT ATTACK ON THE ENEMY BEFORE LONG. WHAT DO YOU PREDICT?
THERE WILL BE A BIG BREAK-THROUGH, HERR FUEHRER!
BUT IT WILL END UP WITH HIS BIGGEST DEFEAT! THAT WILL BE THE BATTLE OF THE BULGE!
BUT THE VERY NEXT DAY, AS JIMMY RETURNS TO HEADQUARTERS AGAIN...
MEIN FUEHRER! WHAT HAPPENED?
SOMEONE TRIED TO KILL ME WITH A BOMB! YOU AND YOUR CRYSTAL BALL SHOULD HAVE WARNED ME! YOU MUST BE ONE OF THE PLOTTERS... ARREST AND SEARCH HIM!
WHEN JIMMY'S POCKETS ARE EMPTIED...
HE HAD A WHOLE LIST OF DISASTERS PLANNED FOR GERMANY ENDING WITH YOUR SUICIDE AND THE FALL OF BERLIN!
¡ULP!¡ THE LIST OF PREDICTIONS WHICH I PREPARED! BUT I FORGOT ALL ABOUT THE ASSASSINATION ATTEMPT OF JULY 20TH, 1944, WHEN HITLER'S OWN OFFICERS TRIED TO KILL HIM AND END THE WAR!
DESPERATELY, JIMMY MAKES A BREAK...
VON OLSEN IS A SPY! SHOOT, SHOOT!
I'LL GET HIM!
IT'S LOTTE LUTZ! MAYBE THIS LL WILL BE MY DOON AFTER ALL! USUALLY, LL'S BRING ME LUCK!
BUT THE BULLETS RICOCHET, AND...
TALK ABOUT BREAKS! THE BULLETS SMASHED THAT SWASTIKA AND TWO CHUNKS KNOCKED OUT GOERING AND HIMMLER!
OH, OH! AN S.S. GUARD! HE'S TOSSED A GRENADE AT ME!
TAKE COVER, FRAULEIN!
8

VOOOMM!
UHHH! THAT GRENADE GOT ME! MY BODY MUST BE PARALYZED! I CAN'T FEEL A THING!
BUT AMAZINGLY, JIMMY FINDS HIMSELF BACK IN METROPOLIS...
WHAT A BREAK! THE POWER SUPPLY OF THE "TIME-BOMB" WAS USED UP, BRINGING ME BACK INTO THE PRESENT!... IT WAS I WHOSE PICTURE WAS ON THAT NEWSREEL AS ONE OF HITLER'S CRONIES!
THE PENTAGON WILL NEVER BELIEVE ME AND... HEY, WHAT GIVES? THE ROLL OF FILM CRUMBLED TO DUS IT MUST HAVE BEEN AFFECTED BY BEING TOO CLOSE TO THE TIME-BOMB WHEN IT WENT OFF. THE EVIDENCE OF MY LIFE AS A NAZI OFFICER IS GONE FOR GOOD!
HOLY COW! I JUST REALIZED THOSE PIECES OF THE SWASTIKA THAT KNOCKED OUT MY PURSUERS WERE SHAPED LIKE TWO L'S! ONCE AGAIN, THE COMBINATION OF LL HAS BEEN LUCKY FOR ME!
THE END
9

SUPERMAN

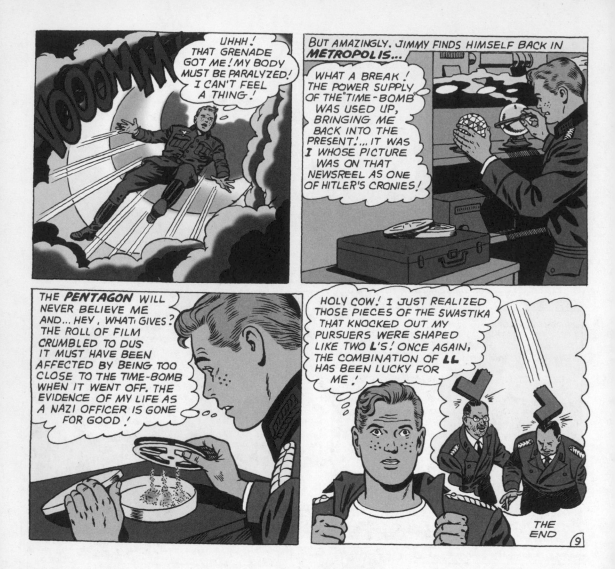

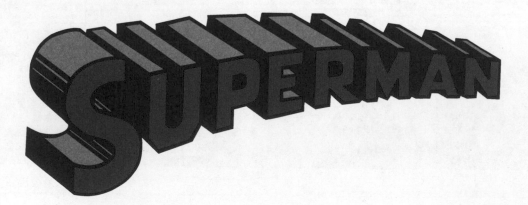

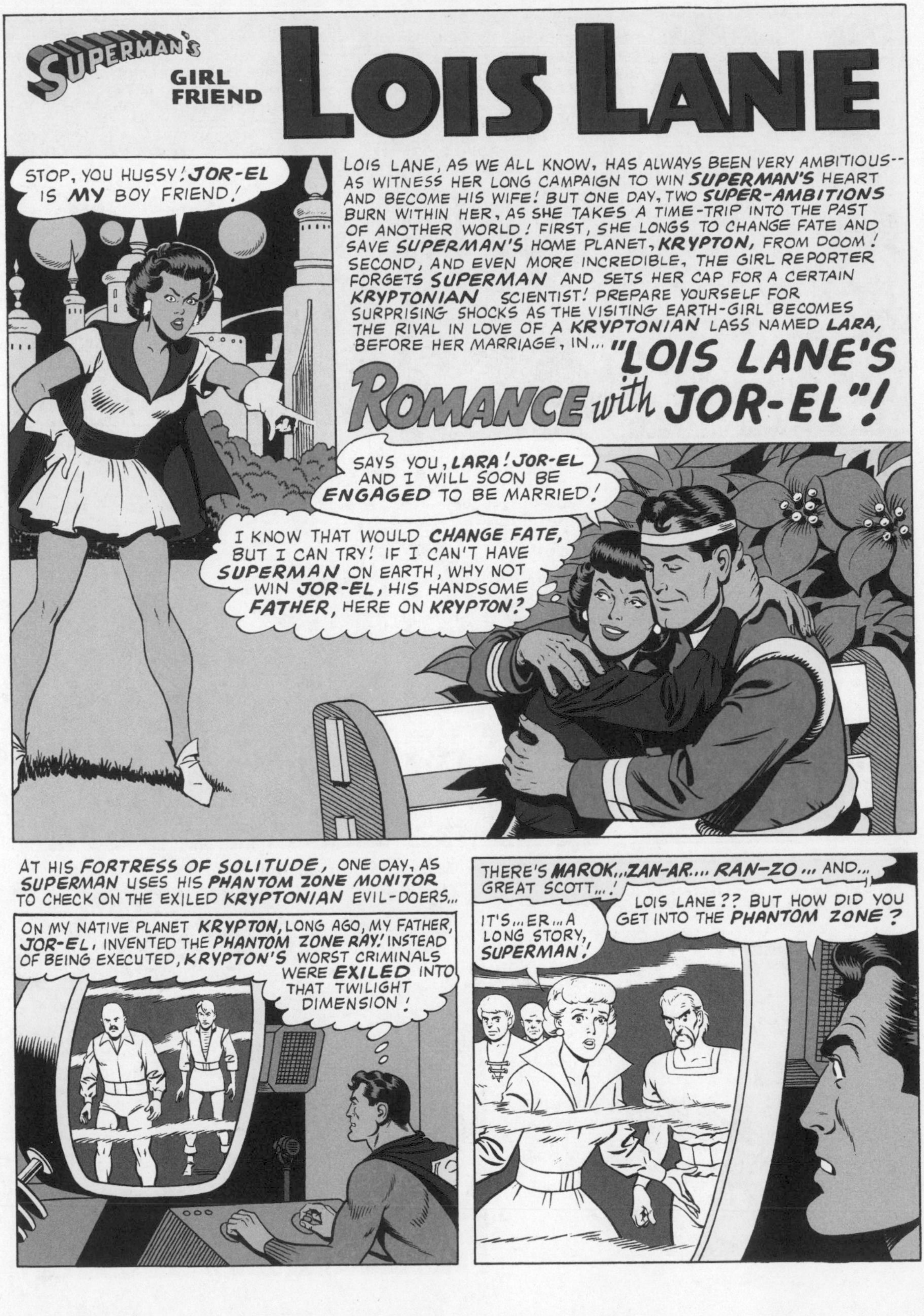
SUPERMAN'S GIRL FRIEND
LOIS LANE
STOP, YOU HUSSY! JOR-EL IS MY BOY FRIEND!
LOIS LANE, AS WE ALL KNOW, HAS ALWAYS BEEN VERY AMBITIOUS-- AS WITNESS HER LONG CAMPAIGN TO WIN SUPERMAN'S HEART AND BECOME HIS WIFE! BUT ONE DAY, TWO SUPER-AMBITIONS BURN WITHIN HER, AS SHE TAKES A TIME-TRIP INTO THE PAST OF ANOTHER WORLD! FIRST, SHE LONGS TO CHANGE FATE AND SAVE SUPERMAN'S HOME PLANET, KRYPTON, FROM DOOM! SECOND, AND EVEN MORE INCREDIBLE, THE GIRL REPORTER FORGETS SUPERMAN AND SETS HER CAP FOR A CERTAIN KRYPTONIAN SCIENTIST! PREPARE YOURSELF FOR SURPRISING SHOCKS AS THE VISITING EARTH-GIRL BECOMES THE RIVAL IN LOVE OF A KRYPTONIAN LASS NAMED LARA, BEFORE HER MARRIAGE, IN... "LOIS LANE'S ROMANCE with JOR-EL"!
SAYS YOU, LARA! JOR-EL AND I WILL SOON BE ENGAGED TO BE MARRIED!
I KNOW THAT WOULD CHANGE FATE, BUT I CAN TRY! IF I CAN'T HAVE SUPERMAN ON EARTH, WHY NOT WIN JOR-EL, HIS HANDSOME FATHER, HERE ON KRYPTON?
AT HIS FORTRESS OF SOLITUDE, ONE DAY, AS SUPERMAN USES HIS PHANTOM ZONE MONITOR TO CHECK ON THE EXILED KRYPTONIAN EVIL-DOERS...
ON MY NATIVE PLANET KRYPTON, LONG AGO, MY FATHER, JOR-EL, INVENTED THE PHANTOM ZONE RAY! INSTEAD OF BEING EXECUTED, KRYPTON'S WORST CRIMINALS WERE EXILED INTO THAT TWILIGHT DIMENSION!
THERE'S MAROK... ZAN-AR.... RAN-ZO... AND... GREAT SCOTT...!
LOIS LANE?? BUT HOW DID YOU GET INTO THE PHANTOM ZONE?
IT'S... ER... A LONG STORY, SUPERMAN!

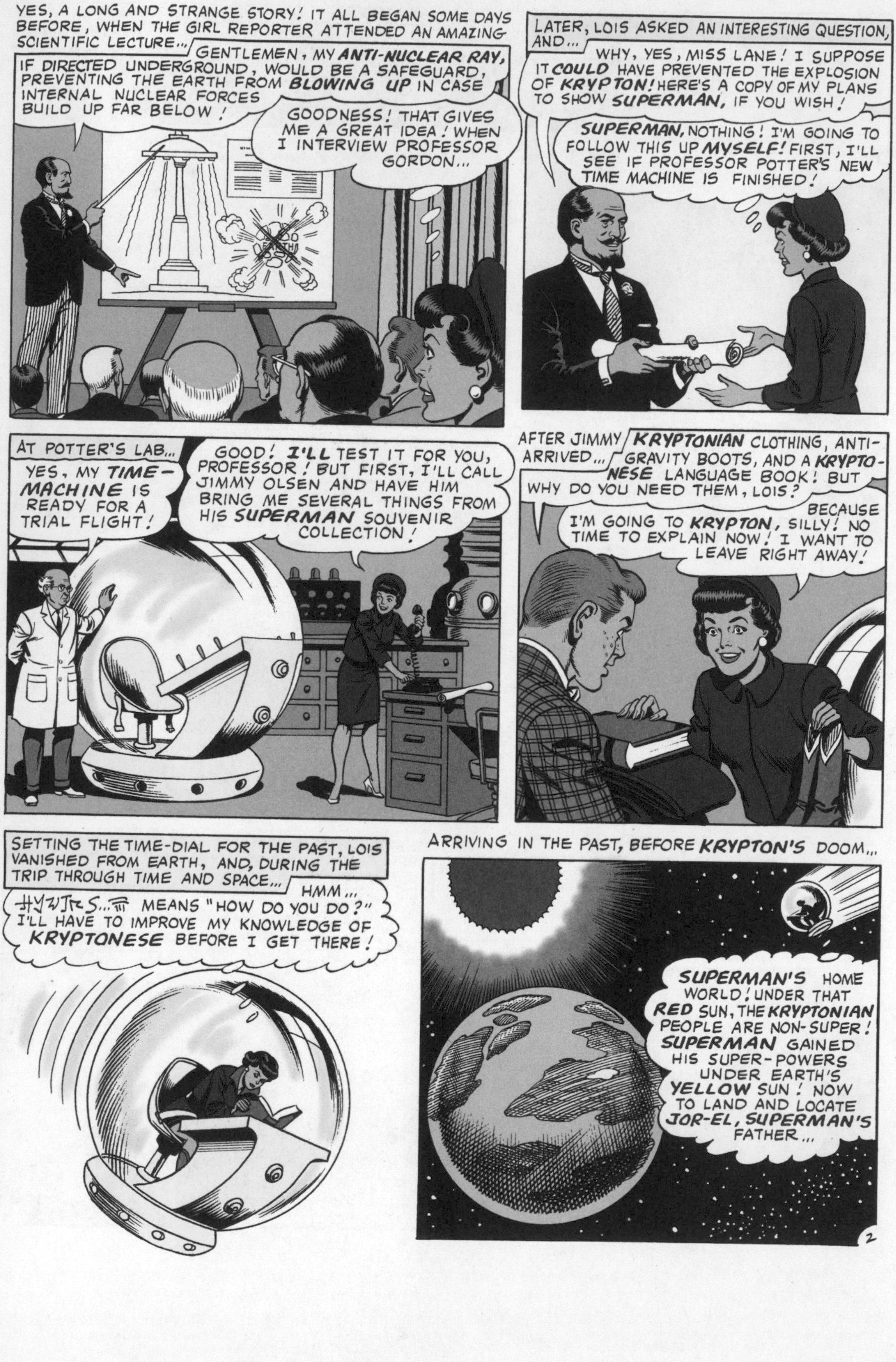
YES, A LONG AND STRANGE STORY! IT ALL BEGAN SOME DAYS BEFORE, WHEN THE GIRL REPORTER ATTENDED AN AMAZING SCIENTIFIC LECTURE...
GENTLEMEN, MY ANTI-NUCLEAR RAY, IF DIRECTED UNDERGROUND, WOULD BE A SAFEGUARD, PREVENTING THE EARTH FROM BLOWING UP IN CASE INTERNAL NUCLEAR FORCES BUILD UP FAR BELOW!
GOODNESS! THAT GIVES ME A GREAT IDEA! WHEN I INTERVIEW PROFESSOR GORDON...
LATER, LOIS ASKED AN INTERESTING QUESTION, AND...
WHY, YES, MISS LANE! I SUPPOSE IT COULD HAVE PREVENTED THE EXPLOSION OF KRYPTON! HERE'S A COPY OF MY PLANS TO SHOW SUPERMAN, IF YOU WISH!
SUPERMAN, NOTHING! I'M GOING TO FOLLOW THIS UP MYSELF! FIRST, I'LL SEE IF PROFESSOR POTTER'S NEW TIME MACHINE IS FINISHED!
AT POTTER'S LAB...
YES, MY TIME-MACHINE IS READY FOR A TRIAL FLIGHT!
GOOD! I'LL TEST IT FOR YOU, PROFESSOR! BUT FIRST, I'LL CALL JIMMY OLSEN AND HAVE HIM BRING ME SEVERAL THINGS FROM HIS SUPERMAN SOUVENIR COLLECTION!
AFTER JIMMY ARRIVED...
KRYPTONIAN CLOTHING, ANTI-GRAVITY BOOTS, AND A KRYPTONESE LANGUAGE BOOK! BUT WHY DO YOU NEED THEM, LOIS?
BECAUSE I'M GOING TO KRYPTON, SILLY! NO TIME TO EXPLAIN NOW! I WANT TO LEAVE RIGHT AWAY!
SETTING THE TIME-DIAL FOR THE PAST, LOIS VANISHED FROM EARTH, AND, DURING THE TRIP THROUGH TIME AND SPACE...
HMM... MEANS "HOW DO YOU DO?" I'LL HAVE TO IMPROVE MY KNOWLEDGE OF KRYPTONESE BEFORE I GET THERE!
ARRIVING IN THE PAST, BEFORE KRYPTON'S DOOM...
SUPERMAN'S HOME WORLD! UNDER THAT RED SUN, THE KRYPTONIAN PEOPLE ARE NON-SUPER! SUPERMAN GAINED HIS SUPER-POWERS UNDER EARTH'S YELLOW SUN! NOW TO LAND AND LOCATE JOR-EL, SUPERMAN'S FATHER...
2

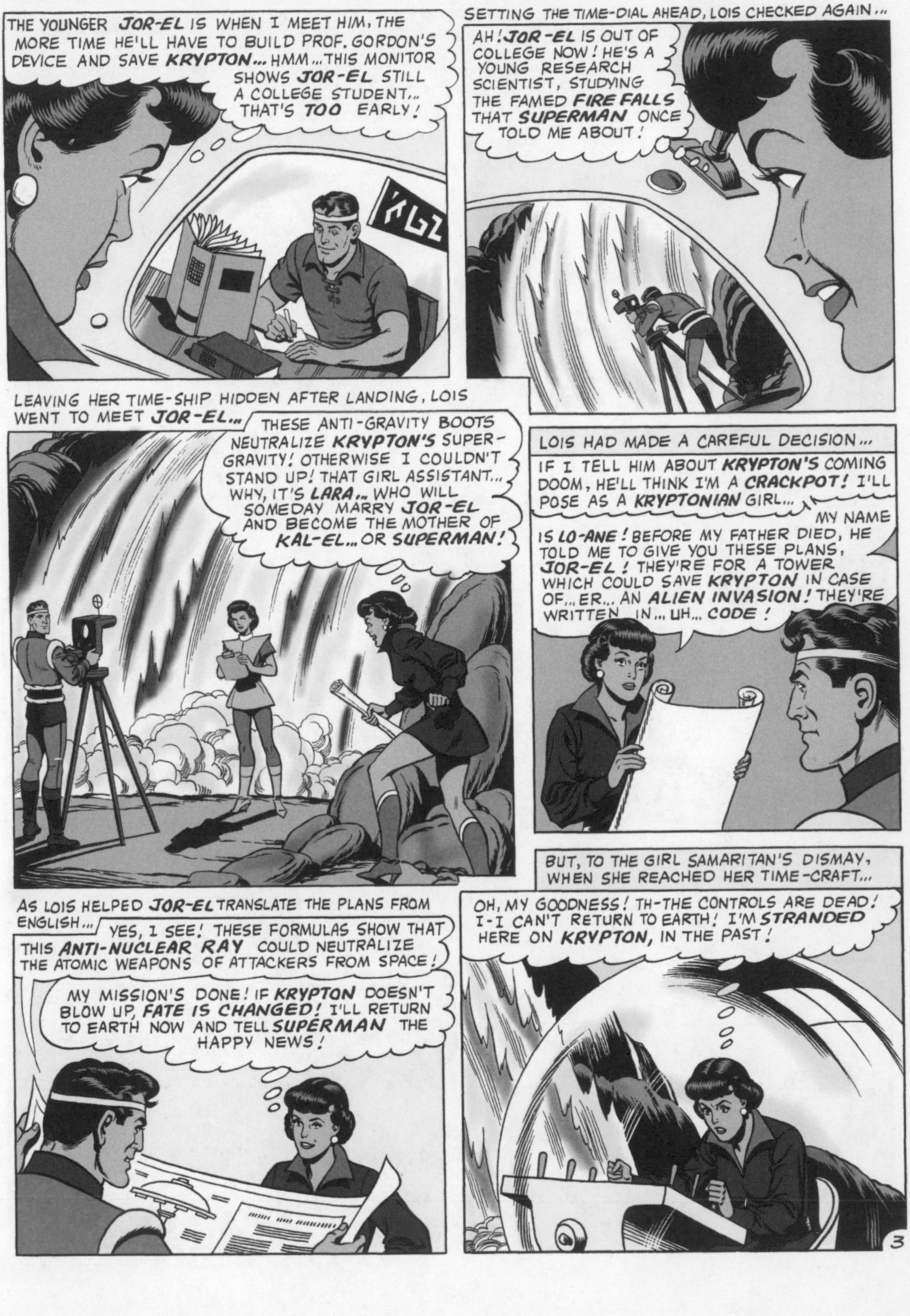
THE YOUNGER JOR-EL IS WHEN I MEET HIM, THE MORE TIME HE'LL HAVE TO BUILD PROF. GORDON'S DEVICE AND SAVE KRYPTON... HMM... THIS MONITOR SHOWS JOR-EL STILL A COLLEGE STUDENT... THAT'S TOO EARLY!
SETTING THE TIME-DIAL AHEAD, LOIS CHECKED AGAIN...
AH! JOR-EL IS OUT OF COLLEGE NOW! HE'S A YOUNG RESEARCH SCIENTIST, STUDYING THE FAMED FIRE FALLS THAT SUPERMAN ONCE TOLD ME ABOUT!
LEAVING HER TIME-SHIP HIDDEN AFTER LANDING, LOIS WENT TO MEET JOR-EL...
THESE ANTI-GRAVITY BOOTS NEUTRALIZE KRYPTON'S SUPER-GRAVITY! OTHERWISE I COULDN'T STAND UP! THAT GIRL ASSISTANT... WHY, IT'S LARA... WHO WILL SOMEDAY MARRY JOR-EL AND BECOME THE MOTHER OF KAL-EL... OR SUPERMAN!
LOIS HAD MADE A CAREFUL DECISION...
IF I TELL HIM ABOUT KRYPTON'S COMING DOOM, HE'LL THINK I'M A CRACKPOT! I'LL POSE AS A KRYPTONIAN GIRL...
MY NAME IS LO-ANE! BEFORE MY FATHER DIED, HE TOLD ME TO GIVE YOU THESE PLANS, JOR-EL! THEY'RE FOR A TOWER WHICH COULD SAVE KRYPTON IN CASE OF... ER... AN ALIEN INVASION! THEY'RE WRITTEN IN... UH... CODE!
AS LOIS HELPED JOR-EL TRANSLATE THE PLANS FROM ENGLISH...
YES, I SEE! THESE FORMULAS SHOW THAT THIS ANTI-NUCLEAR RAY COULD NEUTRALIZE THE ATOMIC WEAPONS OF ATTACKERS FROM SPACE!
MY MISSION'S DONE! IF KRYPTON DOESN'T BLOW UP, FATE IS CHANGED! I'LL RETURN TO EARTH NOW AND TELL SUPERMAN THE HAPPY NEWS!
BUT, TO THE GIRL SAMARITAN'S DISMAY, WHEN SHE REACHED HER TIME-CRAFT...
OH, MY GOODNESS! TH-THE CONTROLS ARE DEAD! I-I CAN'T RETURN TO EARTH! I'M STRANDED HERE ON KRYPTON, IN THE PAST!
3

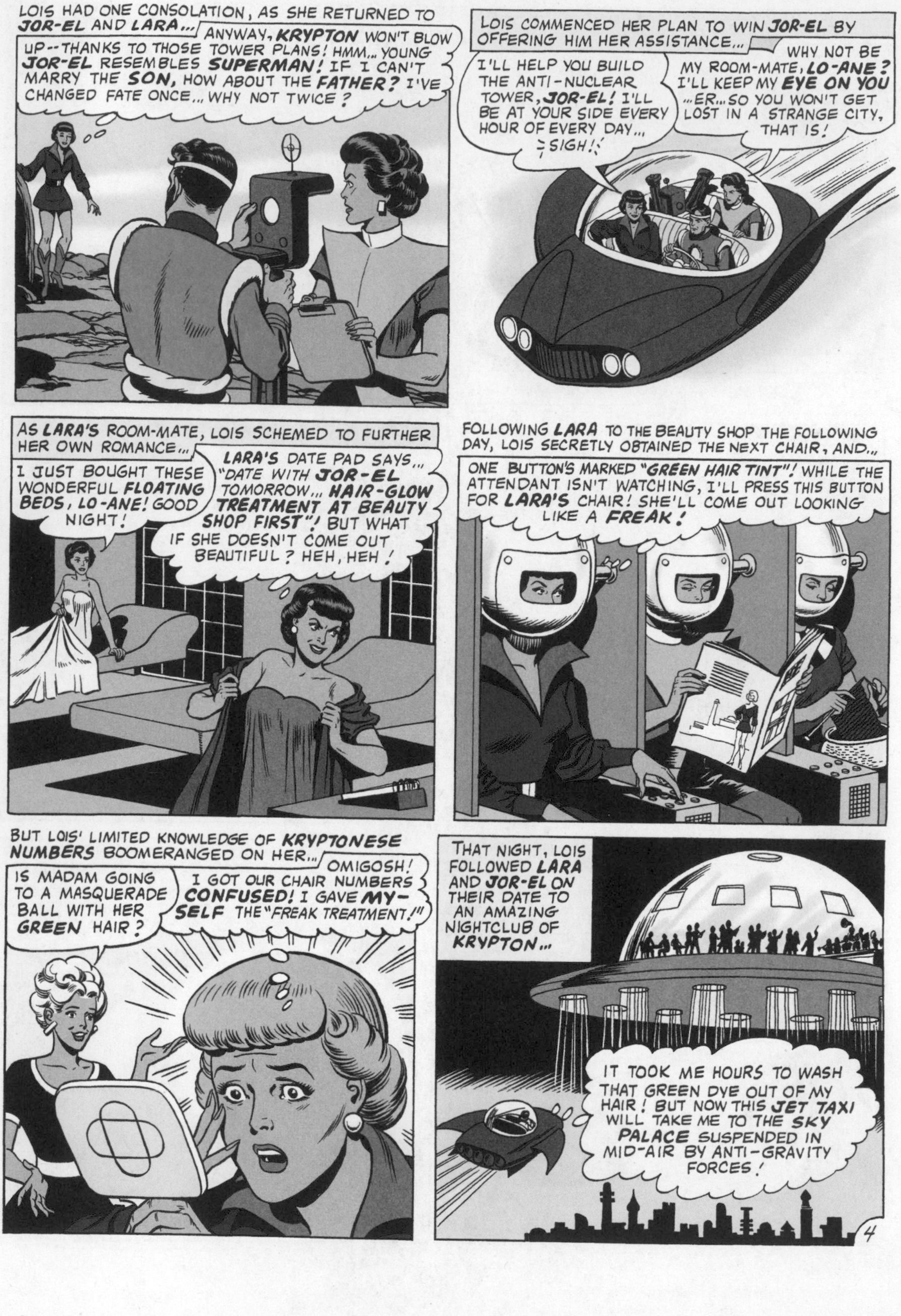
LOIS HAD ONE CONSOLATION, AS SHE RETURNED TO JOR-EL AND LARA...
ANYWAY, KRYPTON WON'T BLOW UP--THANKS TO THOSE TOWER PLANS! HMM... YOUNG JOR-EL RESEMBLES SUPERMAN! IF I CAN'T MARRY THE SON, HOW ABOUT THE FATHER? I'VE CHANGED FATE ONCE... WHY NOT TWICE?
LOIS COMMENCED HER PLAN TO WIN JOR-EL BY OFFERING HIM HER ASSISTANCE...
I'LL HELP YOU BUILD THE ANTI-NUCLEAR TOWER, JOR-EL! I'LL BE AT YOUR SIDE EVERY HOUR OF EVERY DAY... -SIGH!-
WHY NOT BE MY ROOM-MATE, LO-ANE? I'LL KEEP MY EYE ON YOU ...ER... SO YOU WON'T GET LOST IN A STRANGE CITY, THAT IS!
AS LARA'S ROOM-MATE, LOIS SCHEMED TO FURTHER HER OWN ROMANCE...
I JUST BOUGHT THESE WONDERFUL FLOATING BEDS, LO-ANE! GOOD NIGHT!
LARA'S DATE PAD SAYS... "DATE WITH JOR-EL TOMORROW... HAIR-GLOW TREATMENT AT BEAUTY SHOP FIRST"! BUT WHAT IF SHE DOESN'T COME OUT BEAUTIFUL? HEH, HEH!
FOLLOWING LARA TO THE BEAUTY SHOP THE FOLLOWING DAY, LOIS SECRETLY OBTAINED THE NEXT CHAIR, AND...
ONE BUTTON'S MARKED "GREEN HAIR TINT"! WHILE THE ATTENDANT ISN'T WATCHING, I'LL PRESS THIS BUTTON FOR LARA'S CHAIR! SHE'LL COME OUT LOOKING LIKE A FREAK!
BUT LOIS' LIMITED KNOWLEDGE OF KRYPTONESE NUMBERS BOOMERANGED ON HER...
IS MADAM GOING TO A MASQUERADE BALL WITH HER GREEN HAIR?
OMIGOSH! I GOT OUR CHAIR NUMBERS CONFUSED! I GAVE MYSELF THE "FREAK TREATMENT!"
THAT NIGHT, LOIS FOLLOWED LARA AND JOR-EL ON THEIR DATE TO AN AMAZING NIGHTCLUB OF KRYPTON...
IT TOOK ME HOURS TO WASH THAT GREEN DYE OUT OF MY HAIR! BUT NOW THIS JET TAXI WILL TAKE ME TO THE SKY PALACE SUSPENDED IN MID-AIR BY ANTI-GRAVITY FORCES!
4

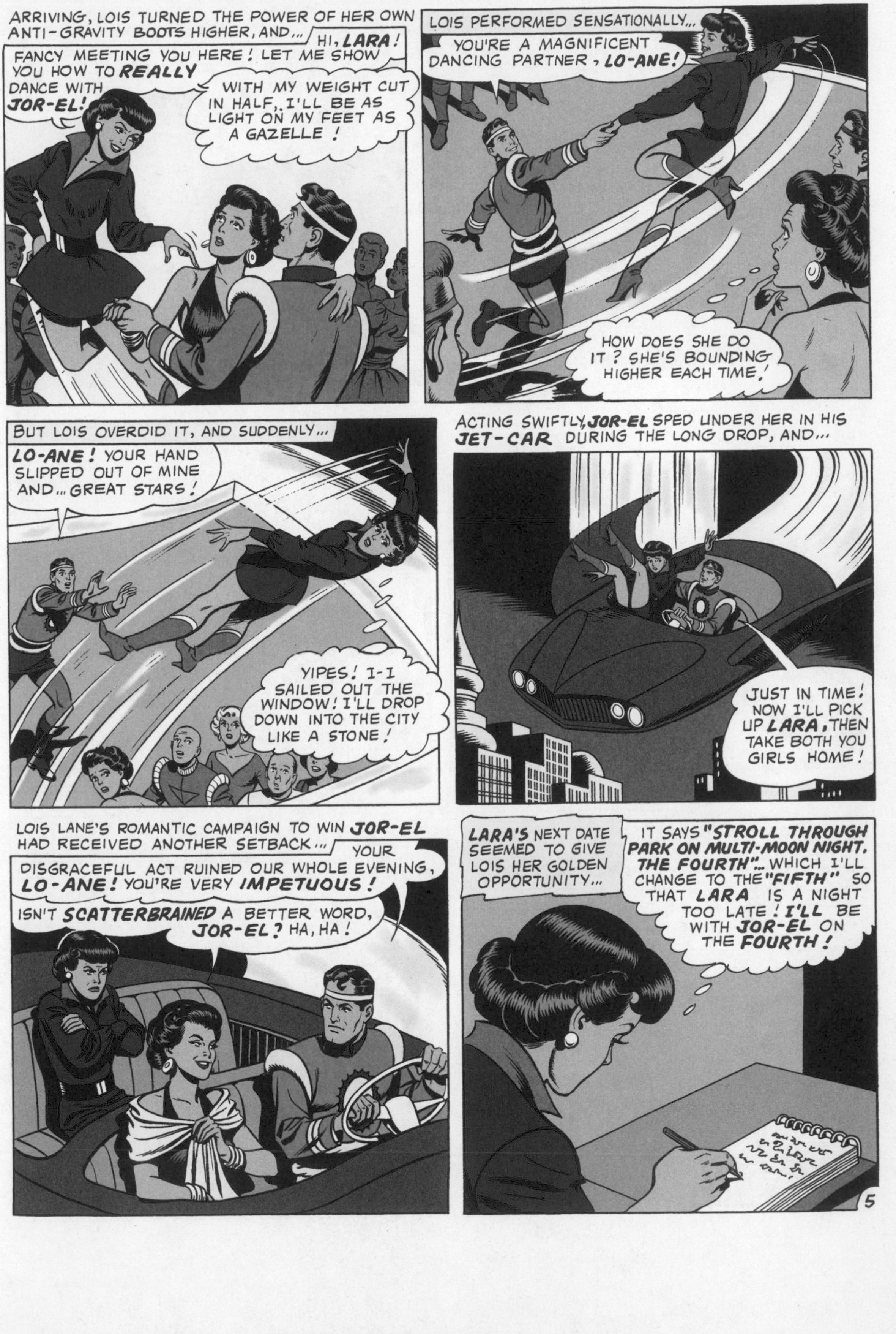
ARRIVING, LOIS TURNED THE POWER OF HER OWN ANTI-GRAVITY BOOTS HIGHER, AND...
HI, LARA! FANCY MEETING YOU HERE! LET ME SHOW YOU HOW TO REALLY DANCE WITH JOR-EL!
WITH MY WEIGHT CUT IN HALF, I'LL BE AS LIGHT ON MY FEET AS A GAZELLE!
LOIS PERFORMED SENSATIONALLY...
YOU'RE A MAGNIFICENT DANCING PARTNER, LO-ANE!
HOW DOES SHE DO IT? SHE'S BOUNDING HIGHER EACH TIME!
BUT LOIS OVERDID IT, AND SUDDENLY...
LO-ANE! YOUR HAND SLIPPED OUT OF MINE AND... GREAT STARS!
YIPES! I-I SAILED OUT THE WINDOW! I'LL DROP DOWN INTO THE CITY LIKE A STONE!
ACTING SWIFTLY, JOR-EL SPED UNDER HER IN HIS JET-CAR DURING THE LONG DROP, AND...
JUST IN TIME! NOW I'LL PICK UP LARA, THEN TAKE BOTH YOU GIRLS HOME!
LOIS LANE'S ROMANTIC CAMPAIGN TO WIN JOR-EL HAD RECEIVED ANOTHER SETBACK...
YOUR DISGRACEFUL ACT RUINED OUR WHOLE EVENING, LO-ANE! YOU'RE VERY IMPETUOUS!
ISN'T SCATTERBRAINED A BETTER WORD, JOR-EL? HA, HA!
LARA'S NEXT DATE SEEMED TO GIVE LOIS HER GOLDEN OPPORTUNITY...
IT SAYS "STROLL THROUGH PARK ON MULTI-MOON NIGHT, THE FOURTH"... WHICH I'LL CHANGE TO THE "FIFTH" SO THAT LARA IS A NIGHT TOO LATE! I'LL BE WITH JOR-EL ON THE FOURTH!
5

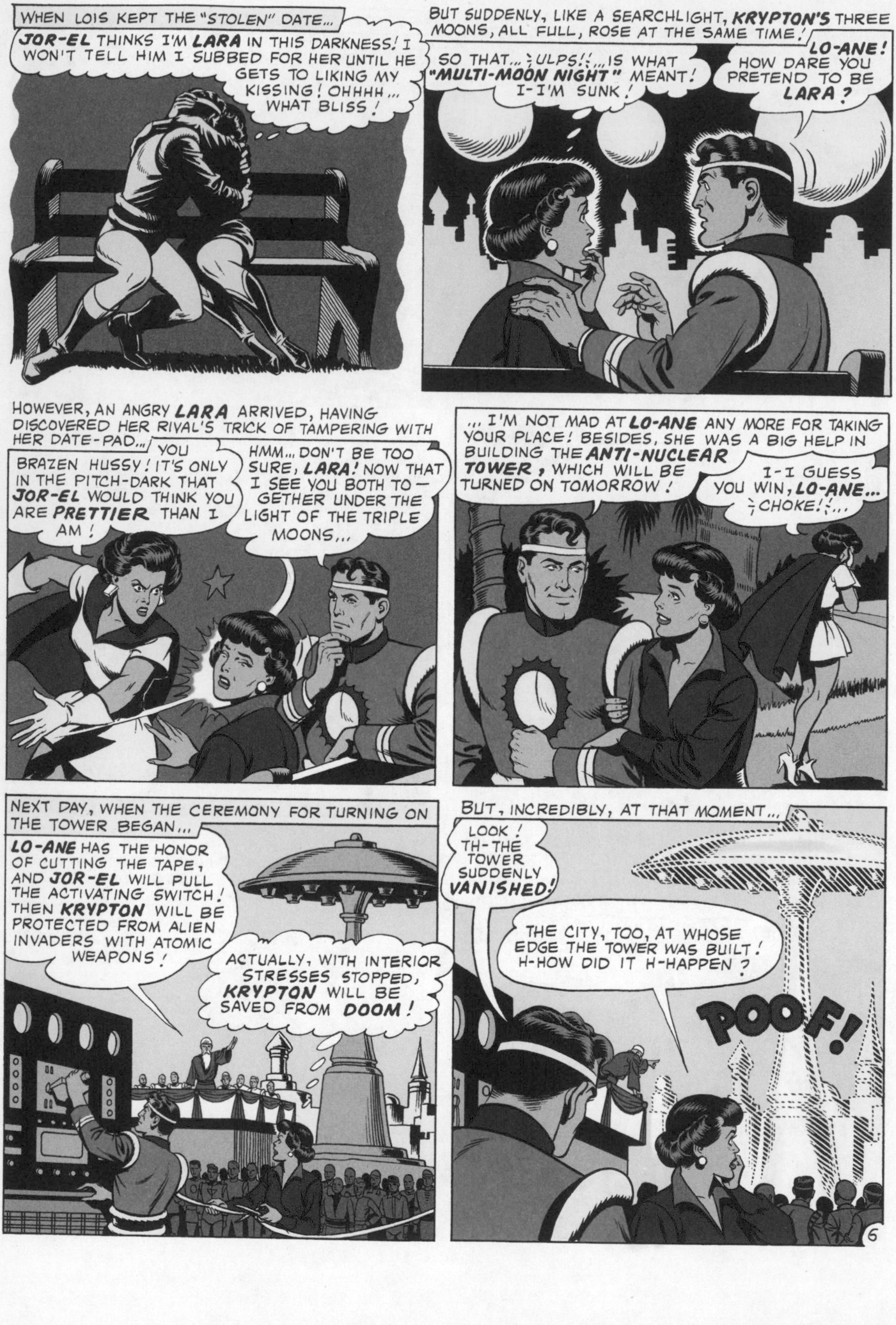
WHEN LOIS KEPT THE "STOLEN" DATE...
JOR-EL THINKS I'M LARA IN THIS DARKNESS! I WON'T TELL HIM I SUBBED FOR HER UNTIL HE GETS TO LIKING MY KISSING! OHHHH... WHAT BLISS!
BUT SUDDENLY, LIKE A SEARCHLIGHT, KRYPTON'S THREE MOONS, ALL FULL, ROSE AT THE SAME TIME!
SO THAT... ;ULPS!;... IS WHAT "MULTI-MOON NIGHT" MEANT! I-I'M SUNK!
LO-ANE! HOW DARE YOU PRETEND TO BE LARA?
HOWEVER, AN ANGRY LARA ARRIVED, HAVING DISCOVERED HER RIVAL'S TRICK OF TAMPERING WITH HER DATE-PAD...
BRAZEN HUSSY! IT'S ONLY IN THE PITCH-DARK THAT JOR-EL WOULD THINK YOU ARE PRETTIER THAN I AM!
HMM... DON'T BE TOO SURE, LARA! NOW THAT I SEE YOU BOTH TO-GETHER UNDER THE LIGHT OF THE TRIPLE MOONS...
... I'M NOT MAD AT LO-ANE ANY MORE FOR TAKING YOUR PLACE! BESIDES, SHE WAS A BIG HELP IN BUILDING THE ANTI-NUCLEAR TOWER, WHICH WILL BE TURNED ON TOMORROW!
I-I GUESS YOU WIN, LO-ANE... ;CHOKE!;...
NEXT DAY, WHEN THE CEREMONY FOR TURNING ON THE TOWER BEGAN...
LO-ANE HAS THE HONOR OF CUTTING THE TAPE, AND JOR-EL WILL PULL THE ACTIVATING SWITCH! THEN KRYPTON WILL BE PROTECTED FROM ALIEN INVADERS WITH ATOMIC WEAPONS!
ACTUALLY, WITH INTERIOR STRESSES STOPPED, KRYPTON WILL BE SAVED FROM DOOM!
BUT, INCREDIBLY, AT THAT MOMENT...
LOOK! TH-THE TOWER SUDDENLY VANISHED!
THE CITY, TOO, AT WHOSE EDGE THE TOWER WAS BUILT! H-HOW DID IT H-HAPPEN?
POOF!
6

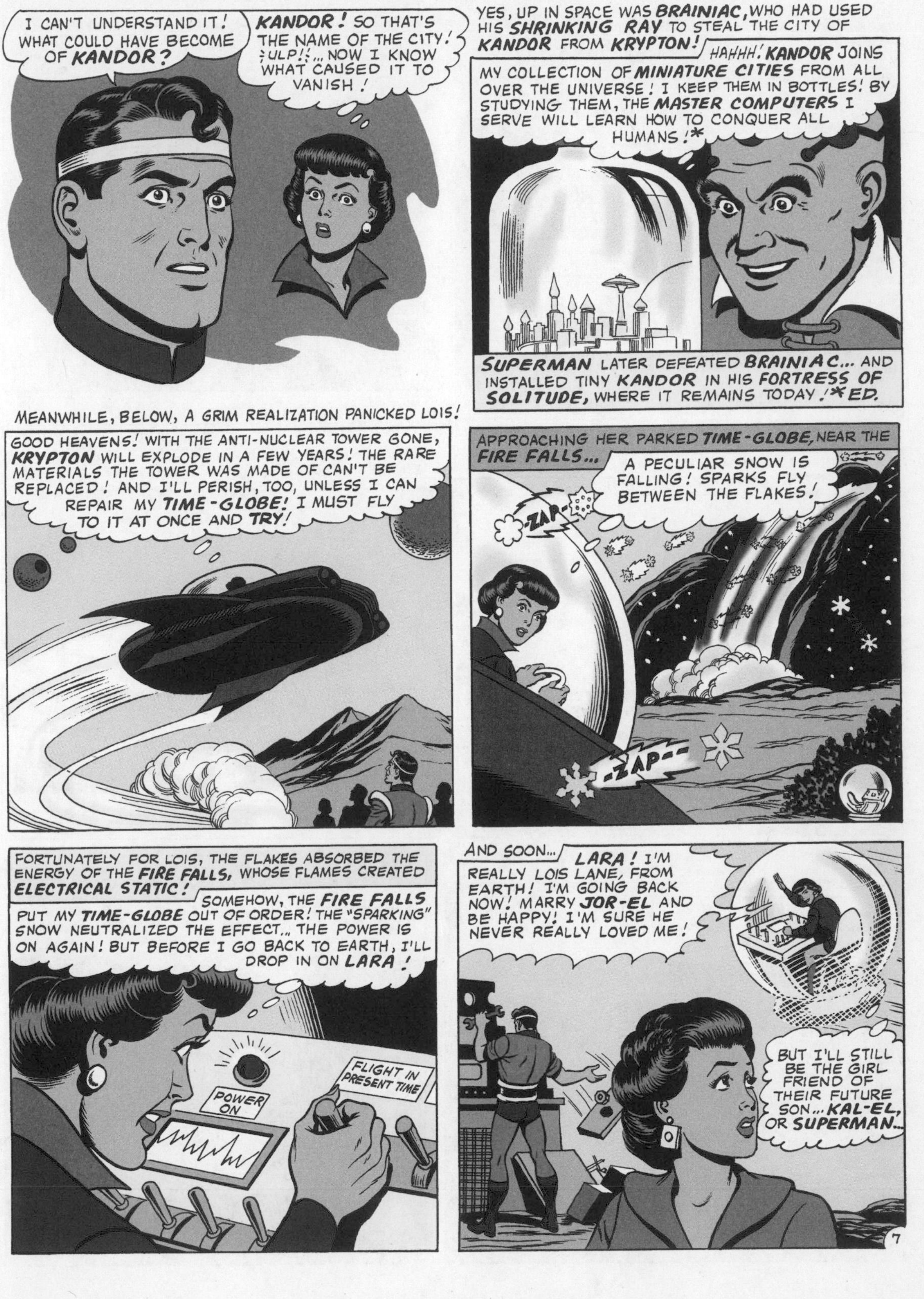

I CAN'T UNDERSTAND IT! WHAT COULD HAVE BECOME OF KANDOR?
KANDOR! SO THAT'S THE NAME OF THE CITY! ULP!! ... NOW I KNOW WHAT CAUSED IT TO VANISH!
YES, UP IN SPACE WAS BRAINIAC, WHO HAD USED HIS SHRINKING RAY TO STEAL THE CITY OF KANDOR FROM KRYPTON!
HAHHH! KANDOR JOINS MY COLLECTION OF MINIATURE CITIES FROM ALL OVER THE UNIVERSE! I KEEP THEM IN BOTTLES! BY STUDYING THEM, THE MASTER COMPUTERS I SERVE WILL LEARN HOW TO CONQUER ALL HUMANS!*
SUPERMAN LATER DEFEATED BRAINIAC... AND INSTALLED TINY KANDOR IN HIS FORTRESS OF SOLITUDE, WHERE IT REMAINS TODAY! *ED.
MEANWHILE, BELOW, A GRIM REALIZATION PANICKED LOIS!
GOOD HEAVENS! WITH THE ANTI-NUCLEAR TOWER GONE, KRYPTON WILL EXPLODE IN A FEW YEARS! THE RARE MATERIALS THE TOWER WAS MADE OF CAN'T BE REPLACED! AND I'LL PERISH, TOO, UNLESS I CAN REPAIR MY TIME-GLOBE! I MUST FLY TO IT AT ONCE AND TRY!
APPROACHING HER PARKED TIME-GLOBE, NEAR THE FIRE FALLS...
A PECULIAR SNOW IS FALLING! SPARKS FLY BETWEEN THE FLAKES!
ZAP
ZAP
FORTUNATELY FOR LOIS, THE FLAKES ABSORBED THE ENERGY OF THE FIRE FALLS, WHOSE FLAMES CREATED ELECTRICAL STATIC!
SOMEHOW, THE FIRE FALLS PUT MY TIME-GLOBE OUT OF ORDER! THE "SPARKING" SNOW NEUTRALIZED THE EFFECT... THE POWER IS ON AGAIN! BUT BEFORE I GO BACK TO EARTH, I'LL DROP IN ON LARA!
POWER ON
FLIGHT IN PRESENT TIME
AND SOON...
LARA! I'M REALLY LOIS LANE, FROM EARTH! I'M GOING BACK NOW! MARRY JOR-EL AND BE HAPPY! I'M SURE HE NEVER REALLY LOVED ME!
BUT I'LL STILL BE THE GIRL FRIEND OF THEIR FUTURE SON... KAL-EL, OR SUPERMAN...
7

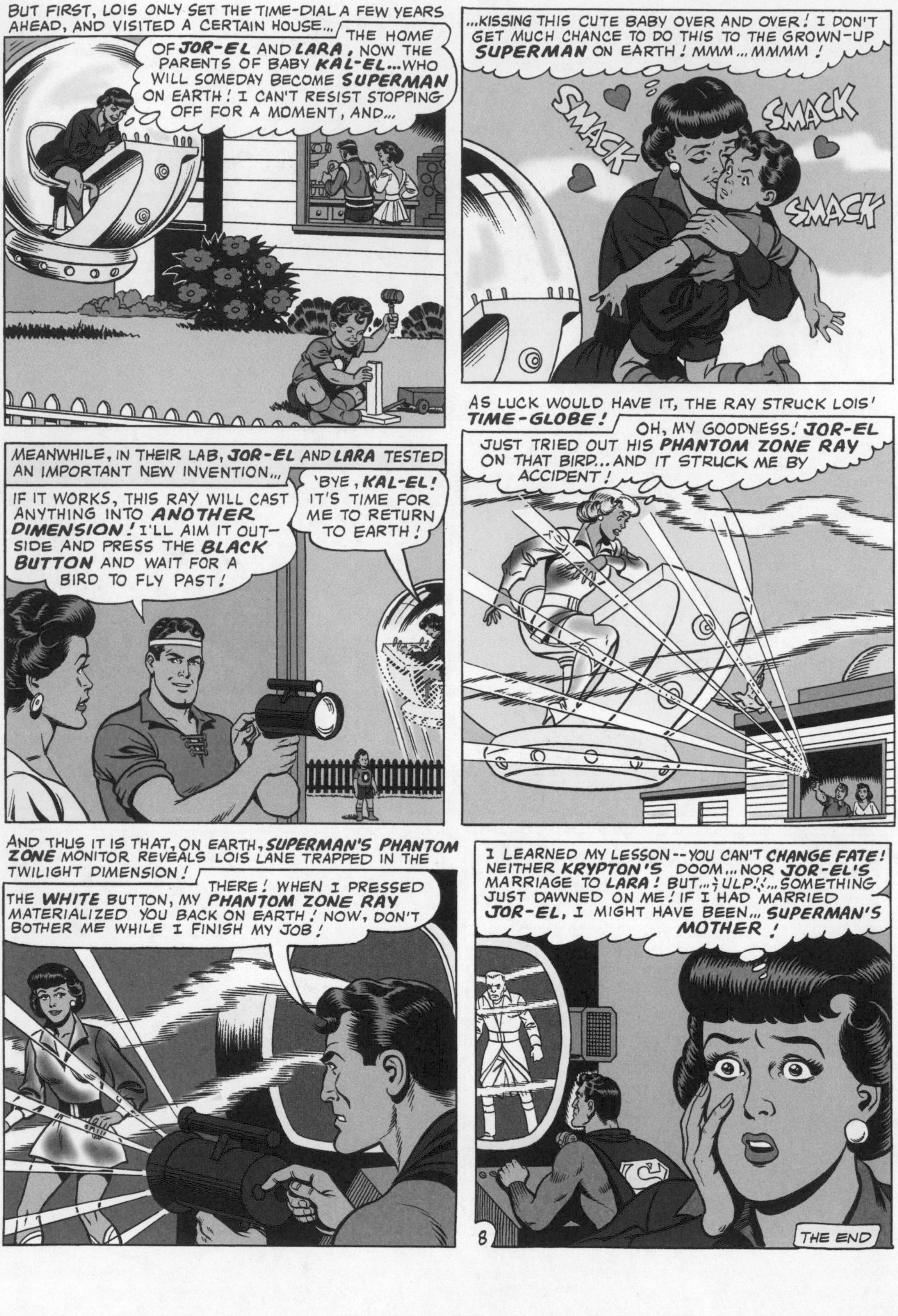

BUT FIRST, LOIS ONLY SET THE TIME-DIAL A FEW YEARS AHEAD, AND VISITED A CERTAIN HOUSE...
THE HOME OF JOR-EL AND LARA, NOW THE PARENTS OF BABY KAL-EL...WHO WILL SOMEDAY BECOME SUPERMAN ON EARTH! I CAN'T RESIST STOPPING OFF FOR A MOMENT, AND...
...KISSING THIS CUTE BABY OVER AND OVER! I DON'T GET MUCH CHANCE TO DO THIS TO THE GROWN-UP SUPERMAN ON EARTH! MMM... MMMM!
SMACK
SMACK
SMACK
MEANWHILE, IN THEIR LAB, JOR-EL AND LARA TESTED AN IMPORTANT NEW INVENTION...
IF IT WORKS, THIS RAY WILL CAST ANYTHING INTO ANOTHER DIMENSION! I'LL AIM IT OUTSIDE AND PRESS THE BLACK BUTTON AND WAIT FOR A BIRD TO FLY PAST!
'BYE, KAL-EL! IT'S TIME FOR ME TO RETURN TO EARTH!
AS LUCK WOULD HAVE IT, THE RAY STRUCK LOIS' TIME-GLOBE!
OH, MY GOODNESS! JOR-EL JUST TRIED OUT HIS PHANTOM ZONE RAY ON THAT BIRD...AND IT STRUCK ME BY ACCIDENT!
AND THUS IT IS THAT, ON EARTH, SUPERMAN'S PHANTOM ZONE MONITOR REVEALS LOIS LANE TRAPPED IN THE TWILIGHT DIMENSION!
THERE! WHEN I PRESSED THE WHITE BUTTON, MY PHANTOM ZONE RAY MATERIALIZED YOU BACK ON EARTH! NOW, DON'T BOTHER ME WHILE I FINISH MY JOB!
I LEARNED MY LESSON--YOU CAN'T CHANGE FATE! NEITHER KRYPTON'S DOOM... NOR JOR-EL'S MARRIAGE TO LARA! BUT... ULP!... SOMETHING JUST DAWNED ON ME! IF I HAD MARRIED JOR-EL, I MIGHT HAVE BEEN... SUPERMAN'S MOTHER!
8
THE END

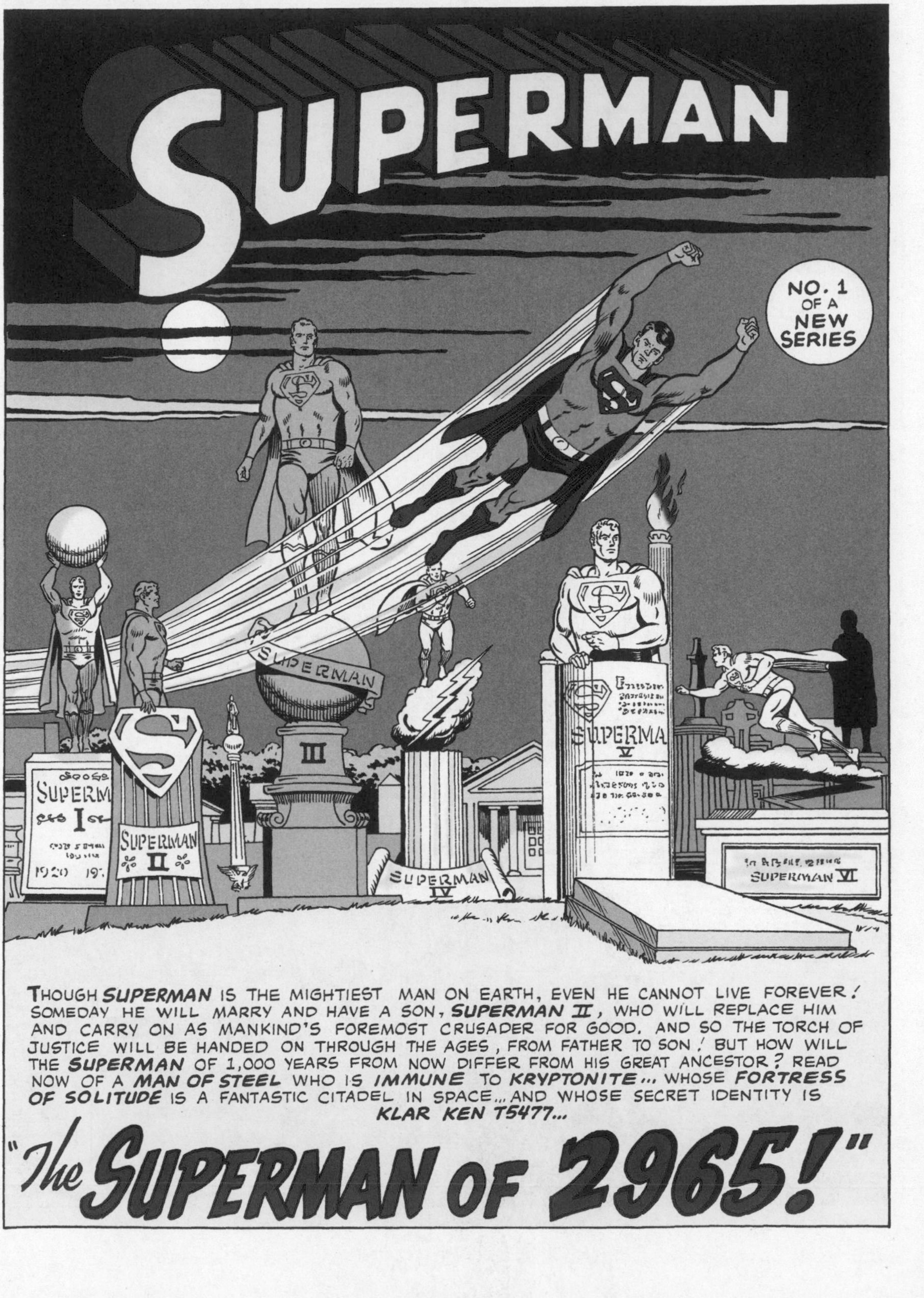
SUPERMAN
NO. 1 OF A NEW SERIES
SUPERM I 1920 19
SUPERMAN II
SUPERMAN
III
SUPERMAN IV
SUPERMA V
SUPERMAN VI
THOUGH SUPERMAN IS THE MIGHTIEST MAN ON EARTH, EVEN HE CANNOT LIVE FOREVER! SOMEDAY HE WILL MARRY AND HAVE A SON, SUPERMAN II, WHO WILL REPLACE HIM AND CARRY ON AS MANKIND'S FOREMOST CRUSADER FOR GOOD. AND SO THE TORCH OF JUSTICE WILL BE HANDED ON THROUGH THE AGES, FROM FATHER TO SON! BUT HOW WILL THE SUPERMAN OF 1,000 YEARS FROM NOW DIFFER FROM HIS GREAT ANCESTOR? READ NOW OF A MAN OF STEEL WHO IS IMMUNE TO KRYPTONITE... WHOSE FORTRESS OF SOLITUDE IS A FANTASTIC CITADEL IN SPACE... AND WHOSE SECRET IDENTITY IS KLAR KEN T5477...
"The SUPERMAN OF 2965!"

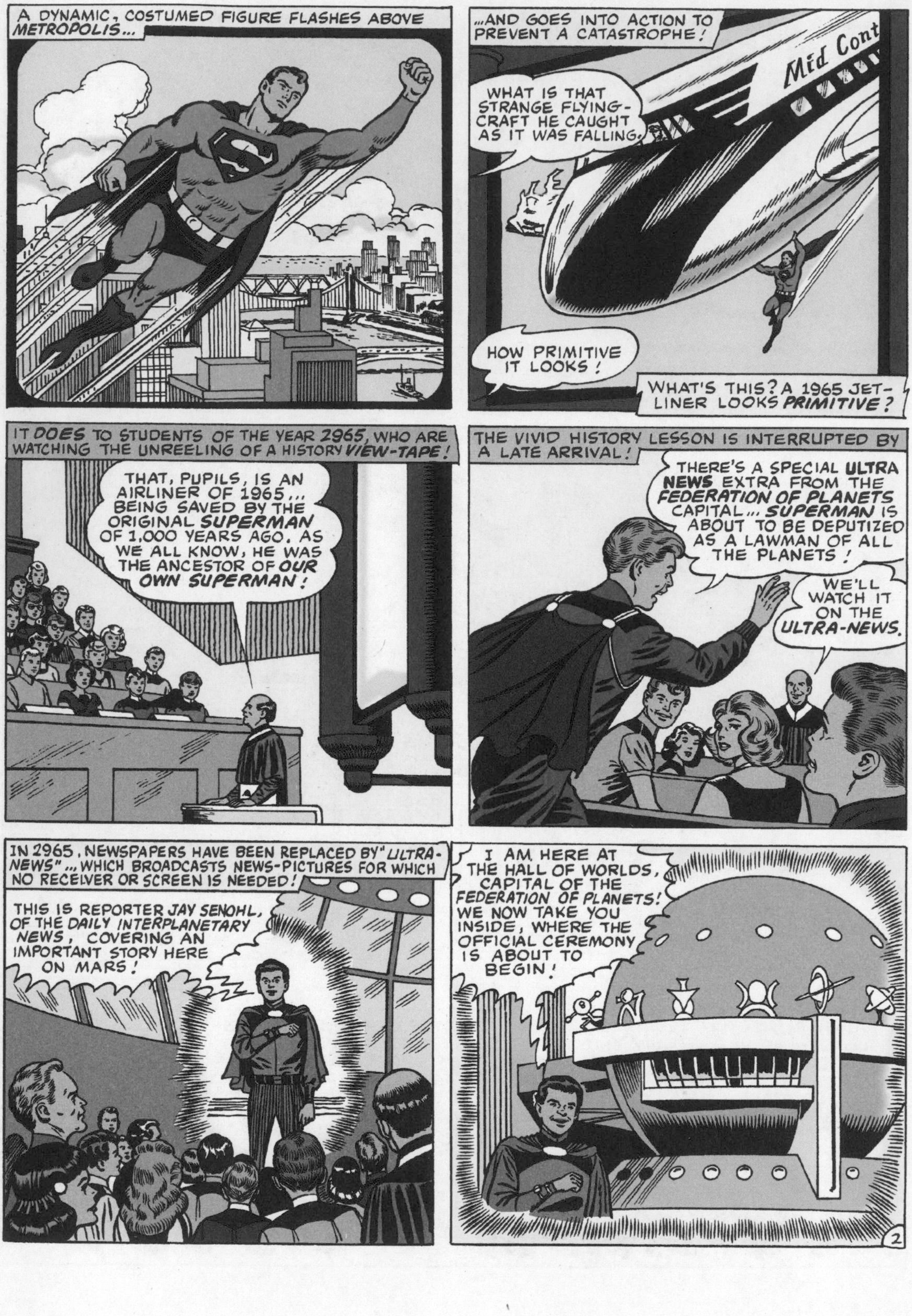
A DYNAMIC, COSTUMED FIGURE FLASHES ABOVE METROPOLIS...
...AND GOES INTO ACTION TO PREVENT A CATASTROPHE!
Mid Cont
WHAT IS THAT STRANGE FLYING-CRAFT HE CAUGHT AS IT WAS FALLING.
HOW PRIMITIVE IT LOOKS!
WHAT'S THIS? A 1965 JET-LINER LOOKS PRIMITIVE?
IT DOES TO STUDENTS OF THE YEAR 2965, WHO ARE WATCHING THE UNREELING OF A HISTORY VIEW-TAPE!
THAT, PUPILS, IS AN AIRLINER OF 1965... BEING SAVED BY THE ORIGINAL SUPERMAN OF 1,000 YEARS AGO. AS WE ALL KNOW, HE WAS THE ANCESTOR OF OUR OWN SUPERMAN!
THE VIVID HISTORY LESSON IS INTERRUPTED BY A LATE ARRIVAL!
THERE'S A SPECIAL ULTRA NEWS EXTRA FROM THE FEDERATION OF PLANETS CAPITAL... SUPERMAN IS ABOUT TO BE DEPUTIZED AS A LAWMAN OF ALL THE PLANETS!
WE'LL WATCH IT ON THE ULTRA-NEWS.
IN 2965, NEWSPAPERS HAVE BEEN REPLACED BY "ULTRA-NEWS"... WHICH BROADCASTS NEWS-PICTURES FOR WHICH NO RECEIVER OR SCREEN IS NEEDED!
THIS IS REPORTER JAY SENOHL, OF THE DAILY INTERPLANETARY NEWS, COVERING AN IMPORTANT STORY HERE ON MARS!
I AM HERE AT THE HALL OF WORLDS, CAPITAL OF THE FEDERATION OF PLANETS! WE NOW TAKE YOU INSIDE, WHERE THE OFFICIAL CEREMONY IS ABOUT TO BEGIN!
2

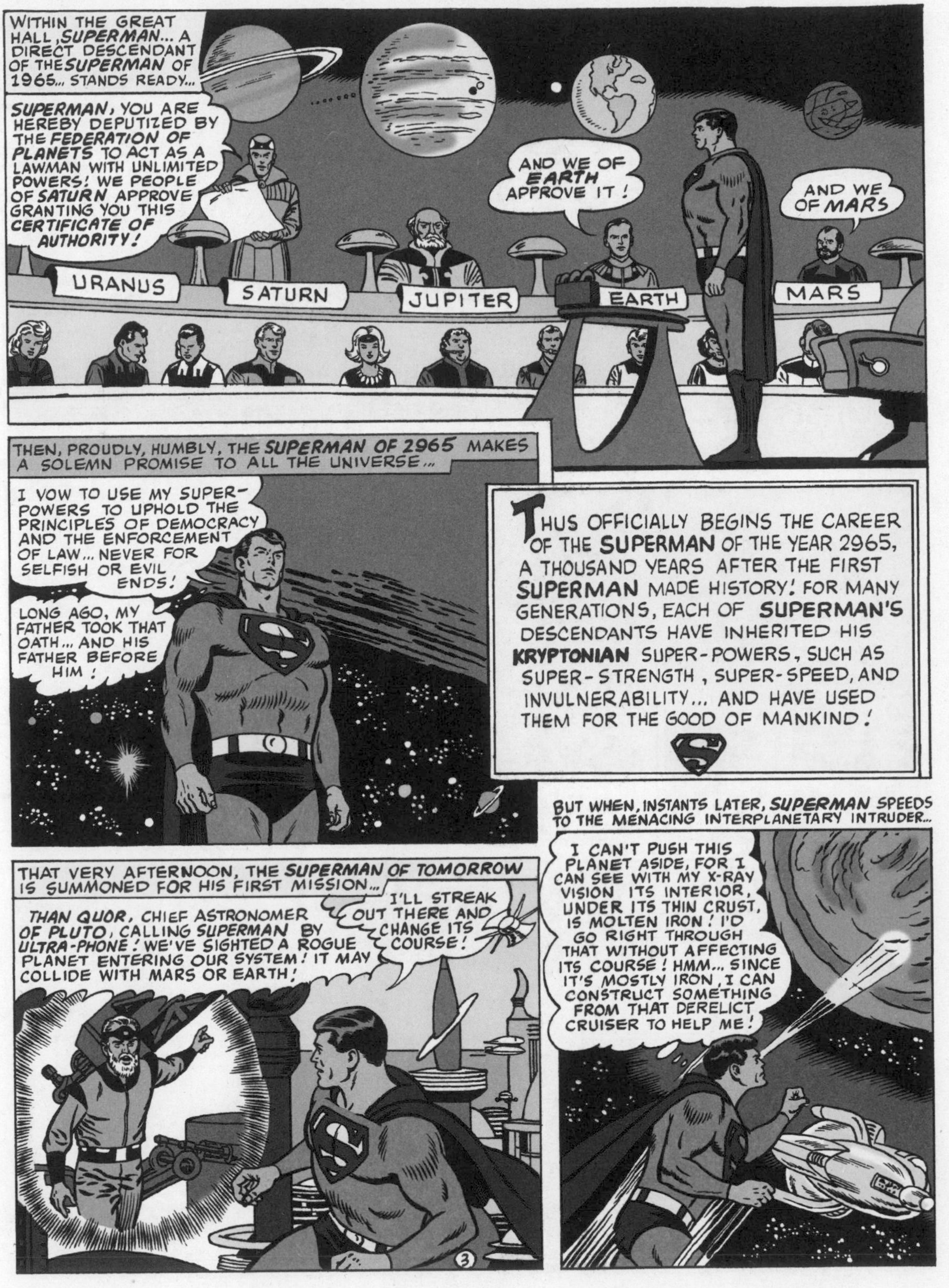
WITHIN THE GREAT HALL, SUPERMAN... A DIRECT DESCENDANT OF THE SUPERMAN OF 1965... STANDS READY...
SUPERMAN, YOU ARE HEREBY DEPUTIZED BY THE FEDERATION OF PLANETS TO ACT AS A LAWMAN WITH UNLIMITED POWERS! WE PEOPLE OF SATURN APPROVE GRANTING YOU THIS CERTIFICATE OF AUTHORITY!
AND WE OF EARTH APPROVE IT!
AND WE OF MARS
URANUS
SATURN
JUPITER
EARTH
MARS
THEN, PROUDLY, HUMBLY, THE SUPERMAN OF 2965 MAKES A SOLEMN PROMISE TO ALL THE UNIVERSE...
I VOW TO USE MY SUPER-POWERS TO UPHOLD THE PRINCIPLES OF DEMOCRACY AND THE ENFORCEMENT OF LAW... NEVER FOR SELFISH OR EVIL ENDS!
LONG AGO, MY FATHER TOOK THAT OATH... AND HIS FATHER BEFORE HIM!
THUS OFFICIALLY BEGINS THE CAREER OF THE SUPERMAN OF THE YEAR 2965, A THOUSAND YEARS AFTER THE FIRST SUPERMAN MADE HISTORY! FOR MANY GENERATIONS, EACH OF SUPERMAN'S DESCENDANTS HAVE INHERITED HIS KRYPTONIAN SUPER-POWERS, SUCH AS SUPER-STRENGTH, SUPER-SPEED, AND INVULNERABILITY... AND HAVE USED THEM FOR THE GOOD OF MANKIND!
THAT VERY AFTERNOON, THE SUPERMAN OF TOMORROW IS SUMMONED FOR HIS FIRST MISSION...
THAN QUOR, CHIEF ASTRONOMER OF PLUTO, CALLING SUPERMAN BY ULTRA-PHONE! WE'VE SIGHTED A ROGUE PLANET ENTERING OUR SYSTEM! IT MAY COLLIDE WITH MARS OR EARTH!
I'LL STREAK OUT THERE AND CHANGE ITS COURSE!
3
BUT WHEN, INSTANTS LATER, SUPERMAN SPEEDS TO THE MENACING INTERPLANETARY INTRUDER...
I CAN'T PUSH THIS PLANET ASIDE, FOR I CAN SEE WITH MY X-RAY VISION ITS INTERIOR, UNDER ITS THIN CRUST, IS MOLTEN IRON! I'D GO RIGHT THROUGH THAT WITHOUT AFFECTING ITS COURSE! HMM... SINCE IT'S MOSTLY IRON, I CAN CONSTRUCT SOMETHING FROM THAT DERELICT CRUISER TO HELP ME!

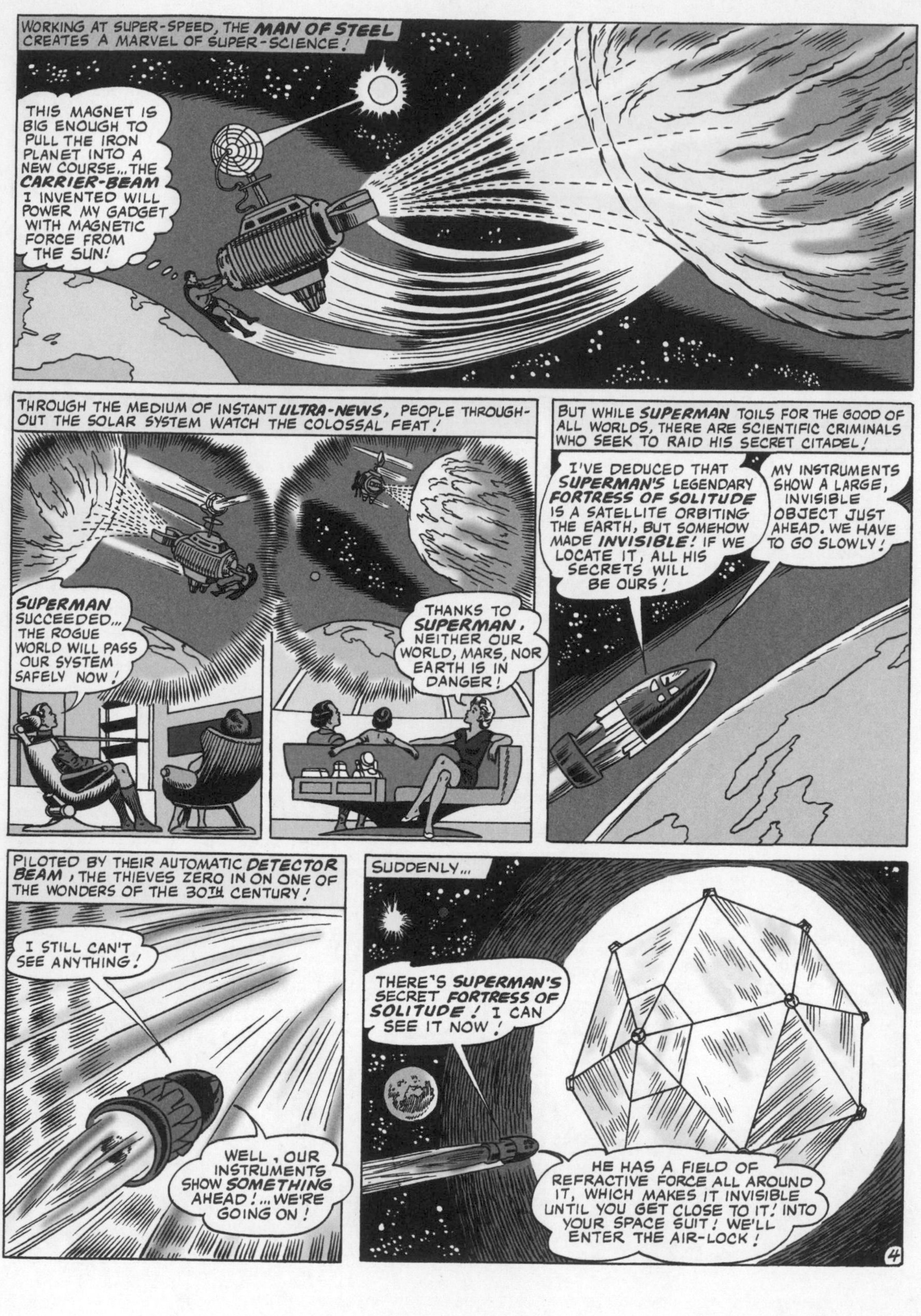
WORKING AT SUPER-SPEED, THE MAN OF STEEL CREATES A MARVEL OF SUPER-SCIENCE!
THIS MAGNET IS BIG ENOUGH TO PULL THE IRON PLANET INTO A NEW COURSE...THE CARRIER-BEAM I INVENTED WILL POWER MY GADGET WITH MAGNETIC FORCE FROM THE SUN!
THROUGH THE MEDIUM OF INSTANT ULTRA-NEWS, PEOPLE THROUGH-OUT THE SOLAR SYSTEM WATCH THE COLOSSAL FEAT!
SUPERMAN SUCCEEDED... THE ROGUE WORLD WILL PASS OUR SYSTEM SAFELY NOW!
THANKS TO SUPERMAN, NEITHER OUR WORLD, MARS, NOR EARTH IS IN DANGER!
BUT WHILE SUPERMAN TOILS FOR THE GOOD OF ALL WORLDS, THERE ARE SCIENTIFIC CRIMINALS WHO SEEK TO RAID HIS SECRET CITADEL!
I'VE DEDUCED THAT SUPERMAN'S LEGENDARY FORTRESS OF SOLITUDE IS A SATELLITE ORBITING THE EARTH, BUT SOMEHOW MADE INVISIBLE! IF WE LOCATE IT, ALL HIS SECRETS WILL BE OURS!
MY INSTRUMENTS SHOW A LARGE, INVISIBLE OBJECT JUST AHEAD. WE HAVE TO GO SLOWLY!
PILOTED BY THEIR AUTOMATIC DETECTOR BEAM, THE THIEVES ZERO IN ON ONE OF THE WONDERS OF THE 30TH CENTURY!
I STILL CAN'T SEE ANYTHING!
WELL, OUR INSTRUMENTS SHOW SOMETHING AHEAD!...WE'RE GOING ON!
SUDDENLY...
THERE'S SUPERMAN'S SECRET FORTRESS OF SOLITUDE! I CAN SEE IT NOW!
HE HAS A FIELD OF REFRACTIVE FORCE ALL AROUND IT, WHICH MAKES IT INVISIBLE UNTIL YOU GET CLOSE TO IT! INTO YOUR SPACE SUIT! WE'LL ENTER THE AIR-LOCK!
4

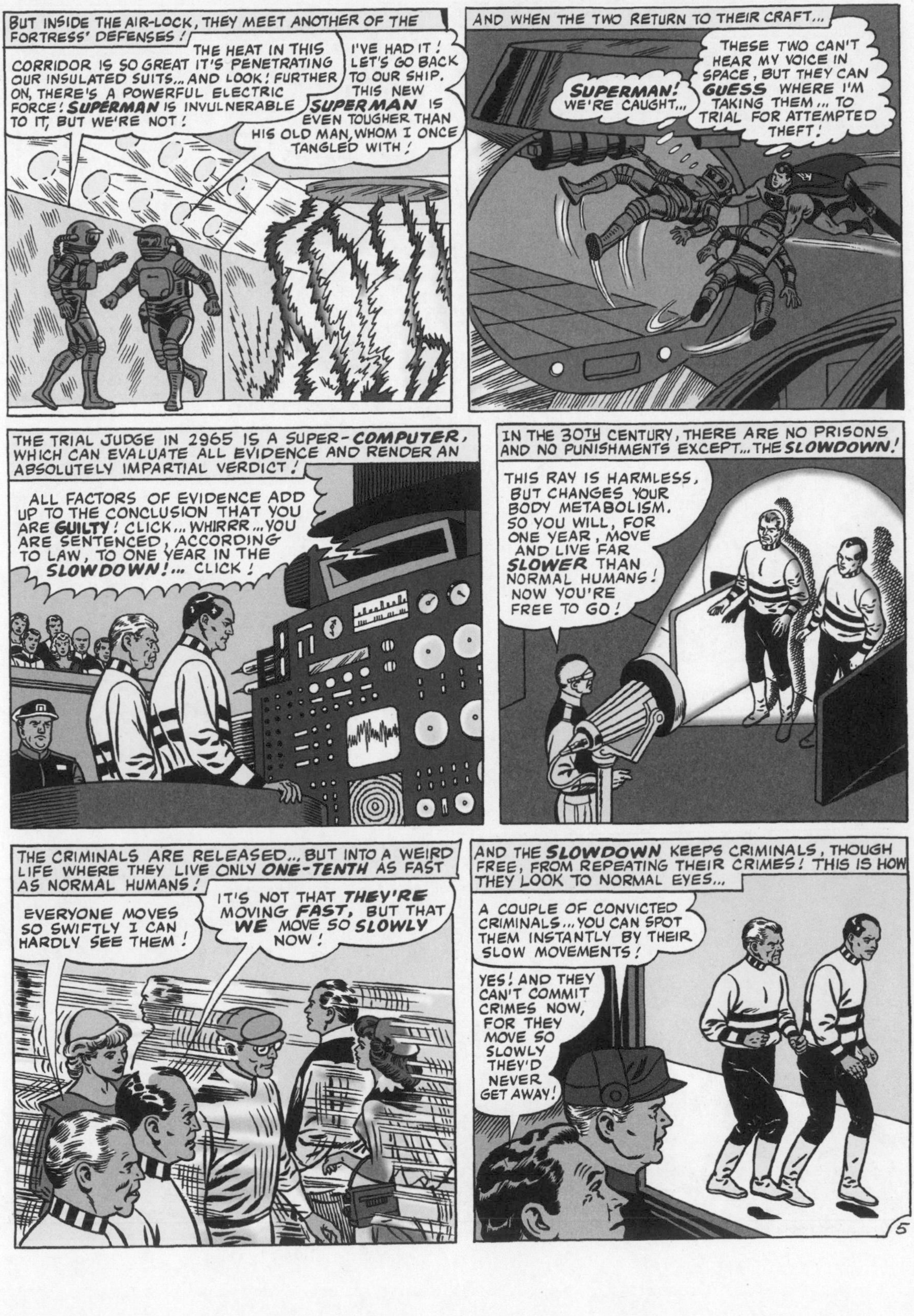
BUT INSIDE THE AIR-LOCK, THEY MEET ANOTHER OF THE FORTRESS' DEFENSES!
THE HEAT IN THIS CORRIDOR IS SO GREAT IT'S PENETRATING OUR INSULATED SUITS... AND LOOK! FURTHER ON, THERE'S A POWERFUL ELECTRIC FORCE! SUPERMAN IS INVULNERABLE TO IT, BUT WE'RE NOT!
I'VE HAD IT! LET'S GO BACK TO OUR SHIP. THIS NEW SUPERMAN IS EVEN TOUGHER THAN HIS OLD MAN, WHOM I ONCE TANGLED WITH!
AND WHEN THE TWO RETURN TO THEIR CRAFT...
SUPERMAN! WE'RE CAUGHT...
THESE TWO CAN'T HEAR MY VOICE IN SPACE, BUT THEY CAN GUESS WHERE I'M TAKING THEM... TO TRIAL FOR ATTEMPTED THEFT!
THE TRIAL JUDGE IN 2965 IS A SUPER-COMPUTER, WHICH CAN EVALUATE ALL EVIDENCE AND RENDER AN ABSOLUTELY IMPARTIAL VERDICT!
ALL FACTORS OF EVIDENCE ADD UP TO THE CONCLUSION THAT YOU ARE GUILTY! CLICK... WHIRRR... YOU ARE SENTENCED, ACCORDING TO LAW, TO ONE YEAR IN THE SLOWDOWN!... CLICK!
IN THE 30TH CENTURY, THERE ARE NO PRISONS AND NO PUNISHMENTS EXCEPT... THE SLOWDOWN!
THIS RAY IS HARMLESS, BUT CHANGES YOUR BODY METABOLISM. SO YOU WILL, FOR ONE YEAR, MOVE AND LIVE FAR SLOWER THAN NORMAL HUMANS! NOW YOU'RE FREE TO GO!
THE CRIMINALS ARE RELEASED... BUT INTO A WEIRD LIFE WHERE THEY LIVE ONLY ONE-TENTH AS FAST AS NORMAL HUMANS!
EVERYONE MOVES SO SWIFTLY I CAN HARDLY SEE THEM!
IT'S NOT THAT THEY'RE MOVING FAST, BUT THAT WE MOVE SO SLOWLY NOW!
AND THE SLOWDOWN KEEPS CRIMINALS, THOUGH FREE, FROM REPEATING THEIR CRIMES! THIS IS HOW THEY LOOK TO NORMAL EYES...
A COUPLE OF CONVICTED CRIMINALS... YOU CAN SPOT THEM INSTANTLY BY THEIR SLOW MOVEMENTS!
YES! AND THEY CAN'T COMMIT CRIMES NOW, FOR THEY MOVE SO SLOWLY THEY'D NEVER GET AWAY!
5

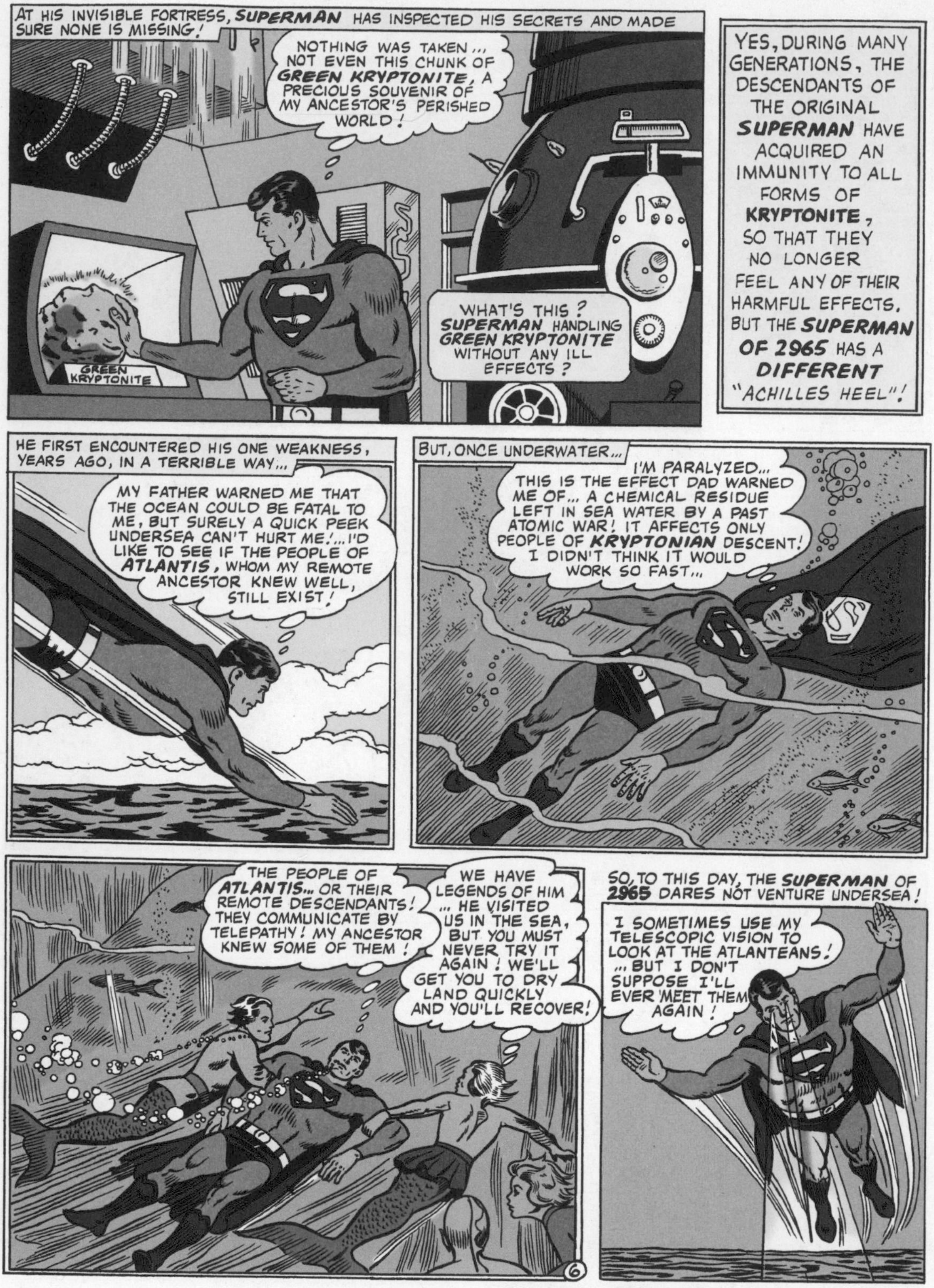
AT HIS INVISIBLE FORTRESS, SUPERMAN HAS INSPECTED HIS SECRETS AND MADE SURE NONE IS MISSING!
NOTHING WAS TAKEN... NOT EVEN THIS CHUNK OF GREEN KRYPTONITE, A PRECIOUS SOUVENIR OF MY ANCESTOR'S PERISHED WORLD!
GREEN KRYPTONITE
WHAT'S THIS? SUPERMAN HANDLING GREEN KRYPTONITE WITHOUT ANY ILL EFFECTS?
YES, DURING MANY GENERATIONS, THE DESCENDANTS OF THE ORIGINAL SUPERMAN HAVE ACQUIRED AN IMMUNITY TO ALL FORMS OF KRYPTONITE, SO THAT THEY NO LONGER FEEL ANY OF THEIR HARMFUL EFFECTS. BUT THE SUPERMAN OF 2965 HAS A DIFFERENT "ACHILLES HEEL"!
HE FIRST ENCOUNTERED HIS ONE WEAKNESS, YEARS AGO, IN A TERRIBLE WAY...
MY FATHER WARNED ME THAT THE OCEAN COULD BE FATAL TO ME, BUT SURELY A QUICK PEEK UNDERSEA CAN'T HURT ME!... I'D LIKE TO SEE IF THE PEOPLE OF ATLANTIS, WHOM MY REMOTE ANCESTOR KNEW WELL, STILL EXIST!
BUT, ONCE UNDERWATER...
I'M PARALYZED... THIS IS THE EFFECT DAD WARNED ME OF... A CHEMICAL RESIDUE LEFT IN SEA WATER BY A PAST ATOMIC WAR! IT AFFECTS ONLY PEOPLE OF KRYPTONIAN DESCENT! I DIDN'T THINK IT WOULD WORK SO FAST...
THE PEOPLE OF ATLANTIS... OR THEIR REMOTE DESCENDANTS! THEY COMMUNICATE BY TELEPATHY! MY ANCESTOR KNEW SOME OF THEM!
WE HAVE LEGENDS OF HIM ... HE VISITED US IN THE SEA, BUT YOU MUST NEVER TRY IT AGAIN! WE'LL GET YOU TO DRY LAND QUICKLY AND YOU'LL RECOVER!
6
SO, TO THIS DAY, THE SUPERMAN OF 2965 DARES NOT VENTURE UNDERSEA!
I SOMETIMES USE MY TELESCOPIC VISION TO LOOK AT THE ATLANTEANS! ... BUT I DON'T SUPPOSE I'LL EVER MEET THEM AGAIN!

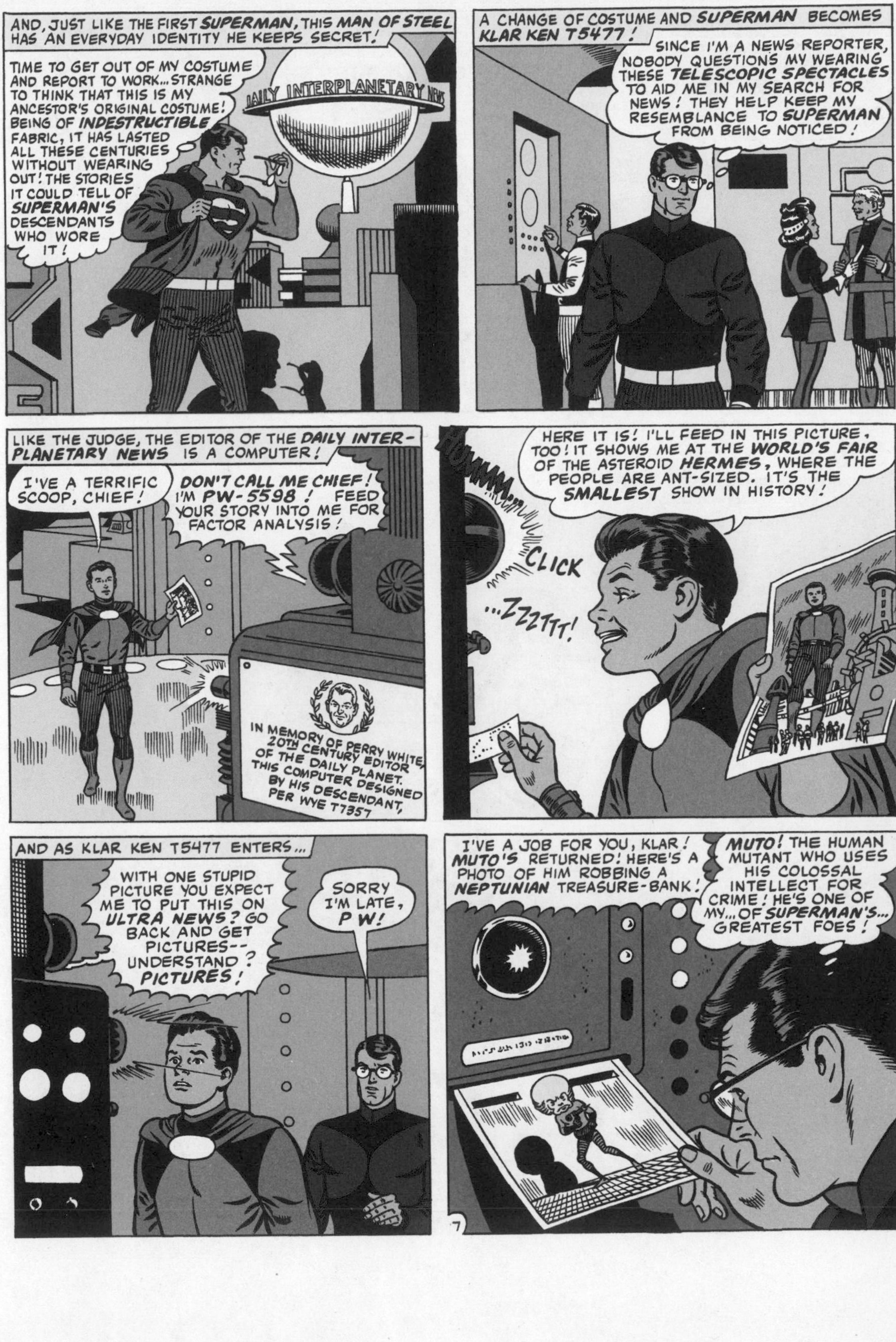
AND, JUST LIKE THE FIRST SUPERMAN, THIS MAN OF STEEL HAS AN EVERYDAY IDENTITY HE KEEPS SECRET!
TIME TO GET OUT OF MY COSTUME AND REPORT TO WORK... STRANGE TO THINK THAT THIS IS MY ANCESTOR'S ORIGINAL COSTUME! BEING OF INDESTRUCTIBLE FABRIC, IT HAS LASTED ALL THESE CENTURIES WITHOUT WEARING OUT! THE STORIES IT COULD TELL OF SUPERMAN'S DESCENDANTS WHO WORE IT!
DAILY INTERPLANETARY NEWS
A CHANGE OF COSTUME AND SUPERMAN BECOMES KLAR KEN T5477!
SINCE I'M A NEWS REPORTER, NOBODY QUESTIONS MY WEARING THESE TELESCOPIC SPECTACLES TO AID ME IN MY SEARCH FOR NEWS! THEY HELP KEEP MY RESEMBLANCE TO SUPERMAN FROM BEING NOTICED!
LIKE THE JUDGE, THE EDITOR OF THE DAILY INTER-PLANETARY NEWS IS A COMPUTER!
I'VE A TERRIFIC SCOOP, CHIEF!
DON'T CALL ME CHIEF! I'M PW-5598! FEED YOUR STORY INTO ME FOR FACTOR ANALYSIS!
IN MEMORY OF PERRY WHITE, 20TH CENTURY EDITOR OF THE DAILY PLANET. THIS COMPUTER DESIGNED BY HIS DESCENDANT, PER WYE T7357
HUMMM...
HERE IT IS! I'LL FEED IN THIS PICTURE, TOO! IT SHOWS ME AT THE WORLD'S FAIR OF THE ASTEROID HERMES, WHERE THE PEOPLE ARE ANT-SIZED. IT'S THE SMALLEST SHOW IN HISTORY!
CLICK
...ZZZTTT!
AND AS KLAR KEN T5477 ENTERS...
WITH ONE STUPID PICTURE YOU EXPECT ME TO PUT THIS ON ULTRA NEWS? GO BACK AND GET PICTURES-- UNDERSTAND? PICTURES!
SORRY I'M LATE, PW!
I'VE A JOB FOR YOU, KLAR! MUTO'S RETURNED! HERE'S A PHOTO OF HIM ROBBING A NEPTUNIAN TREASURE-BANK!
MUTO! THE HUMAN MUTANT WHO USES HIS COLOSSAL INTELLECT FOR CRIME! HE'S ONE OF MY... OF SUPERMAN'S... GREATEST FOES!
7

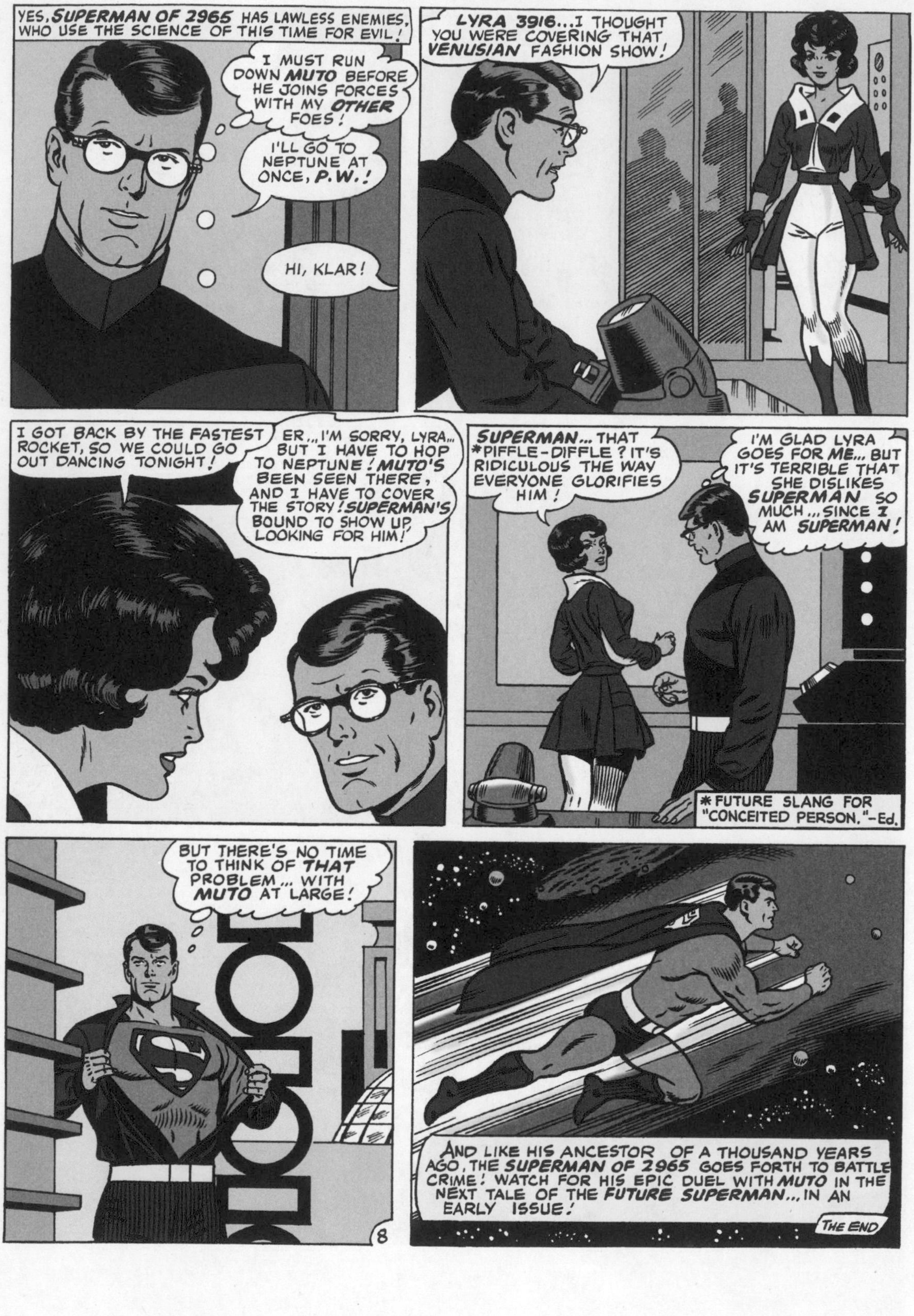
YES, SUPERMAN OF 2965 HAS LAWLESS ENEMIES, WHO USE THE SCIENCE OF THIS TIME FOR EVIL!
I MUST RUN DOWN MUTO BEFORE HE JOINS FORCES WITH MY OTHER FOES!
I'LL GO TO NEPTUNE AT ONCE, P.W.!
HI, KLAR!
LYRA 3916...I THOUGHT YOU WERE COVERING THAT VENUSIAN FASHION SHOW!
I GOT BACK BY THE FASTEST ROCKET, SO WE COULD GO OUT DANCING TONIGHT!
ER... I'M SORRY, LYRA... BUT I HAVE TO HOP TO NEPTUNE! MUTO'S BEEN SEEN THERE, AND I HAVE TO COVER THE STORY! SUPERMAN'S BOUND TO SHOW UP LOOKING FOR HIM!
SUPERMAN... THAT *PIFFLE-DIFFLE? IT'S RIDICULOUS THE WAY EVERYONE GLORIFIES HIM!
I'M GLAD LYRA GOES FOR ME... BUT IT'S TERRIBLE THAT SHE DISLIKES SUPERMAN SO MUCH... SINCE I AM SUPERMAN!
*FUTURE SLANG FOR "CONCEITED PERSON."-Ed.
BUT THERE'S NO TIME TO THINK OF THAT PROBLEM... WITH MUTO AT LARGE!
8
AND LIKE HIS ANCESTOR OF A THOUSAND YEARS AGO, THE SUPERMAN OF 2965 GOES FORTH TO BATTLE CRIME! WATCH FOR HIS EPIC DUEL WITH MUTO IN THE NEXT TALE OF THE FUTURE SUPERMAN... IN AN EARLY ISSUE!
THE END

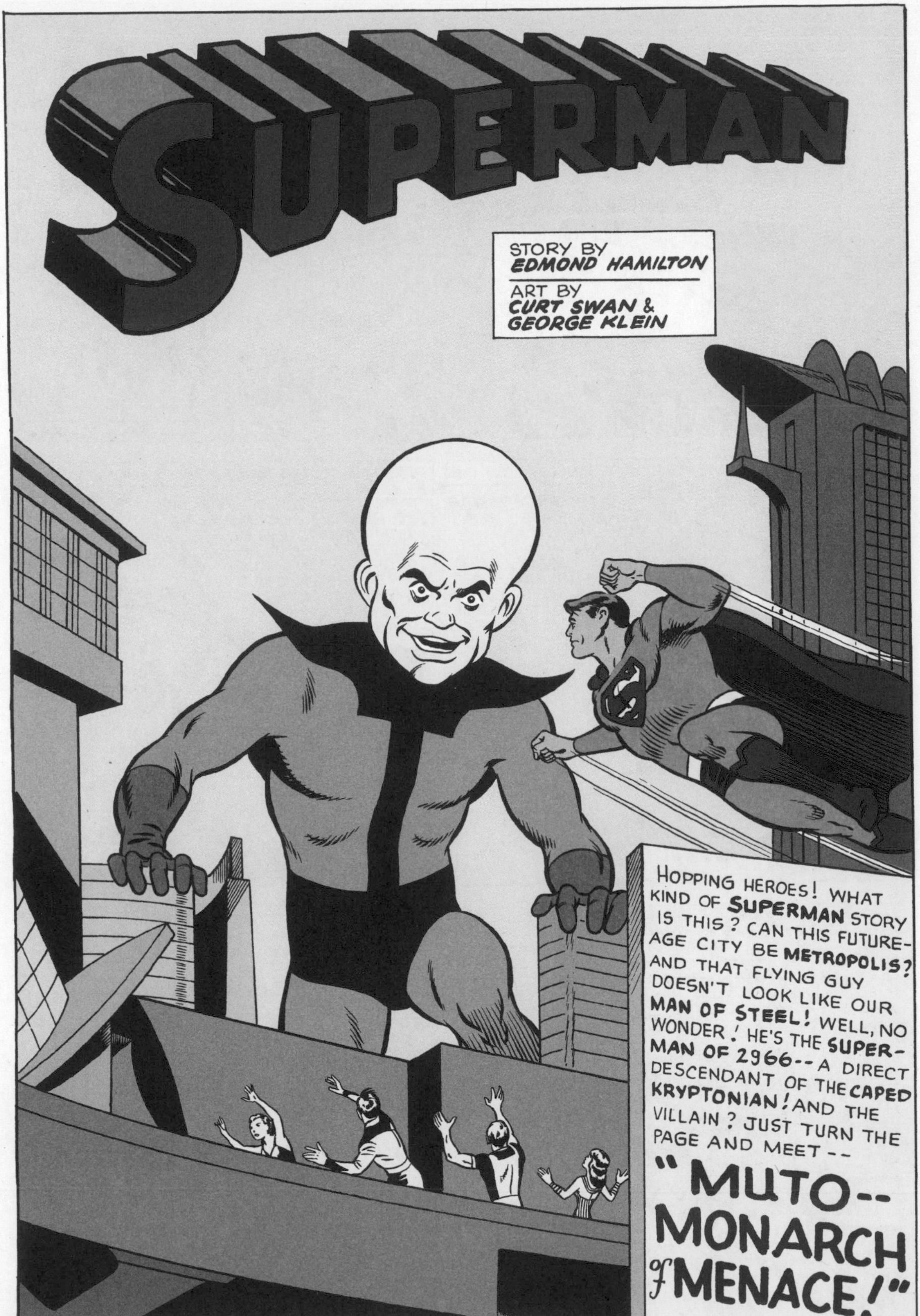
SUPERMAN
STORY BY EDMOND HAMILTON
ART BY CURT SWAN & GEORGE KLEIN
HOPPING HEROES! WHAT KIND OF SUPERMAN STORY IS THIS? CAN THIS FUTURE-AGE CITY BE METROPOLIS? AND THAT FLYING GUY DOESN'T LOOK LIKE OUR MAN OF STEEL! WELL, NO WONDER! HE'S THE SUPER-MAN OF 2966-- A DIRECT DESCENDANT OF THE CAPED KRYPTONIAN! AND THE VILLAIN? JUST TURN THE PAGE AND MEET --
"MUTO-- MONARCH of MENACE!"

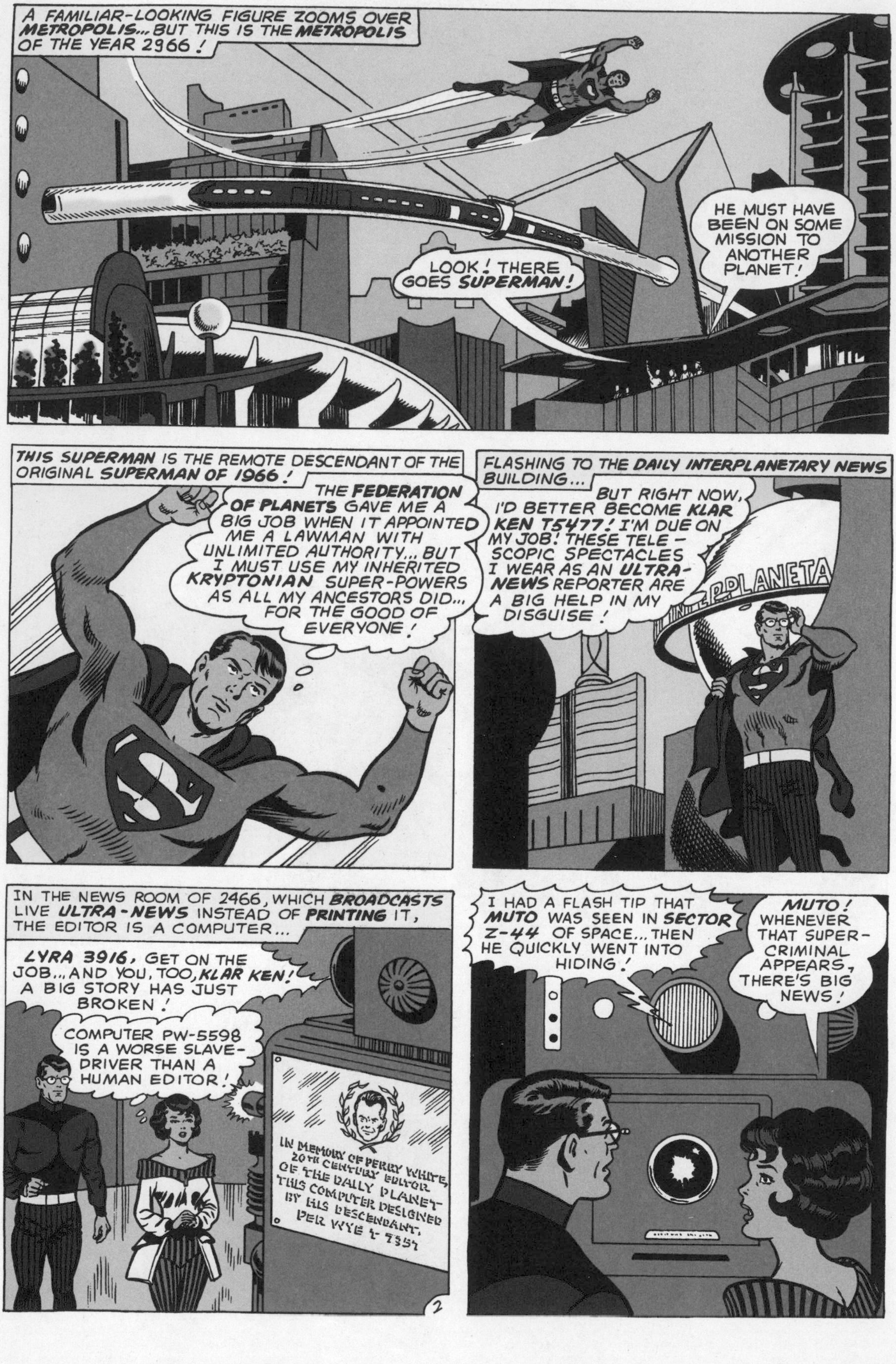
A FAMILIAR-LOOKING FIGURE ZOOMS OVER METROPOLIS... BUT THIS IS THE METROPOLIS OF THE YEAR 2966!
LOOK! THERE GOES SUPERMAN!
HE MUST HAVE BEEN ON SOME MISSION TO ANOTHER PLANET!
THIS SUPERMAN IS THE REMOTE DESCENDANT OF THE ORIGINAL SUPERMAN OF 1966!
THE FEDERATION OF PLANETS GAVE ME A BIG JOB WHEN IT APPOINTED ME A LAWMAN WITH UNLIMITED AUTHORITY... BUT I MUST USE MY INHERITED KRYPTONIAN SUPER-POWERS AS ALL MY ANCESTORS DID... FOR THE GOOD OF EVERYONE!
FLASHING TO THE DAILY INTERPLANETARY NEWS BUILDING...
BUT RIGHT NOW, I'D BETTER BECOME KLAR KEN T5477! I'M DUE ON MY JOB! THESE TELE-SCOPIC SPECTACLES I WEAR AS AN ULTRA-NEWS REPORTER ARE A BIG HELP IN MY DISGUISE!
IN THE NEWS ROOM OF 2466, WHICH BROADCASTS LIVE ULTRA-NEWS INSTEAD OF PRINTING IT, THE EDITOR IS A COMPUTER...
LYRA 3916, GET ON THE JOB... AND YOU, TOO, KLAR KEN! A BIG STORY HAS JUST BROKEN!
COMPUTER PW-5598 IS A WORSE SLAVE-DRIVER THAN A HUMAN EDITOR!
IN MEMORY OF PERRY WHITE, 20TH CENTURY EDITOR OF THE DAILY PLANET THIS COMPUTER DESIGNED BY HIS DESCENDANT, PER WYE T-7351
2
I HAD A FLASH TIP THAT MUTO WAS SEEN IN SECTOR Z-44 OF SPACE... THEN HE QUICKLY WENT INTO HIDING!
MUTO! WHENEVER THAT SUPER-CRIMINAL APPEARS, THERE'S BIG NEWS!

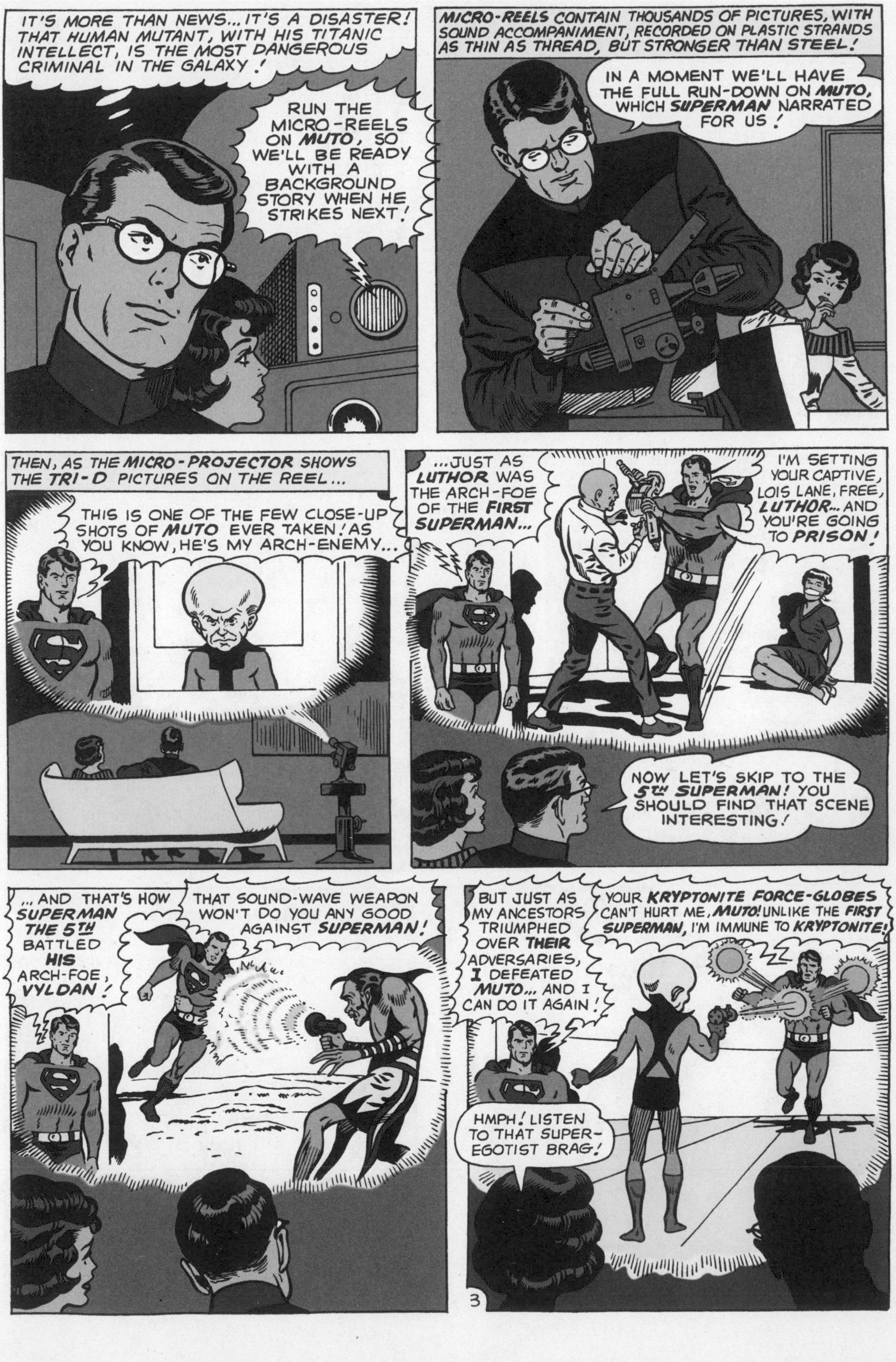

IT'S MORE THAN NEWS... IT'S A DISASTER! THAT HUMAN MUTANT, WITH HIS TITANIC INTELLECT, IS THE MOST DANGEROUS CRIMINAL IN THE GALAXY!
RUN THE MICRO-REELS ON MUTO, SO WE'LL BE READY WITH A BACKGROUND STORY WHEN HE STRIKES NEXT!
MICRO-REELS CONTAIN THOUSANDS OF PICTURES, WITH SOUND ACCOMPANIMENT, RECORDED ON PLASTIC STRANDS AS THIN AS THREAD, BUT STRONGER THAN STEEL!
IN A MOMENT WE'LL HAVE THE FULL RUN-DOWN ON MUTO, WHICH SUPERMAN NARRATED FOR US!
THEN, AS THE MICRO-PROJECTOR SHOWS THE TRI-D PICTURES ON THE REEL...
THIS IS ONE OF THE FEW CLOSE-UP SHOTS OF MUTO EVER TAKEN! AS YOU KNOW, HE'S MY ARCH-ENEMY...
...JUST AS LUTHOR WAS THE ARCH-FOE OF THE FIRST SUPERMAN...
I'M SETTING YOUR CAPTIVE, LOIS LANE, FREE, LUTHOR... AND YOU'RE GOING TO PRISON!
NOW LET'S SKIP TO THE 5TH SUPERMAN! YOU SHOULD FIND THAT SCENE INTERESTING!
...AND THAT'S HOW SUPERMAN THE 5TH BATTLED HIS ARCH-FOE, VYLDAN!
THAT SOUND-WAVE WEAPON WON'T DO YOU ANY GOOD AGAINST SUPERMAN!
BUT JUST AS MY ANCESTORS TRIUMPHED OVER THEIR ADVERSARIES, I DEFEATED MUTO... AND I CAN DO IT AGAIN!
YOUR KRYPTONITE FORCE-GLOBES CAN'T HURT ME, MUTO! UNLIKE THE FIRST SUPERMAN, I'M IMMUNE TO KRYPTONITE!
HMPH! LISTEN TO THAT SUPER-EGOTIST BRAG!
3

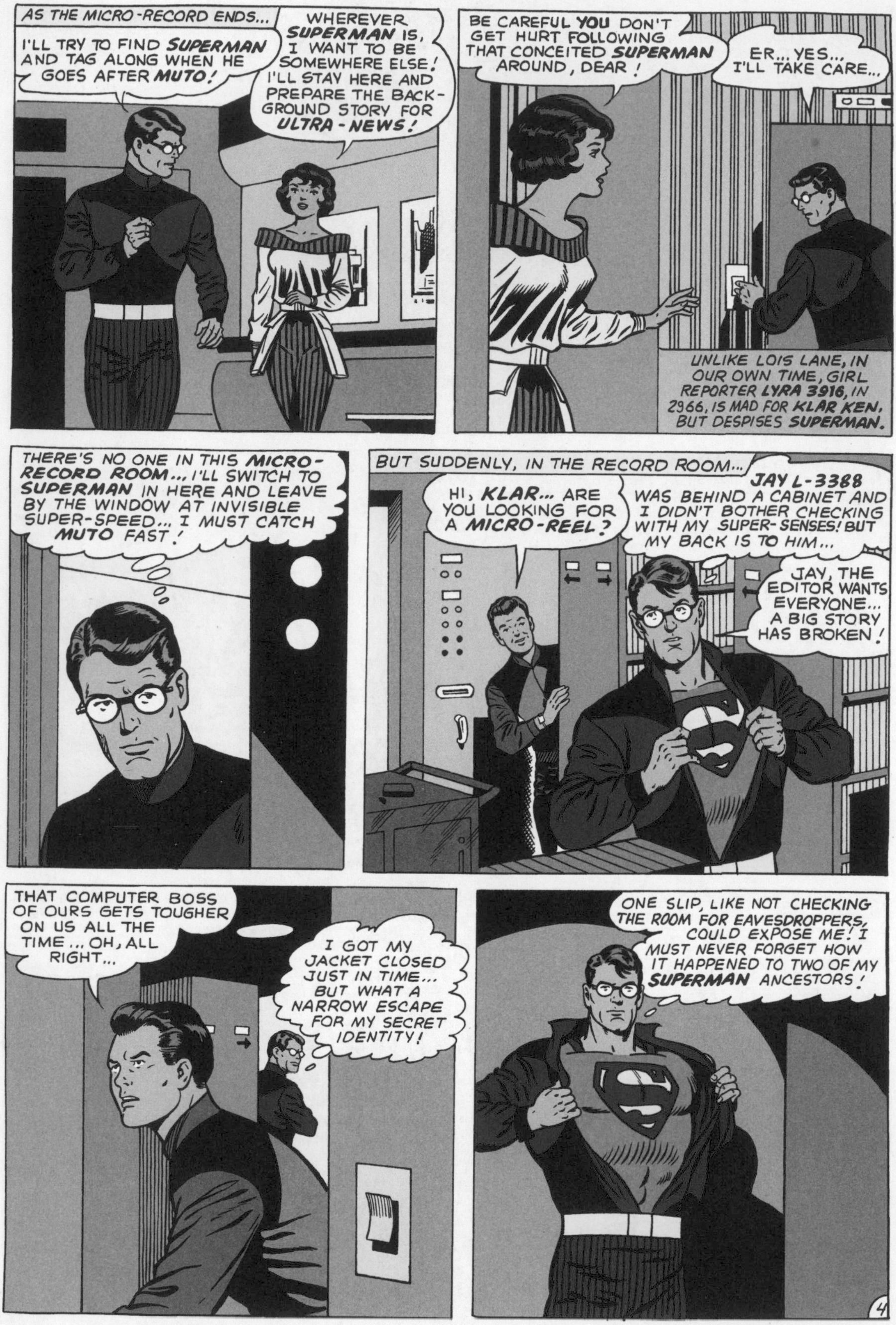

AS THE MICRO-RECORD ENDS...
I'LL TRY TO FIND SUPERMAN AND TAG ALONG WHEN HE GOES AFTER MUTO!
WHEREVER SUPERMAN IS, I WANT TO BE SOMEWHERE ELSE! I'LL STAY HERE AND PREPARE THE BACK-GROUND STORY FOR ULTRA-NEWS!
BE CAREFUL YOU DON'T GET HURT FOLLOWING THAT CONCEITED SUPERMAN AROUND, DEAR!
ER... YES... I'LL TAKE CARE...
UNLIKE LOIS LANE, IN OUR OWN TIME, GIRL REPORTER LYRA 3916, IN 2966, IS MAD FOR KLAR KEN, BUT DESPISES SUPERMAN.
THERE'S NO ONE IN THIS MICRO-RECORD ROOM..., I'LL SWITCH TO SUPERMAN IN HERE AND LEAVE BY THE WINDOW AT INVISIBLE SUPER-SPEED... I MUST CATCH MUTO FAST!
BUT SUDDENLY, IN THE RECORD ROOM...
HI, KLAR... ARE YOU LOOKING FOR A MICRO-REEL?
JAY L-3388 WAS BEHIND A CABINET AND I DIDN'T BOTHER CHECKING WITH MY SUPER-SENSES! BUT MY BACK IS TO HIM...
JAY, THE EDITOR WANTS EVERYONE... A BIG STORY HAS BROKEN!
THAT COMPUTER BOSS OF OURS GETS TOUGHER ON US ALL THE TIME... OH, ALL RIGHT...
I GOT MY JACKET CLOSED JUST IN TIME... BUT WHAT A NARROW ESCAPE FOR MY SECRET IDENTITY!
ONE SLIP, LIKE NOT CHECKING THE ROOM FOR EAVESDROPPERS, COULD EXPOSE ME! I MUST NEVER FORGET HOW IT HAPPENED TO TWO OF MY SUPERMAN ANCESTORS!
4

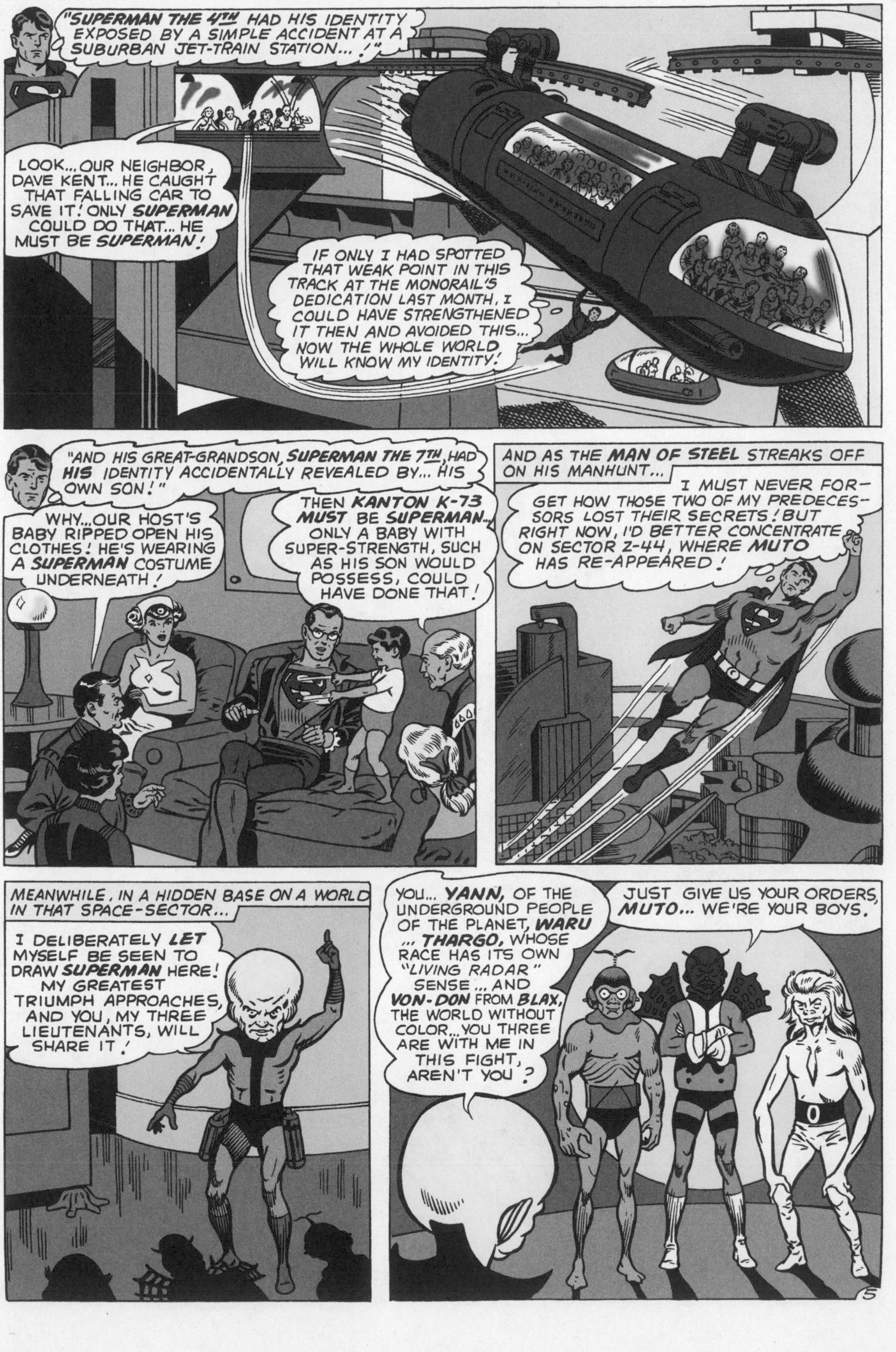
"SUPERMAN THE 4TH HAD HIS IDENTITY EXPOSED BY A SIMPLE ACCIDENT AT A SUBURBAN JET-TRAIN STATION... !"
LOOK... OUR NEIGHBOR, DAVE KENT... HE CAUGHT THAT FALLING CAR TO SAVE IT! ONLY SUPERMAN COULD DO THAT... HE MUST BE SUPERMAN!
IF ONLY I HAD SPOTTED THAT WEAK POINT IN THIS TRACK AT THE MONORAIL'S DEDICATION LAST MONTH, I COULD HAVE STRENGTHENED IT THEN AND AVOIDED THIS... NOW THE WHOLE WORLD WILL KNOW MY IDENTITY!
"AND HIS GREAT-GRANDSON, SUPERMAN THE 7TH, HAD HIS IDENTITY ACCIDENTALLY REVEALED BY... HIS OWN SON!"
WHY... OUR HOST'S BABY RIPPED OPEN HIS CLOTHES! HE'S WEARING A SUPERMAN COSTUME UNDERNEATH!
THEN KANTON K-73 MUST BE SUPERMAN... ONLY A BABY WITH SUPER-STRENGTH, SUCH AS HIS SON WOULD POSSESS, COULD HAVE DONE THAT!
AND AS THE MAN OF STEEL STREAKS OFF ON HIS MANHUNT...
I MUST NEVER FORGET HOW THOSE TWO OF MY PREDECESSORS LOST THEIR SECRETS! BUT RIGHT NOW, I'D BETTER CONCENTRATE ON SECTOR Z-44, WHERE MUTO HAS RE-APPEARED!
MEANWHILE, IN A HIDDEN BASE ON A WORLD IN THAT SPACE-SECTOR...
I DELIBERATELY LET MYSELF BE SEEN TO DRAW SUPERMAN HERE! MY GREATEST TRIUMPH APPROACHES, AND YOU, MY THREE LIEUTENANTS, WILL SHARE IT!
YOU... YANN, OF THE UNDERGROUND PEOPLE OF THE PLANET, WARU ... THARGO, WHOSE RACE HAS ITS OWN "LIVING RADAR" SENSE... AND VON-DON FROM BLAX, THE WORLD WITHOUT COLOR... YOU THREE ARE WITH ME IN THIS FIGHT, AREN'T YOU?
JUST GIVE US YOUR ORDERS, MUTO... WE'RE YOUR BOYS.
5

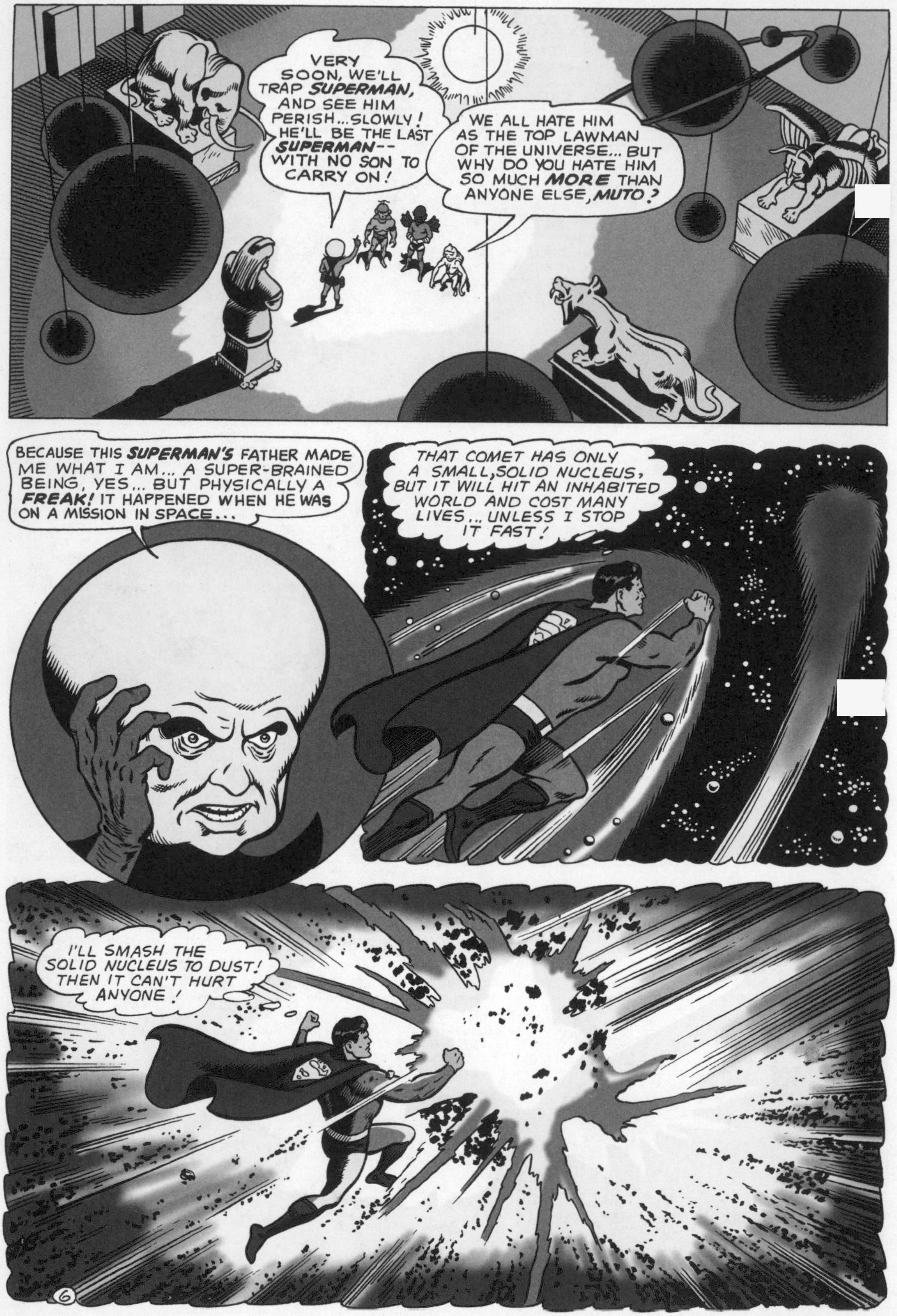
VERY SOON, WE'LL TRAP SUPERMAN, AND SEE HIM PERISH...SLOWLY! HE'LL BE THE LAST SUPERMAN-- WITH NO SON TO CARRY ON!
WE ALL HATE HIM AS THE TOP LAWMAN OF THE UNIVERSE... BUT WHY DO YOU HATE HIM SO MUCH MORE THAN ANYONE ELSE, MUTO?
BECAUSE THIS SUPERMAN'S FATHER MADE ME WHAT I AM... A SUPER-BRAINED BEING, YES... BUT PHYSICALLY A FREAK! IT HAPPENED WHEN HE WAS ON A MISSION IN SPACE...
THAT COMET HAS ONLY A SMALL, SOLID NUCLEUS, BUT IT WILL HIT AN INHABITED WORLD AND COST MANY LIVES... UNLESS I STOP IT FAST!
I'LL SMASH THE SOLID NUCLEUS TO DUST! THEN IT CAN'T HURT ANYONE!
6

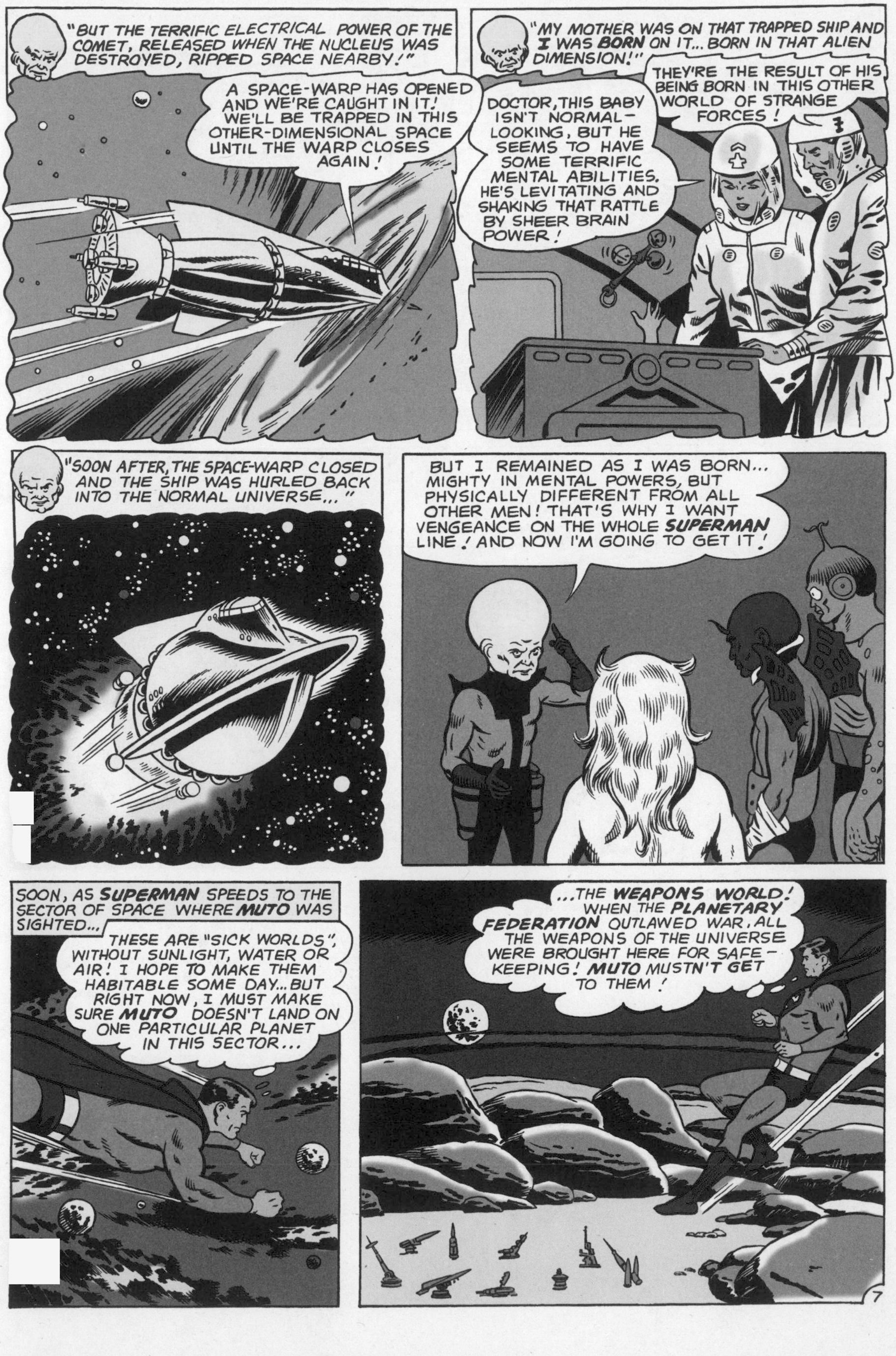
"BUT THE TERRIFIC ELECTRICAL POWER OF THE COMET, RELEASED WHEN THE NUCLEUS WAS DESTROYED, RIPPED SPACE NEARBY!"
A SPACE-WARP HAS OPENED AND WE'RE CAUGHT IN IT! WE'LL BE TRAPPED IN THIS OTHER-DIMENSIONAL SPACE UNTIL THE WARP CLOSES AGAIN!
"MY MOTHER WAS ON THAT TRAPPED SHIP AND I WAS BORN ON IT... BORN IN THAT ALIEN DIMENSION!"
DOCTOR, THIS BABY ISN'T NORMAL-LOOKING, BUT HE SEEMS TO HAVE SOME TERRIFIC MENTAL ABILITIES. HE'S LEVITATING AND SHAKING THAT RATTLE BY SHEER BRAIN POWER!
THEY'RE THE RESULT OF HIS BEING BORN IN THIS OTHER WORLD OF STRANGE FORCES!
"SOON AFTER, THE SPACE-WARP CLOSED AND THE SHIP WAS HURLED BACK INTO THE NORMAL UNIVERSE..."
BUT I REMAINED AS I WAS BORN... MIGHTY IN MENTAL POWERS, BUT PHYSICALLY DIFFERENT FROM ALL OTHER MEN! THAT'S WHY I WANT VENGEANCE ON THE WHOLE SUPERMAN LINE! AND NOW I'M GOING TO GET IT!
SOON, AS SUPERMAN SPEEDS TO THE SECTOR OF SPACE WHERE MUTO WAS SIGHTED...
THESE ARE "SICK WORLDS", WITHOUT SUNLIGHT, WATER OR AIR! I HOPE TO MAKE THEM HABITABLE SOME DAY... BUT RIGHT NOW, I MUST MAKE SURE MUTO DOESN'T LAND ON ONE PARTICULAR PLANET IN THIS SECTOR...
...THE WEAPONS WORLD! WHEN THE PLANETARY FEDERATION OUTLAWED WAR, ALL THE WEAPONS OF THE UNIVERSE WERE BROUGHT HERE FOR SAFE-KEEPING! MUTO MUSTN'T GET TO THEM!
7

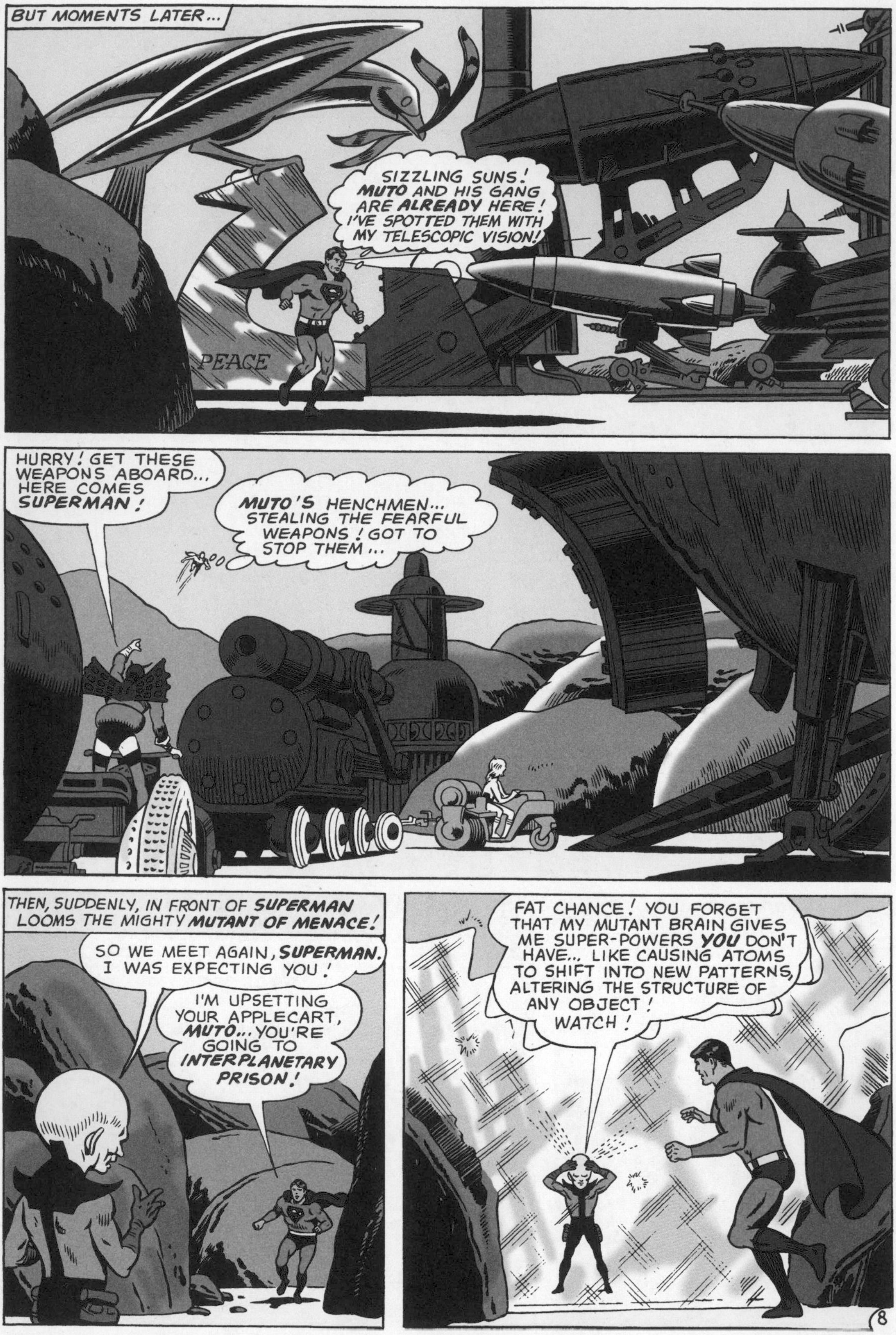
BUT MOMENTS LATER...
SIZZLING SUNS! MUTO AND HIS GANG ARE ALREADY HERE! I'VE SPOTTED THEM WITH MY TELESCOPIC VISION!
PEACE
HURRY! GET THESE WEAPONS ABOARD... HERE COMES SUPERMAN!
MUTO'S HENCHMEN... STEALING THE FEARFUL WEAPONS! GOT TO STOP THEM...
THEN, SUDDENLY, IN FRONT OF SUPERMAN LOOMS THE MIGHTY MUTANT OF MENACE!
SO WE MEET AGAIN, SUPERMAN. I WAS EXPECTING YOU!
I'M UPSETTING YOUR APPLECART, MUTO... YOU'RE GOING TO INTERPLANETARY PRISON!
FAT CHANCE! YOU FORGET THAT MY MUTANT BRAIN GIVES ME SUPER-POWERS YOU DON'T HAVE... LIKE CAUSING ATOMS TO SHIFT INTO NEW PATTERNS, ALTERING THE STRUCTURE OF ANY OBJECT! WATCH!
8

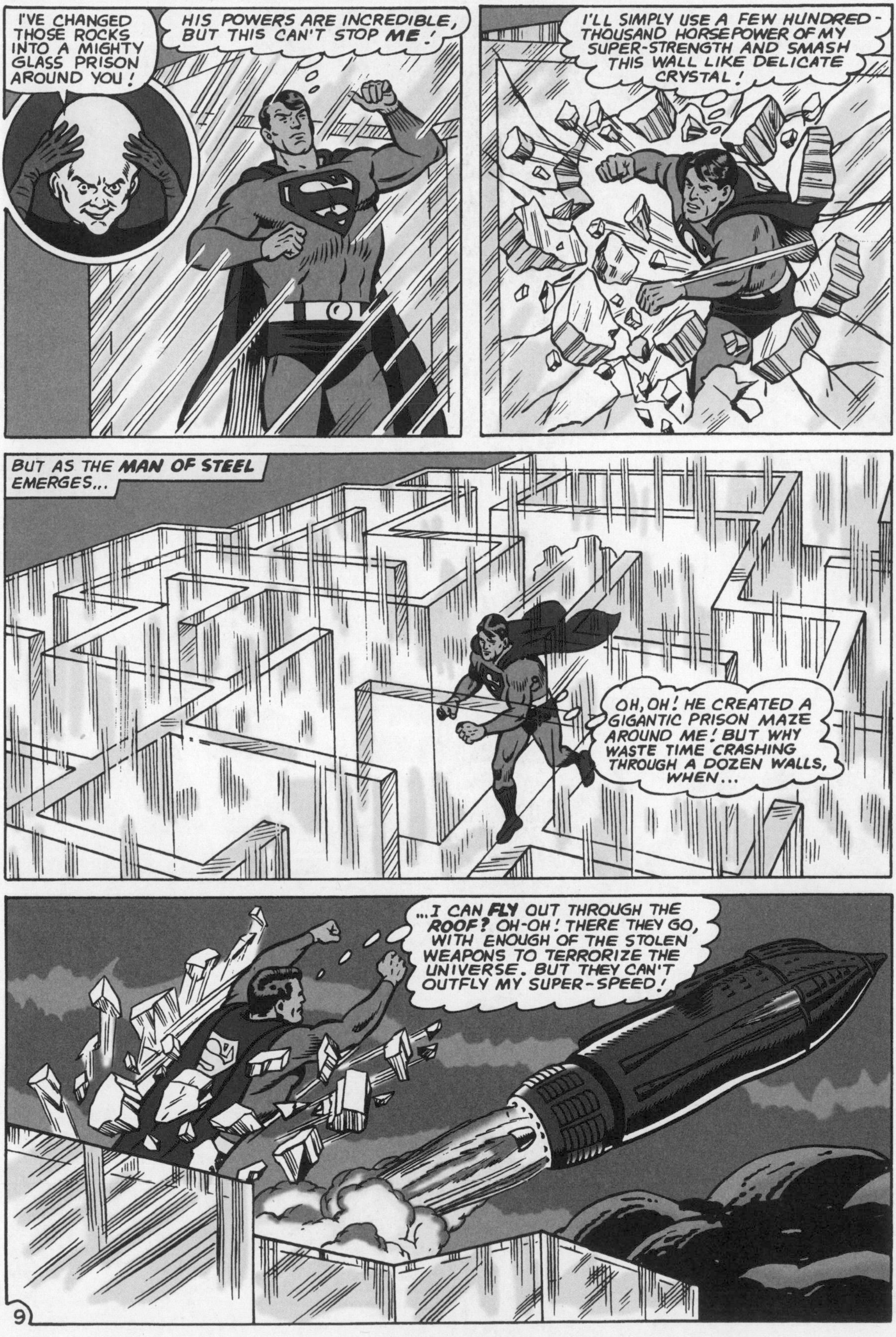
I'VE CHANGED THOSE ROCKS INTO A MIGHTY GLASS PRISON AROUND YOU!
HIS POWERS ARE INCREDIBLE, BUT THIS CAN'T STOP ME!
I'LL SIMPLY USE A FEW HUNDRED-THOUSAND HORSEPOWER OF MY SUPER-STRENGTH AND SMASH THIS WALL LIKE DELICATE CRYSTAL!
BUT AS THE MAN OF STEEL EMERGES...
OH, OH! HE CREATED A GIGANTIC PRISON MAZE AROUND ME! BUT WHY WASTE TIME CRASHING THROUGH A DOZEN WALLS, WHEN...
...I CAN FLY OUT THROUGH THE ROOF? OH-OH! THERE THEY GO, WITH ENOUGH OF THE STOLEN WEAPONS TO TERRORIZE THE UNIVERSE. BUT THEY CAN'T OUTFLY MY SUPER-SPEED!
9

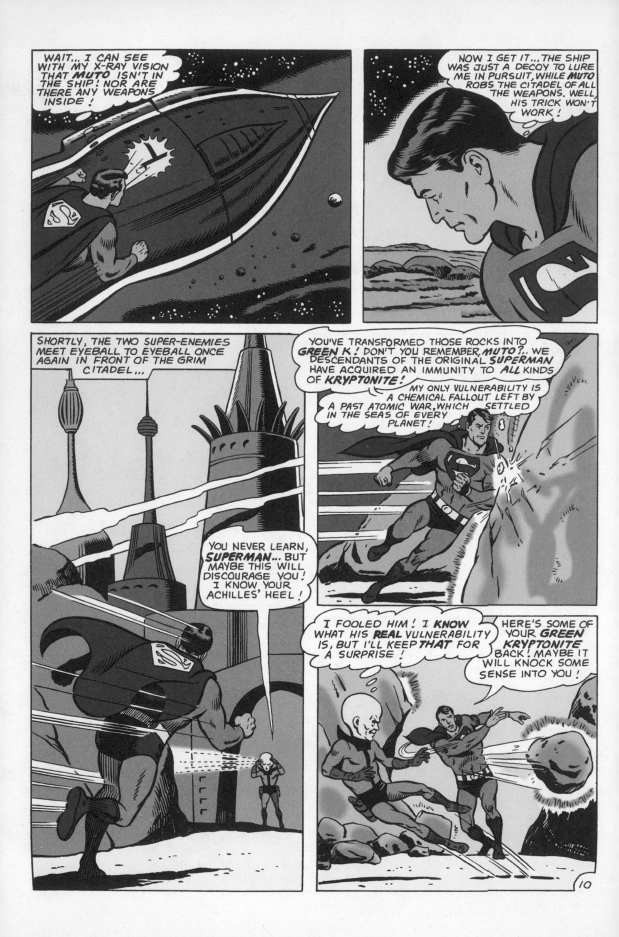

WAIT... I CAN SEE WITH MY X-RAY VISION THAT *MUTO* ISN'T IN THE SHIP! NOR ARE THERE ANY WEAPONS INSIDE!

NOW I GET IT... THE SHIP WAS JUST A DECOY TO LURE ME IN PURSUIT, WHILE *MUTO* ROBS THE CITADEL OF ALL THE WEAPONS. WELL HIS TRICK WON'T WORK!

SHORTLY, THE TWO SUPER-ENEMIES MEET EYEBALL TO EYEBALL ONCE AGAIN IN FRONT OF THE GRIM CITADEL...

YOU'VE TRANSFORMED THOSE ROCKS INTO *GREEN K*! DON'T YOU REMEMBER, *MUTO?*... WE DESCENDANTS OF THE ORIGINAL *SUPERMAN* HAVE ACQUIRED AN IMMUNITY TO *ALL* KINDS OF *KRYPTONITE*!

MY ONLY VULNERABILITY IS A CHEMICAL FALLOUT LEFT BY A PAST ATOMIC WAR, WHICH SETTLED IN THE SEAS OF EVERY PLANET!

YOU NEVER LEARN, *SUPERMAN*... BUT MAYBE THIS WILL DISCOURAGE YOU! I KNOW YOUR ACHILLES' HEEL!

I FOOLED HIM! I *KNOW* WHAT HIS *REAL* VULNERABILITY IS, BUT I'LL KEEP *THAT* FOR A SURPRISE!

HERE'S SOME OF YOUR *GREEN KRYPTONITE* BACK! MAYBE IT WILL KNOCK SOME SENSE INTO YOU!

10

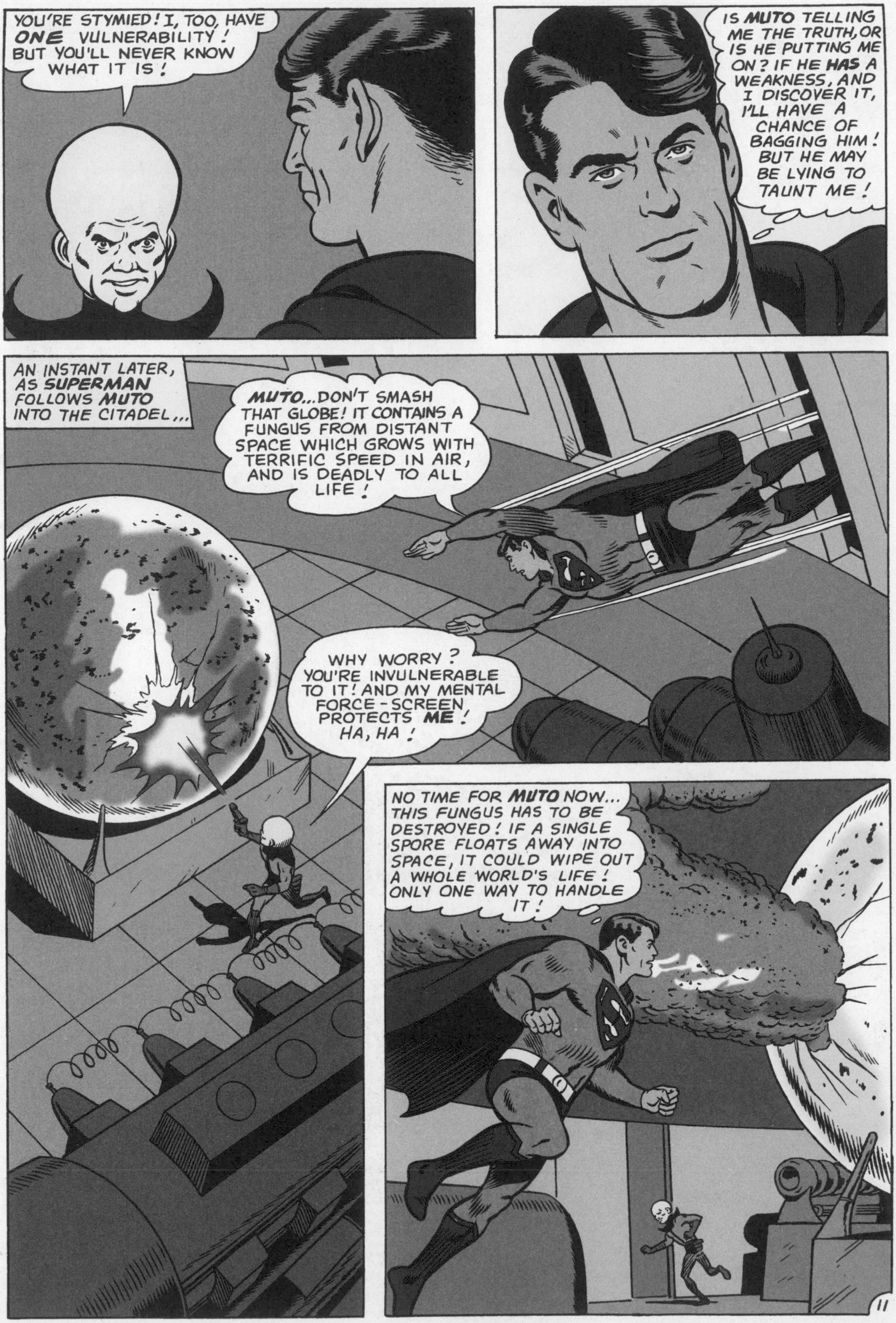

YOU'RE STYMIED! I, TOO, HAVE ONE VULNERABILITY! BUT YOU'LL NEVER KNOW WHAT IT IS!
IS MUTO TELLING ME THE TRUTH, OR IS HE PUTTING ME ON? IF HE HAS A WEAKNESS, AND I DISCOVER IT, I'LL HAVE A CHANCE OF BAGGING HIM! BUT HE MAY BE LYING TO TAUNT ME!
AN INSTANT LATER, AS SUPERMAN FOLLOWS MUTO INTO THE CITADEL...
MUTO... DON'T SMASH THAT GLOBE! IT CONTAINS A FUNGUS FROM DISTANT SPACE WHICH GROWS WITH TERRIFIC SPEED IN AIR, AND IS DEADLY TO ALL LIFE!
WHY WORRY? YOU'RE INVULNERABLE TO IT! AND MY MENTAL FORCE-SCREEN PROTECTS ME! HA, HA!
NO TIME FOR MUTO NOW... THIS FUNGUS HAS TO BE DESTROYED! IF A SINGLE SPORE FLOATS AWAY INTO SPACE, IT COULD WIPE OUT A WHOLE WORLD'S LIFE! ONLY ONE WAY TO HANDLE IT!
11

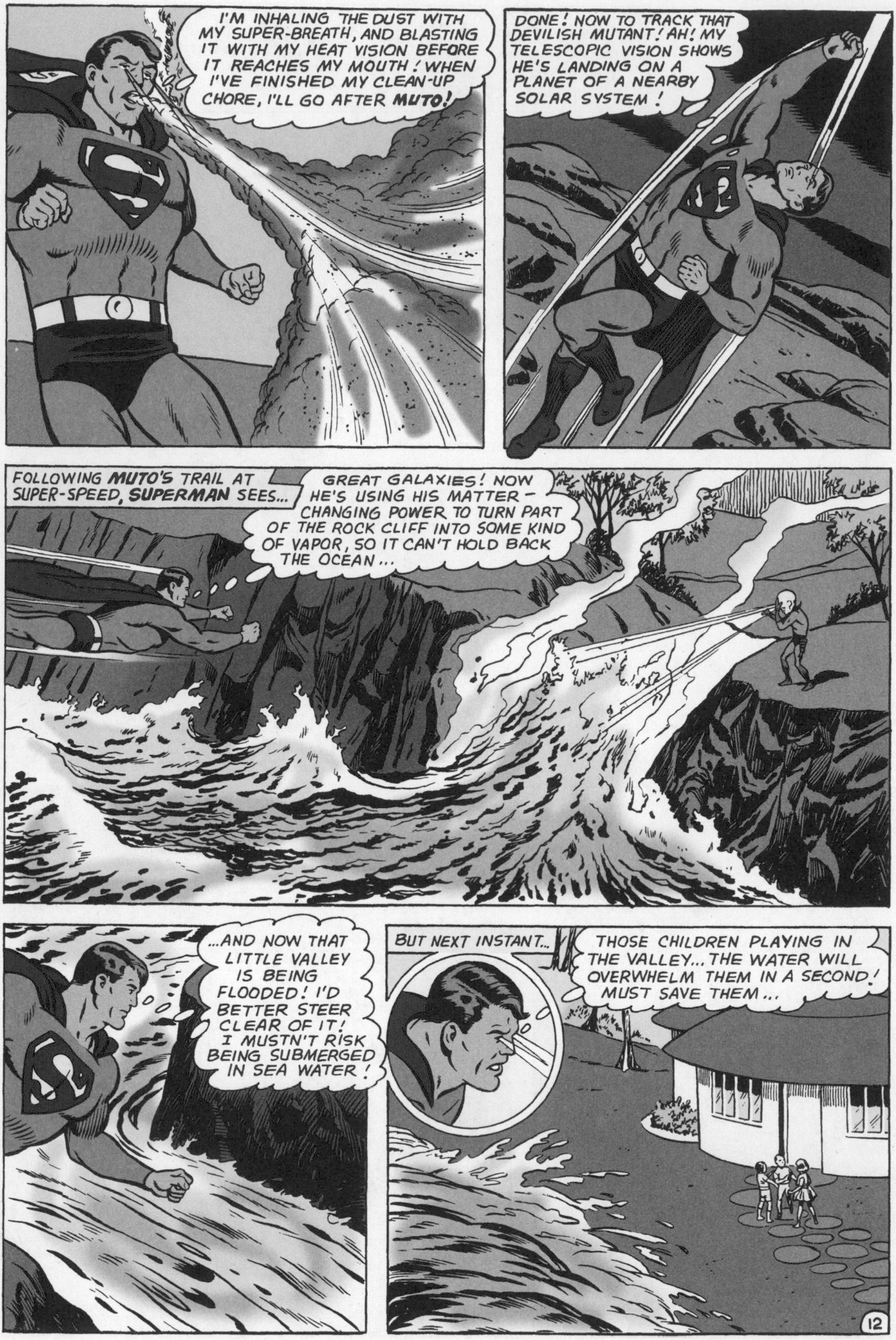
I'M INHALING THE DUST WITH MY SUPER-BREATH, AND BLASTING IT WITH MY HEAT VISION BEFORE IT REACHES MY MOUTH! WHEN I'VE FINISHED MY CLEAN-UP CHORE, I'LL GO AFTER MUTO!
DONE! NOW TO TRACK THAT DEVILISH MUTANT! AH! MY TELESCOPIC VISION SHOWS HE'S LANDING ON A PLANET OF A NEARBY SOLAR SYSTEM!
FOLLOWING MUTO'S TRAIL AT SUPER-SPEED, SUPERMAN SEES...
GREAT GALAXIES! NOW HE'S USING HIS MATTER-CHANGING POWER TO TURN PART OF THE ROCK CLIFF INTO SOME KIND OF VAPOR, SO IT CAN'T HOLD BACK THE OCEAN...
...AND NOW THAT LITTLE VALLEY IS BEING FLOODED! I'D BETTER STEER CLEAR OF IT! I MUSTN'T RISK BEING SUBMERGED IN SEA WATER!
BUT NEXT INSTANT...
THOSE CHILDREN PLAYING IN THE VALLEY... THE WATER WILL OVERWHELM THEM IN A SECOND! MUST SAVE THEM...
12

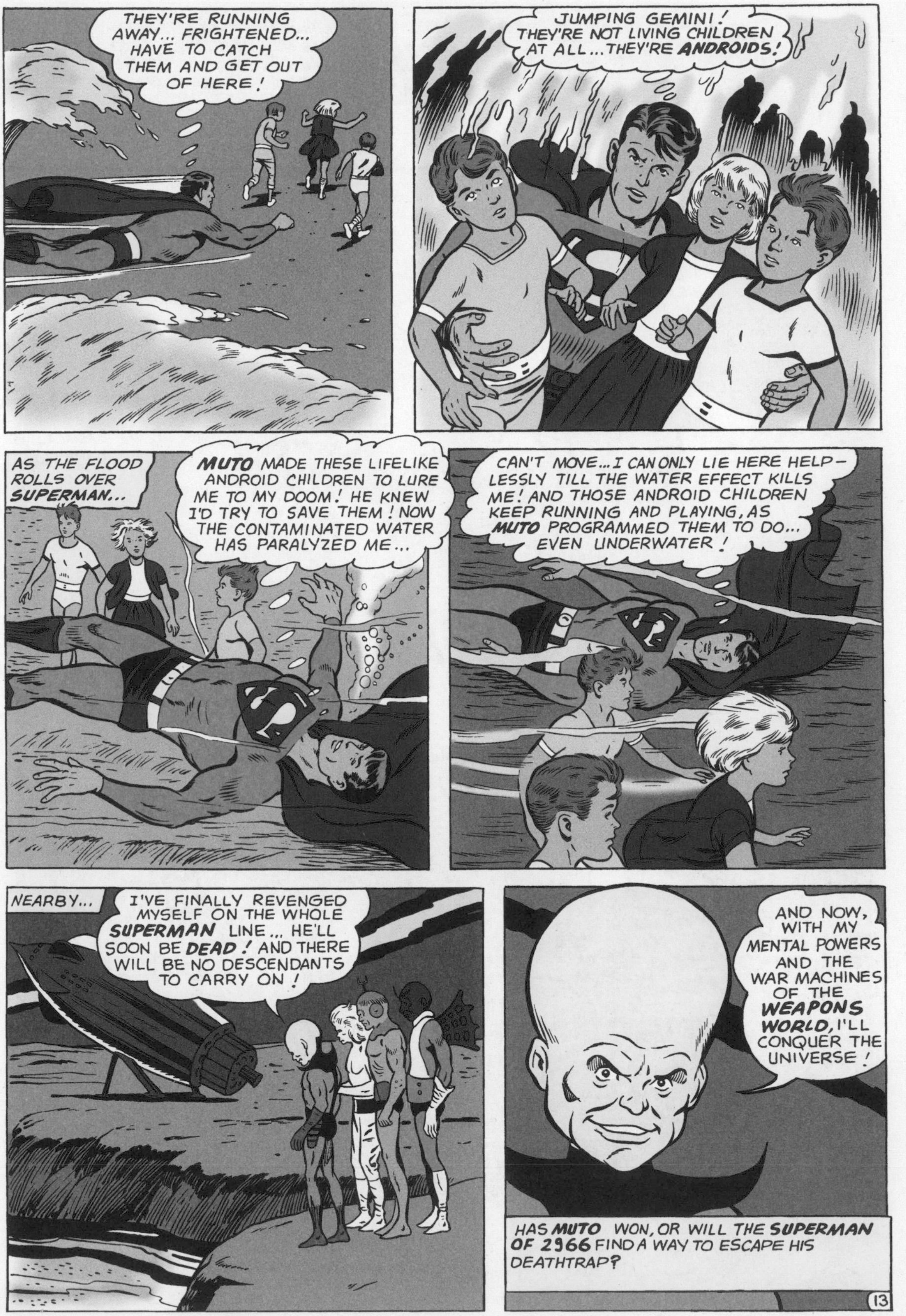
THEY'RE RUNNING AWAY... FRIGHTENED... HAVE TO CATCH THEM AND GET OUT OF HERE!
JUMPING GEMINI! THEY'RE NOT LIVING CHILDREN AT ALL... THEY'RE ANDROIDS!
AS THE FLOOD ROLLS OVER SUPERMAN...
MUTO MADE THESE LIFELIKE ANDROID CHILDREN TO LURE ME TO MY DOOM! HE KNEW I'D TRY TO SAVE THEM! NOW THE CONTAMINATED WATER HAS PARALYZED ME...
CAN'T MOVE... I CAN ONLY LIE HERE HELP-LESSLY TILL THE WATER EFFECT KILLS ME! AND THOSE ANDROID CHILDREN KEEP RUNNING AND PLAYING, AS MUTO PROGRAMMED THEM TO DO... EVEN UNDERWATER!
NEARBY...
I'VE FINALLY REVENGED MYSELF ON THE WHOLE SUPERMAN LINE... HE'LL SOON BE DEAD! AND THERE WILL BE NO DESCENDANTS TO CARRY ON!
AND NOW, WITH MY MENTAL POWERS AND THE WAR MACHINES OF THE WEAPONS WORLD, I'LL CONQUER THE UNIVERSE!
HAS MUTO WON, OR WILL THE SUPERMAN OF 2966 FIND A WAY TO ESCAPE HIS DEATHTRAP?
13

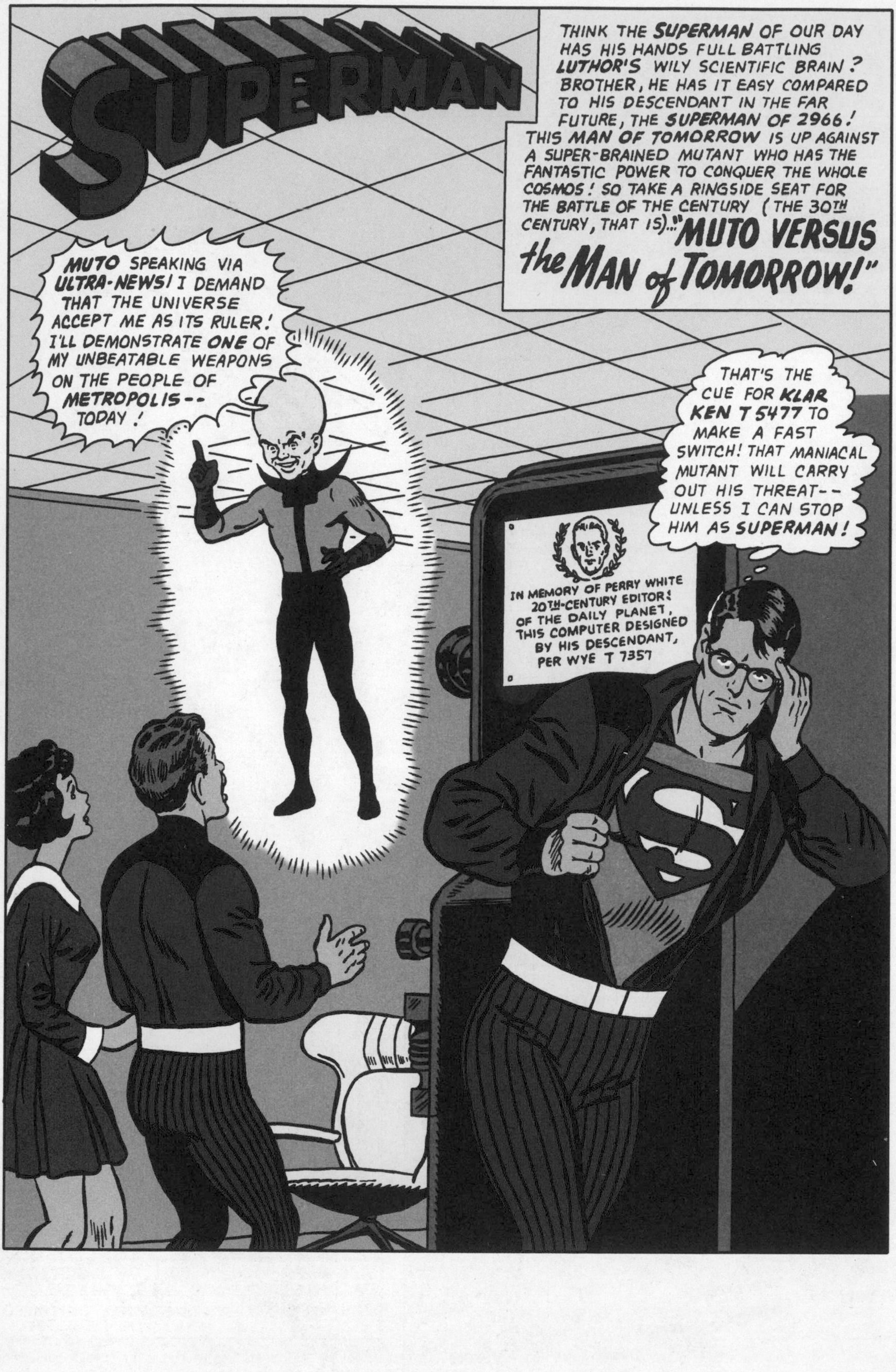
SUPERMAN
THINK THE SUPERMAN OF OUR DAY HAS HIS HANDS FULL BATTLING LUTHOR'S WILY SCIENTIFIC BRAIN? BROTHER, HE HAS IT EASY COMPARED TO HIS DESCENDANT IN THE FAR FUTURE, THE SUPERMAN OF 2966! THIS MAN OF TOMORROW IS UP AGAINST A SUPER-BRAINED MUTANT WHO HAS THE FANTASTIC POWER TO CONQUER THE WHOLE COSMOS! SO TAKE A RINGSIDE SEAT FOR THE BATTLE OF THE CENTURY (THE 30TH CENTURY, THAT IS)..."MUTO VERSUS the MAN of TOMORROW!"
MUTO SPEAKING VIA ULTRA-NEWS! I DEMAND THAT THE UNIVERSE ACCEPT ME AS ITS RULER! I'LL DEMONSTRATE ONE OF MY UNBEATABLE WEAPONS ON THE PEOPLE OF METROPOLIS--TODAY!
THAT'S THE CUE FOR KLAR KEN T 5477 TO MAKE A FAST SWITCH! THAT MANIACAL MUTANT WILL CARRY OUT HIS THREAT--UNLESS I CAN STOP HIM AS SUPERMAN!
IN MEMORY OF PERRY WHITE 20TH-CENTURY EDITOR OF THE DAILY PLANET, THIS COMPUTER DESIGNED BY HIS DESCENDANT, PER WYE T 7357

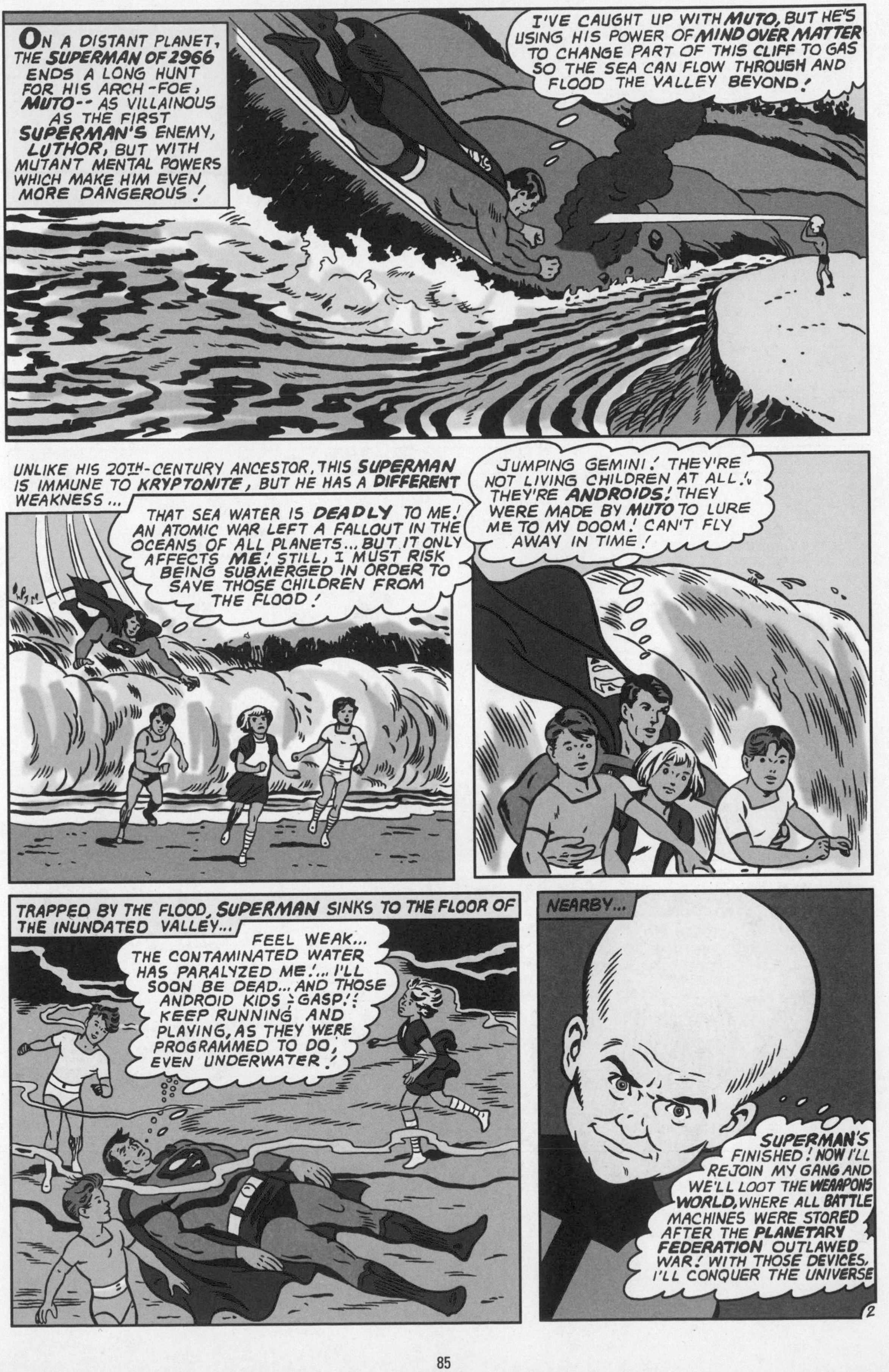
ON A DISTANT PLANET, THE SUPERMAN OF 2966 ENDS A LONG HUNT FOR HIS ARCH-FOE, MUTO-- AS VILLAINOUS AS THE FIRST SUPERMAN'S ENEMY, LUTHOR, BUT WITH MUTANT MENTAL POWERS WHICH MAKE HIM EVEN MORE DANGEROUS!
I'VE CAUGHT UP WITH MUTO, BUT HE'S USING HIS POWER OF MIND OVER MATTER TO CHANGE PART OF THIS CLIFF TO GAS SO THE SEA CAN FLOW THROUGH AND FLOOD THE VALLEY BEYOND!
UNLIKE HIS 20TH-CENTURY ANCESTOR, THIS SUPERMAN IS IMMUNE TO KRYPTONITE, BUT HE HAS A DIFFERENT WEAKNESS...
THAT SEA WATER IS DEADLY TO ME! AN ATOMIC WAR LEFT A FALLOUT IN THE OCEANS OF ALL PLANETS... BUT IT ONLY AFFECTS ME! STILL, I MUST RISK BEING SUBMERGED IN ORDER TO SAVE THOSE CHILDREN FROM THE FLOOD!
JUMPING GEMINI! THEY'RE NOT LIVING CHILDREN AT ALL! THEY'RE ANDROIDS! THEY WERE MADE BY MUTO TO LURE ME TO MY DOOM! CAN'T FLY AWAY IN TIME!
TRAPPED BY THE FLOOD, SUPERMAN SINKS TO THE FLOOR OF THE INUNDATED VALLEY...
FEEL WEAK... THE CONTAMINATED WATER HAS PARALYZED ME!... I'LL SOON BE DEAD... AND THOSE ANDROID KIDS -GASP!- KEEP RUNNING AND PLAYING, AS THEY WERE PROGRAMMED TO DO, EVEN UNDERWATER!
NEARBY...
SUPERMAN'S FINISHED! NOW I'LL REJOIN MY GANG AND WE'LL LOOT THE WEAPONS WORLD, WHERE ALL BATTLE MACHINES WERE STORED AFTER THE PLANETARY FEDERATION OUTLAWED WAR! WITH THOSE DEVICES, I'LL CONQUER THE UNIVERSE
2

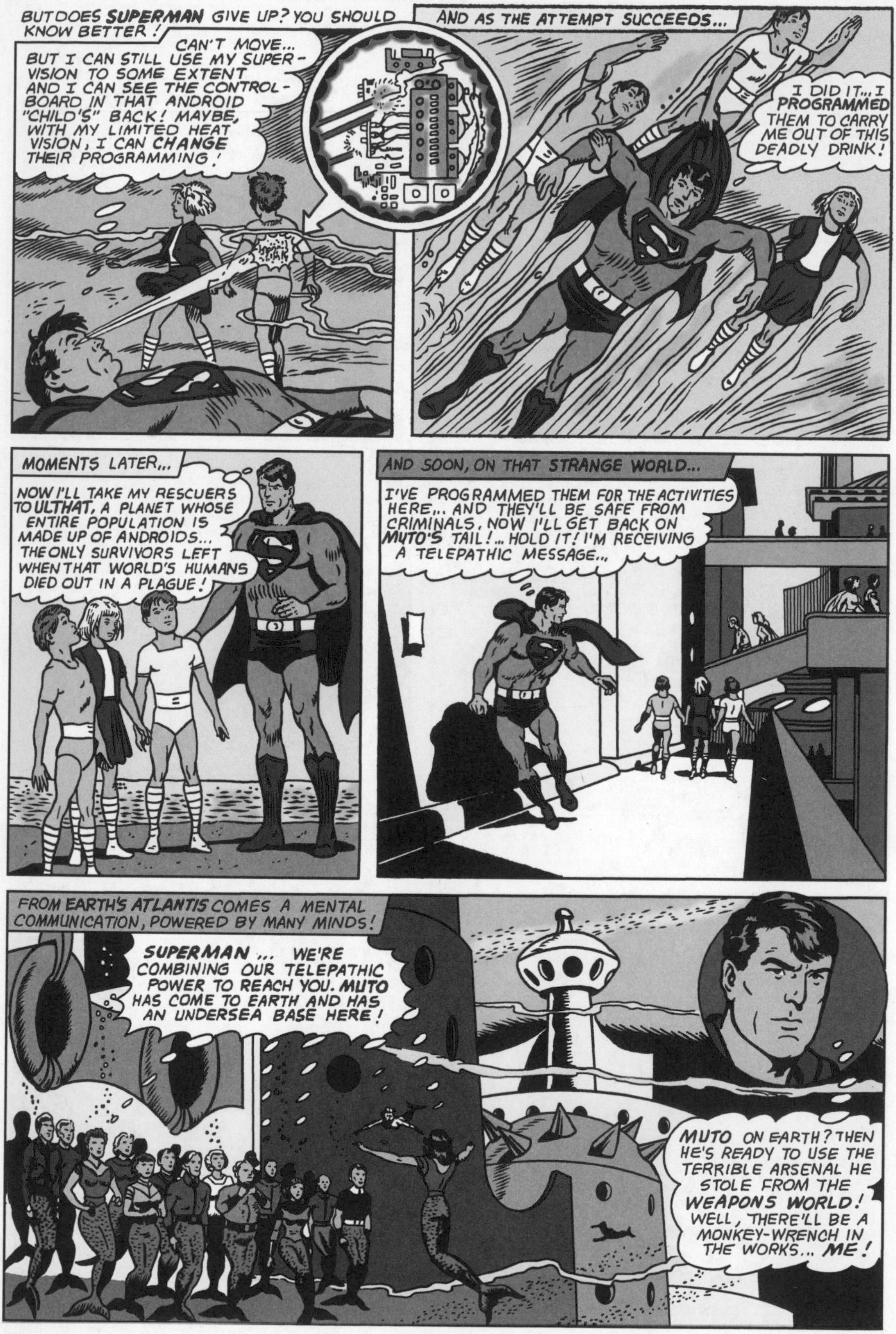
BUT DOES SUPERMAN GIVE UP? YOU SHOULD KNOW BETTER!
CAN'T MOVE... BUT I CAN STILL USE MY SUPER-VISION TO SOME EXTENT AND I CAN SEE THE CONTROL-BOARD IN THAT ANDROID "CHILD'S" BACK! MAYBE, WITH MY LIMITED HEAT VISION, I CAN CHANGE THEIR PROGRAMMING!
AND AS THE ATTEMPT SUCCEEDS...
I DID IT... I PROGRAMMED THEM TO CARRY ME OUT OF THIS DEADLY DRINK!
MOMENTS LATER...
NOW I'LL TAKE MY RESCUERS TO ULTHAT, A PLANET WHOSE ENTIRE POPULATION IS MADE UP OF ANDROIDS... THE ONLY SURVIVORS LEFT WHEN THAT WORLD'S HUMANS DIED OUT IN A PLAGUE!
AND SOON, ON THAT STRANGE WORLD...
I'VE PROGRAMMED THEM FOR THE ACTIVITIES HERE... AND THEY'LL BE SAFE FROM CRIMINALS. NOW I'LL GET BACK ON MUTO'S TAIL!... HOLD IT! I'M RECEIVING A TELEPATHIC MESSAGE...
FROM EARTH'S ATLANTIS COMES A MENTAL COMMUNICATION, POWERED BY MANY MINDS!
SUPERMAN... WE'RE COMBINING OUR TELEPATHIC POWER TO REACH YOU. MUTO HAS COME TO EARTH AND HAS AN UNDERSEA BASE HERE!
MUTO ON EARTH? THEN HE'S READY TO USE THE TERRIBLE ARSENAL HE STOLE FROM THE WEAPONS WORLD! WELL, THERE'LL BE A MONKEY-WRENCH IN THE WORKS... ME!

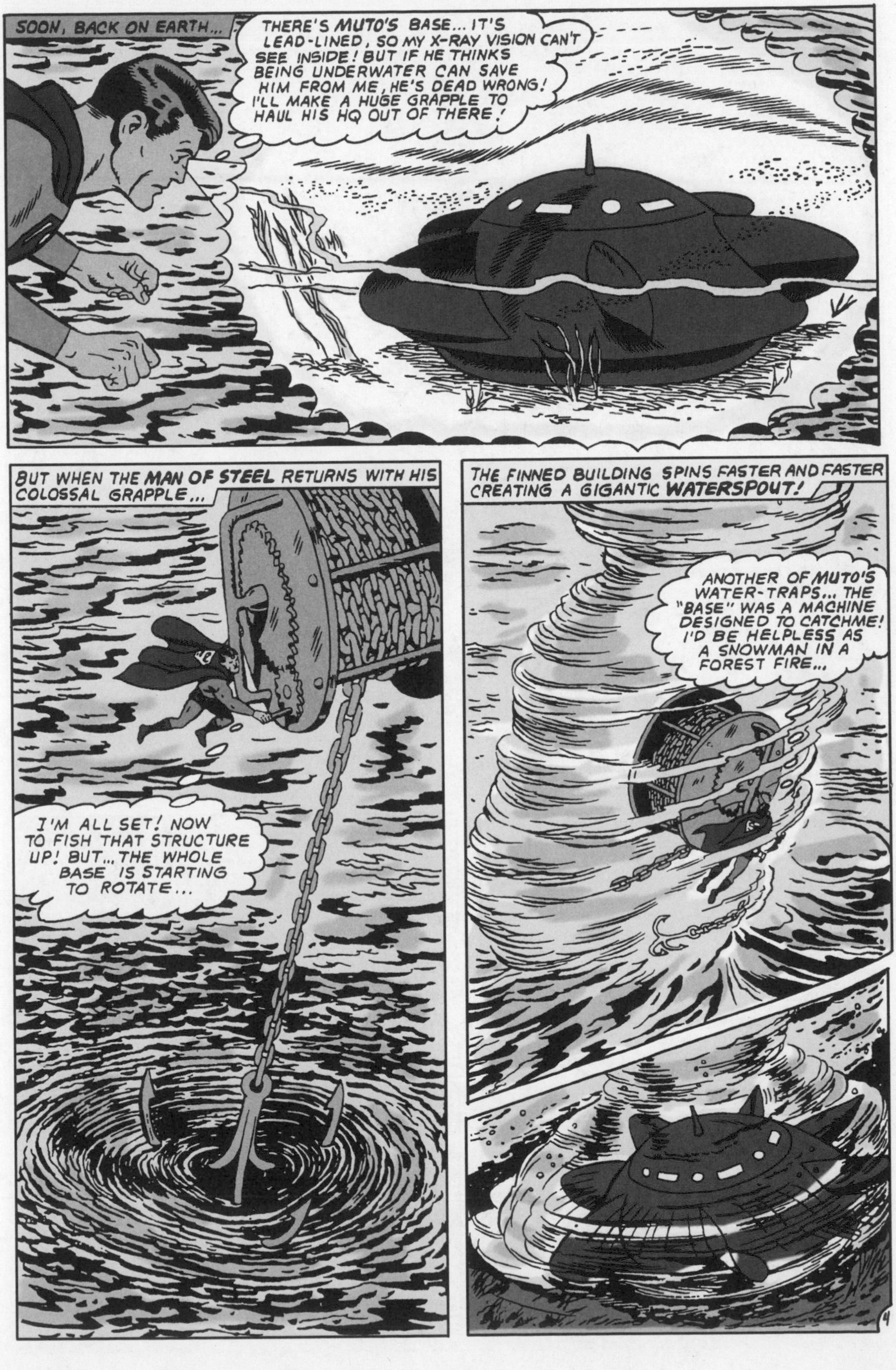
SOON, BACK ON EARTH...
THERE'S MUTO'S BASE... IT'S LEAD-LINED, SO MY X-RAY VISION CAN'T SEE INSIDE! BUT IF HE THINKS BEING UNDERWATER CAN SAVE HIM FROM ME, HE'S DEAD WRONG! I'LL MAKE A HUGE GRAPPLE TO HAUL HIS HQ OUT OF THERE!
BUT WHEN THE MAN OF STEEL RETURNS WITH HIS COLOSSAL GRAPPLE...
I'M ALL SET! NOW TO FISH THAT STRUCTURE UP! BUT... THE WHOLE BASE IS STARTING TO ROTATE...
THE FINNED BUILDING SPINS FASTER AND FASTER CREATING A GIGANTIC WATERSPOUT!
ANOTHER OF MUTO'S WATER-TRAPS... THE "BASE" WAS A MACHINE DESIGNED TO CATCHME! I'D BE HELPLESS AS A SNOWMAN IN A FOREST FIRE...
4

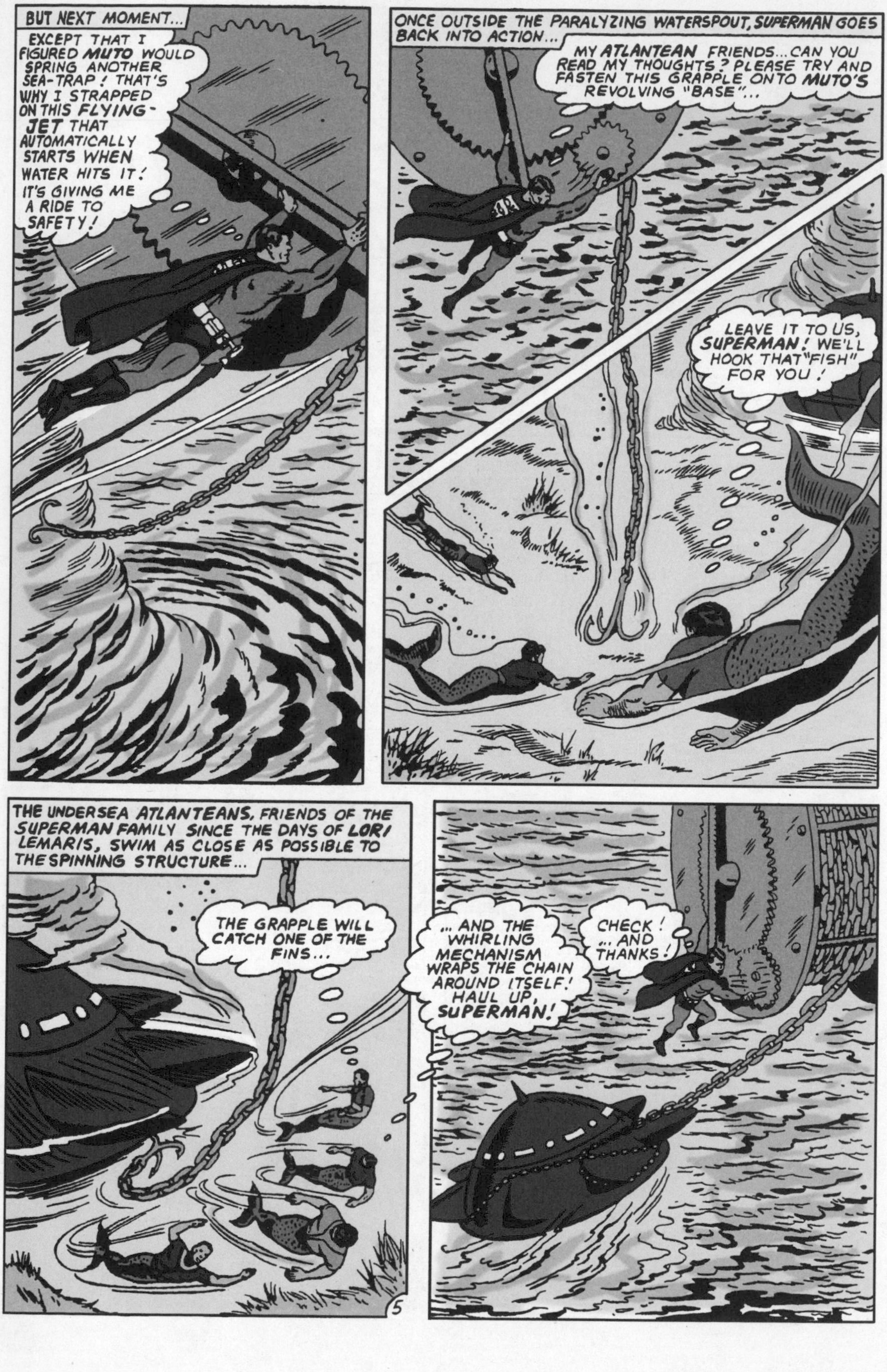
BUT NEXT MOMENT...
EXCEPT THAT I FIGURED MUTO WOULD SPRING ANOTHER SEA-TRAP! THAT'S WHY I STRAPPED ON THIS FLYING-JET THAT AUTOMATICALLY STARTS WHEN WATER HITS IT! IT'S GIVING ME A RIDE TO SAFETY!
ONCE OUTSIDE THE PARALYZING WATERSPOUT, SUPERMAN GOES BACK INTO ACTION...
MY ATLANTEAN FRIENDS... CAN YOU READ MY THOUGHTS? PLEASE TRY AND FASTEN THIS GRAPPLE ONTO MUTO'S REVOLVING "BASE"...
LEAVE IT TO US, SUPERMAN! WE'LL HOOK THAT "FISH" FOR YOU!
THE UNDERSEA ATLANTEANS, FRIENDS OF THE SUPERMAN FAMILY SINCE THE DAYS OF LORI LEMARIS, SWIM AS CLOSE AS POSSIBLE TO THE SPINNING STRUCTURE...
THE GRAPPLE WILL CATCH ONE OF THE FINS...
... AND THE WHIRLING MECHANISM WRAPS THE CHAIN AROUND ITSELF! HAUL UP, SUPERMAN!
CHECK! ... AND THANKS!
5

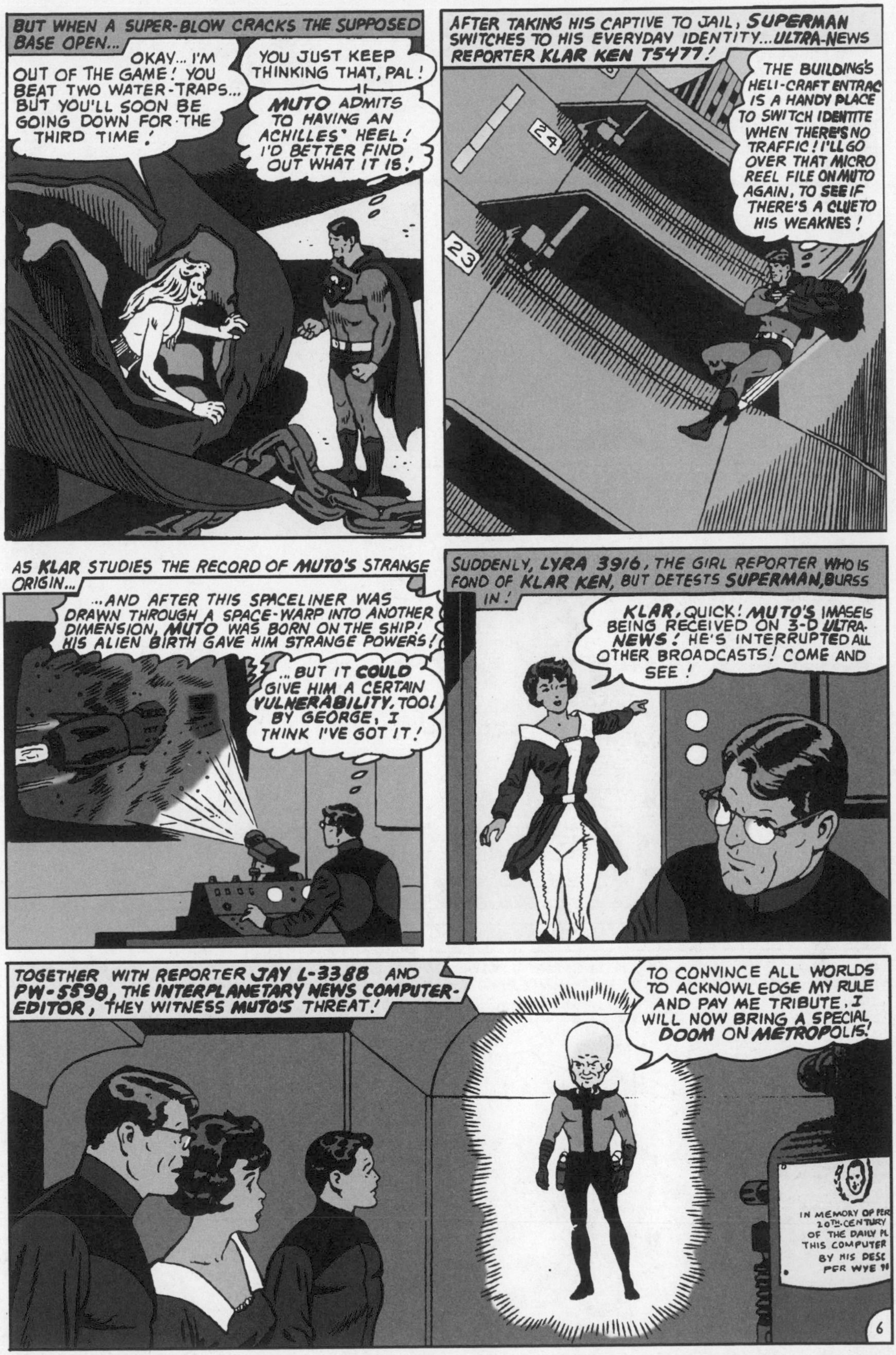
BUT WHEN A SUPER-BLOW CRACKS THE SUPPOSED BASE OPEN...
OKAY... I'M OUT OF THE GAME! YOU BEAT TWO WATER-TRAPS... BUT YOU'LL SOON BE GOING DOWN FOR THE THIRD TIME!
YOU JUST KEEP THINKING THAT, PAL!
MUTO ADMITS TO HAVING AN ACHILLES' HEEL! I'D BETTER FIND OUT WHAT IT IS!
AFTER TAKING HIS CAPTIVE TO JAIL, SUPERMAN SWITCHES TO HIS EVERYDAY IDENTITY... ULTRA-NEWS REPORTER KLAR KEN T5477!
THE BUILDING'S HELI-CRAFT ENTRAC IS A HANDY PLACE TO SWITCH IDENTITE WHEN THERE'S NO TRAFFIC! I'LL GO OVER THAT MICRO REEL FILE ON MUTO AGAIN, TO SEE IF THERE'S A CLUE TO HIS WEAKNES!
24
23
AS KLAR STUDIES THE RECORD OF MUTO'S STRANGE ORIGIN...
...AND AFTER THIS SPACELINER WAS DRAWN THROUGH A SPACE-WARP INTO ANOTHER DIMENSION, MUTO WAS BORN ON THE SHIP! HIS ALIEN BIRTH GAVE HIM STRANGE POWERS!
...BUT IT COULD GIVE HIM A CERTAIN VULNERABILITY, TOO! BY GEORGE, I THINK I'VE GOT IT!
SUDDENLY, LYRA 3916, THE GIRL REPORTER WHO IS FOND OF KLAR KEN, BUT DETESTS SUPERMAN, BURSS IN!
KLAR, QUICK! MUTO'S IMAGE IS BEING RECEIVED ON 3-D ULTRA-NEWS! HE'S INTERRUPTED ALL OTHER BROADCASTS! COME AND SEE!
TOGETHER WITH REPORTER JAY L-3388 AND PW-5598, THE INTERPLANETARY NEWS COMPUTER-EDITOR, THEY WITNESS MUTO'S THREAT!
TO CONVINCE ALL WORLDS TO ACKNOWLEDGE MY RULE AND PAY ME TRIBUTE, I WILL NOW BRING A SPECIAL DOOM ON METROPOLIS!
IN MEMORY OF PER 20TH CENTURY OF THE DAILY PL THIS COMPUTER BY HIS DESC PER WYE 90
6

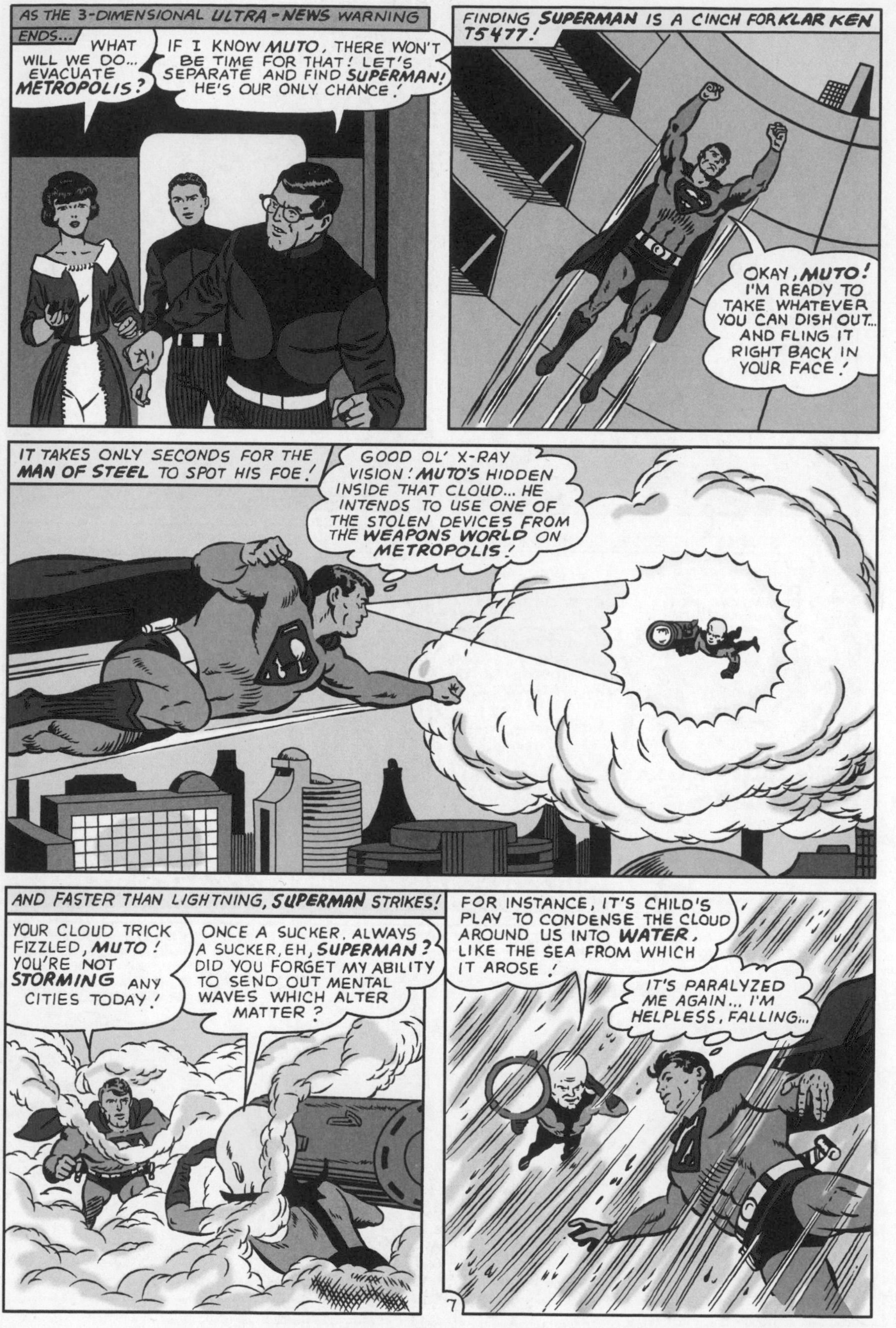
AS THE 3-DIMENSIONAL ULTRA-NEWS WARNING ENDS...
WHAT WILL WE DO... EVACUATE METROPOLIS?
IF I KNOW MUTO, THERE WON'T BE TIME FOR THAT! LET'S SEPARATE AND FIND SUPERMAN! HE'S OUR ONLY CHANCE!
FINDING SUPERMAN IS A CINCH FOR KLAR KEN T5477!
OKAY, MUTO! I'M READY TO TAKE WHATEVER YOU CAN DISH OUT... AND FLING IT RIGHT BACK IN YOUR FACE!
IT TAKES ONLY SECONDS FOR THE MAN OF STEEL TO SPOT HIS FOE!
GOOD OL' X-RAY VISION! MUTO'S HIDDEN INSIDE THAT CLOUD... HE INTENDS TO USE ONE OF THE STOLEN DEVICES FROM THE WEAPONS WORLD ON METROPOLIS!
AND FASTER THAN LIGHTNING, SUPERMAN STRIKES!
YOUR CLOUD TRICK FIZZLED, MUTO! YOU'RE NOT STORMING ANY CITIES TODAY!
ONCE A SUCKER, ALWAYS A SUCKER, EH, SUPERMAN? DID YOU FORGET MY ABILITY TO SEND OUT MENTAL WAVES WHICH ALTER MATTER?
FOR INSTANCE, IT'S CHILD'S PLAY TO CONDENSE THE CLOUD AROUND US INTO WATER, LIKE THE SEA FROM WHICH IT AROSE!
IT'S PARALYZED ME AGAIN... I'M HELPLESS, FALLING...
7

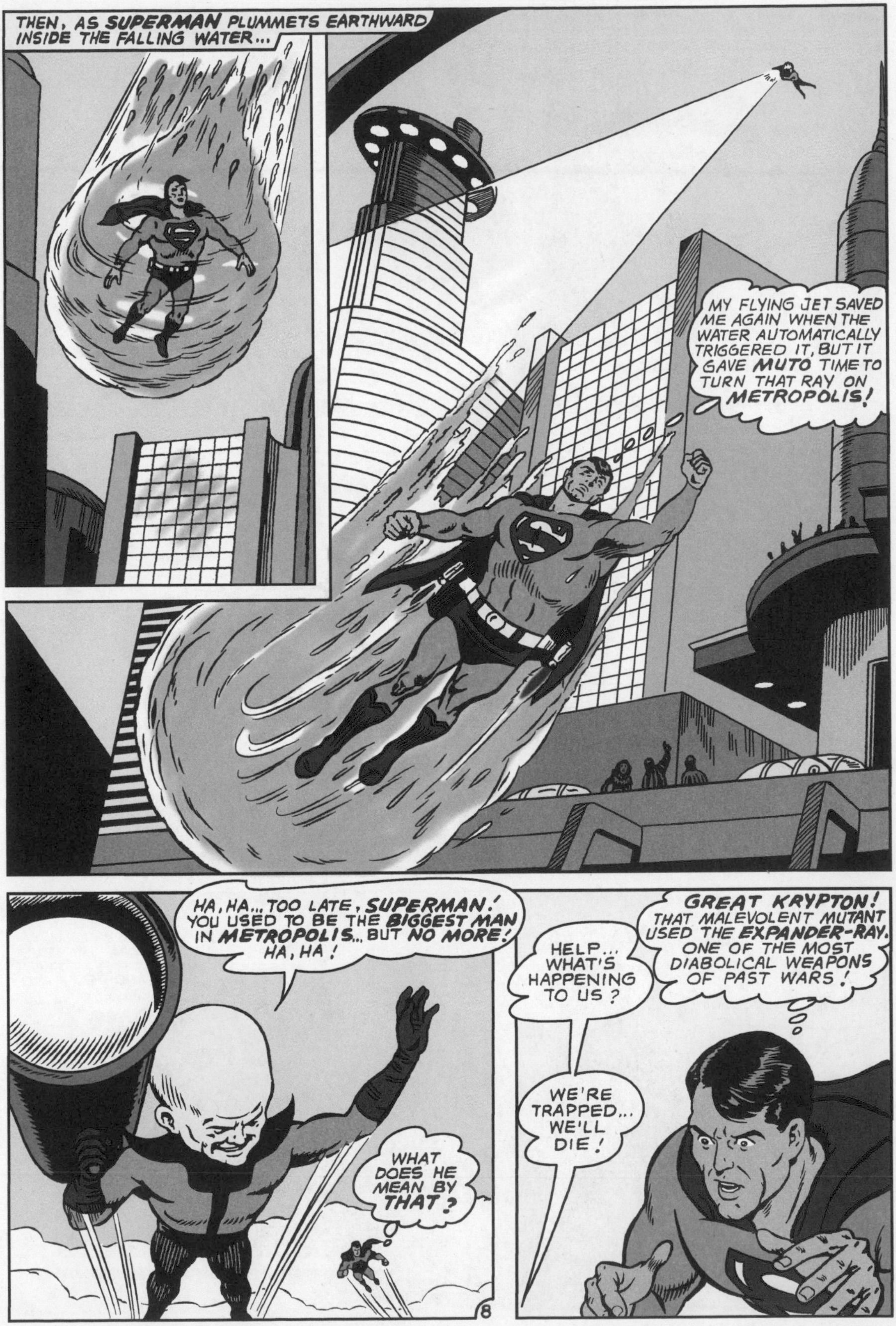
THEN, AS SUPERMAN PLUMMETS EARTHWARD INSIDE THE FALLING WATER...
MY FLYING JET SAVED ME AGAIN WHEN THE WATER AUTOMATICALLY TRIGGERED IT, BUT IT GAVE MUTO TIME TO TURN THAT RAY ON METROPOLIS!
HA, HA... TOO LATE, SUPERMAN! YOU USED TO BE THE BIGGEST MAN IN METROPOLIS... BUT NO MORE! HA, HA!
WHAT DOES HE MEAN BY THAT?
8
HELP... WHAT'S HAPPENING TO US?
WE'RE TRAPPED... WE'LL DIE!
GREAT KRYPTON! THAT MALEVOLENT MUTANT USED THE EXPANDER-RAY. ONE OF THE MOST DIABOLICAL WEAPONS OF PAST WARS!

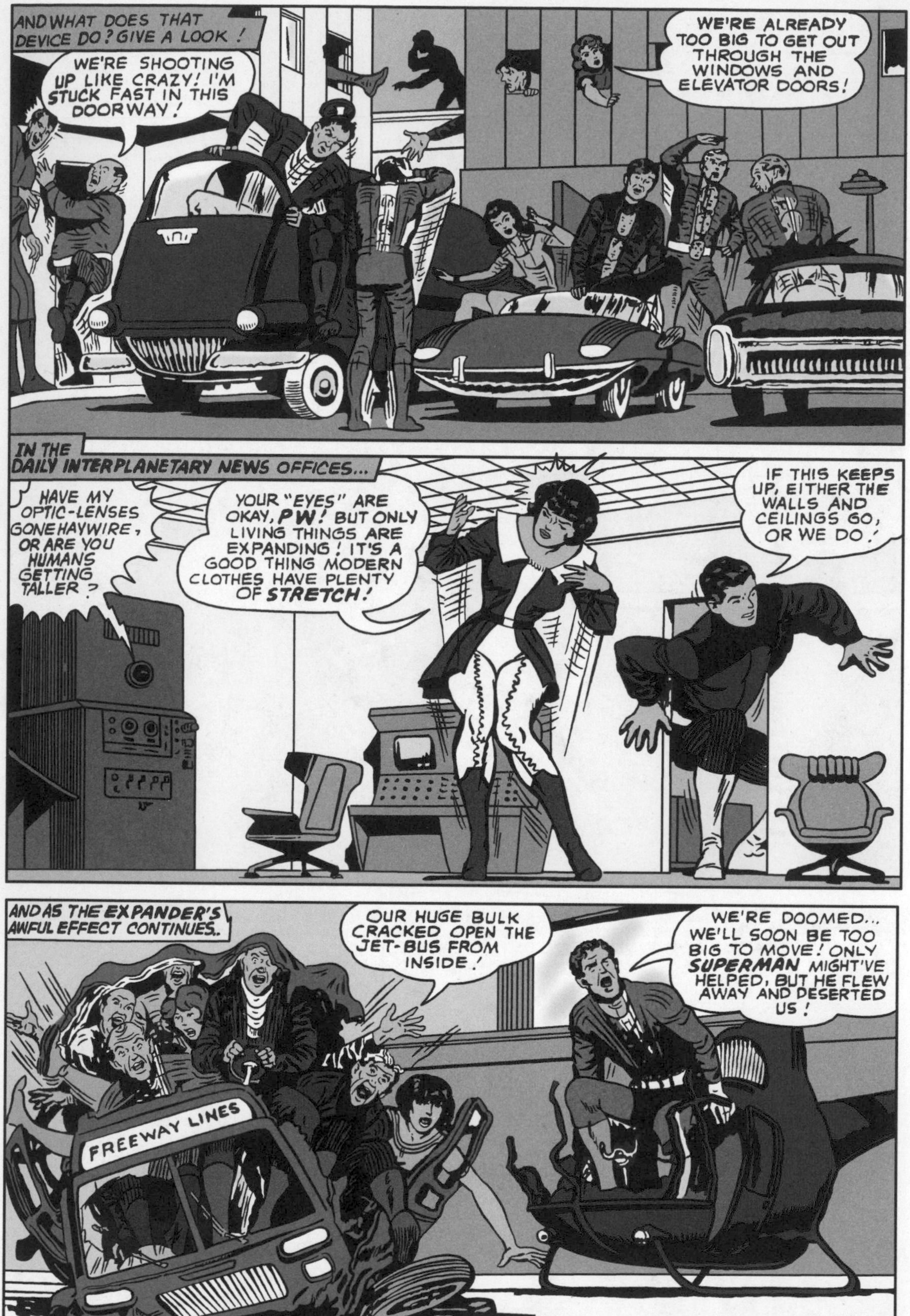
AND WHAT DOES THAT DEVICE DO? GIVE A LOOK!
WE'RE SHOOTING UP LIKE CRAZY! I'M STUCK FAST IN THIS DOORWAY!
WE'RE ALREADY TOO BIG TO GET OUT THROUGH THE WINDOWS AND ELEVATOR DOORS!
IN THE DAILY INTERPLANETARY NEWS OFFICES...
HAVE MY OPTIC-LENSES GONE HAYWIRE, OR ARE YOU HUMANS GETTING TALLER?
YOUR "EYES" ARE OKAY, PW! BUT ONLY LIVING THINGS ARE EXPANDING! IT'S A GOOD THING MODERN CLOTHES HAVE PLENTY OF STRETCH!
IF THIS KEEPS UP, EITHER THE WALLS AND CEILINGS GO, OR WE DO!
AND AS THE EXPANDER'S AWFUL EFFECT CONTINUES..
OUR HUGE BULK CRACKED OPEN THE JET-BUS FROM INSIDE!
WE'RE DOOMED... WE'LL SOON BE TOO BIG TO MOVE! ONLY SUPERMAN MIGHT'VE HELPED, BUT HE FLEW AWAY AND DESERTED US!
FREEWAY LINES
9

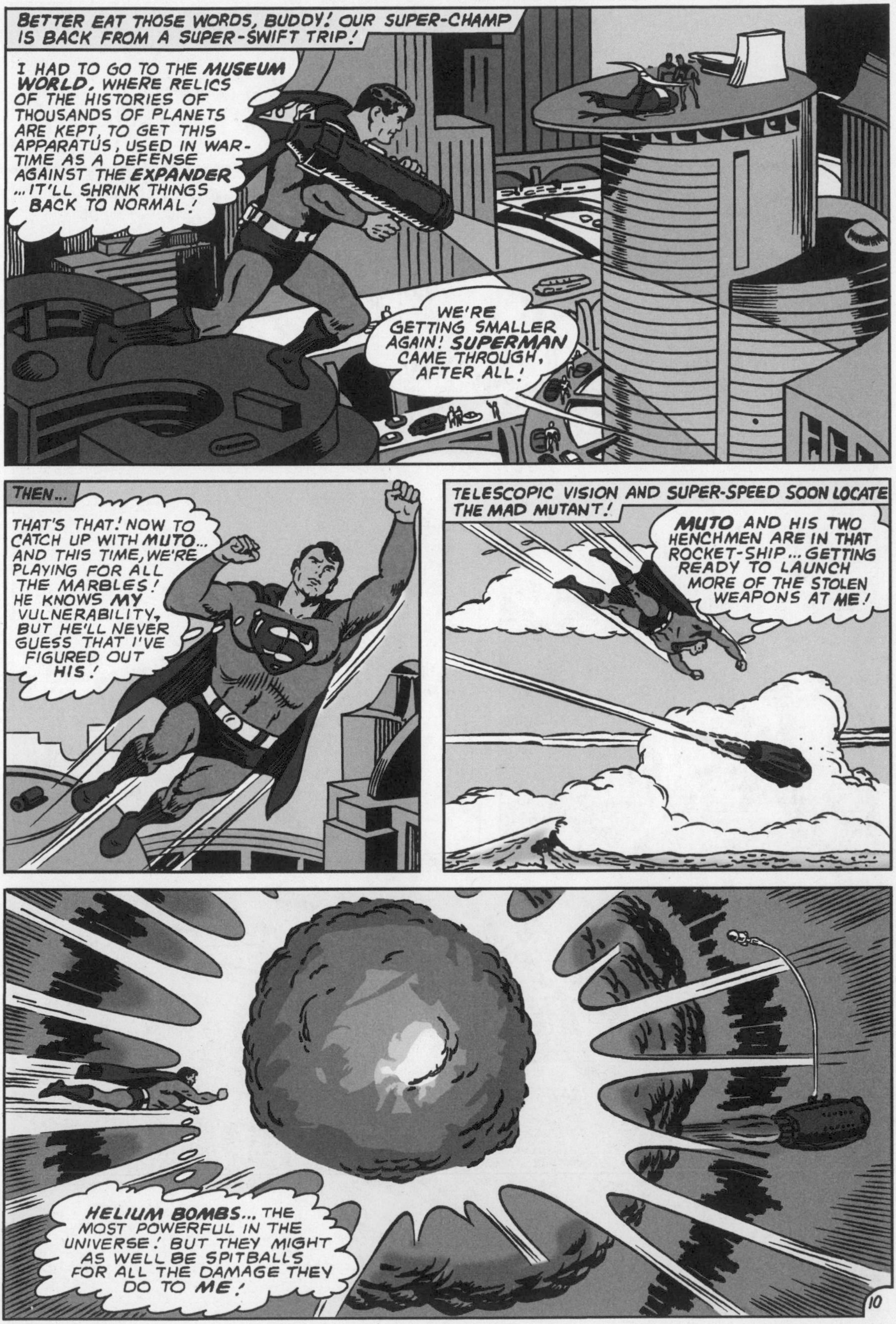
BETTER EAT THOSE WORDS, BUDDY! OUR SUPER-CHAMP IS BACK FROM A SUPER-SWIFT TRIP!
I HAD TO GO TO THE MUSEUM WORLD, WHERE RELICS OF THE HISTORIES OF THOUSANDS OF PLANETS ARE KEPT, TO GET THIS APPARATUS, USED IN WAR-TIME AS A DEFENSE AGAINST THE EXPANDER ...IT'LL SHRINK THINGS BACK TO NORMAL!
WE'RE GETTING SMALLER AGAIN! SUPERMAN CAME THROUGH, AFTER ALL!
THEN...
THAT'S THAT! NOW TO CATCH UP WITH MUTO... AND THIS TIME, WE'RE PLAYING FOR ALL THE MARBLES! HE KNOWS MY VULNERABILITY, BUT HE'LL NEVER GUESS THAT I'VE FIGURED OUT HIS!
TELESCOPIC VISION AND SUPER-SPEED SOON LOCATE THE MAD MUTANT!
MUTO AND HIS TWO HENCHMEN ARE IN THAT ROCKET-SHIP... GETTING READY TO LAUNCH MORE OF THE STOLEN WEAPONS AT ME!
HELIUM BOMBS... THE MOST POWERFUL IN THE UNIVERSE! BUT THEY MIGHT AS WELL BE SPITBALLS FOR ALL THE DAMAGE THEY DO TO ME!
10

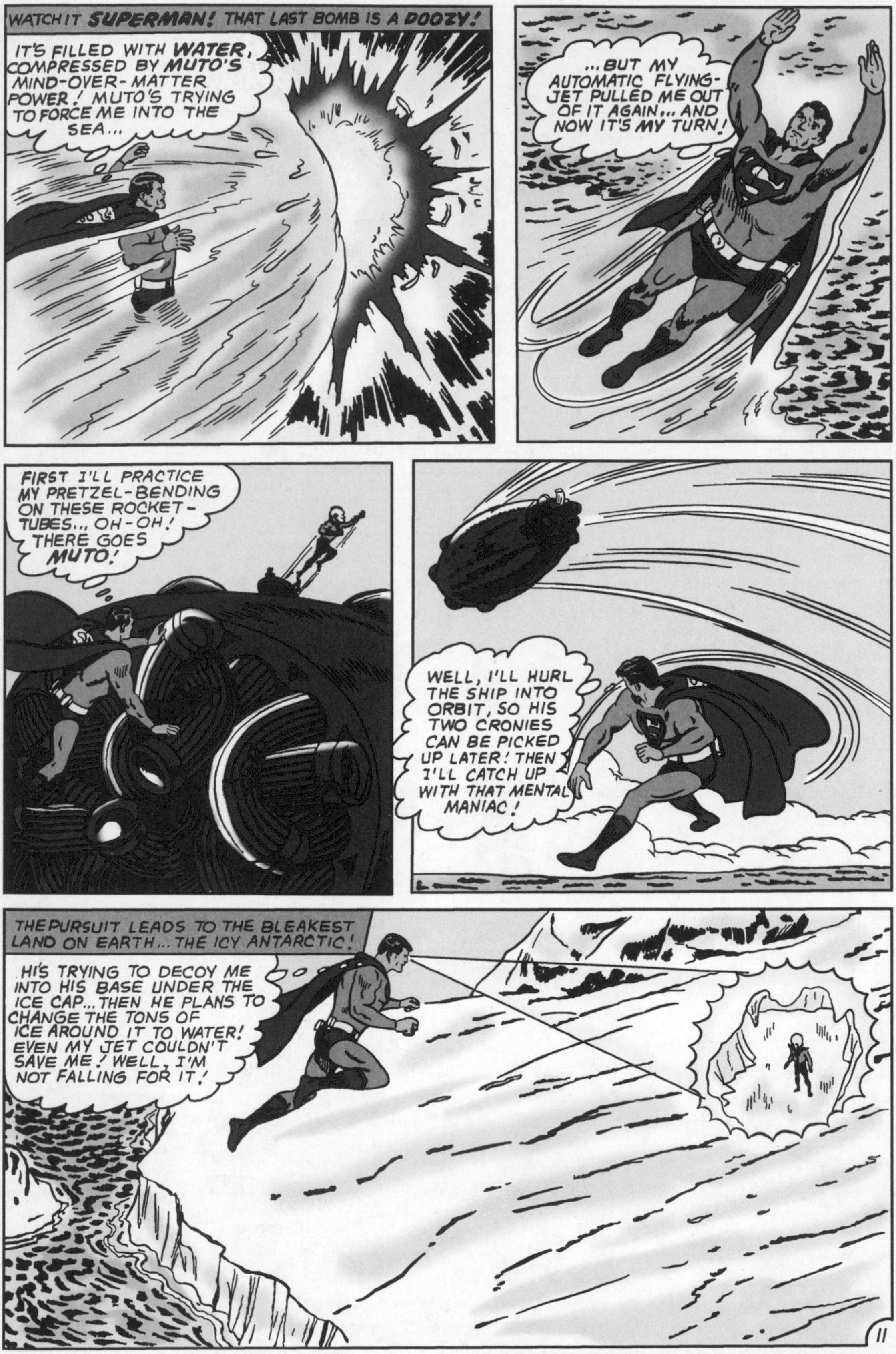
WATCH IT SUPERMAN! THAT LAST BOMB IS A DOOZY!
IT'S FILLED WITH WATER, COMPRESSED BY MUTO'S MIND-OVER-MATTER POWER! MUTO'S TRYING TO FORCE ME INTO THE SEA...
...BUT MY AUTOMATIC FLYING-JET PULLED ME OUT OF IT AGAIN... AND NOW IT'S MY TURN!
FIRST I'LL PRACTICE MY PRETZEL-BENDING ON THESE ROCKET-TUBES... OH-OH! THERE GOES MUTO!
WELL, I'LL HURL THE SHIP INTO ORBIT, SO HIS TWO CRONIES CAN BE PICKED UP LATER! THEN I'LL CATCH UP WITH THAT MENTAL MANIAC!
THE PURSUIT LEADS TO THE BLEAKEST LAND ON EARTH... THE ICY ANTARCTIC!
HE'S TRYING TO DECOY ME INTO HIS BASE UNDER THE ICE CAP... THEN HE PLANS TO CHANGE THE TONS OF ICE AROUND IT TO WATER! EVEN MY JET COULDN'T SAVE ME! WELL, I'M NOT FALLING FOR IT!
11

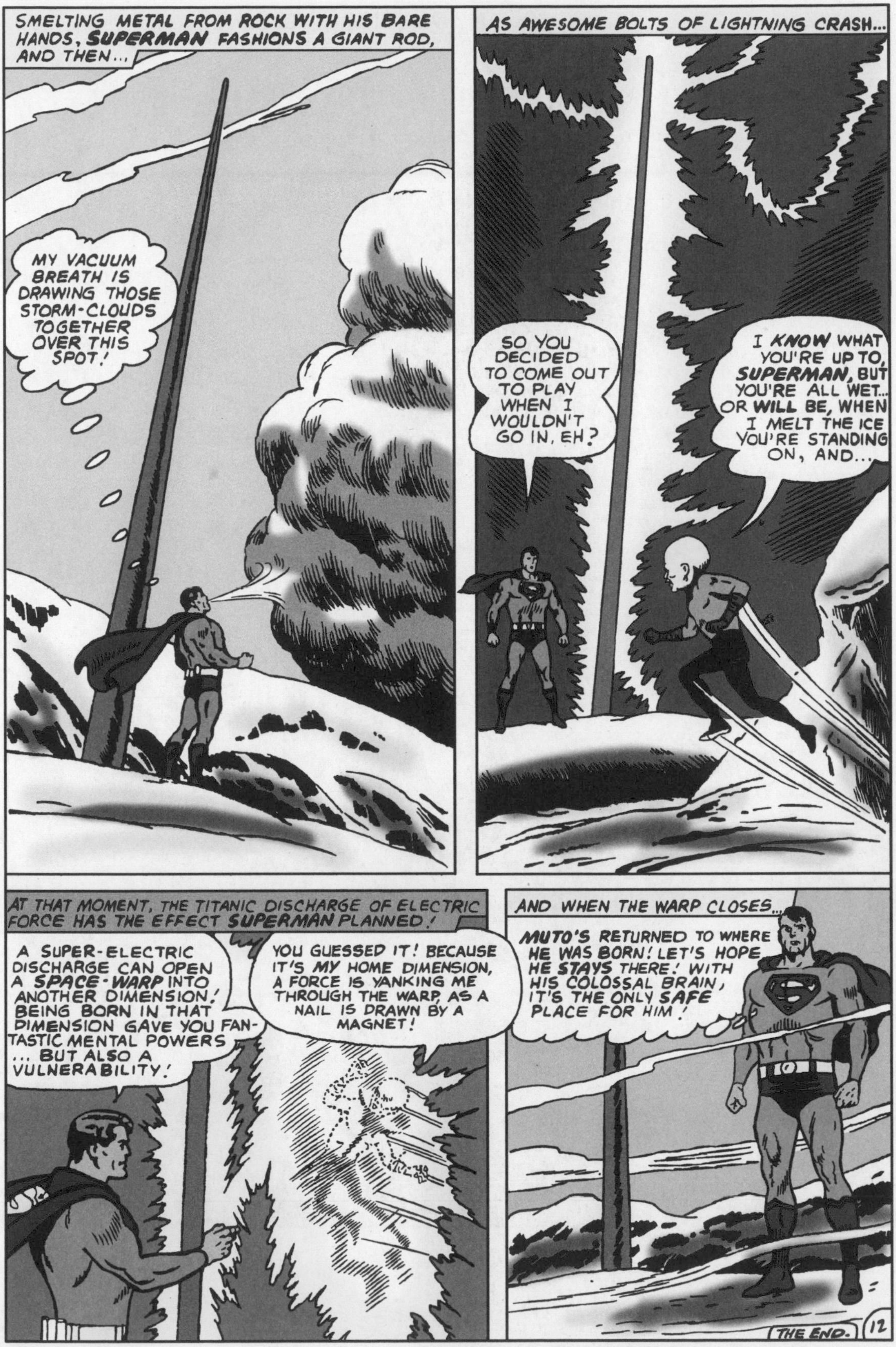
SMELTING METAL FROM ROCK WITH HIS BARE HANDS, SUPERMAN FASHIONS A GIANT ROD, AND THEN...
MY VACUUM BREATH IS DRAWING THOSE STORM-CLOUDS TOGETHER OVER THIS SPOT!
AS AWESOME BOLTS OF LIGHTNING CRASH...
SO YOU DECIDED TO COME OUT TO PLAY WHEN I WOULDN'T GO IN, EH?
I KNOW WHAT YOU'RE UP TO, SUPERMAN, BUT YOU'RE ALL WET... OR WILL BE, WHEN I MELT THE ICE YOU'RE STANDING ON, AND...
AT THAT MOMENT, THE TITANIC DISCHARGE OF ELECTRIC FORCE HAS THE EFFECT SUPERMAN PLANNED!
A SUPER-ELECTRIC DISCHARGE CAN OPEN A SPACE-WARP INTO ANOTHER DIMENSION! BEING BORN IN THAT DIMENSION GAVE YOU FANTASTIC MENTAL POWERS ... BUT ALSO A VULNERABILITY!
YOU GUESSED IT! BECAUSE IT'S MY HOME DIMENSION, A FORCE IS YANKING ME THROUGH THE WARP, AS A NAIL IS DRAWN BY A MAGNET!
AND WHEN THE WARP CLOSES...
MUTO'S RETURNED TO WHERE HE WAS BORN! LET'S HOPE HE STAYS THERE! WITH HIS COLOSSAL BRAIN, IT'S THE ONLY SAFE PLACE FOR HIM!
THE END.
12

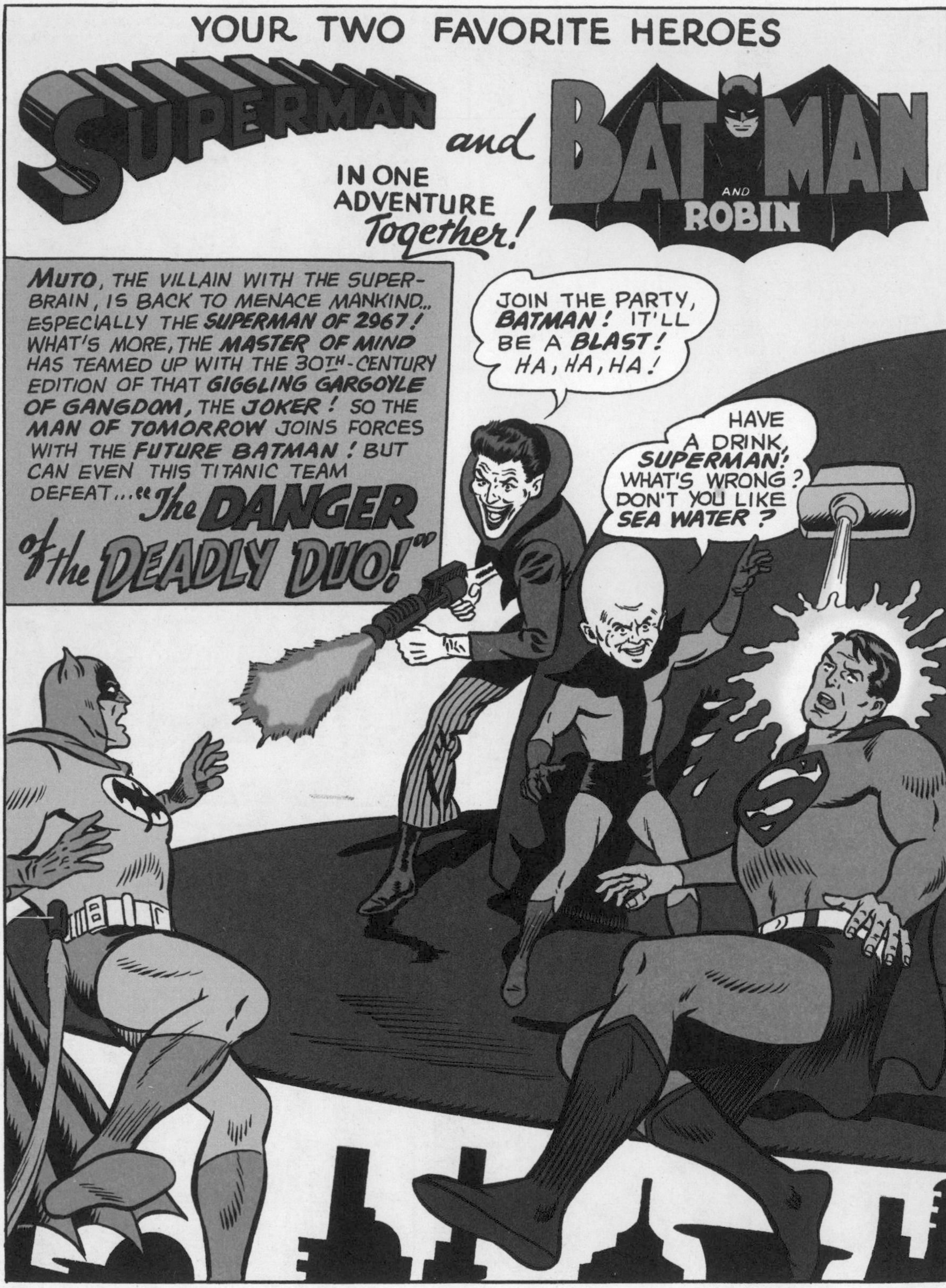
YOUR TWO FAVORITE HEROES
SUPERMAN and BATMAN AND ROBIN
IN ONE ADVENTURE Together!
MUTO, THE VILLAIN WITH THE SUPER-BRAIN, IS BACK TO MENACE MANKIND... ESPECIALLY THE SUPERMAN OF 2967! WHAT'S MORE, THE MASTER OF MIND HAS TEAMED UP WITH THE 30TH-CENTURY EDITION OF THAT GIGGLING GARGOYLE OF GANGDOM, THE JOKER! SO THE MAN OF TOMORROW JOINS FORCES WITH THE FUTURE BATMAN! BUT CAN EVEN THIS TITANIC TEAM DEFEAT... "The DANGER of the DEADLY DUO!"
JOIN THE PARTY, BATMAN! IT'LL BE A BLAST! HA, HA, HA!
HAVE A DRINK, SUPERMAN! WHAT'S WRONG? DON'T YOU LIKE SEA WATER?

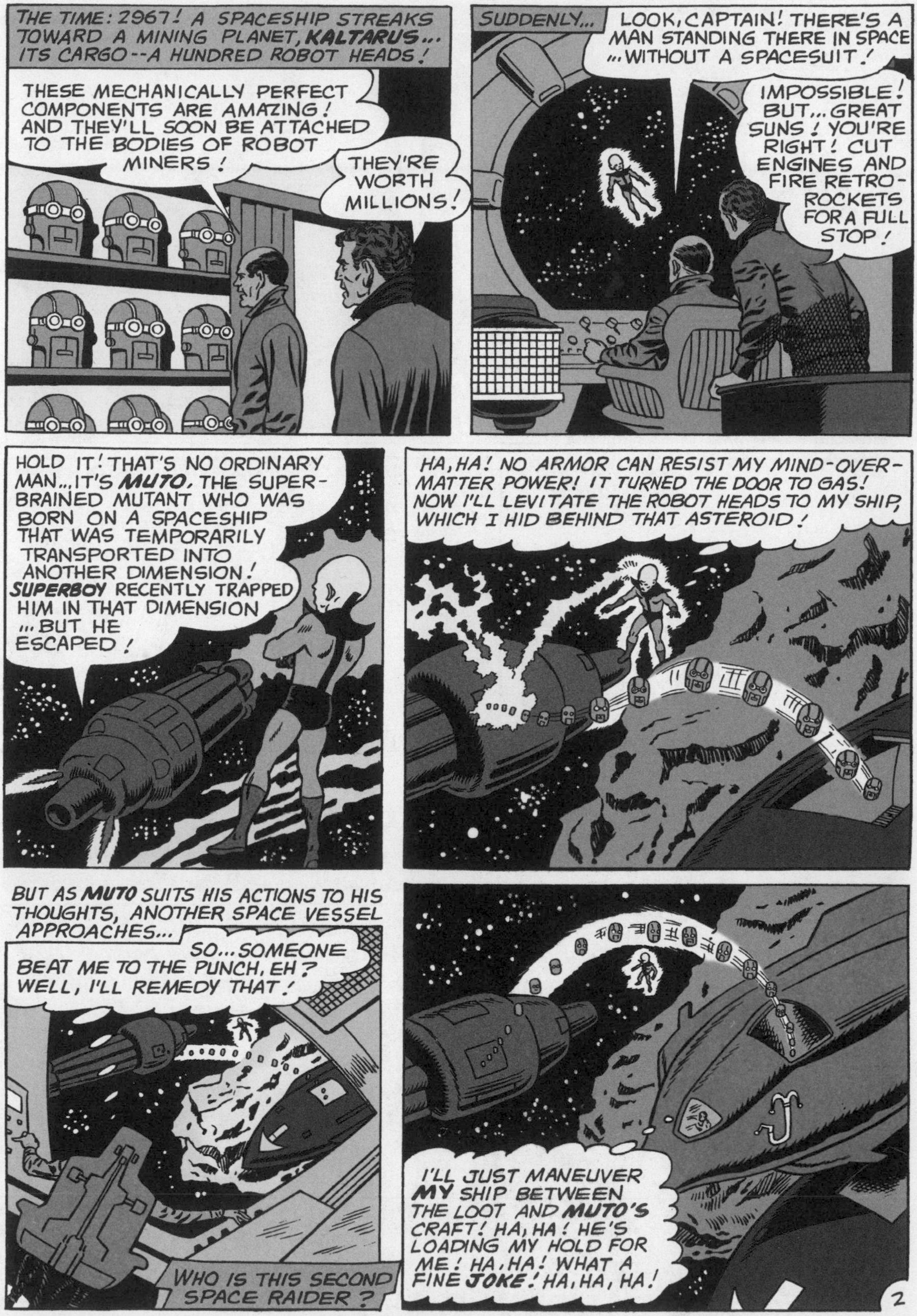
THE TIME: 2967! A SPACESHIP STREAKS TOWARD A MINING PLANET, KALTARUS... ITS CARGO--A HUNDRED ROBOT HEADS!
THESE MECHANICALLY PERFECT COMPONENTS ARE AMAZING! AND THEY'LL SOON BE ATTACHED TO THE BODIES OF ROBOT MINERS!
THEY'RE WORTH MILLIONS!
SUDDENLY...
LOOK, CAPTAIN! THERE'S A MAN STANDING THERE IN SPACE ...WITHOUT A SPACESUIT!
IMPOSSIBLE! BUT... GREAT SUNS! YOU'RE RIGHT! CUT ENGINES AND FIRE RETRO-ROCKETS FOR A FULL STOP!
HOLD IT! THAT'S NO ORDINARY MAN... IT'S MUTO, THE SUPER-BRAINED MUTANT WHO WAS BORN ON A SPACESHIP THAT WAS TEMPORARILY TRANSPORTED INTO ANOTHER DIMENSION! SUPERBOY RECENTLY TRAPPED HIM IN THAT DIMENSION ...BUT HE ESCAPED!
HA, HA! NO ARMOR CAN RESIST MY MIND-OVER-MATTER POWER! IT TURNED THE DOOR TO GAS! NOW I'LL LEVITATE THE ROBOT HEADS TO MY SHIP, WHICH I HID BEHIND THAT ASTEROID!
BUT AS MUTO SUITS HIS ACTIONS TO HIS THOUGHTS, ANOTHER SPACE VESSEL APPROACHES...
SO... SOMEONE BEAT ME TO THE PUNCH, EH? WELL, I'LL REMEDY THAT!
WHO IS THIS SECOND SPACE RAIDER?
I'LL JUST MANEUVER MY SHIP BETWEEN THE LOOT AND MUTO'S CRAFT! HA, HA! HE'S LOADING MY HOLD FOR ME! HA, HA! WHAT A FINE JOKE! HA, HA, HA!
2

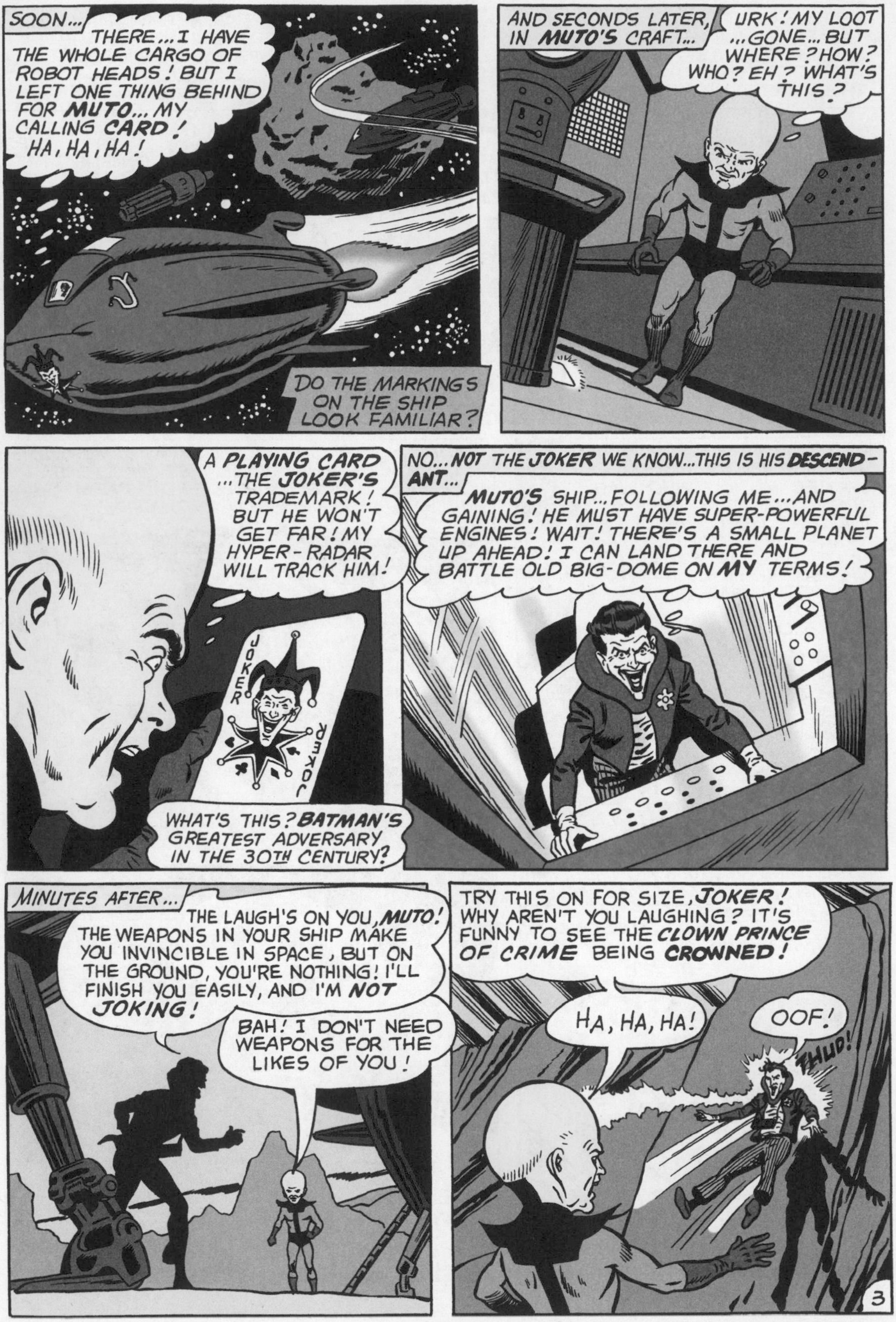
SOON...
THERE...I HAVE THE WHOLE CARGO OF ROBOT HEADS! BUT I LEFT ONE THING BEHIND FOR MUTO... MY CALLING CARD! HA, HA, HA!
DO THE MARKINGS ON THE SHIP LOOK FAMILIAR?
AND SECONDS LATER, IN MUTO'S CRAFT...
URK! MY LOOT ...GONE... BUT WHERE? HOW? WHO? EH? WHAT'S THIS?
A PLAYING CARD ...THE JOKER'S TRADEMARK! BUT HE WON'T GET FAR! MY HYPER-RADAR WILL TRACK HIM!
JOKER
WHAT'S THIS? BATMAN'S GREATEST ADVERSARY IN THE 30TH CENTURY?
NO...NOT THE JOKER WE KNOW...THIS IS HIS DESCENDANT...
MUTO'S SHIP...FOLLOWING ME...AND GAINING! HE MUST HAVE SUPER-POWERFUL ENGINES! WAIT! THERE'S A SMALL PLANET UP AHEAD! I CAN LAND THERE AND BATTLE OLD BIG-DOME ON MY TERMS!
MINUTES AFTER...
THE LAUGH'S ON YOU, MUTO! THE WEAPONS IN YOUR SHIP MAKE YOU INVINCIBLE IN SPACE, BUT ON THE GROUND, YOU'RE NOTHING! I'LL FINISH YOU EASILY, AND I'M NOT JOKING!
BAH! I DON'T NEED WEAPONS FOR THE LIKES OF YOU!
TRY THIS ON FOR SIZE, JOKER! WHY AREN'T YOU LAUGHING? IT'S FUNNY TO SEE THE CLOWN PRINCE OF CRIME BEING CROWNED!
HA, HA, HA!
OOF!
THUD!
3

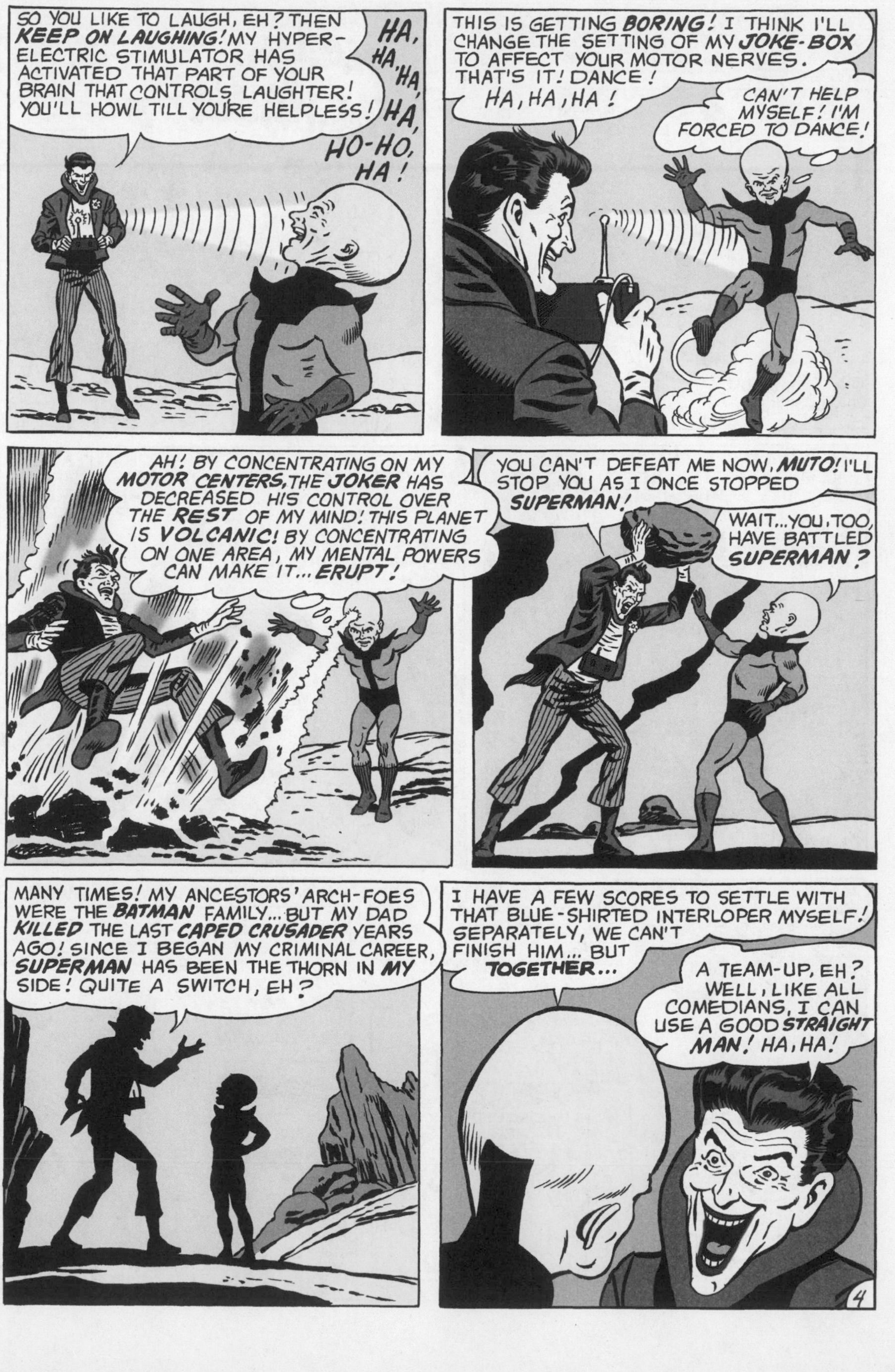
SO YOU LIKE TO LAUGH, EH? THEN KEEP ON LAUGHING! MY HYPER-ELECTRIC STIMULATOR HAS ACTIVATED THAT PART OF YOUR BRAIN THAT CONTROLS LAUGHTER! YOU'LL HOWL TILL YOU'RE HELPLESS!
HA, HA, HA, HA, HO-HO, HA!
THIS IS GETTING BORING! I THINK I'LL CHANGE THE SETTING OF MY JOKE-BOX TO AFFECT YOUR MOTOR NERVES. THAT'S IT! DANCE! HA, HA, HA!
CAN'T HELP MYSELF! I'M FORCED TO DANCE!
AH! BY CONCENTRATING ON MY MOTOR CENTERS, THE JOKER HAS DECREASED HIS CONTROL OVER THE REST OF MY MIND! THIS PLANET IS VOLCANIC! BY CONCENTRATING ON ONE AREA, MY MENTAL POWERS CAN MAKE IT... ERUPT!
YOU CAN'T DEFEAT ME NOW, MUTO! I'LL STOP YOU AS I ONCE STOPPED SUPERMAN!
WAIT... YOU, TOO, HAVE BATTLED SUPERMAN?
MANY TIMES! MY ANCESTORS' ARCH-FOES WERE THE BATMAN FAMILY... BUT MY DAD KILLED THE LAST CAPED CRUSADER YEARS AGO! SINCE I BEGAN MY CRIMINAL CAREER, SUPERMAN HAS BEEN THE THORN IN MY SIDE! QUITE A SWITCH, EH?
I HAVE A FEW SCORES TO SETTLE WITH THAT BLUE-SHIRTED INTERLOPER MYSELF! SEPARATELY, WE CAN'T FINISH HIM... BUT TOGETHER...
A TEAM-UP, EH? WELL, LIKE ALL COMEDIANS, I CAN USE A GOOD STRAIGHT MAN! HA, HA!
4

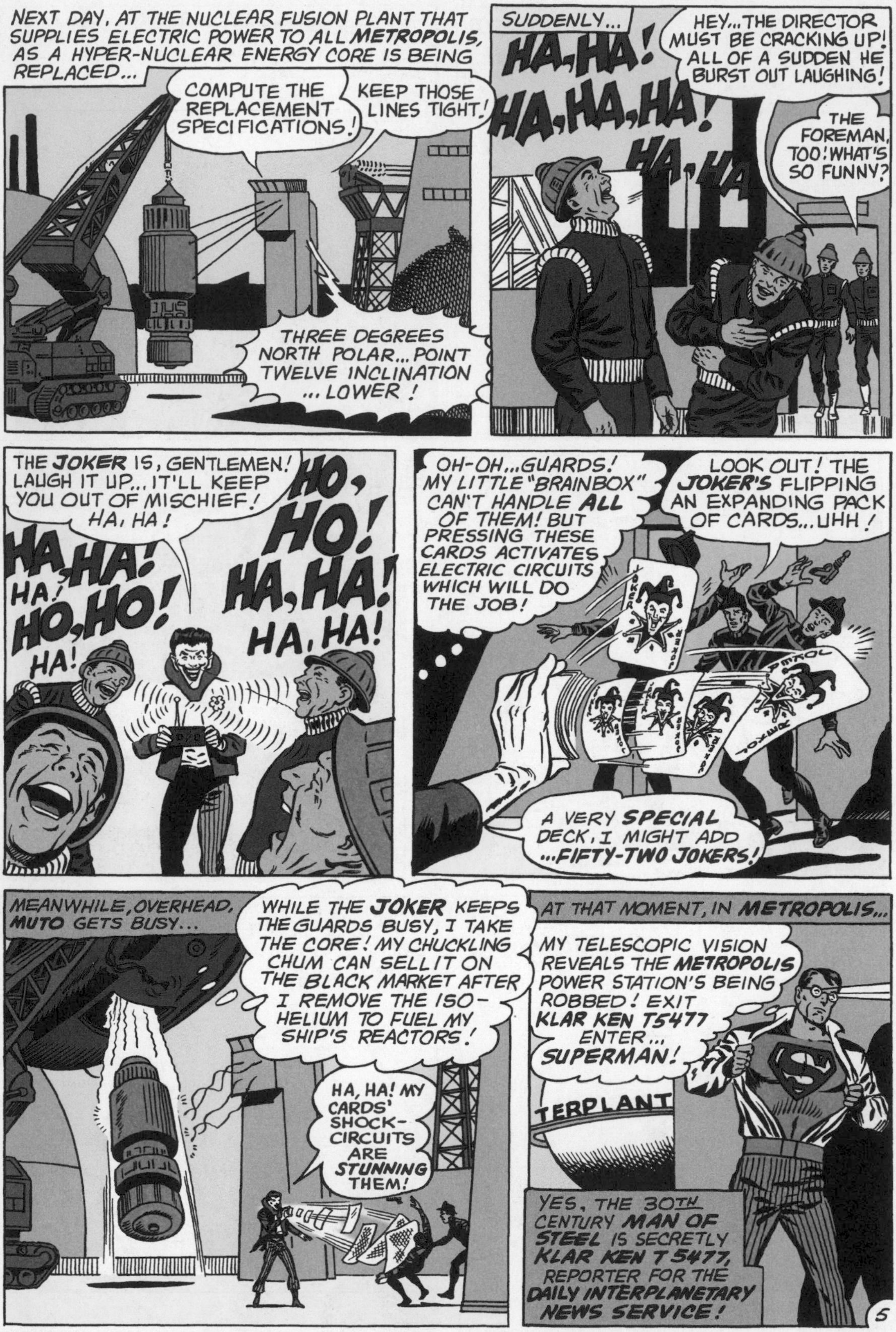
NEXT DAY, AT THE NUCLEAR FUSION PLANT THAT SUPPLIES ELECTRIC POWER TO ALL METROPOLIS, AS A HYPER-NUCLEAR ENERGY CORE IS BEING REPLACED...
COMPUTE THE REPLACEMENT SPECIFICATIONS!
KEEP THOSE LINES TIGHT!
THREE DEGREES NORTH POLAR... POINT TWELVE INCLINATION ...LOWER!
SUDDENLY...
HA-HA! HA-HA-HA! HA-HA
HEY... THE DIRECTOR MUST BE CRACKING UP! ALL OF A SUDDEN HE BURST OUT LAUGHING!
THE FOREMAN, TOO! WHAT'S SO FUNNY?
THE JOKER IS, GENTLEMEN! LAUGH IT UP... IT'LL KEEP YOU OUT OF MISCHIEF! HA, HA!
HA, HA! HA! HO, HO! HA!
HO, HO! HA, HA! HA, HA!
OH-OH... GUARDS! MY LITTLE "BRAINBOX" CAN'T HANDLE ALL OF THEM! BUT PRESSING THESE CARDS ACTIVATES ELECTRIC CIRCUITS WHICH WILL DO THE JOB!
LOOK OUT! THE JOKER'S FLIPPING AN EXPANDING PACK OF CARDS... UHH!
A VERY SPECIAL DECK, I MIGHT ADD ...FIFTY-TWO JOKERS!
MEANWHILE, OVERHEAD, MUTO GETS BUSY...
WHILE THE JOKER KEEPS THE GUARDS BUSY, I TAKE THE CORE! MY CHUCKLING CHUM CAN SELL IT ON THE BLACK MARKET AFTER I REMOVE THE ISO-HELIUM TO FUEL MY SHIP'S REACTORS!
HA, HA! MY CARDS' SHOCK-CIRCUITS ARE STUNNING THEM!
AT THAT MOMENT, IN METROPOLIS...
MY TELESCOPIC VISION REVEALS THE METROPOLIS POWER STATION'S BEING ROBBED! EXIT KLAR KEN T5477 ENTER... SUPERMAN!
TERPLANT
YES, THE 30TH CENTURY MAN OF STEEL IS SECRETLY KLAR KEN T 5477, REPORTER FOR THE DAILY INTERPLANETARY NEWS SERVICE!
5

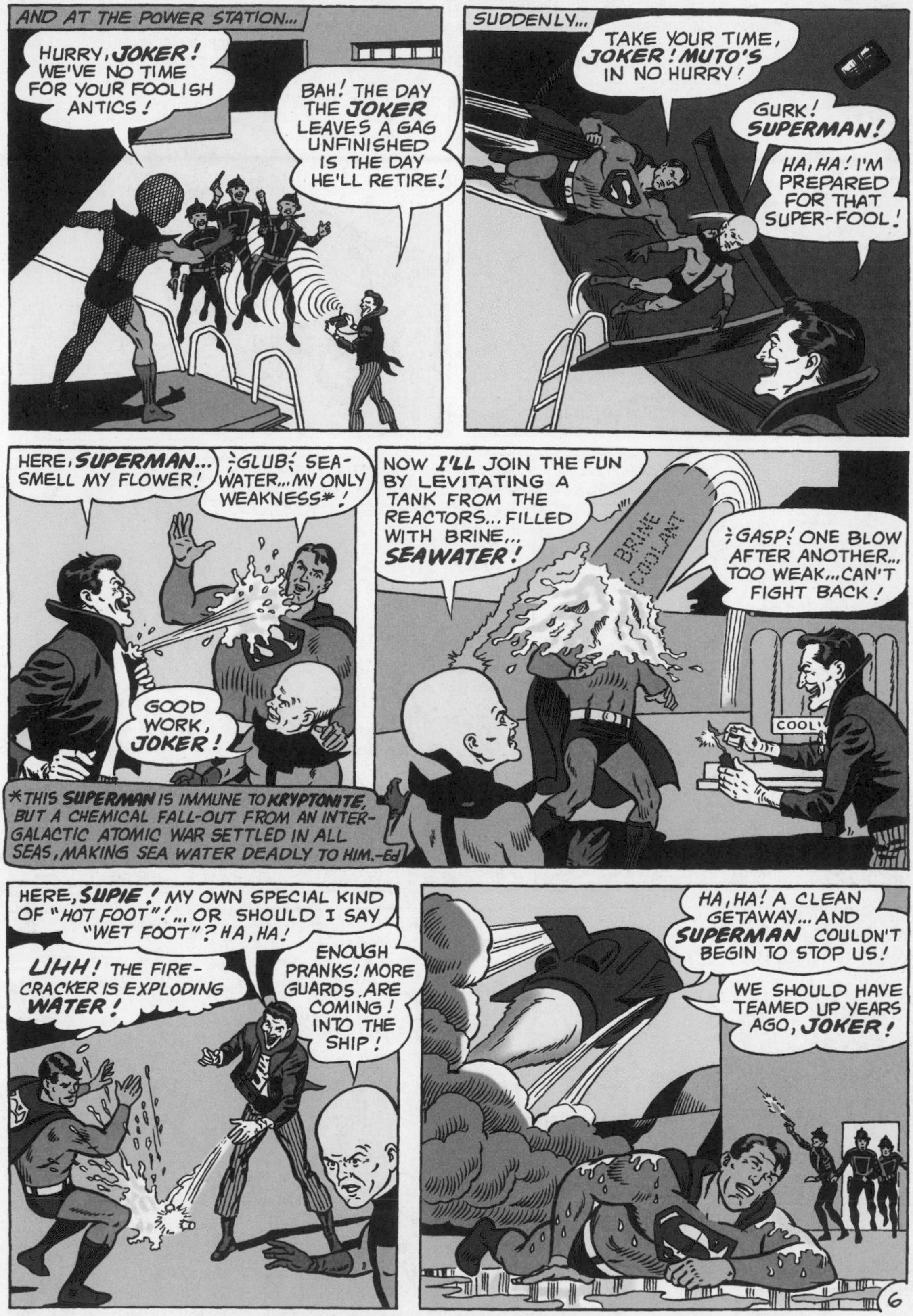
AND AT THE POWER STATION...
HURRY, JOKER! WE'VE NO TIME FOR YOUR FOOLISH ANTICS!
BAH! THE DAY THE JOKER LEAVES A GAG UNFINISHED IS THE DAY HE'LL RETIRE!
SUDDENLY...
TAKE YOUR TIME, JOKER! MUTO'S IN NO HURRY!
GURK! SUPERMAN!
HA, HA! I'M PREPARED FOR THAT SUPER-FOOL!
HERE, SUPERMAN... SMELL MY FLOWER!
GLUB! SEA-WATER... MY ONLY WEAKNESS*!
GOOD WORK, JOKER!
*THIS SUPERMAN IS IMMUNE TO KRYPTONITE, BUT A CHEMICAL FALL-OUT FROM AN INTER-GALACTIC ATOMIC WAR SETTLED IN ALL SEAS, MAKING SEA WATER DEADLY TO HIM. -Ed
NOW I'LL JOIN THE FUN BY LEVITATING A TANK FROM THE REACTORS... FILLED WITH BRINE... SEAWATER!
BRINE COOLANT
GASP! ONE BLOW AFTER ANOTHER... TOO WEAK... CAN'T FIGHT BACK!
COOL
HERE, SUPIE! MY OWN SPECIAL KIND OF "HOT FOOT"! ... OR SHOULD I SAY "WET FOOT"? HA, HA!
UHH! THE FIRE-CRACKER IS EXPLODING WATER!
ENOUGH PRANKS! MORE GUARDS ARE COMING! INTO THE SHIP!
HA, HA! A CLEAN GETAWAY... AND SUPERMAN COULDN'T BEGIN TO STOP US!
WE SHOULD HAVE TEAMED UP YEARS AGO, JOKER!
6

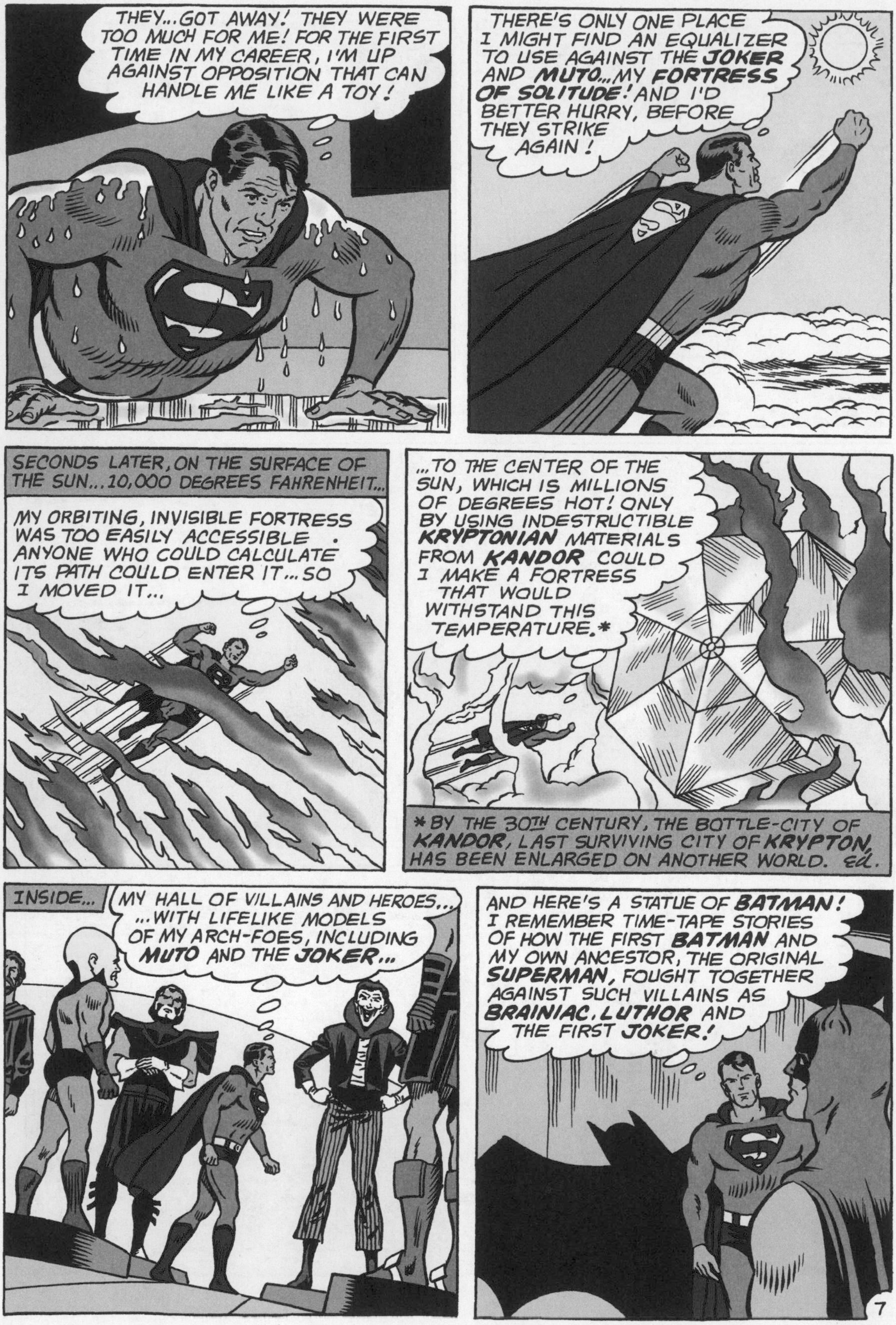
THEY...GOT AWAY! THEY WERE TOO MUCH FOR ME! FOR THE FIRST TIME IN MY CAREER, I'M UP AGAINST OPPOSITION THAT CAN HANDLE ME LIKE A TOY!
THERE'S ONLY ONE PLACE I MIGHT FIND AN EQUALIZER TO USE AGAINST THE JOKER AND MUTO...MY FORTRESS OF SOLITUDE! AND I'D BETTER HURRY, BEFORE THEY STRIKE AGAIN!
SECONDS LATER, ON THE SURFACE OF THE SUN...10,000 DEGREES FAHRENHEIT...
MY ORBITING, INVISIBLE FORTRESS WAS TOO EASILY ACCESSIBLE. ANYONE WHO COULD CALCULATE ITS PATH COULD ENTER IT...SO I MOVED IT...
...TO THE CENTER OF THE SUN, WHICH IS MILLIONS OF DEGREES HOT! ONLY BY USING INDESTRUCTIBLE KRYPTONIAN MATERIALS FROM KANDOR COULD I MAKE A FORTRESS THAT WOULD WITHSTAND THIS TEMPERATURE.*
* BY THE 30TH CENTURY, THE BOTTLE-CITY OF KANDOR, LAST SURVIVING CITY OF KRYPTON, HAS BEEN ENLARGED ON ANOTHER WORLD. Ed.
INSIDE...
MY HALL OF VILLAINS AND HEROES... ...WITH LIFELIKE MODELS OF MY ARCH-FOES, INCLUDING MUTO AND THE JOKER...
AND HERE'S A STATUE OF BATMAN! I REMEMBER TIME-TAPE STORIES OF HOW THE FIRST BATMAN AND MY OWN ANCESTOR, THE ORIGINAL SUPERMAN, FOUGHT TOGETHER AGAINST SUCH VILLAINS AS BRAINIAC, LUTHOR AND THE FIRST JOKER!
7

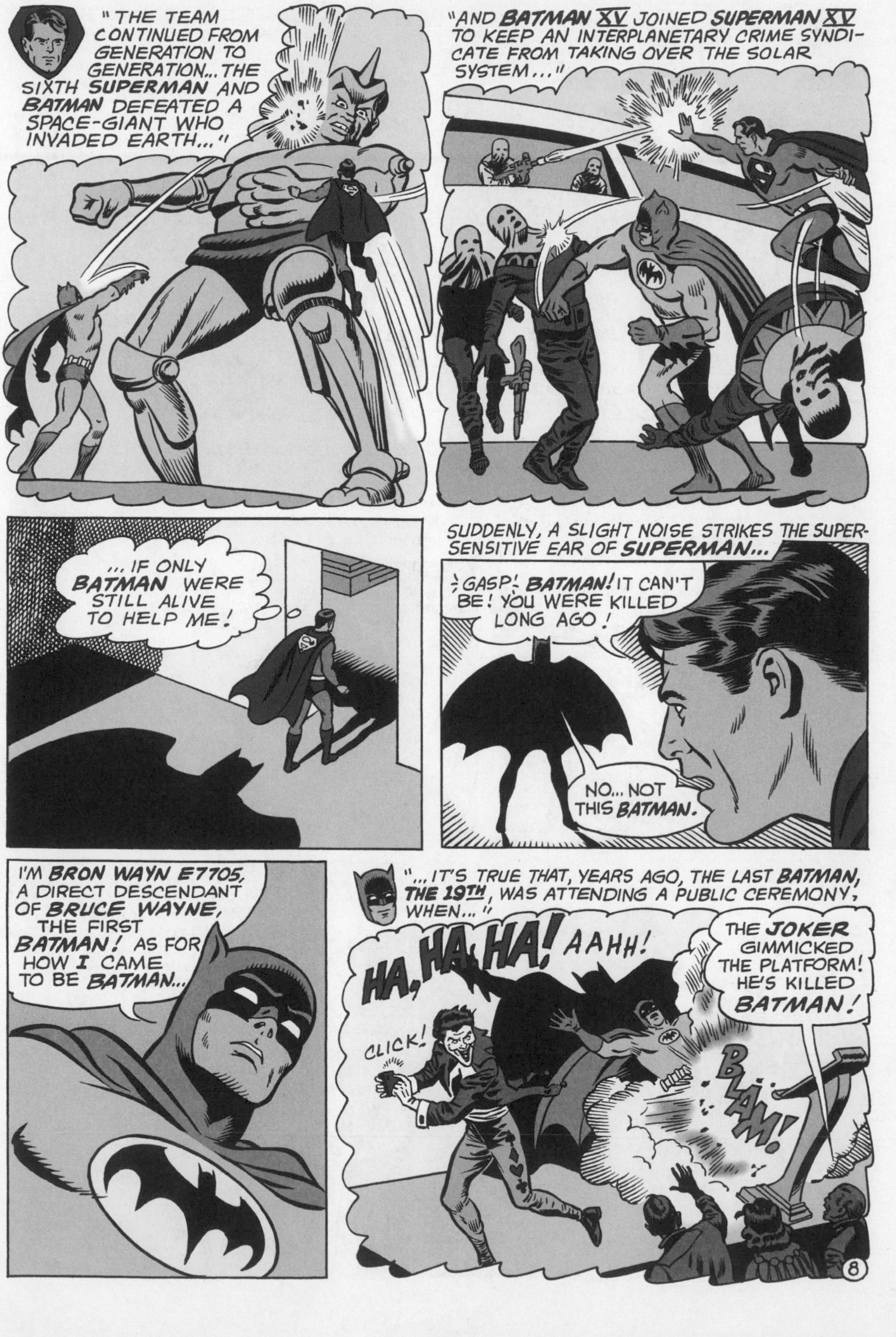
"THE TEAM CONTINUED FROM GENERATION TO GENERATION... THE SIXTH SUPERMAN AND BATMAN DEFEATED A SPACE-GIANT WHO INVADED EARTH..."
"AND BATMAN XV JOINED SUPERMAN XV TO KEEP AN INTERPLANETARY CRIME SYNDICATE FROM TAKING OVER THE SOLAR SYSTEM..."
... IF ONLY BATMAN WERE STILL ALIVE TO HELP ME!
SUDDENLY, A SLIGHT NOISE STRIKES THE SUPER-SENSITIVE EAR OF SUPERMAN...
-GASP!- BATMAN! IT CAN'T BE! YOU WERE KILLED LONG AGO!
NO... NOT THIS BATMAN.
I'M BRON WAYN E7705, A DIRECT DESCENDANT OF BRUCE WAYNE, THE FIRST BATMAN! AS FOR HOW I CAME TO BE BATMAN...
"... IT'S TRUE THAT, YEARS AGO, THE LAST BATMAN, THE 19TH, WAS ATTENDING A PUBLIC CEREMONY, WHEN..."
HA, HA, HA! AAHH!
THE JOKER GIMMICKED THE PLATFORM! HE'S KILLED BATMAN!
CLICK!
BLAM!
8

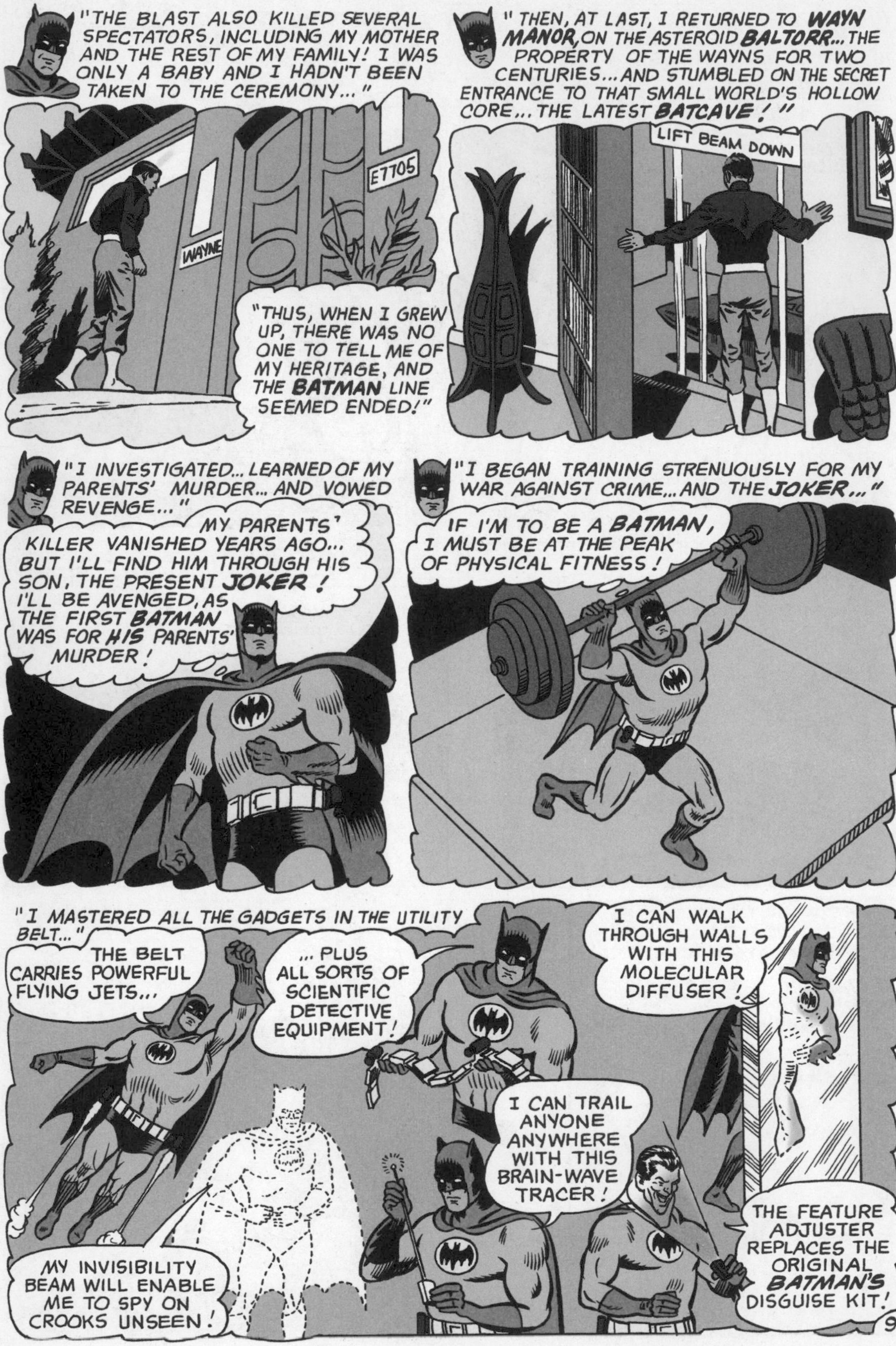
"THE BLAST ALSO KILLED SEVERAL SPECTATORS, INCLUDING MY MOTHER AND THE REST OF MY FAMILY! I WAS ONLY A BABY AND I HADN'T BEEN TAKEN TO THE CEREMONY..."
E7705
WAYNE
"THUS, WHEN I GREW UP, THERE WAS NO ONE TO TELL ME OF MY HERITAGE, AND THE BATMAN LINE SEEMED ENDED!"
"THEN, AT LAST, I RETURNED TO WAYN MANOR, ON THE ASTEROID BALTORR... THE PROPERTY OF THE WAYNS FOR TWO CENTURIES... AND STUMBLED ON THE SECRET ENTRANCE TO THAT SMALL WORLD'S HOLLOW CORE... THE LATEST BATCAVE!"
LIFT BEAM DOWN
"I INVESTIGATED... LEARNED OF MY PARENTS' MURDER... AND VOWED REVENGE..."
MY PARENTS' KILLER VANISHED YEARS AGO... BUT I'LL FIND HIM THROUGH HIS SON, THE PRESENT JOKER! I'LL BE AVENGED, AS THE FIRST BATMAN WAS FOR HIS PARENTS' MURDER!
"I BEGAN TRAINING STRENUOUSLY FOR MY WAR AGAINST CRIME... AND THE JOKER..."
IF I'M TO BE A BATMAN, I MUST BE AT THE PEAK OF PHYSICAL FITNESS!
"I MASTERED ALL THE GADGETS IN THE UTILITY BELT..."
THE BELT CARRIES POWERFUL FLYING JETS...
... PLUS ALL SORTS OF SCIENTIFIC DETECTIVE EQUIPMENT!
I CAN WALK THROUGH WALLS WITH THIS MOLECULAR DIFFUSER!
I CAN TRAIL ANYONE ANYWHERE WITH THIS BRAIN-WAVE TRACER!
MY INVISIBILITY BEAM WILL ENABLE ME TO SPY ON CROOKS UNSEEN!
THE FEATURE ADJUSTER REPLACES THE ORIGINAL BATMAN'S DISGUISE KIT!
9

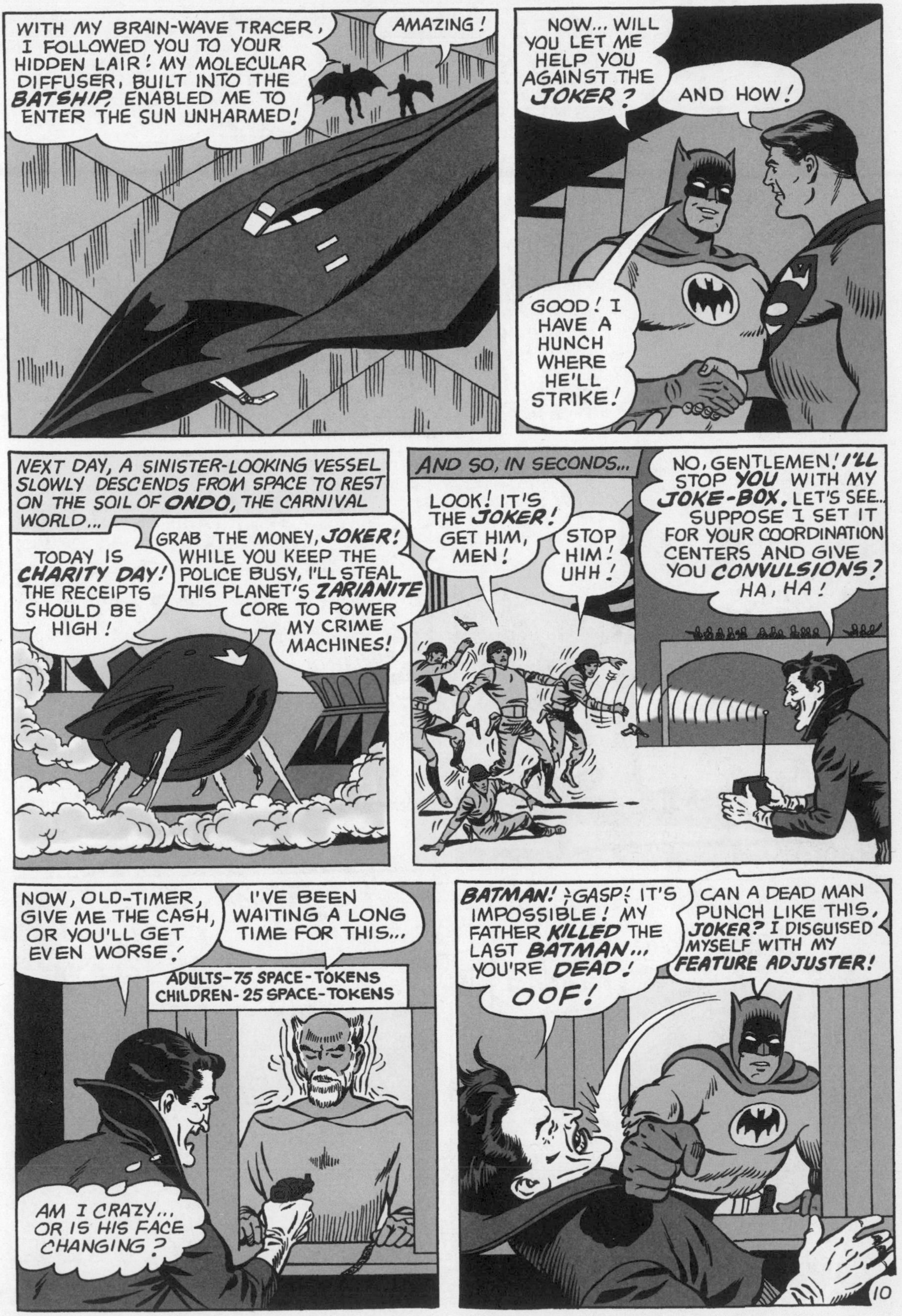

WITH MY BRAIN-WAVE TRACER, I FOLLOWED YOU TO YOUR HIDDEN LAIR! MY MOLECULAR DIFFUSER, BUILT INTO THE BATSHIP, ENABLED ME TO ENTER THE SUN UNHARMED!
AMAZING!
NOW... WILL YOU LET ME HELP YOU AGAINST THE JOKER?
AND HOW!
GOOD! I HAVE A HUNCH WHERE HE'LL STRIKE!
NEXT DAY, A SINISTER-LOOKING VESSEL SLOWLY DESCENDS FROM SPACE TO REST ON THE SOIL OF ONDO, THE CARNIVAL WORLD...
TODAY IS CHARITY DAY! THE RECEIPTS SHOULD BE HIGH!
GRAB THE MONEY, JOKER! WHILE YOU KEEP THE POLICE BUSY, I'LL STEAL THIS PLANET'S ZARIANITE CORE TO POWER MY CRIME MACHINES!
AND SO, IN SECONDS...
LOOK! IT'S THE JOKER! GET HIM, MEN!
STOP HIM! UHH!
NO, GENTLEMEN! I'LL STOP YOU WITH MY JOKE-BOX. LET'S SEE... SUPPOSE I SET IT FOR YOUR COORDINATION CENTERS AND GIVE YOU CONVULSIONS? HA, HA!
NOW, OLD-TIMER, GIVE ME THE CASH, OR YOU'LL GET EVEN WORSE!
I'VE BEEN WAITING A LONG TIME FOR THIS...
ADULTS-75 SPACE-TOKENS
CHILDREN-25 SPACE-TOKENS
AM I CRAZY... OR IS HIS FACE CHANGING?
BATMAN! -GASP- IT'S IMPOSSIBLE! MY FATHER KILLED THE LAST BATMAN... YOU'RE DEAD!
OOF!
CAN A DEAD MAN PUNCH LIKE THIS, JOKER? I DISGUISED MYSELF WITH MY FEATURE ADJUSTER!
10

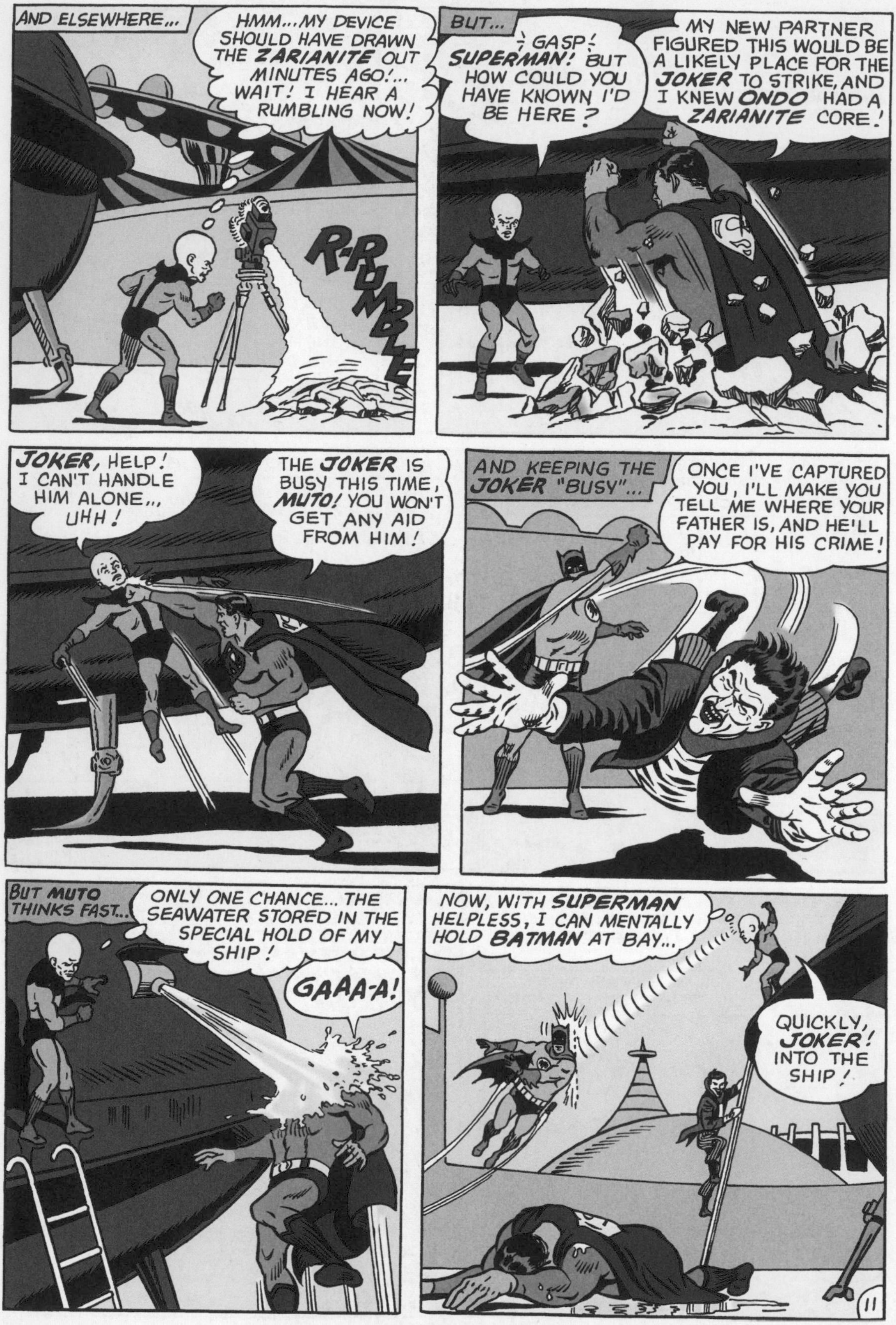
AND ELSEWHERE...
HMM... MY DEVICE SHOULD HAVE DRAWN THE ZARIANITE OUT MINUTES AGO!... WAIT! I HEAR A RUMBLING NOW!
R-RUMBLE
BUT...
GASP! SUPERMAN! BUT HOW COULD YOU HAVE KNOWN I'D BE HERE?
MY NEW PARTNER FIGURED THIS WOULD BE A LIKELY PLACE FOR THE JOKER TO STRIKE, AND I KNEW ONDO HAD A ZARIANITE CORE!
JOKER, HELP! I CAN'T HANDLE HIM ALONE... UHH!
THE JOKER IS BUSY THIS TIME, MUTO! YOU WON'T GET ANY AID FROM HIM!
AND KEEPING THE JOKER "BUSY"...
ONCE I'VE CAPTURED YOU, I'LL MAKE YOU TELL ME WHERE YOUR FATHER IS, AND HE'LL PAY FOR HIS CRIME!
BUT MUTO THINKS FAST...
ONLY ONE CHANCE... THE SEAWATER STORED IN THE SPECIAL HOLD OF MY SHIP!
GAAA-A!
NOW, WITH SUPERMAN HELPLESS, I CAN MENTALLY HOLD BATMAN AT BAY...
QUICKLY, JOKER! INTO THE SHIP!
11

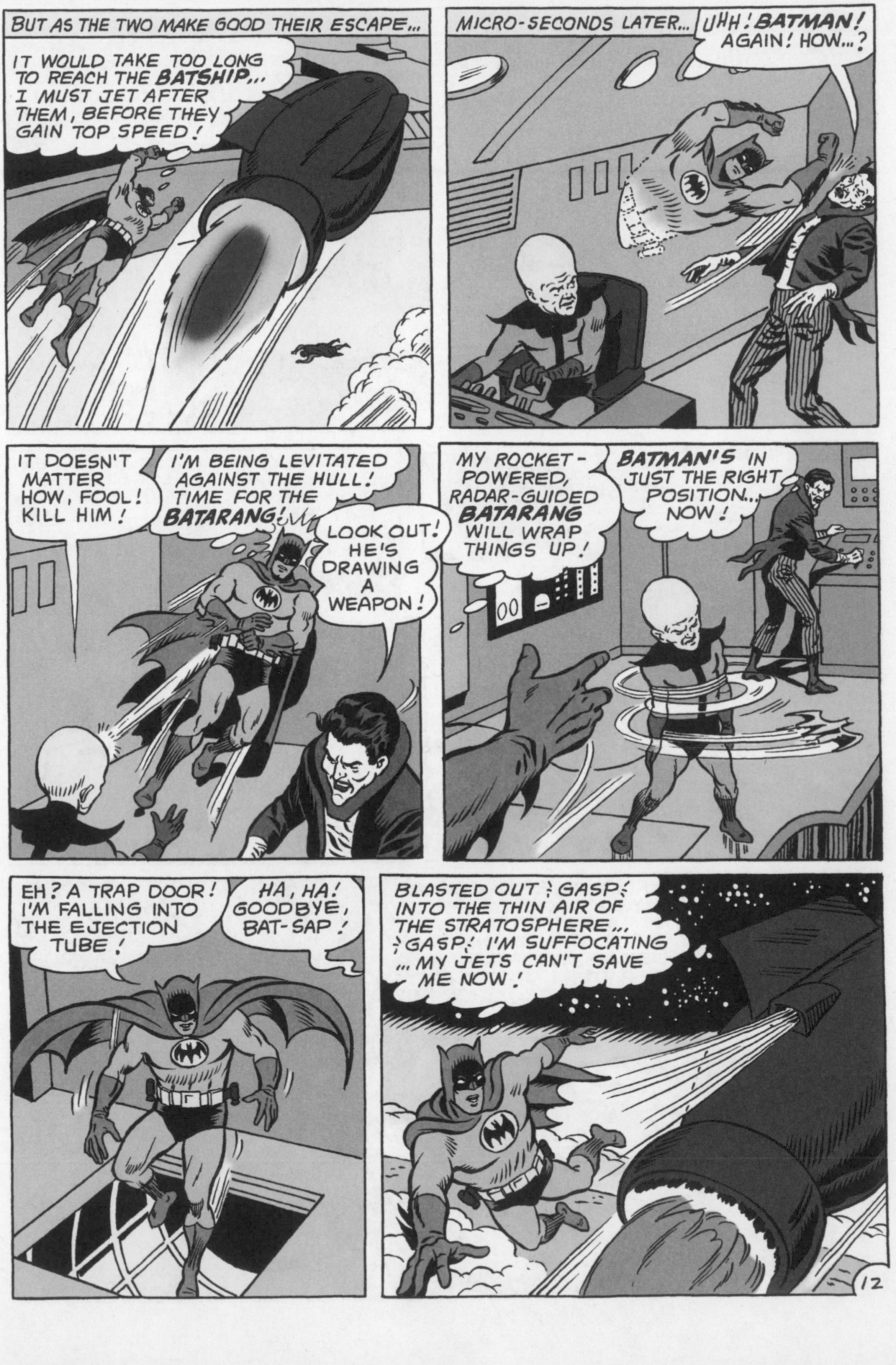
BUT AS THE TWO MAKE GOOD THEIR ESCAPE...
IT WOULD TAKE TOO LONG TO REACH THE BATSHIP... I MUST JET AFTER THEM, BEFORE THEY GAIN TOP SPEED!
MICRO-SECONDS LATER...
UHH! BATMAN! AGAIN! HOW...?
IT DOESN'T MATTER HOW, FOOL! KILL HIM!
I'M BEING LEVITATED AGAINST THE HULL! TIME FOR THE BATARANG!
LOOK OUT! HE'S DRAWING A WEAPON!
MY ROCKET-POWERED, RADAR-GUIDED BATARANG WILL WRAP THINGS UP!
BATMAN'S IN JUST THE RIGHT POSITION... NOW!
EH? A TRAP DOOR! I'M FALLING INTO THE EJECTION TUBE!
HA, HA! GOODBYE, BAT-SAP!
BLASTED OUT ;GASP; INTO THE THIN AIR OF THE STRATOSPHERE... ;GASP; I'M SUFFOCATING ...MY JETS CAN'T SAVE ME NOW!
12

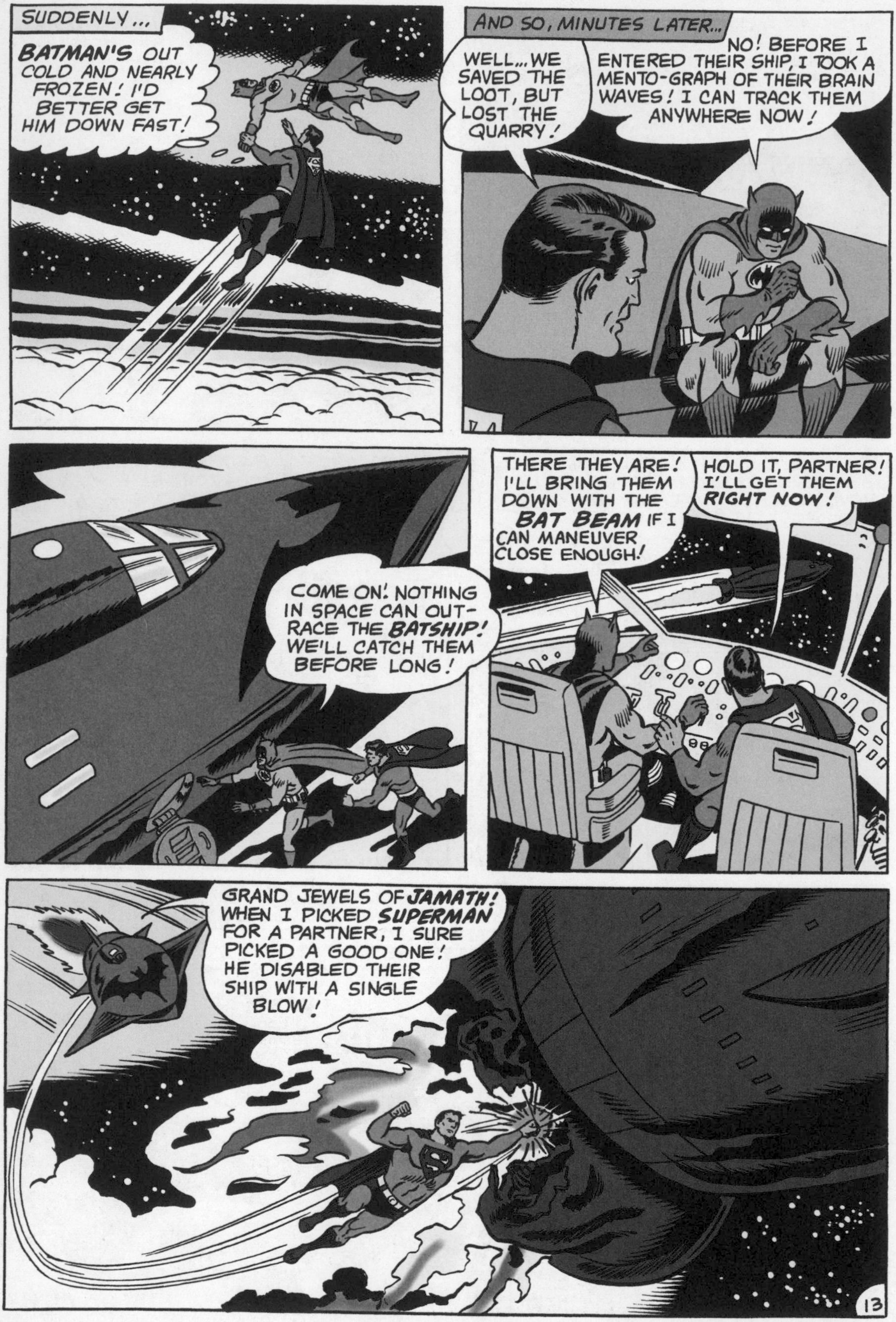
SUDDENLY...
BATMAN'S OUT COLD AND NEARLY FROZEN! I'D BETTER GET HIM DOWN FAST!
AND SO, MINUTES LATER...
WELL... WE SAVED THE LOOT, BUT LOST THE QUARRY!
NO! BEFORE I ENTERED THEIR SHIP, I TOOK A MENTO-GRAPH OF THEIR BRAIN WAVES! I CAN TRACK THEM ANYWHERE NOW!
COME ON! NOTHING IN SPACE CAN OUT-RACE THE BATSHIP! WE'LL CATCH THEM BEFORE LONG!
THERE THEY ARE! I'LL BRING THEM DOWN WITH THE BAT BEAM IF I CAN MANEUVER CLOSE ENOUGH!
HOLD IT, PARTNER! I'LL GET THEM RIGHT NOW!
GRAND JEWELS OF JAMATH! WHEN I PICKED SUPERMAN FOR A PARTNER, I SURE PICKED A GOOD ONE! HE DISABLED THEIR SHIP WITH A SINGLE BLOW!
13

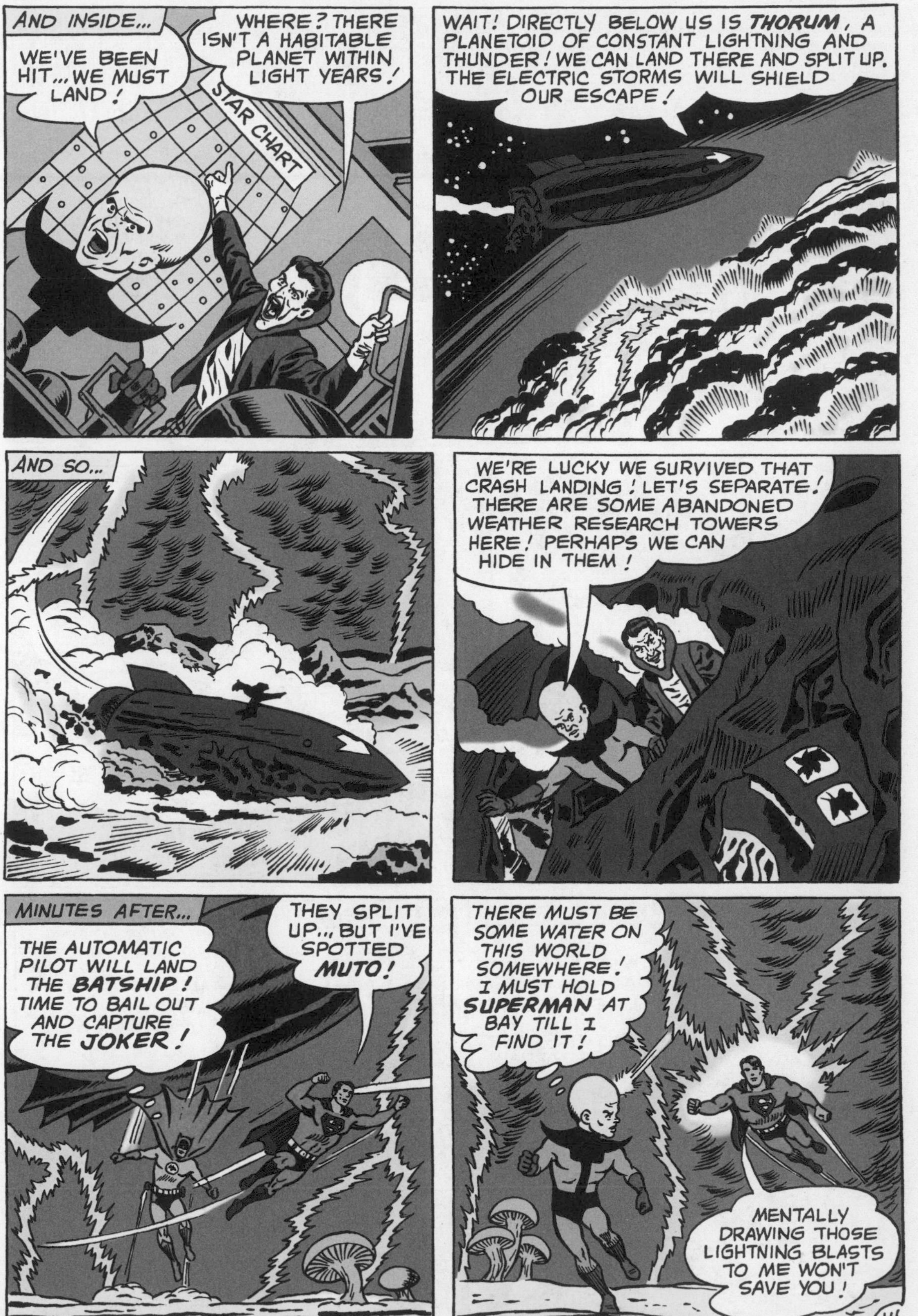
AND INSIDE...
WE'VE BEEN HIT... WE MUST LAND!
WHERE? THERE ISN'T A HABITABLE PLANET WITHIN LIGHT YEARS!
STAR CHART
WAIT! DIRECTLY BELOW US IS THORUM, A PLANETOID OF CONSTANT LIGHTNING AND THUNDER! WE CAN LAND THERE AND SPLIT UP. THE ELECTRIC STORMS WILL SHIELD OUR ESCAPE!
AND SO...
WE'RE LUCKY WE SURVIVED THAT CRASH LANDING! LET'S SEPARATE! THERE ARE SOME ABANDONED WEATHER RESEARCH TOWERS HERE! PERHAPS WE CAN HIDE IN THEM!
MINUTES AFTER...
THE AUTOMATIC PILOT WILL LAND THE BATSHIP! TIME TO BAIL OUT AND CAPTURE THE JOKER!
THEY SPLIT UP..., BUT I'VE SPOTTED MUTO!
THERE MUST BE SOME WATER ON THIS WORLD SOMEWHERE! I MUST HOLD SUPERMAN AT BAY TILL I FIND IT!
MENTALLY DRAWING THOSE LIGHTNING BLASTS TO ME WON'T SAVE YOU!
14

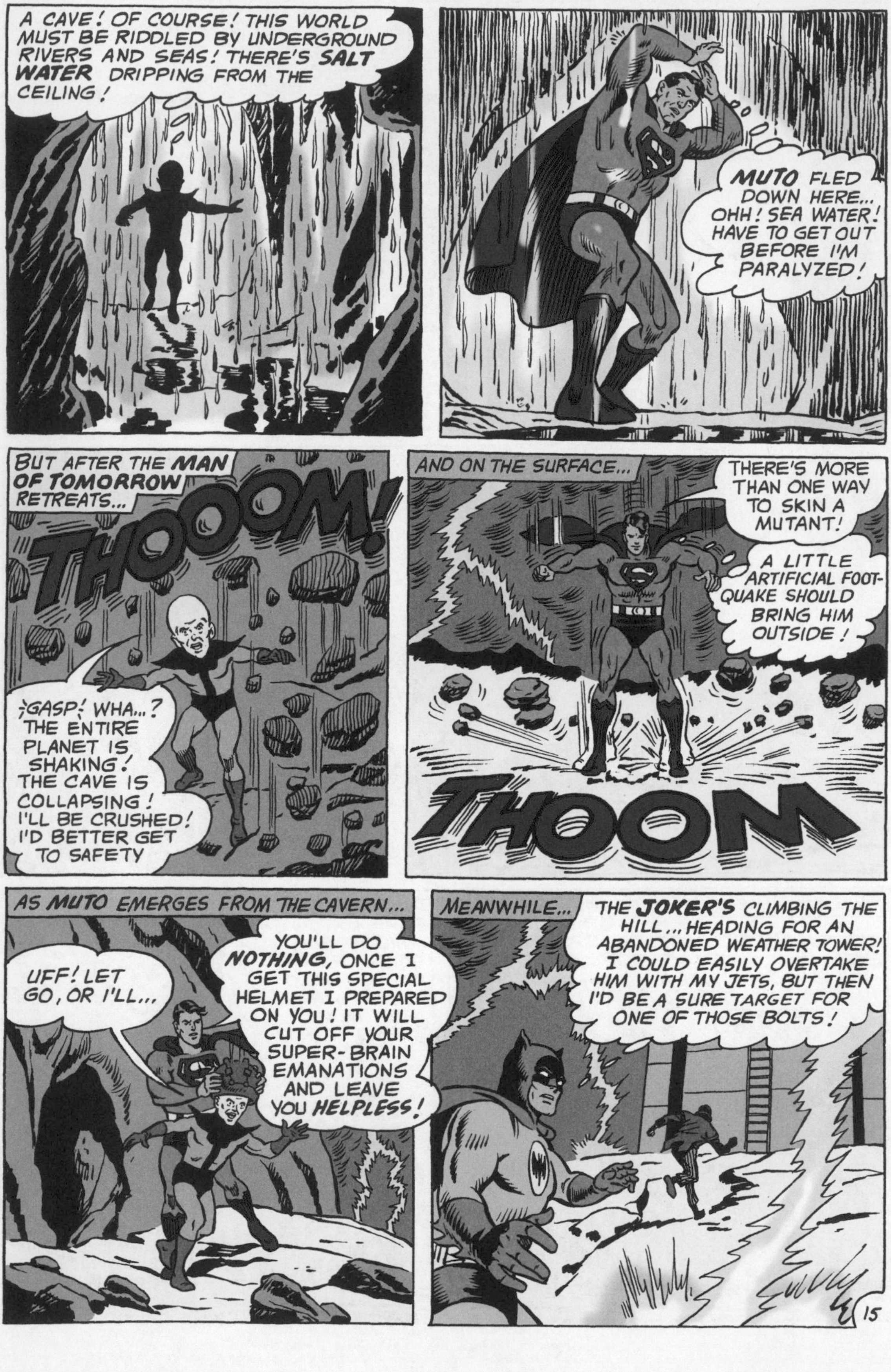
A CAVE! OF COURSE! THIS WORLD MUST BE RIDDLED BY UNDERGROUND RIVERS AND SEAS! THERE'S SALT WATER DRIPPING FROM THE CEILING!
MUTO FLED DOWN HERE... OHH! SEA WATER! HAVE TO GET OUT BEFORE I'M PARALYZED!
BUT AFTER THE MAN OF TOMORROW RETREATS...
THOOOM!
¡GASP! WHA...? THE ENTIRE PLANET IS SHAKING! THE CAVE IS COLLAPSING! I'LL BE CRUSHED! I'D BETTER GET TO SAFETY
AND ON THE SURFACE...
THERE'S MORE THAN ONE WAY TO SKIN A MUTANT!
A LITTLE ARTIFICIAL FOOT-QUAKE SHOULD BRING HIM OUTSIDE!
THOOM
AS MUTO EMERGES FROM THE CAVERN...
UFF! LET GO, OR I'LL...
YOU'LL DO NOTHING, ONCE I GET THIS SPECIAL HELMET I PREPARED ON YOU! IT WILL CUT OFF YOUR SUPER-BRAIN EMANATIONS AND LEAVE YOU HELPLESS!
MEANWHILE...
THE JOKER'S CLIMBING THE HILL... HEADING FOR AN ABANDONED WEATHER TOWER! I COULD EASILY OVERTAKE HIM WITH MY JETS, BUT THEN I'D BE A SURE TARGET FOR ONE OF THOSE BOLTS!
15

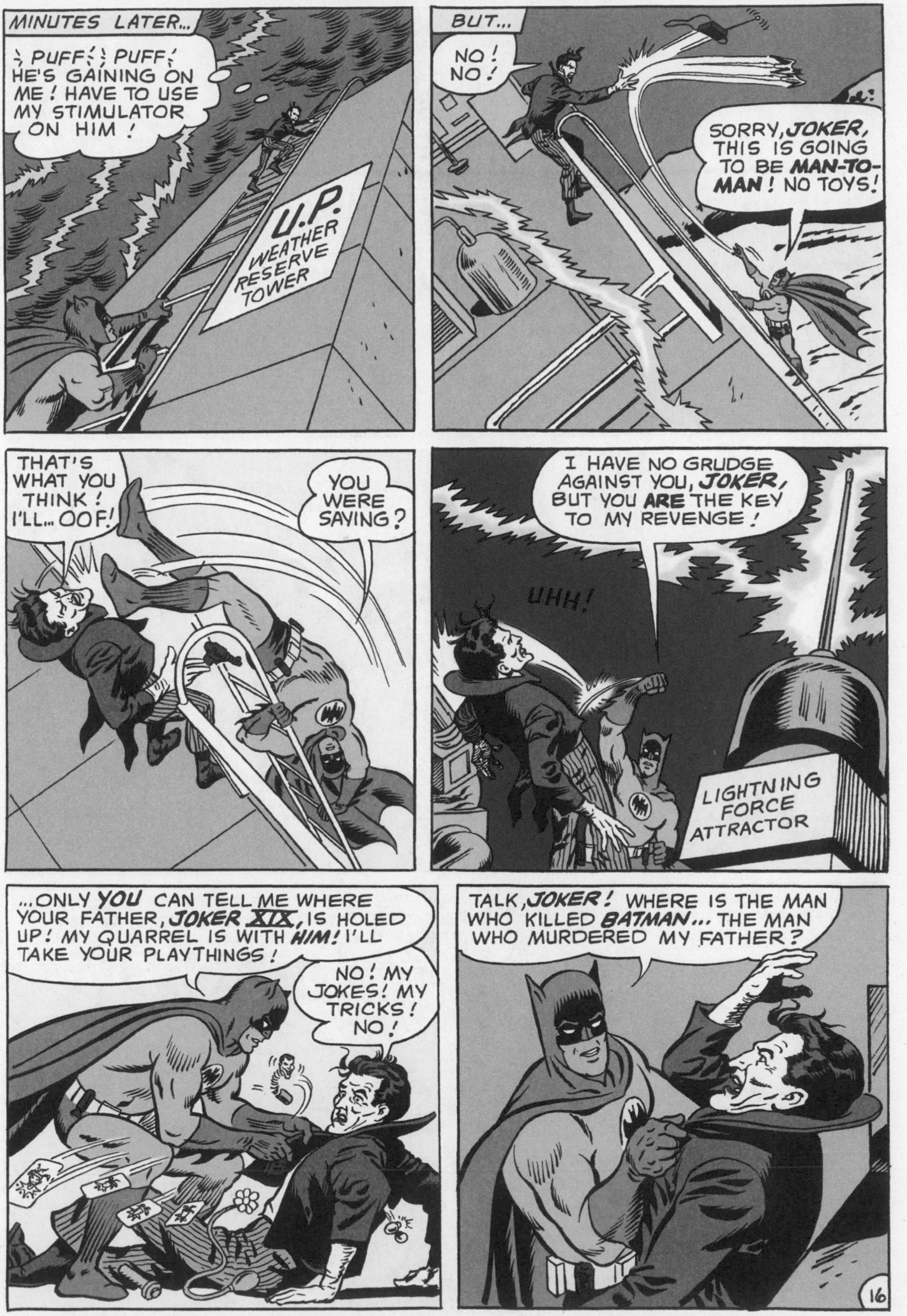
MINUTES LATER...
-PUFF!- -PUFF!- HE'S GAINING ON ME! HAVE TO USE MY STIMULATOR ON HIM!
U.P. WEATHER RESERVE TOWER
BUT...
NO! NO!
SORRY, JOKER, THIS IS GOING TO BE MAN-TO-MAN! NO TOYS!
THAT'S WHAT YOU THINK! I'LL... OOF!
YOU WERE SAYING?
I HAVE NO GRUDGE AGAINST YOU, JOKER, BUT YOU ARE THE KEY TO MY REVENGE!
UHH!
LIGHTNING FORCE ATTRACTOR
...ONLY YOU CAN TELL ME WHERE YOUR FATHER, JOKER XIX, IS HOLED UP! MY QUARREL IS WITH HIM! I'LL TAKE YOUR PLAYTHINGS!
NO! MY JOKES! MY TRICKS! NO!
TALK, JOKER! WHERE IS THE MAN WHO KILLED BATMAN... THE MAN WHO MURDERED MY FATHER?
16

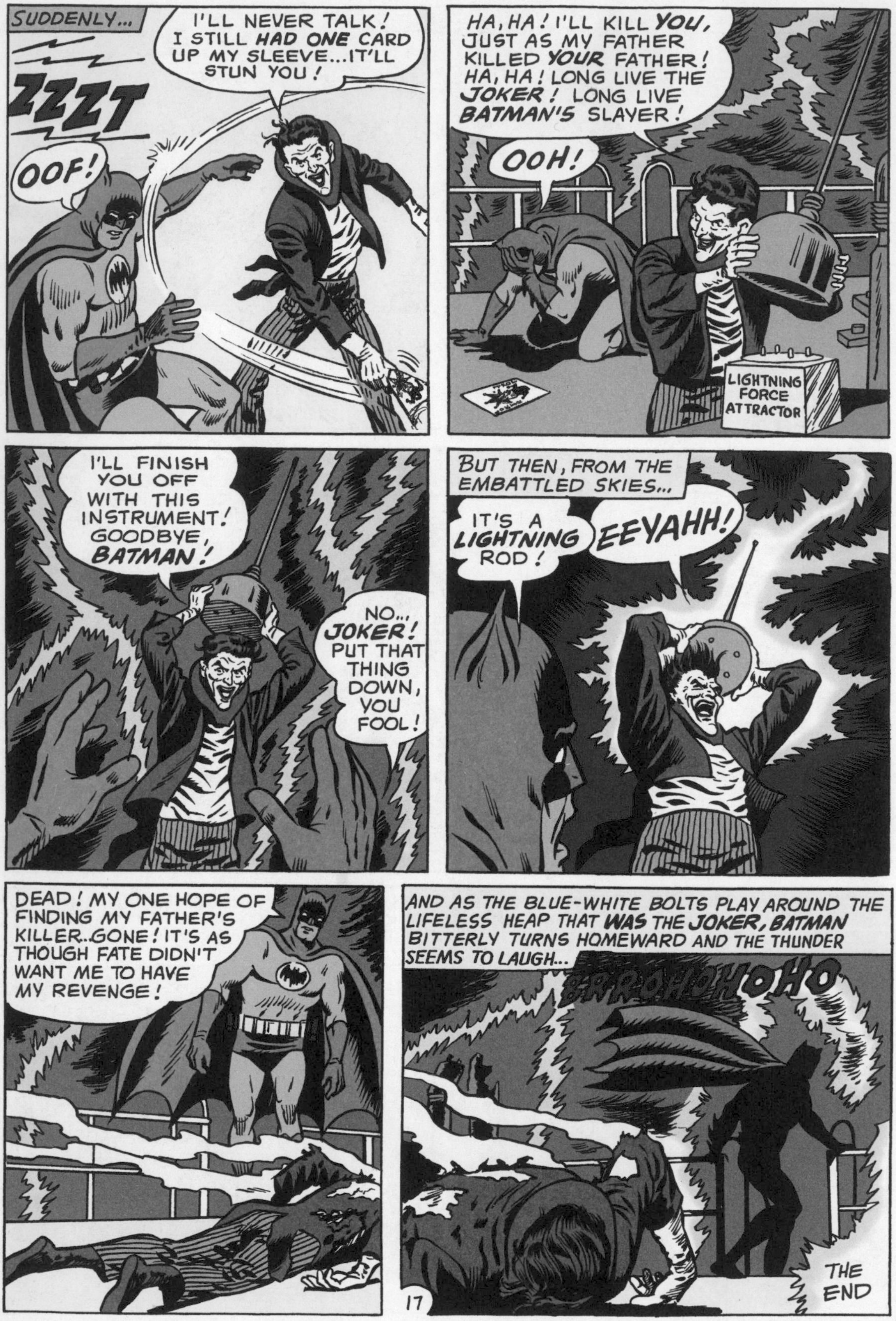
SUDDENLY...
I'LL NEVER TALK! I STILL HAD ONE CARD UP MY SLEEVE...IT'LL STUN YOU!
ZZZT
OOF!
HA, HA! I'LL KILL YOU, JUST AS MY FATHER KILLED YOUR FATHER! HA, HA! LONG LIVE THE JOKER! LONG LIVE BATMAN'S SLAYER!
OOH!
LIGHTNING FORCE ATTRACTOR
I'LL FINISH YOU OFF WITH THIS INSTRUMENT! GOODBYE, BATMAN!
NO... JOKER! PUT THAT THING DOWN, YOU FOOL!
BUT THEN, FROM THE EMBATTLED SKIES...
IT'S A LIGHTNING ROD!
EEYAHH!
DEAD! MY ONE HOPE OF FINDING MY FATHER'S KILLER..GONE! IT'S AS THOUGH FATE DIDN'T WANT ME TO HAVE MY REVENGE!
17
AND AS THE BLUE-WHITE BOLTS PLAY AROUND THE LIFELESS HEAP THAT WAS THE JOKER, BATMAN BITTERLY TURNS HOMEWARD AND THE THUNDER SEEMS TO LAUGH...
BRROHOHOHOHO
THE END

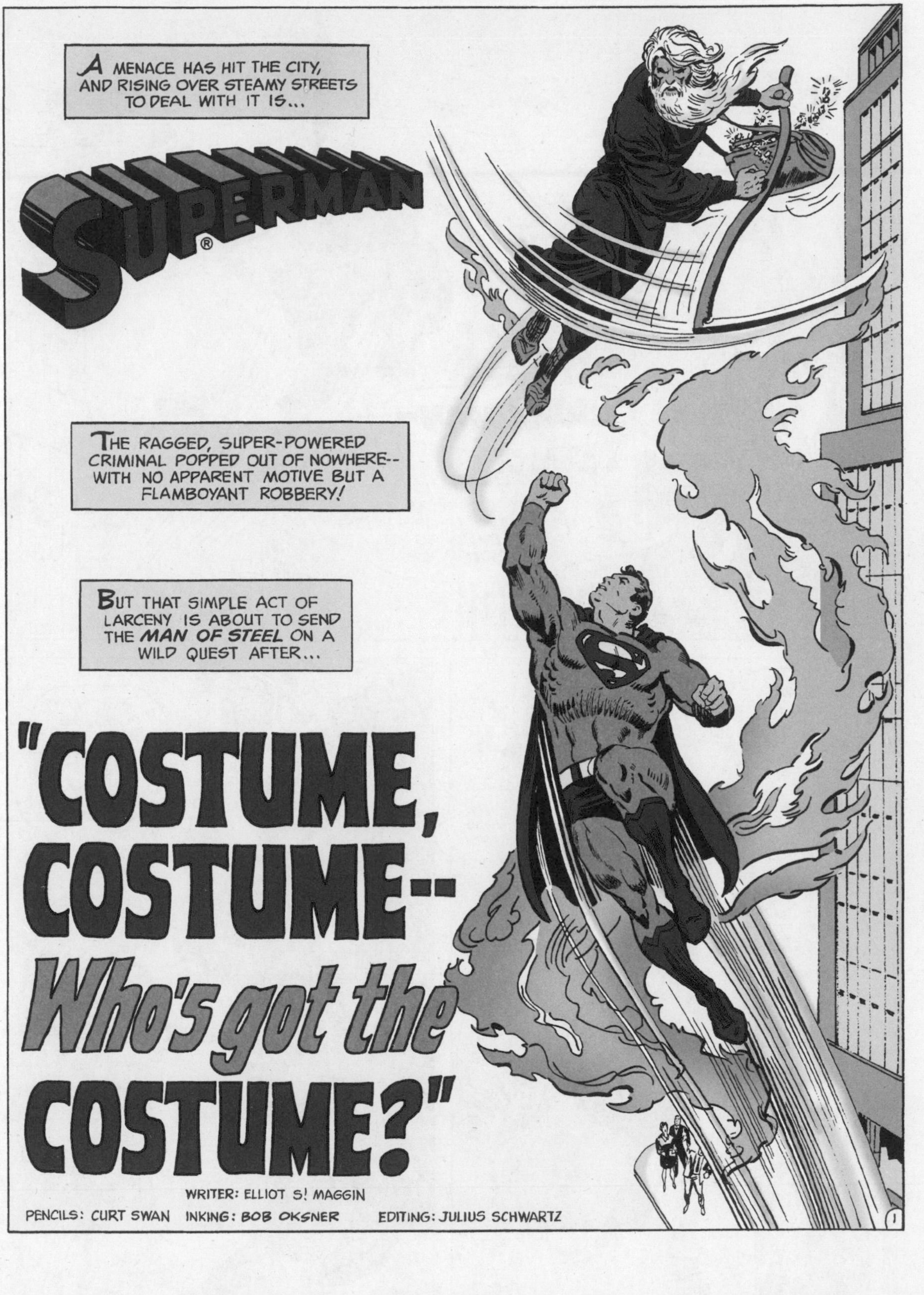
A MENACE HAS HIT THE CITY, AND RISING OVER STEAMY STREETS TO DEAL WITH IT IS...
SUPERMAN®
THE RAGGED, SUPER-POWERED CRIMINAL POPPED OUT OF NOWHERE-- WITH NO APPARENT MOTIVE BUT A FLAMBOYANT ROBBERY!
BUT THAT SIMPLE ACT OF LARCENY IS ABOUT TO SEND THE MAN OF STEEL ON A WILD QUEST AFTER...
"COSTUME, COSTUME-- Who's got the COSTUME?"
WRITER: ELLIOT S! MAGGIN
PENCILS: CURT SWAN INKING: BOB OKSNER EDITING: JULIUS SCHWARTZ
1

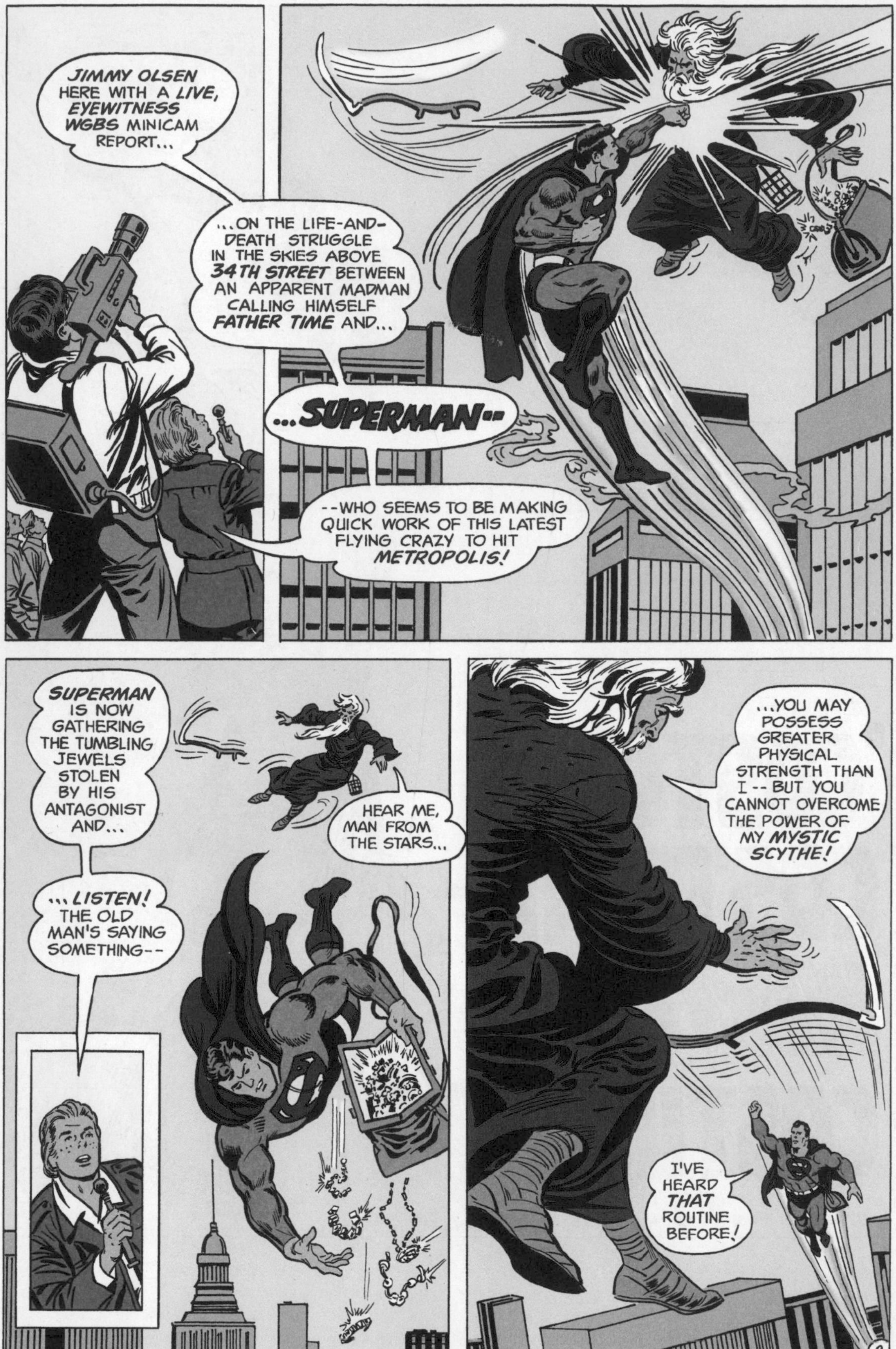
JIMMY OLSEN HERE WITH A LIVE, EYEWITNESS WGBS MINICAM REPORT...
...ON THE LIFE-AND-DEATH STRUGGLE IN THE SKIES ABOVE 34TH STREET BETWEEN AN APPARENT MADMAN CALLING HIMSELF FATHER TIME AND...
...SUPERMAN--
--WHO SEEMS TO BE MAKING QUICK WORK OF THIS LATEST FLYING CRAZY TO HIT METROPOLIS!
SUPERMAN IS NOW GATHERING THE TUMBLING JEWELS STOLEN BY HIS ANTAGONIST AND...
...LISTEN! THE OLD MAN'S SAYING SOMETHING--
HEAR ME, MAN FROM THE STARS...
...YOU MAY POSSESS GREATER PHYSICAL STRENGTH THAN I -- BUT YOU CANNOT OVERCOME THE POWER OF MY MYSTIC SCYTHE!
I'VE HEARD THAT ROUTINE BEFORE!
2

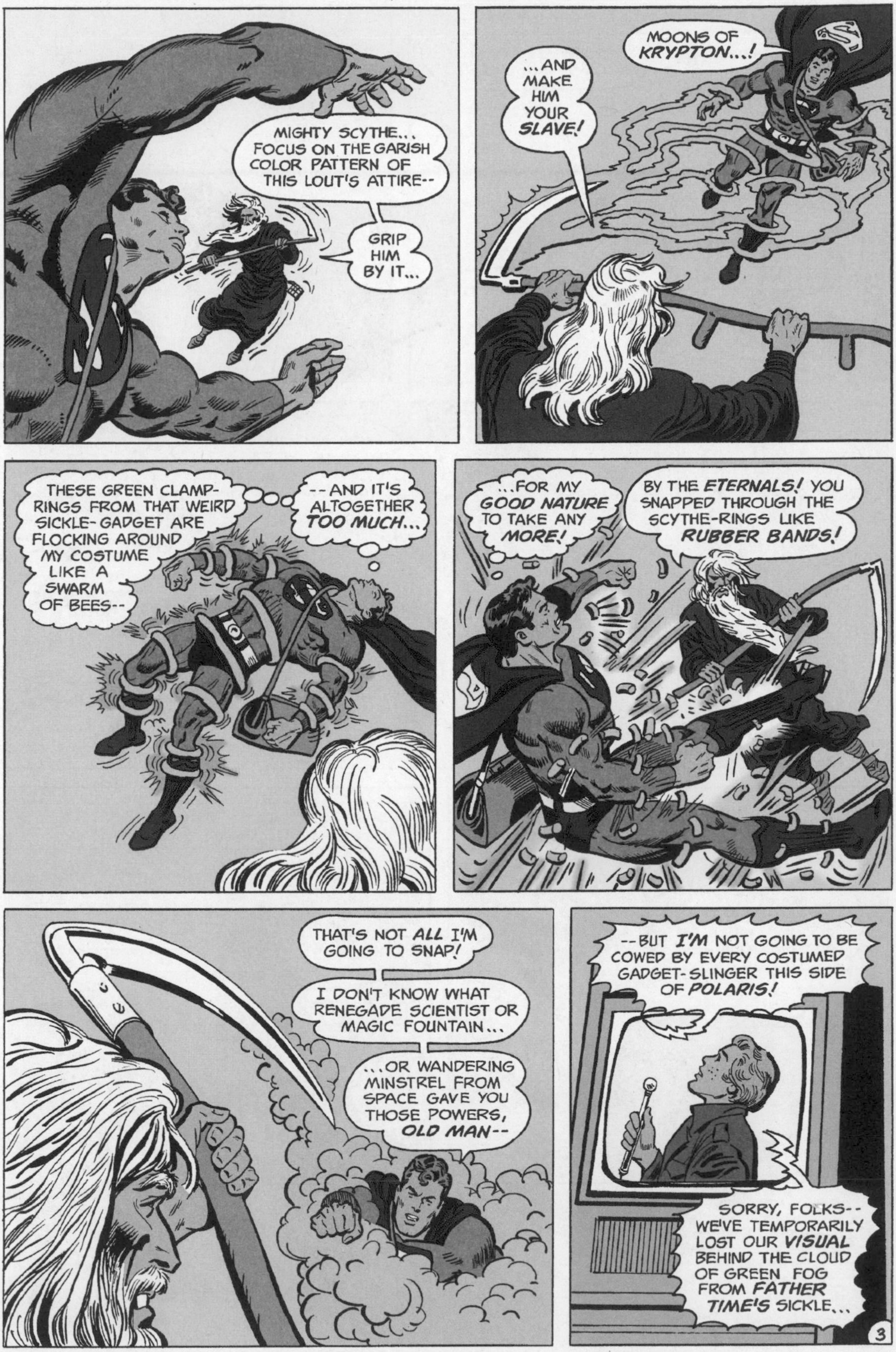
MIGHTY SCYTHE... FOCUS ON THE GARISH COLOR PATTERN OF THIS LOUT'S ATTIRE--
GRIP HIM BY IT...
...AND MAKE HIM YOUR SLAVE!
MOONS OF KRYPTON...!
THESE GREEN CLAMP-RINGS FROM THAT WEIRD SICKLE-GADGET ARE FLOCKING AROUND MY COSTUME LIKE A SWARM OF BEES--
--AND IT'S ALTOGETHER TOO MUCH...
...FOR MY GOOD NATURE TO TAKE ANY MORE!
BY THE ETERNALS! YOU SNAPPED THROUGH THE SCYTHE-RINGS LIKE RUBBER BANDS!
THAT'S NOT ALL I'M GOING TO SNAP!
I DON'T KNOW WHAT RENEGADE SCIENTIST OR MAGIC FOUNTAIN...
...OR WANDERING MINSTREL FROM SPACE GAVE YOU THOSE POWERS, OLD MAN--
--BUT I'M NOT GOING TO BE COWED BY EVERY COSTUMED GADGET-SLINGER THIS SIDE OF POLARIS!
SORRY, FOLKS-- WE'VE TEMPORARILY LOST OUR VISUAL BEHIND THE CLOUD OF GREEN FOG FROM FATHER TIME'S SICKLE...
3

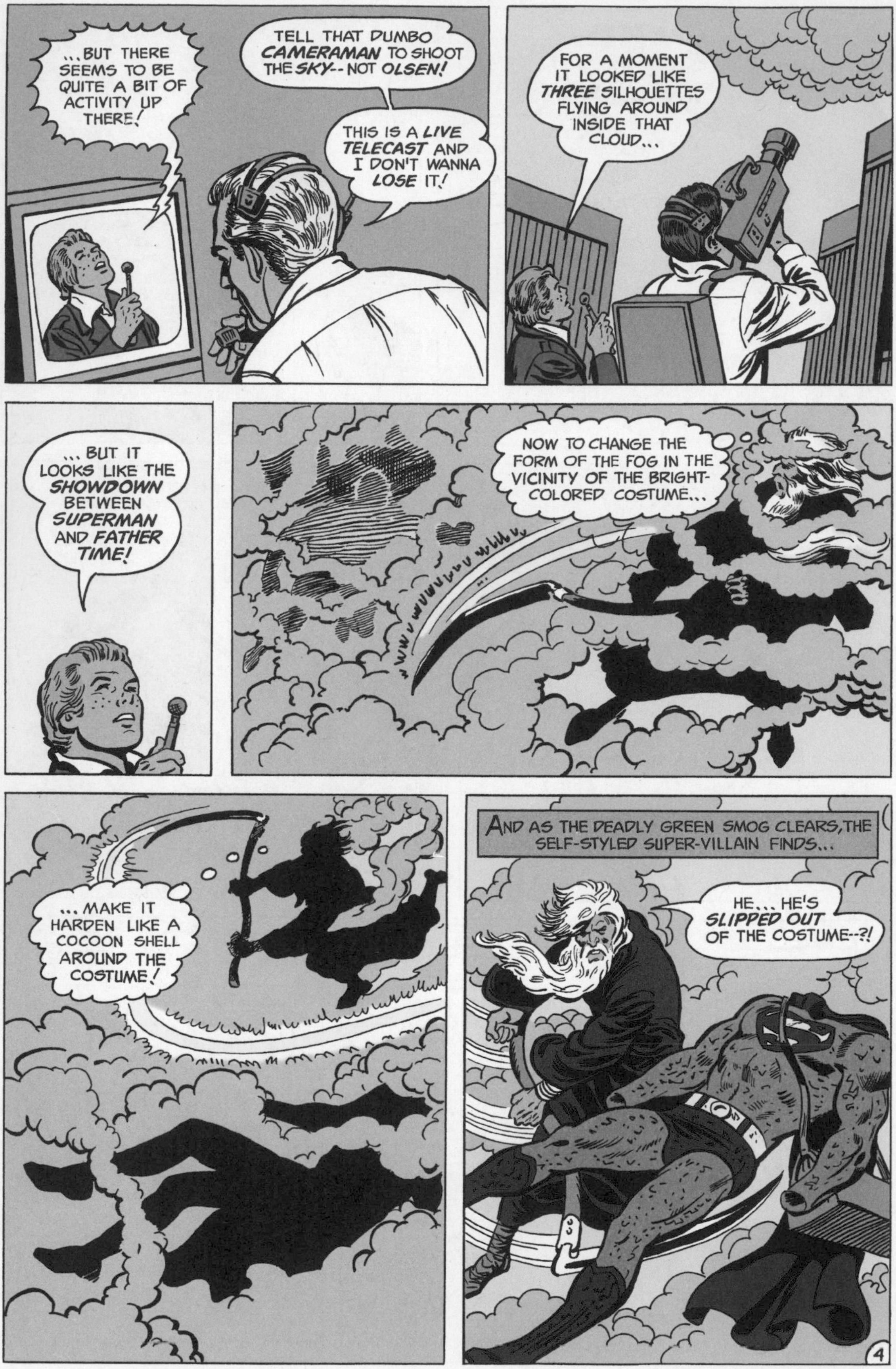
...BUT THERE SEEMS TO BE QUITE A BIT OF ACTIVITY UP THERE!
TELL THAT DUMBO CAMERAMAN TO SHOOT THE SKY-- NOT OLSEN!
THIS IS A LIVE TELECAST AND I DON'T WANNA LOSE IT!
FOR A MOMENT IT LOOKED LIKE THREE SILHOUETTES FLYING AROUND INSIDE THAT CLOUD...
...BUT IT LOOKS LIKE THE SHOWDOWN BETWEEN SUPERMAN AND FATHER TIME!
NOW TO CHANGE THE FORM OF THE FOG IN THE VICINITY OF THE BRIGHT-COLORED COSTUME...
...MAKE IT HARDEN LIKE A COCOON SHELL AROUND THE COSTUME!
AND AS THE DEADLY GREEN SMOG CLEARS, THE SELF-STYLED SUPER-VILLAIN FINDS...
HE... HE'S SLIPPED OUT OF THE COSTUME--?!
4

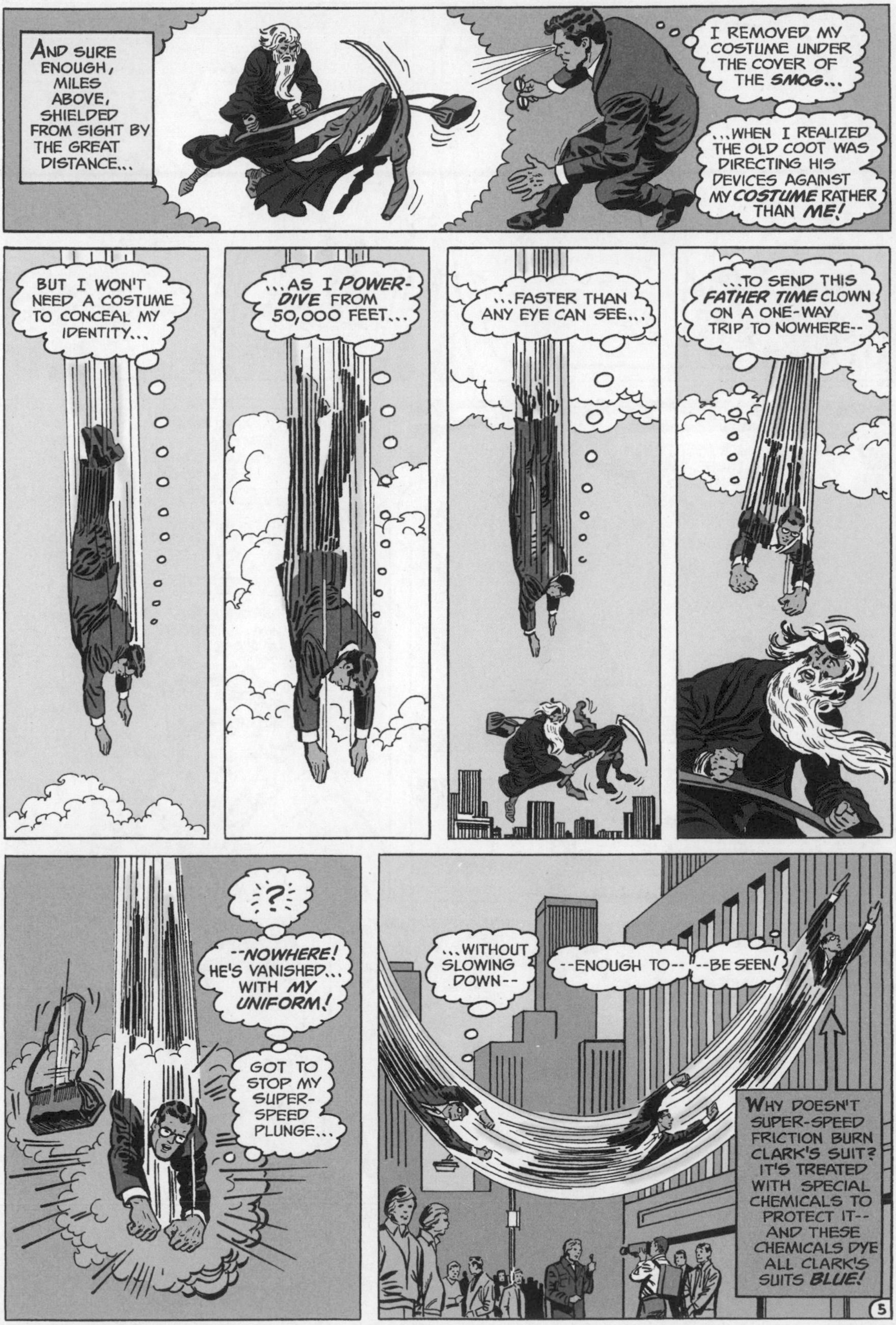
AND SURE ENOUGH, MILES ABOVE, SHIELDED FROM SIGHT BY THE GREAT DISTANCE...
I REMOVED MY COSTUME UNDER THE COVER OF THE SMOG...
...WHEN I REALIZED THE OLD COOT WAS DIRECTING HIS DEVICES AGAINST MY COSTUME RATHER THAN ME!
BUT I WON'T NEED A COSTUME TO CONCEAL MY IDENTITY...
...AS I POWER-DIVE FROM 50,000 FEET...
...FASTER THAN ANY EYE CAN SEE...
...TO SEND THIS FATHER TIME CLOWN ON A ONE-WAY TRIP TO NOWHERE--
?
--NOWHERE! HE'S VANISHED... WITH MY UNIFORM!
GOT TO STOP MY SUPER-SPEED PLUNGE...
...WITHOUT SLOWING DOWN--
--ENOUGH TO--
--BE SEEN!
WHY DOESN'T SUPER-SPEED FRICTION BURN CLARK'S SUIT? IT'S TREATED WITH SPECIAL CHEMICALS TO PROTECT IT-- AND THESE CHEMICALS DYE ALL CLARK'S SUITS BLUE!
5

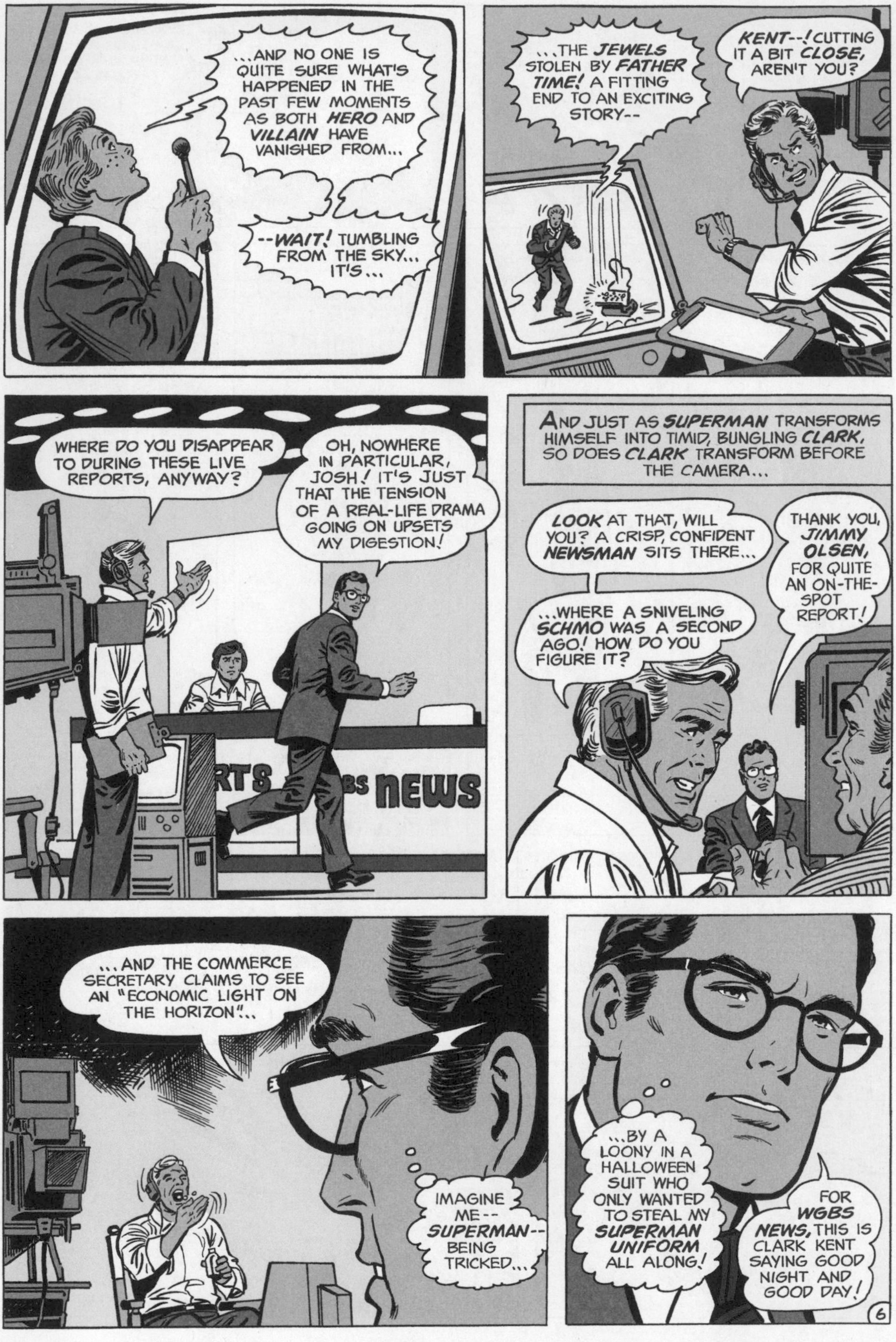
...AND NO ONE IS QUITE SURE WHAT'S HAPPENED IN THE PAST FEW MOMENTS AS BOTH HERO AND VILLAIN HAVE VANISHED FROM...
--WAIT! TUMBLING FROM THE SKY... IT'S...
...THE JEWELS STOLEN BY FATHER TIME! A FITTING END TO AN EXCITING STORY--
KENT--! CUTTING IT A BIT CLOSE, AREN'T YOU?
WHERE DO YOU DISAPPEAR TO DURING THESE LIVE REPORTS, ANYWAY?
OH, NOWHERE IN PARTICULAR, JOSH! IT'S JUST THAT THE TENSION OF A REAL-LIFE DRAMA GOING ON UPSETS MY DIGESTION!
RTS
BS NEWS
AND JUST AS SUPERMAN TRANSFORMS HIMSELF INTO TIMID, BUNGLING CLARK, SO DOES CLARK TRANSFORM BEFORE THE CAMERA...
LOOK AT THAT, WILL YOU? A CRISP, CONFIDENT NEWSMAN SITS THERE...
...WHERE A SNIVELING SCHMO WAS A SECOND AGO! HOW DO YOU FIGURE IT?
THANK YOU, JIMMY OLSEN, FOR QUITE AN ON-THE-SPOT REPORT!
...AND THE COMMERCE SECRETARY CLAIMS TO SEE AN "ECONOMIC LIGHT ON THE HORIZON"...
IMAGINE ME--SUPERMAN--BEING TRICKED...
...BY A LOONY IN A HALLOWEEN SUIT WHO ONLY WANTED TO STEAL MY SUPERMAN UNIFORM ALL ALONG!
FOR WGBS NEWS, THIS IS CLARK KENT SAYING GOOD NIGHT AND GOOD DAY!
6

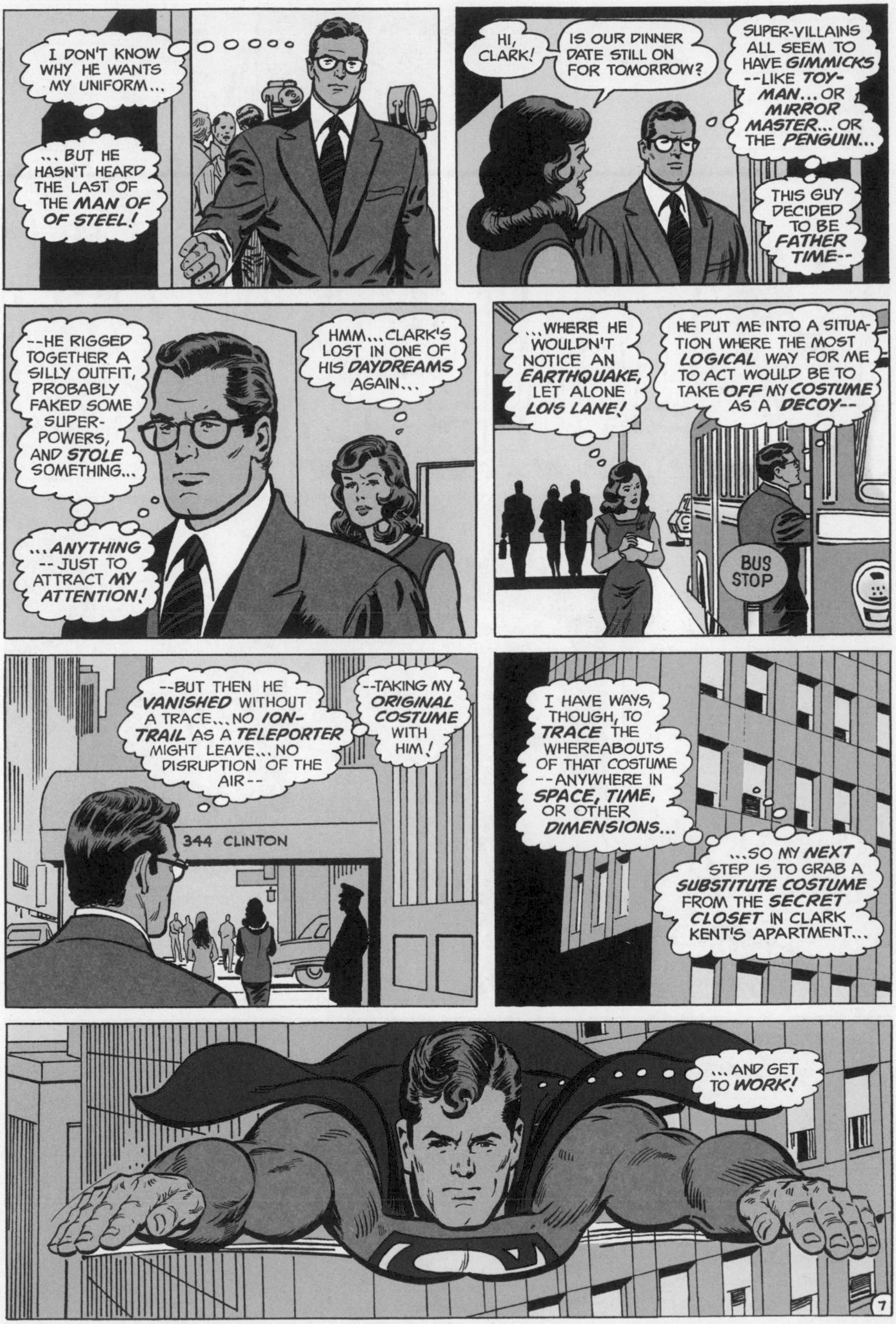

I DON'T KNOW WHY HE WANTS MY UNIFORM...
... BUT HE HASN'T HEARD THE LAST OF THE MAN OF OF STEEL!
HI, CLARK!
IS OUR DINNER DATE STILL ON FOR TOMORROW?
SUPER-VILLAINS ALL SEEM TO HAVE GIMMICKS --LIKE TOY-MAN... OR MIRROR MASTER... OR THE PENGUIN...
THIS GUY DECIDED TO BE FATHER TIME--
--HE RIGGED TOGETHER A SILLY OUTFIT, PROBABLY FAKED SOME SUPER-POWERS, AND STOLE SOMETHING...
...ANYTHING --JUST TO ATTRACT MY ATTENTION!
HMM... CLARK'S LOST IN ONE OF HIS DAYDREAMS AGAIN...
...WHERE HE WOULDN'T NOTICE AN EARTHQUAKE, LET ALONE LOIS LANE!
HE PUT ME INTO A SITUATION WHERE THE MOST LOGICAL WAY FOR ME TO ACT WOULD BE TO TAKE OFF MY COSTUME AS A DECOY--
BUS STOP
--BUT THEN HE VANISHED WITHOUT A TRACE... NO ION-TRAIL AS A TELEPORTER MIGHT LEAVE... NO DISRUPTION OF THE AIR--
--TAKING MY ORIGINAL COSTUME WITH HIM!
344 CLINTON
I HAVE WAYS, THOUGH, TO TRACE THE WHEREABOUTS OF THAT COSTUME --ANYWHERE IN SPACE, TIME, OR OTHER DIMENSIONS...
...SO MY NEXT STEP IS TO GRAB A SUBSTITUTE COSTUME FROM THE SECRET CLOSET IN CLARK KENT'S APARTMENT...
...AND GET TO WORK!
7

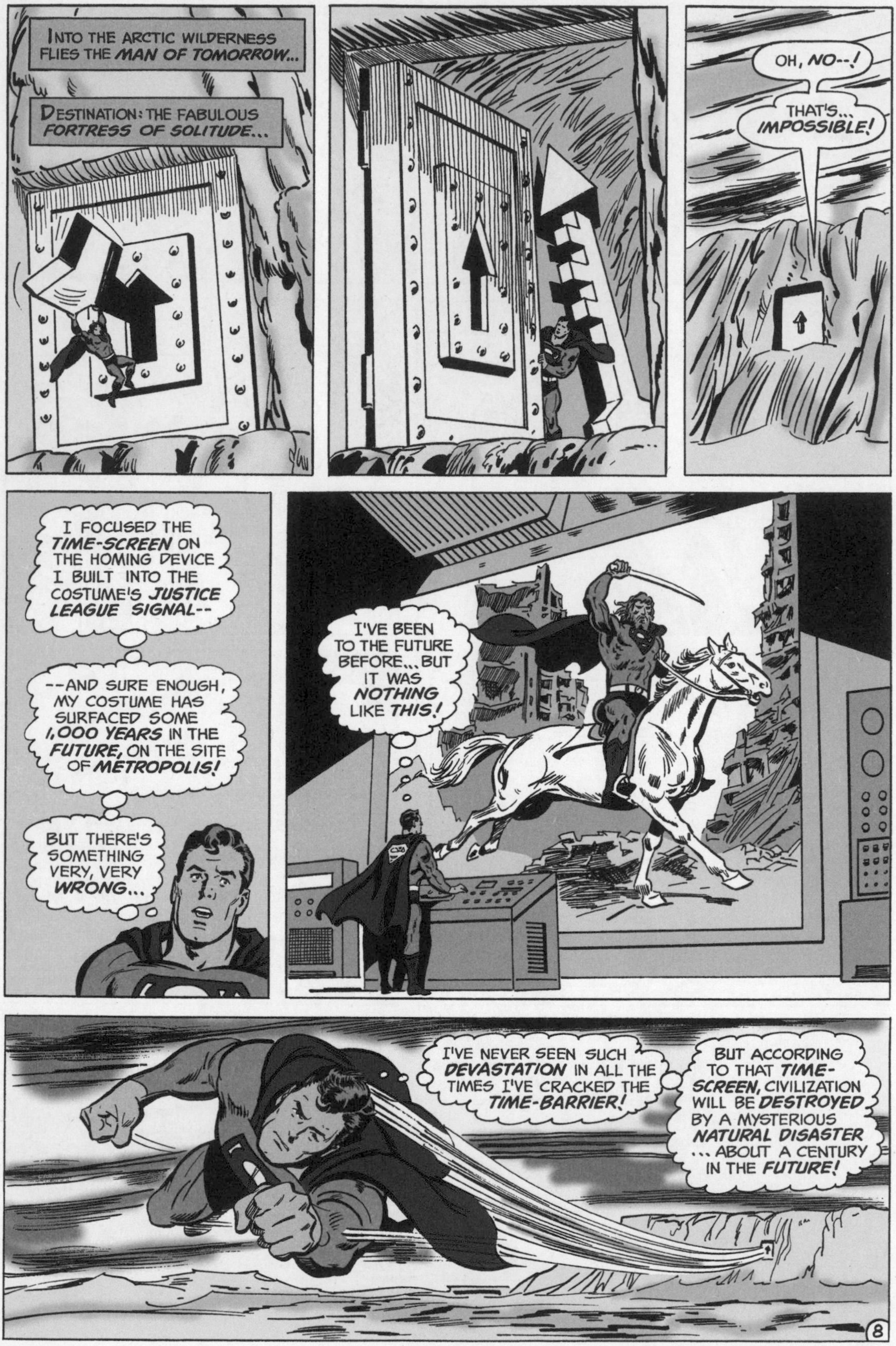
INTO THE ARCTIC WILDERNESS FLIES THE MAN OF TOMORROW...
DESTINATION: THE FABULOUS FORTRESS OF SOLITUDE...
OH, NO--!
THAT'S... IMPOSSIBLE!
I FOCUSED THE TIME-SCREEN ON THE HOMING DEVICE I BUILT INTO THE COSTUME'S JUSTICE LEAGUE SIGNAL--
--AND SURE ENOUGH, MY COSTUME HAS SURFACED SOME 1,000 YEARS IN THE FUTURE, ON THE SITE OF METROPOLIS!
BUT THERE'S SOMETHING VERY, VERY WRONG...
I'VE BEEN TO THE FUTURE BEFORE... BUT IT WAS NOTHING LIKE THIS!
I'VE NEVER SEEN SUCH DEVASTATION IN ALL THE TIMES I'VE CRACKED THE TIME-BARRIER!
BUT ACCORDING TO THAT TIME-SCREEN, CIVILIZATION WILL BE DESTROYED BY A MYSTERIOUS NATURAL DISASTER ... ABOUT A CENTURY IN THE FUTURE!
8

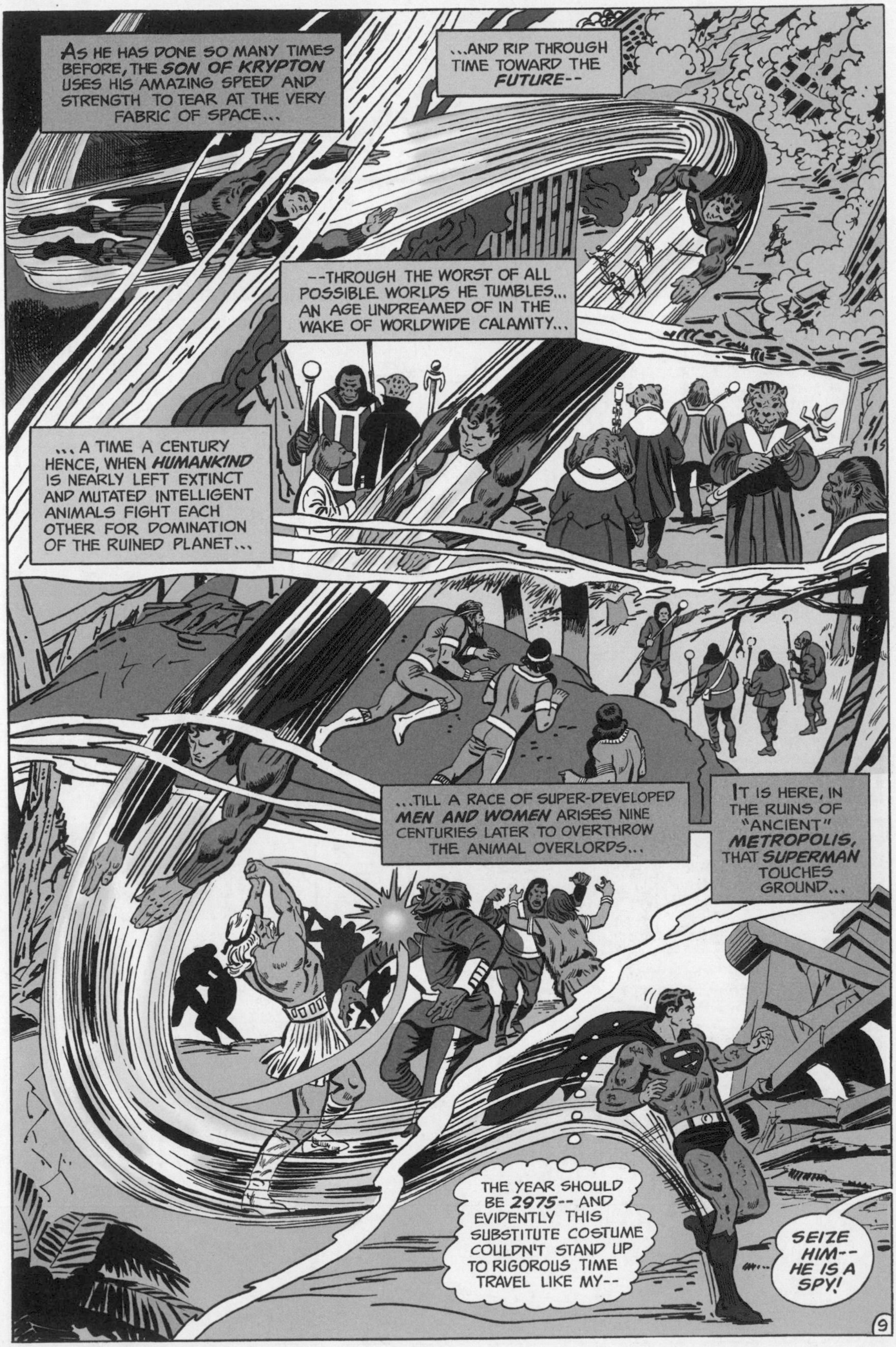
AS HE HAS DONE SO MANY TIMES BEFORE, THE SON OF KRYPTON USES HIS AMAZING SPEED AND STRENGTH TO TEAR AT THE VERY FABRIC OF SPACE...
...AND RIP THROUGH TIME TOWARD THE FUTURE--
--THROUGH THE WORST OF ALL POSSIBLE WORLDS HE TUMBLES... AN AGE UNDREAMED OF IN THE WAKE OF WORLDWIDE CALAMITY...
...A TIME A CENTURY HENCE, WHEN HUMANKIND IS NEARLY LEFT EXTINCT AND MUTATED INTELLIGENT ANIMALS FIGHT EACH OTHER FOR DOMINATION OF THE RUINED PLANET...
...TILL A RACE OF SUPER-DEVELOPED MEN AND WOMEN ARISES NINE CENTURIES LATER TO OVERTHROW THE ANIMAL OVERLORDS...
IT IS HERE, IN THE RUINS OF "ANCIENT" METROPOLIS, THAT SUPERMAN TOUCHES GROUND...
THE YEAR SHOULD BE 2975-- AND EVIDENTLY THIS SUBSTITUTE COSTUME COULDN'T STAND UP TO RIGOROUS TIME TRAVEL LIKE MY--
SEIZE HIM-- HE IS A SPY!
9

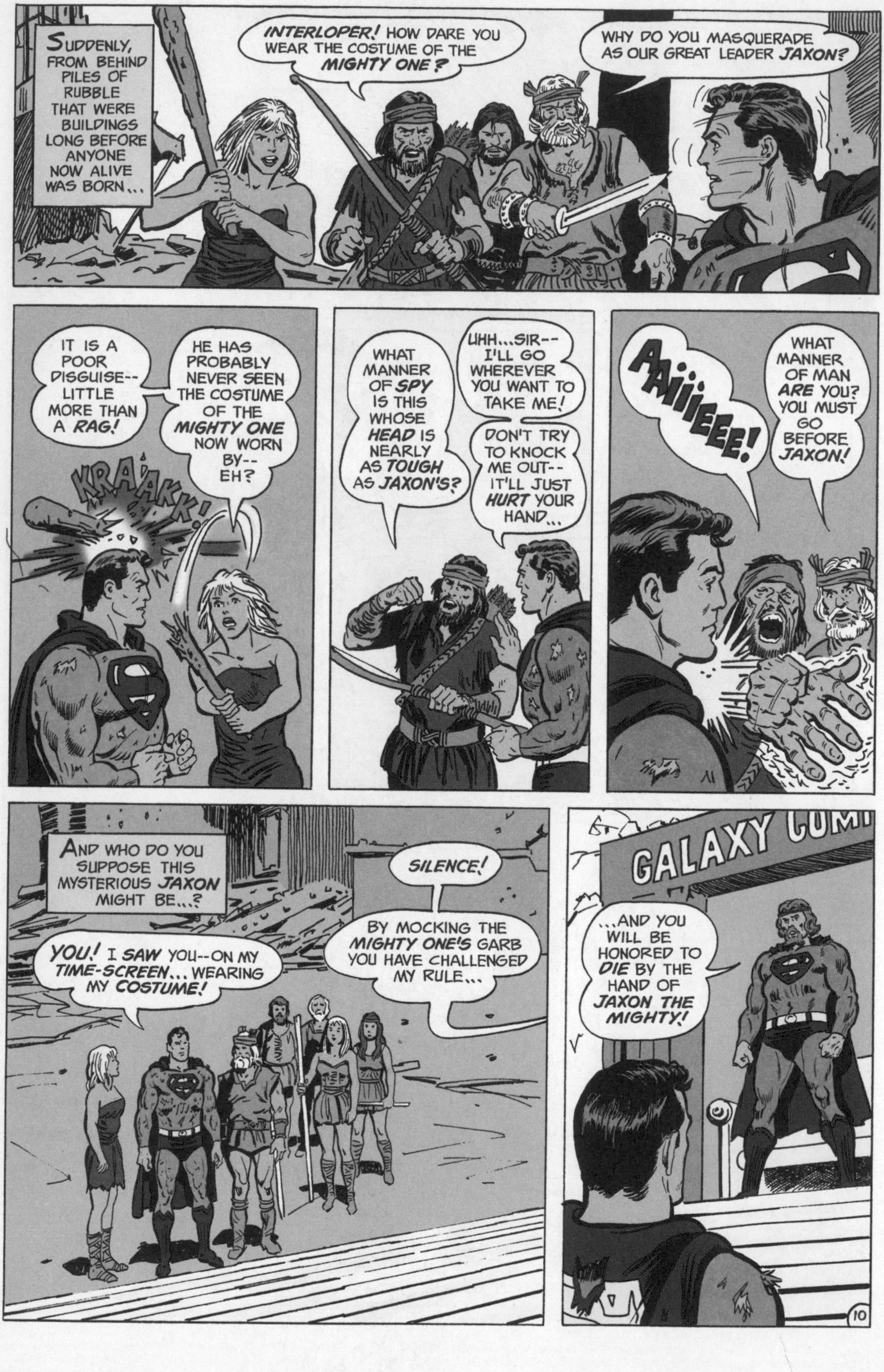

SUDDENLY, FROM BEHIND PILES OF RUBBLE THAT WERE BUILDINGS LONG BEFORE ANYONE NOW ALIVE WAS BORN...
INTERLOPER! HOW DARE YOU WEAR THE COSTUME OF THE MIGHTY ONE?
WHY DO YOU MASQUERADE AS OUR GREAT LEADER JAXON?
IT IS A POOR DISGUISE-- LITTLE MORE THAN A RAG!
HE HAS PROBABLY NEVER SEEN THE COSTUME OF THE MIGHTY ONE NOW WORN BY-- EH?
KRAAKK!
WHAT MANNER OF SPY IS THIS WHOSE HEAD IS NEARLY AS TOUGH AS JAXON'S?
UHH...SIR-- I'LL GO WHEREVER YOU WANT TO TAKE ME!
DON'T TRY TO KNOCK ME OUT-- IT'LL JUST HURT YOUR HAND...
AAIIIEEEE!
WHAT MANNER OF MAN ARE YOU? YOU MUST GO BEFORE JAXON!
AND WHO DO YOU SUPPOSE THIS MYSTERIOUS JAXON MIGHT BE...?
SILENCE!
BY MOCKING THE MIGHTY ONE'S GARB YOU HAVE CHALLENGED MY RULE...
YOU! I SAW YOU--ON MY TIME-SCREEN... WEARING MY COSTUME!
GALAXY COM
...AND YOU WILL BE HONORED TO DIE BY THE HAND OF JAXON THE MIGHTY!
10

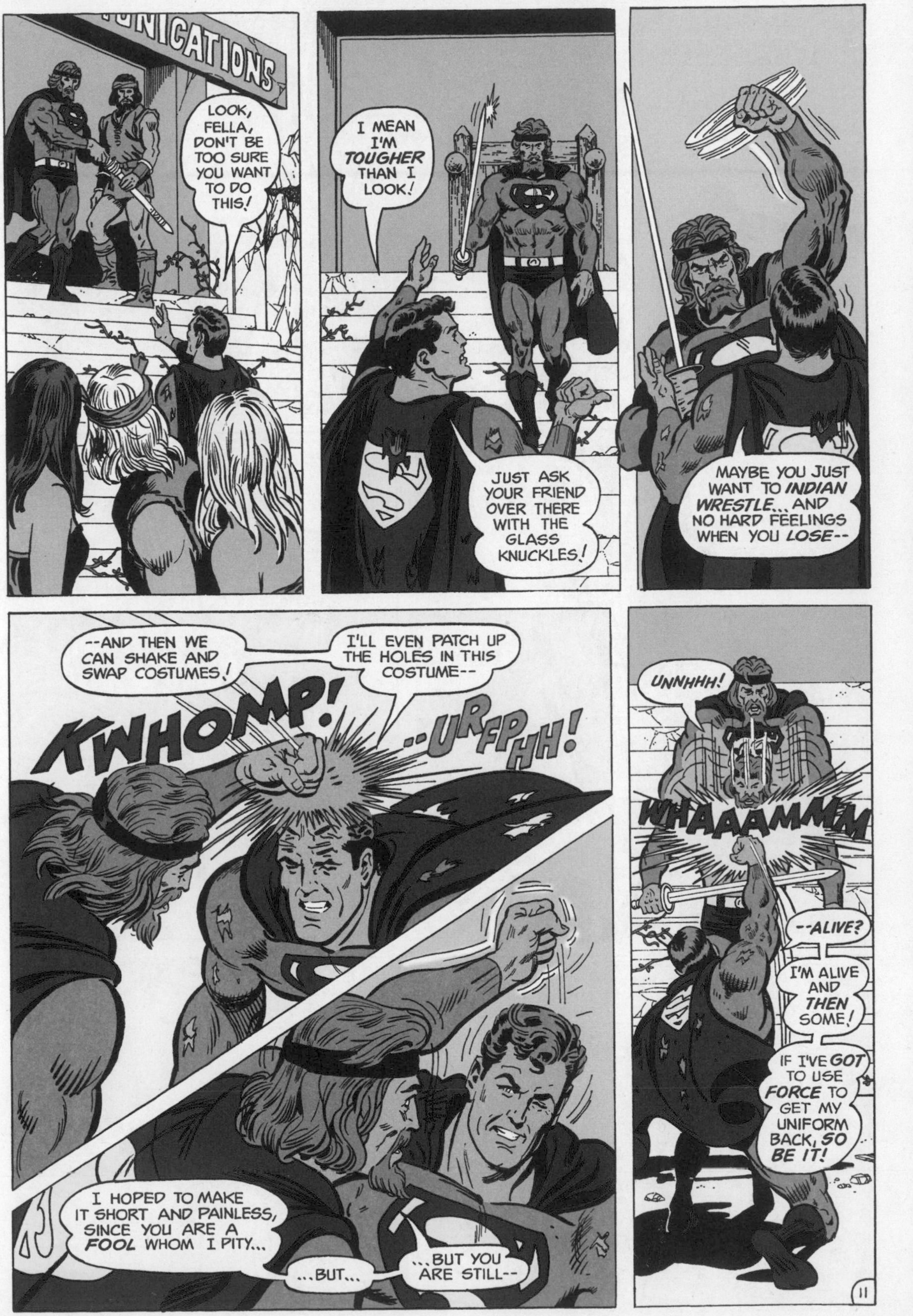

...UNICATIONS
LOOK, FELLA, DON'T BE TOO SURE YOU WANT TO DO THIS!
I MEAN I'M *TOUGHER* THAN I LOOK!
JUST ASK YOUR FRIEND OVER THERE WITH THE GLASS KNUCKLES!
MAYBE YOU JUST WANT TO *INDIAN WRESTLE*... AND NO HARD FEELINGS WHEN YOU *LOSE*--
--AND THEN WE CAN SHAKE AND SWAP COSTUMES!
I'LL EVEN PATCH UP THE HOLES IN THIS COSTUME--
KWHOMP!
..URFPHH!
I HOPED TO MAKE IT SHORT AND PAINLESS, SINCE YOU ARE A *FOOL* WHOM I PITY...
...BUT...
...BUT YOU ARE STILL--
UNNHHH!
WHAAAMMM
--*ALIVE?*
I'M ALIVE AND *THEN* SOME!
IF I'VE *GOT* TO USE *FORCE* TO GET MY UNIFORM BACK, *SO BE IT!*
11

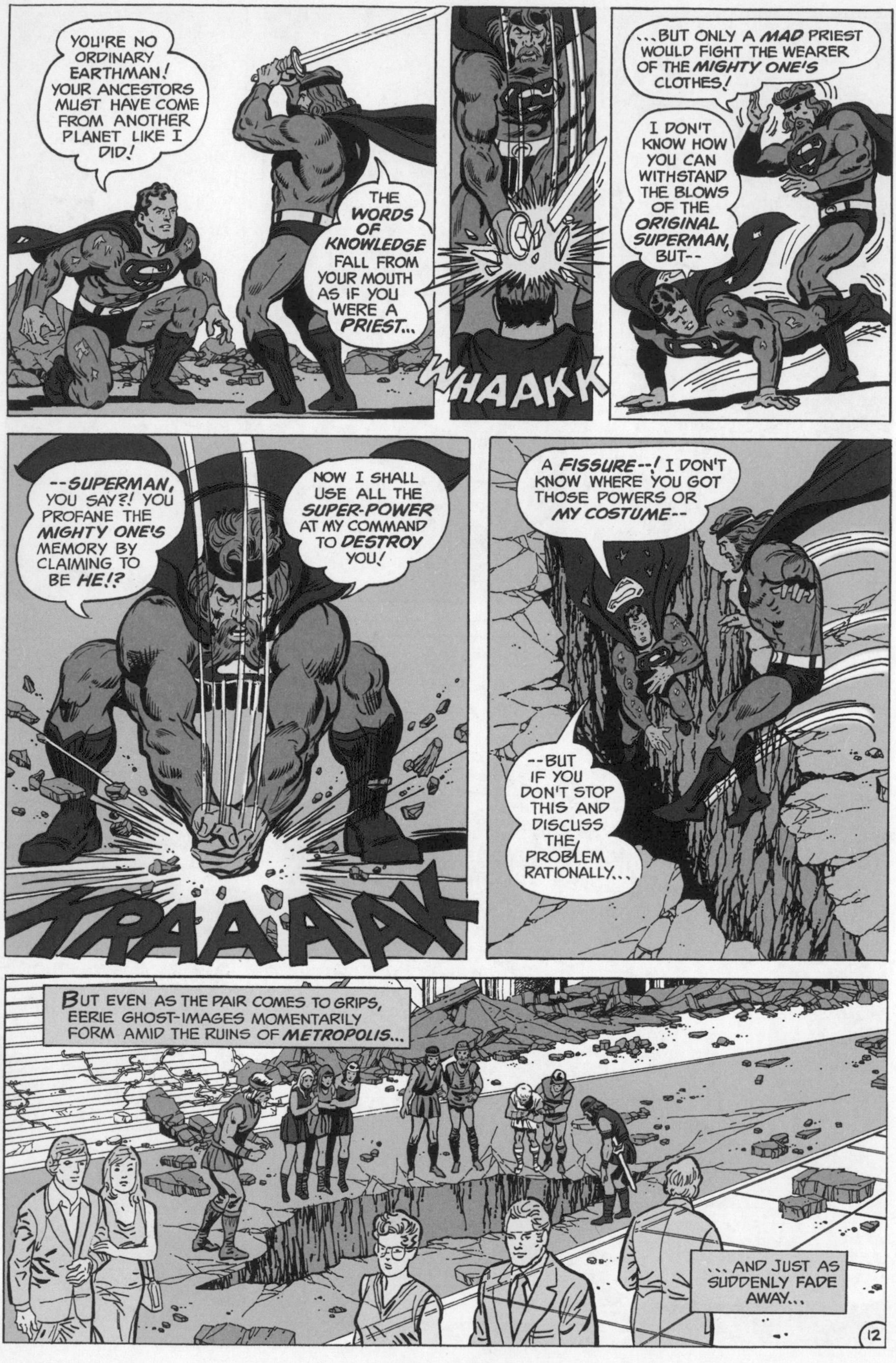
YOU'RE NO ORDINARY EARTHMAN! YOUR ANCESTORS MUST HAVE COME FROM ANOTHER PLANET LIKE I DID!
THE WORDS OF KNOWLEDGE FALL FROM YOUR MOUTH AS IF YOU WERE A PRIEST...
WHAAKK
...BUT ONLY A MAD PRIEST WOULD FIGHT THE WEARER OF THE MIGHTY ONE'S CLOTHES!
I DON'T KNOW HOW YOU CAN WITHSTAND THE BLOWS OF THE ORIGINAL SUPERMAN, BUT--
--SUPERMAN, YOU SAY?! YOU PROFANE THE MIGHTY ONE'S MEMORY BY CLAIMING TO BE HE!?
NOW I SHALL USE ALL THE SUPER-POWER AT MY COMMAND TO DESTROY YOU!
KRAAAAK
A FISSURE--! I DON'T KNOW WHERE YOU GOT THOSE POWERS OR MY COSTUME--
--BUT IF YOU DON'T STOP THIS AND DISCUSS THE PROBLEM RATIONALLY...
BUT EVEN AS THE PAIR COMES TO GRIPS, EERIE GHOST-IMAGES MOMENTARILY FORM AMID THE RUINS OF METROPOLIS...
...AND JUST AS SUDDENLY FADE AWAY...
12

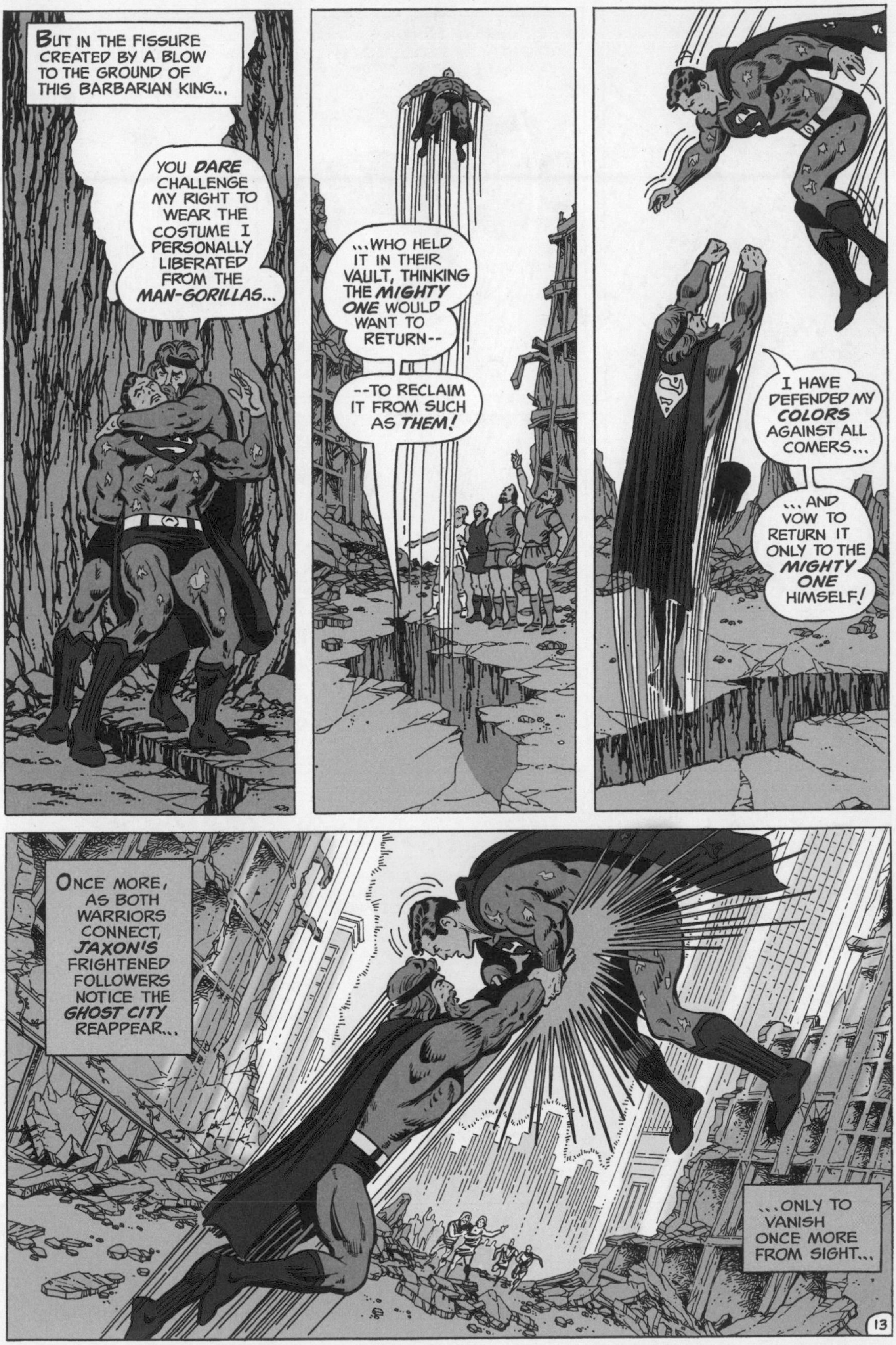

BUT IN THE FISSURE CREATED BY A BLOW TO THE GROUND OF THIS BARBARIAN KING...
YOU DARE CHALLENGE MY RIGHT TO WEAR THE COSTUME I PERSONALLY LIBERATED FROM THE MAN-GORILLAS...
...WHO HELD IT IN THEIR VAULT, THINKING THE MIGHTY ONE WOULD WANT TO RETURN--
--TO RECLAIM IT FROM SUCH AS THEM!
I HAVE DEFENDED MY COLORS AGAINST ALL COMERS...
...AND VOW TO RETURN IT ONLY TO THE MIGHTY ONE HIMSELF!
ONCE MORE, AS BOTH WARRIORS CONNECT, JAXON'S FRIGHTENED FOLLOWERS NOTICE THE GHOST CITY REAPPEAR...
...ONLY TO VANISH ONCE MORE FROM SIGHT...
13

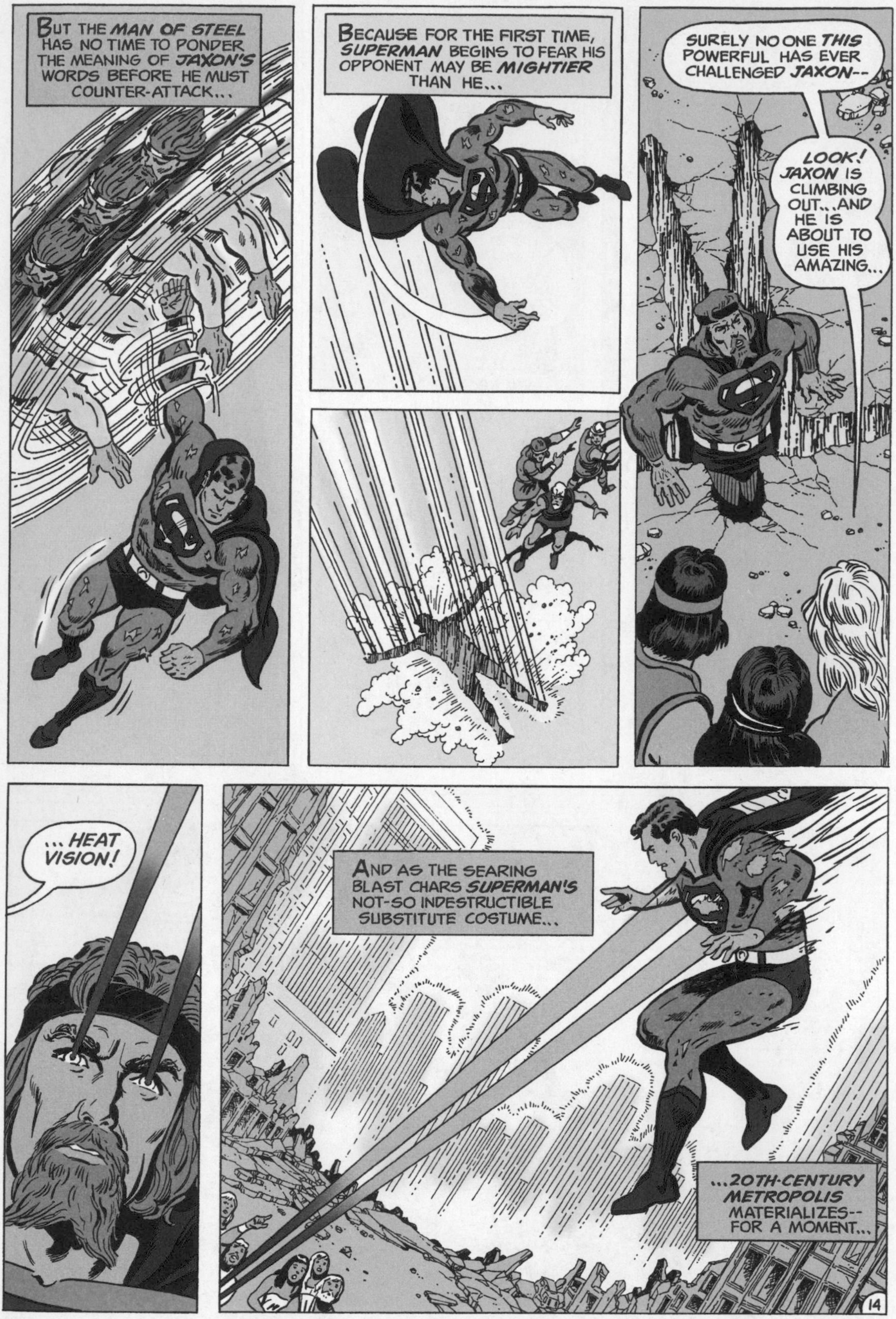
BUT THE MAN OF STEEL HAS NO TIME TO PONDER THE MEANING OF JAXON'S WORDS BEFORE HE MUST COUNTER-ATTACK...
BECAUSE FOR THE FIRST TIME, SUPERMAN BEGINS TO FEAR HIS OPPONENT MAY BE MIGHTIER THAN HE...
SURELY NO ONE THIS POWERFUL HAS EVER CHALLENGED JAXON--
LOOK! JAXON IS CLIMBING OUT...AND HE IS ABOUT TO USE HIS AMAZING...
...HEAT VISION!
AND AS THE SEARING BLAST CHARS SUPERMAN'S NOT-SO INDESTRUCTIBLE SUBSTITUTE COSTUME...
...20TH-CENTURY METROPOLIS MATERIALIZES--FOR A MOMENT...
14

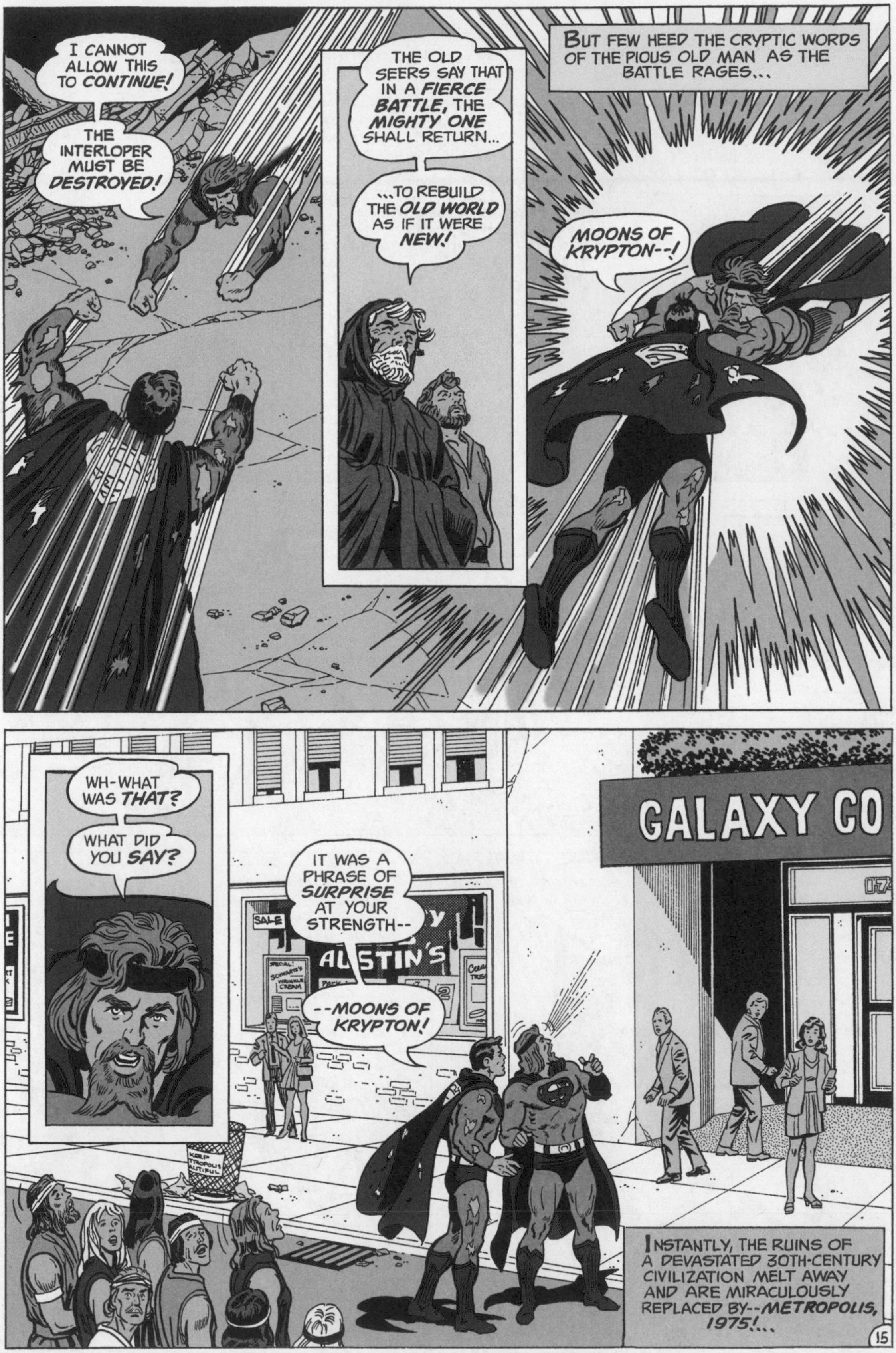
I CANNOT ALLOW THIS TO CONTINUE!
THE INTERLOPER MUST BE DESTROYED!
THE OLD SEERS SAY THAT IN A FIERCE BATTLE, THE MIGHTY ONE SHALL RETURN...
...TO REBUILD THE OLD WORLD AS IF IT WERE NEW!
BUT FEW HEED THE CRYPTIC WORDS OF THE PIOUS OLD MAN AS THE BATTLE RAGES...
MOONS OF KRYPTON--!
WH-WHAT WAS THAT?
WHAT DID YOU SAY?
IT WAS A PHRASE OF SURPRISE AT YOUR STRENGTH--
--MOONS OF KRYPTON!
GALAXY CO
AUSTIN'S
SALE
INSTANTLY, THE RUINS OF A DEVASTATED 30TH-CENTURY CIVILIZATION MELT AWAY AND ARE MIRACULOUSLY REPLACED BY--METROPOLIS, 1975!...
15

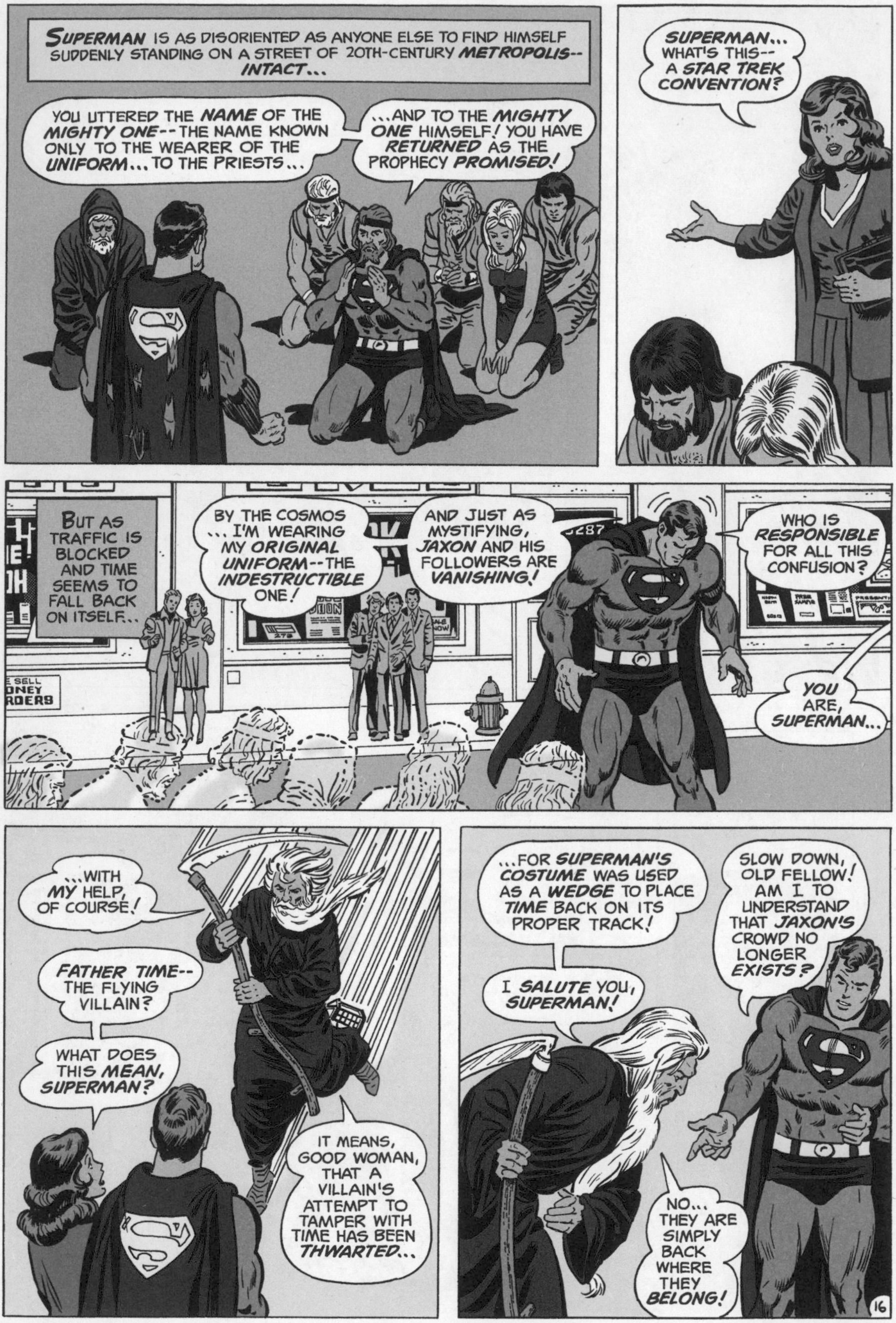
SUPERMAN IS AS DISORIENTED AS ANYONE ELSE TO FIND HIMSELF SUDDENLY STANDING ON A STREET OF 20TH-CENTURY METROPOLIS-- INTACT...
YOU UTTERED THE NAME OF THE MIGHTY ONE--THE NAME KNOWN ONLY TO THE WEARER OF THE UNIFORM... TO THE PRIESTS...
...AND TO THE MIGHTY ONE HIMSELF! YOU HAVE RETURNED AS THE PROPHECY PROMISED!
SUPERMAN... WHAT'S THIS-- A STAR TREK CONVENTION?
BUT AS TRAFFIC IS BLOCKED AND TIME SEEMS TO FALL BACK ON ITSELF...
BY THE COSMOS ...I'M WEARING MY ORIGINAL UNIFORM--THE INDESTRUCTIBLE ONE!
AND JUST AS MYSTIFYING, JAXON AND HIS FOLLOWERS ARE VANISHING!
WHO IS RESPONSIBLE FOR ALL THIS CONFUSION?
YOU ARE, SUPERMAN...
...WITH MY HELP, OF COURSE!
FATHER TIME-- THE FLYING VILLAIN?
WHAT DOES THIS MEAN, SUPERMAN?
IT MEANS, GOOD WOMAN, THAT A VILLAIN'S ATTEMPT TO TAMPER WITH TIME HAS BEEN THWARTED...
...FOR SUPERMAN'S COSTUME WAS USED AS A WEDGE TO PLACE TIME BACK ON ITS PROPER TRACK!
I SALUTE YOU, SUPERMAN!
SLOW DOWN, OLD FELLOW! AM I TO UNDERSTAND THAT JAXON'S CROWD NO LONGER EXISTS?
NO... THEY ARE SIMPLY BACK WHERE THEY BELONG!
16

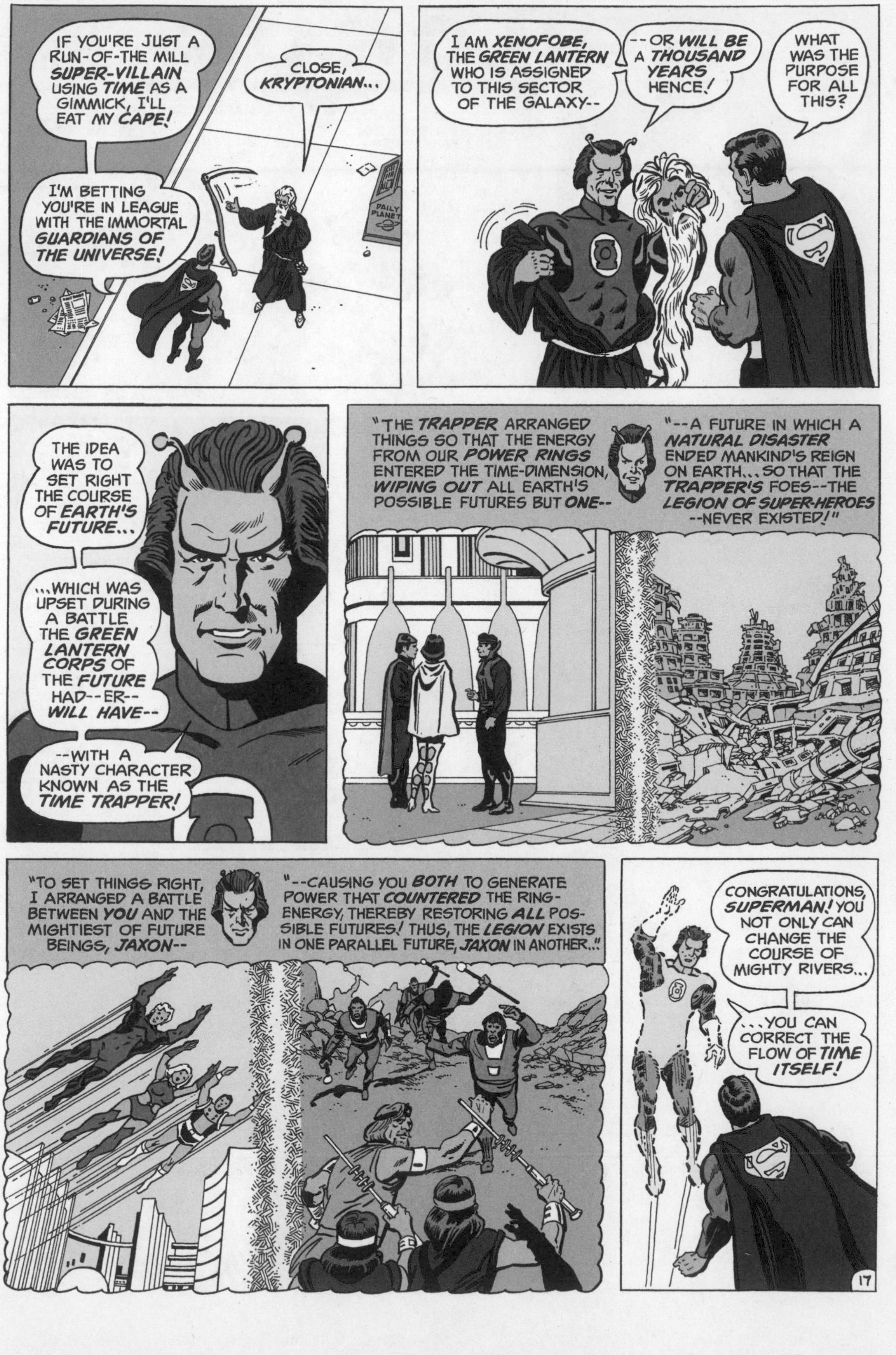
IF YOU'RE JUST A RUN-OF-THE MILL SUPER-VILLAIN USING TIME AS A GIMMICK, I'LL EAT MY CAPE!
I'M BETTING YOU'RE IN LEAGUE WITH THE IMMORTAL GUARDIANS OF THE UNIVERSE!
CLOSE, KRYPTONIAN...
DAILY PLANET
I AM XENOFOBE, THE GREEN LANTERN WHO IS ASSIGNED TO THIS SECTOR OF THE GALAXY--
--OR WILL BE A THOUSAND YEARS HENCE!
WHAT WAS THE PURPOSE FOR ALL THIS?
THE IDEA WAS TO SET RIGHT THE COURSE OF EARTH'S FUTURE...
...WHICH WAS UPSET DURING A BATTLE THE GREEN LANTERN CORPS OF THE FUTURE HAD--ER-- WILL HAVE--
--WITH A NASTY CHARACTER KNOWN AS THE TIME TRAPPER!
"THE TRAPPER ARRANGED THINGS SO THAT THE ENERGY FROM OUR POWER RINGS ENTERED THE TIME-DIMENSION, WIPING OUT ALL EARTH'S POSSIBLE FUTURES BUT ONE--
"--A FUTURE IN WHICH A NATURAL DISASTER ENDED MANKIND'S REIGN ON EARTH... SO THAT THE TRAPPER'S FOES--THE LEGION OF SUPER-HEROES --NEVER EXISTED!"
"TO SET THINGS RIGHT, I ARRANGED A BATTLE BETWEEN YOU AND THE MIGHTIEST OF FUTURE BEINGS, JAXON--
"--CAUSING YOU BOTH TO GENERATE POWER THAT COUNTERED THE RING-ENERGY, THEREBY RESTORING ALL POSSIBLE FUTURES! THUS, THE LEGION EXISTS IN ONE PARALLEL FUTURE, JAXON IN ANOTHER..."
CONGRATULATIONS, SUPERMAN! YOU NOT ONLY CAN CHANGE THE COURSE OF MIGHTY RIVERS...
...YOU CAN CORRECT THE FLOW OF TIME ITSELF!
17

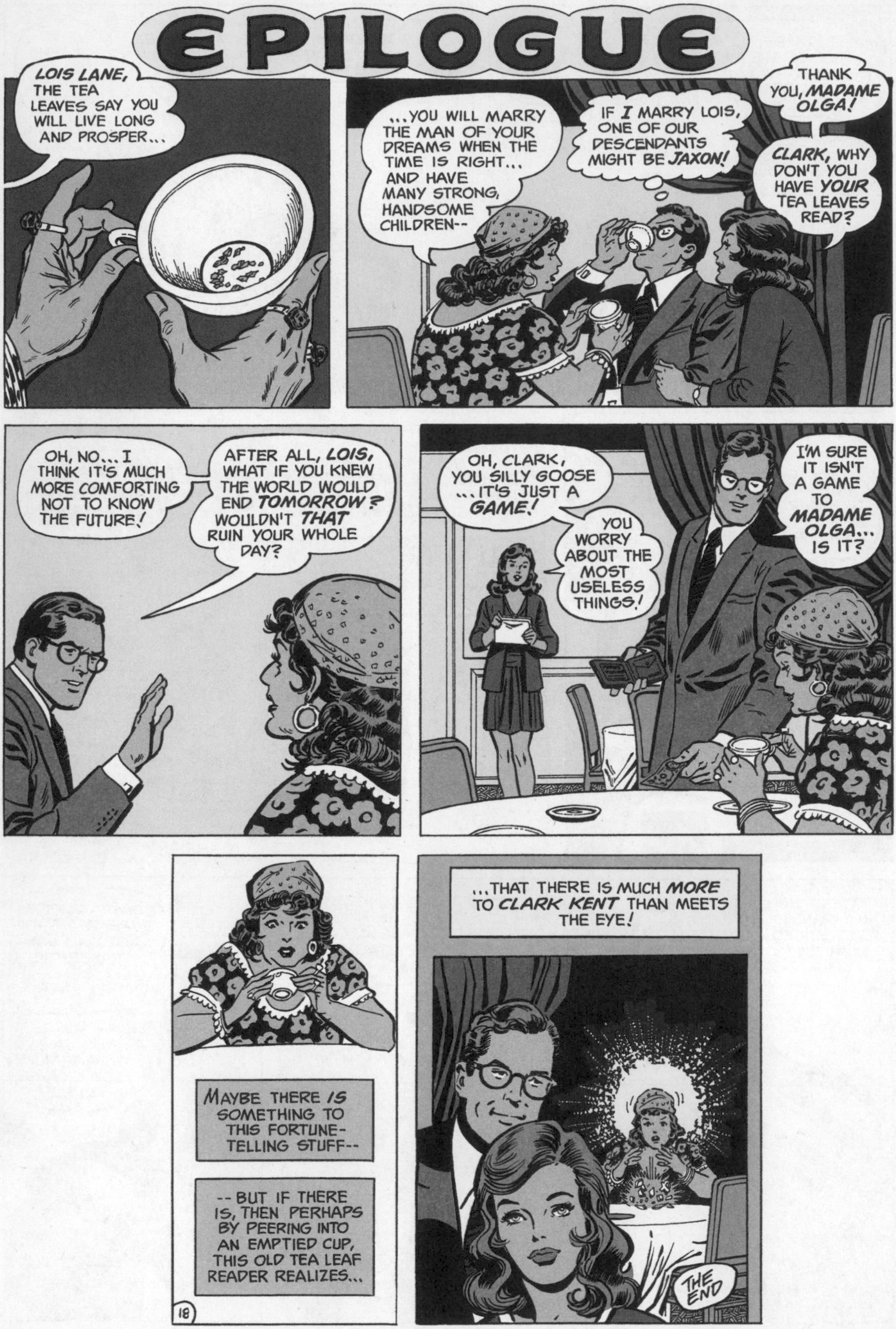
EPILOGUE
LOIS LANE, THE TEA LEAVES SAY YOU WILL LIVE LONG AND PROSPER...
...YOU WILL MARRY THE MAN OF YOUR DREAMS WHEN THE TIME IS RIGHT... AND HAVE MANY STRONG, HANDSOME CHILDREN--
IF I MARRY LOIS, ONE OF OUR DESCENDANTS MIGHT BE JAXON!
THANK YOU, MADAME OLGA!
CLARK, WHY DON'T YOU HAVE YOUR TEA LEAVES READ?
OH, NO... I THINK IT'S MUCH MORE COMFORTING NOT TO KNOW THE FUTURE!
AFTER ALL, LOIS, WHAT IF YOU KNEW THE WORLD WOULD END TOMORROW? WOULDN'T THAT RUIN YOUR WHOLE DAY?
OH, CLARK, YOU SILLY GOOSE ...IT'S JUST A GAME!
YOU WORRY ABOUT THE MOST USELESS THINGS!
I'M SURE IT ISN'T A GAME TO MADAME OLGA... IS IT?
MAYBE THERE IS SOMETHING TO THIS FORTUNE-TELLING STUFF--
-- BUT IF THERE IS, THEN PERHAPS BY PEERING INTO AN EMPTIED CUP, THIS OLD TEA LEAF READER REALIZES...
18
...THAT THERE IS MUCH MORE TO CLARK KENT THAN MEETS THE EYE!
THE END

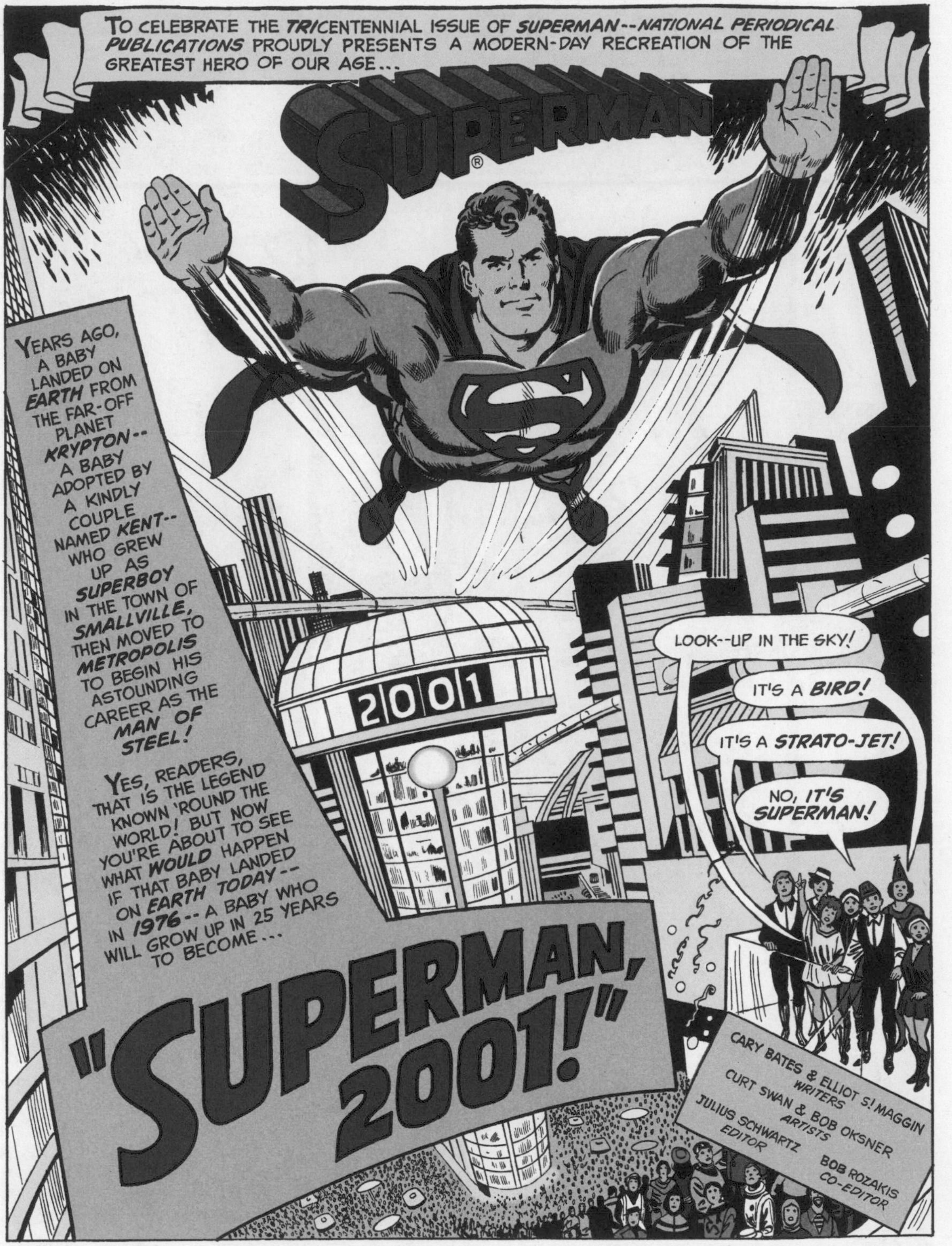

TO CELEBRATE THE TRICENTENNIAL ISSUE OF SUPERMAN--NATIONAL PERIODICAL PUBLICATIONS PROUDLY PRESENTS A MODERN-DAY RECREATION OF THE GREATEST HERO OF OUR AGE...
SUPERMAN®
YEARS AGO, A BABY LANDED ON EARTH FROM THE FAR-OFF PLANET KRYPTON-- A BABY ADOPTED BY A KINDLY COUPLE NAMED KENT-- WHO GREW UP AS SUPERBOY IN THE TOWN OF SMALLVILLE, THEN MOVED TO METROPOLIS TO BEGIN HIS ASTOUNDING CAREER AS THE MAN OF STEEL!
YES, READERS, THAT IS THE LEGEND KNOWN 'ROUND THE WORLD! BUT NOW YOU'RE ABOUT TO SEE WHAT WOULD HAPPEN IF THAT BABY LANDED ON EARTH TODAY-- IN 1976-- A BABY WHO WILL GROW UP IN 25 YEARS TO BECOME...
2001
LOOK--UP IN THE SKY!
IT'S A BIRD!
IT'S A STRATO-JET!
NO, IT'S SUPERMAN!
"SUPERMAN, 2001!"
CARY BATES & ELLIOT S! MAGGIN WRITERS
CURT SWAN & BOB OKSNER ARTISTS
JULIUS SCHWARTZ EDITOR
BOB ROZAKIS CO-EDITOR

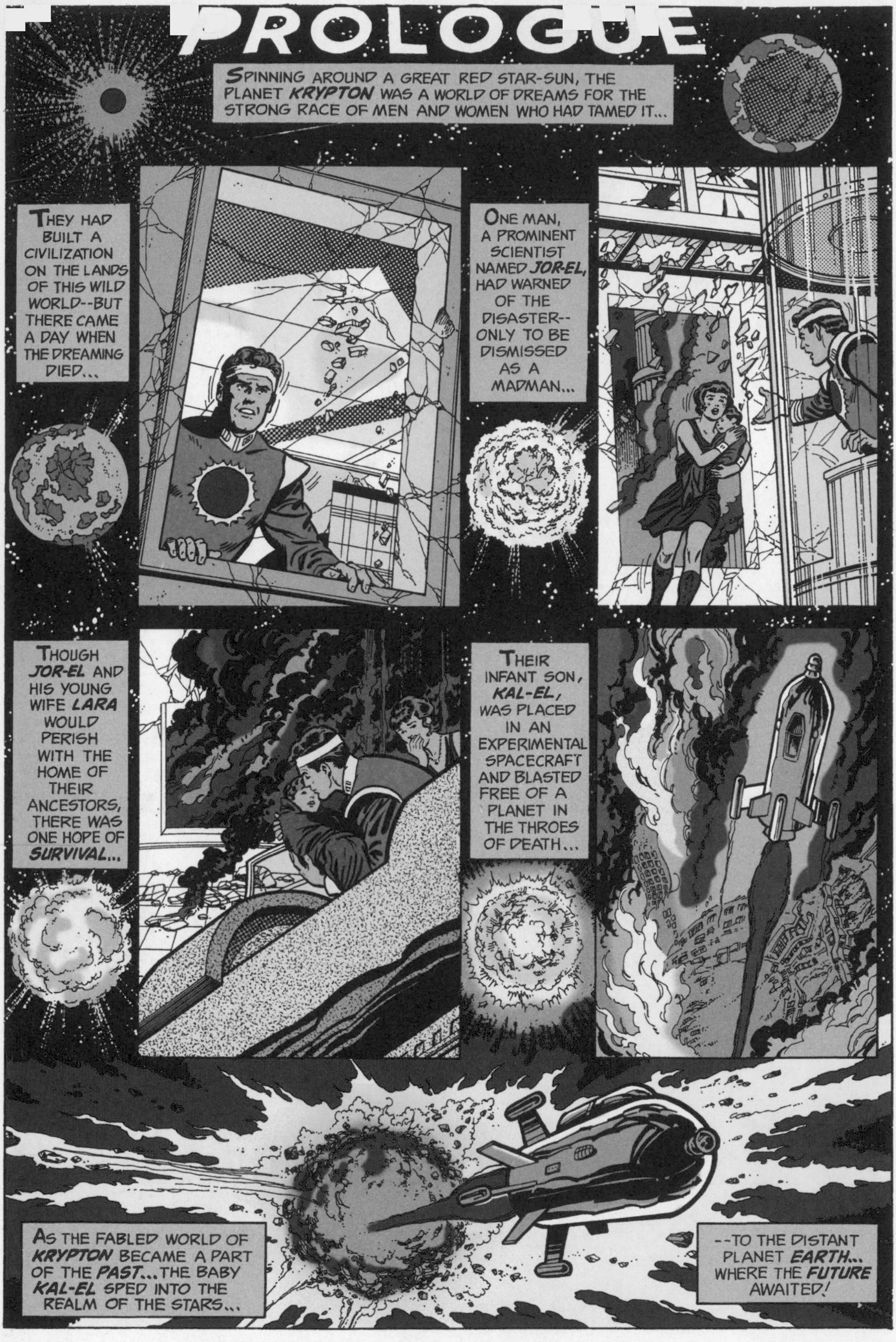
PROLOGUE
SPINNING AROUND A GREAT RED STAR-SUN, THE PLANET KRYPTON WAS A WORLD OF DREAMS FOR THE STRONG RACE OF MEN AND WOMEN WHO HAD TAMED IT...
THEY HAD BUILT A CIVILIZATION ON THE LANDS OF THIS WILD WORLD--BUT THERE CAME A DAY WHEN THE DREAMING DIED...
ONE MAN, A PROMINENT SCIENTIST NAMED JOR-EL, HAD WARNED OF THE DISASTER-- ONLY TO BE DISMISSED AS A MADMAN...
THOUGH JOR-EL AND HIS YOUNG WIFE LARA WOULD PERISH WITH THE HOME OF THEIR ANCESTORS, THERE WAS ONE HOPE OF SURVIVAL...
THEIR INFANT SON, KAL-EL, WAS PLACED IN AN EXPERIMENTAL SPACECRAFT AND BLASTED FREE OF A PLANET IN THE THROES OF DEATH...
AS THE FABLED WORLD OF KRYPTON BECAME A PART OF THE PAST... THE BABY KAL-EL SPED INTO THE REALM OF THE STARS...
--TO THE DISTANT PLANET EARTH... WHERE THE FUTURE AWAITED!

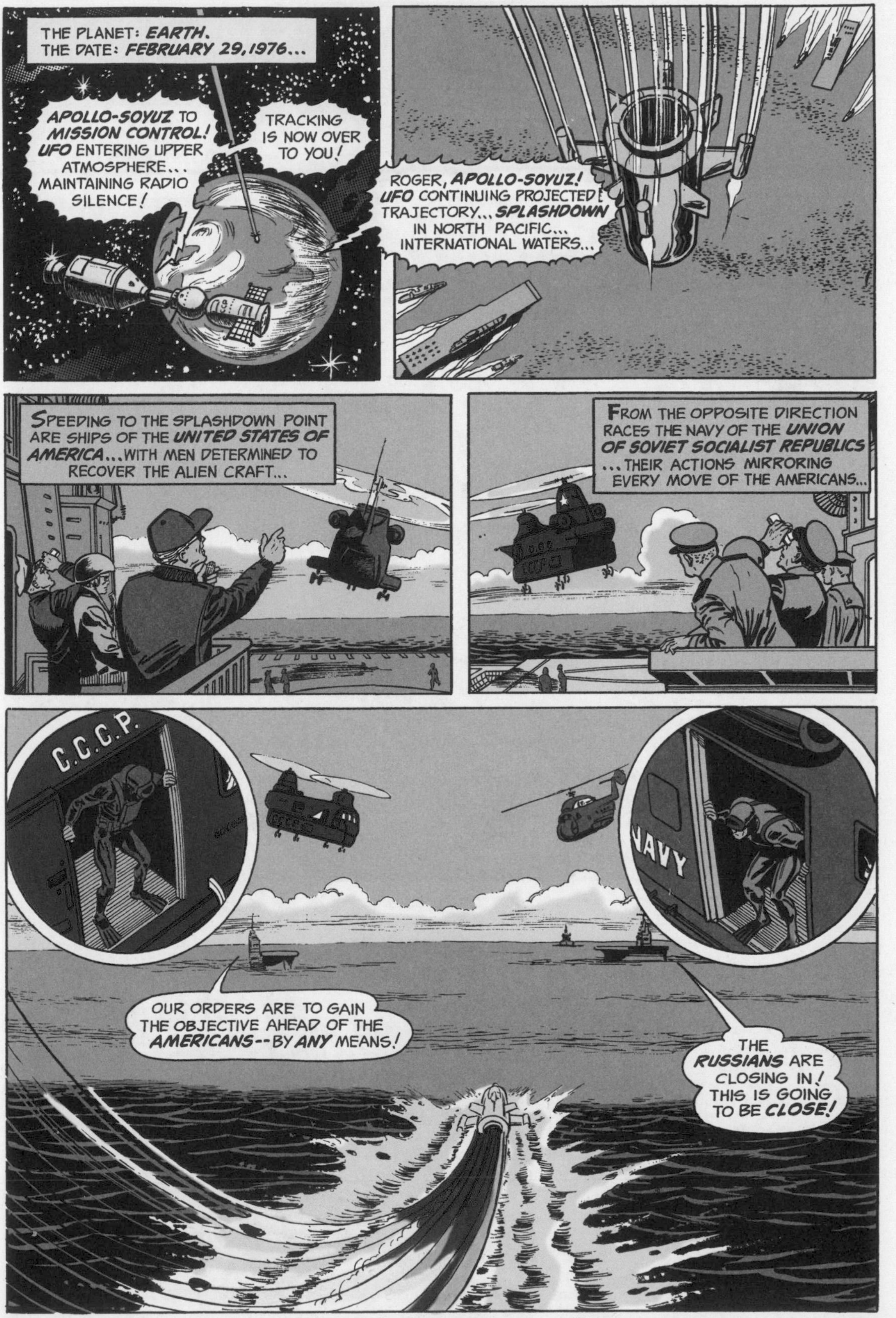
THE PLANET: EARTH.
THE DATE: FEBRUARY 29, 1976...
APOLLO-SOYUZ TO MISSION CONTROL! UFO ENTERING UPPER ATMOSPHERE... MAINTAINING RADIO SILENCE!
TRACKING IS NOW OVER TO YOU!
ROGER, APOLLO-SOYUZ! UFO CONTINUING PROJECTED TRAJECTORY... SPLASHDOWN IN NORTH PACIFIC... INTERNATIONAL WATERS...
SPEEDING TO THE SPLASHDOWN POINT ARE SHIPS OF THE UNITED STATES OF AMERICA... WITH MEN DETERMINED TO RECOVER THE ALIEN CRAFT...
FROM THE OPPOSITE DIRECTION RACES THE NAVY OF THE UNION OF SOVIET SOCIALIST REPUBLICS ... THEIR ACTIONS MIRRORING EVERY MOVE OF THE AMERICANS...
C.C.C.P.
NAVY
OUR ORDERS ARE TO GAIN THE OBJECTIVE AHEAD OF THE AMERICANS--BY ANY MEANS!
THE RUSSIANS ARE CLOSING IN! THIS IS GOING TO BE CLOSE!

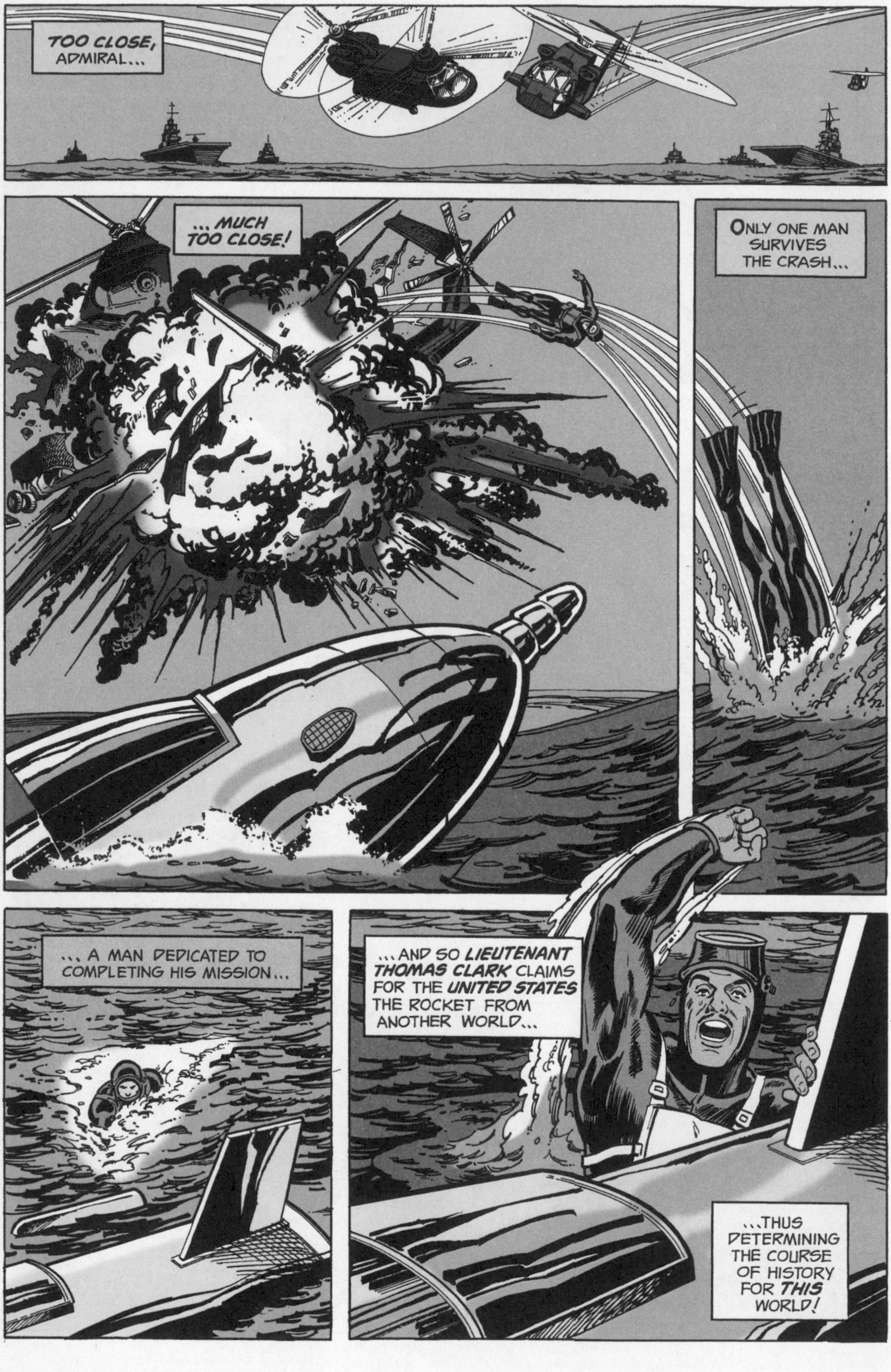
TOO CLOSE, ADMIRAL...
...MUCH TOO CLOSE!
ONLY ONE MAN SURVIVES THE CRASH...
...A MAN DEDICATED TO COMPLETING HIS MISSION...
...AND SO LIEUTENANT THOMAS CLARK CLAIMS FOR THE UNITED STATES THE ROCKET FROM ANOTHER WORLD...
...THUS DETERMINING THE COURSE OF HISTORY FOR THIS WORLD!

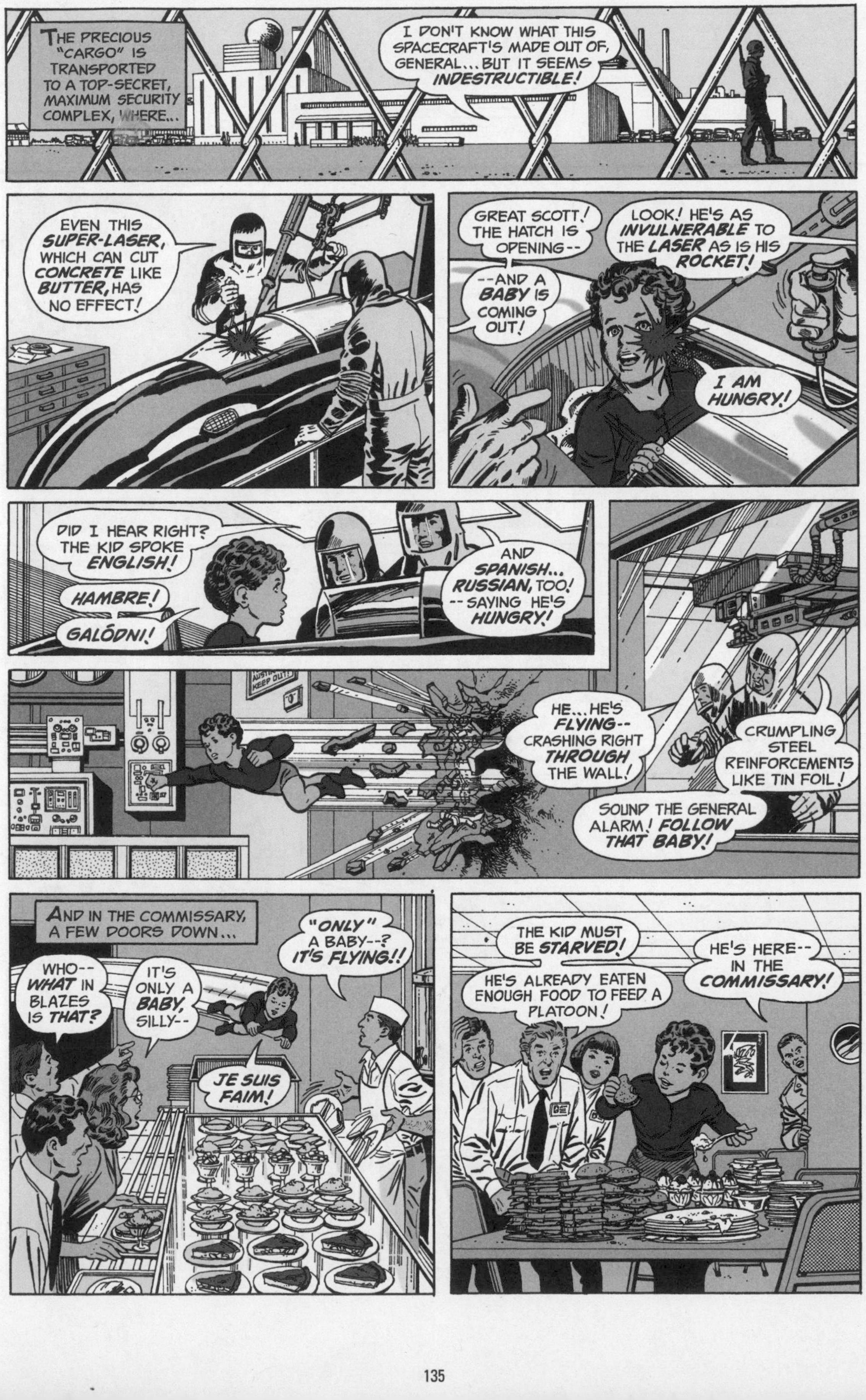
THE PRECIOUS "CARGO" IS TRANSPORTED TO A TOP-SECRET, MAXIMUM SECURITY COMPLEX, WHERE...
I DON'T KNOW WHAT THIS SPACECRAFT'S MADE OUT OF, GENERAL... BUT IT SEEMS INDESTRUCTIBLE!
EVEN THIS SUPER-LASER, WHICH CAN CUT CONCRETE LIKE BUTTER, HAS NO EFFECT!
GREAT SCOTT! THE HATCH IS OPENING--
--AND A BABY IS COMING OUT!
LOOK! HE'S AS INVULNERABLE TO THE LASER AS IS HIS ROCKET!
I AM HUNGRY!
DID I HEAR RIGHT? THE KID SPOKE ENGLISH!
HAMBRE!
GALÓDNI!
AND SPANISH... RUSSIAN, TOO! --SAYING HE'S HUNGRY!
KEEP OUT!
HE... HE'S FLYING-- CRASHING RIGHT THROUGH THE WALL!
CRUMPLING STEEL REINFORCEMENTS LIKE TIN FOIL!
SOUND THE GENERAL ALARM! FOLLOW THAT BABY!
AND IN THE COMMISSARY, A FEW DOORS DOWN...
WHO-- WHAT IN BLAZES IS THAT?
IT'S ONLY A BABY, SILLY--
"ONLY" A BABY--? IT'S FLYING!!
JE SUIS FAIM!
THE KID MUST BE STARVED!
HE'S ALREADY EATEN ENOUGH FOOD TO FEED A PLATOON!
HE'S HERE-- IN THE COMMISSARY!

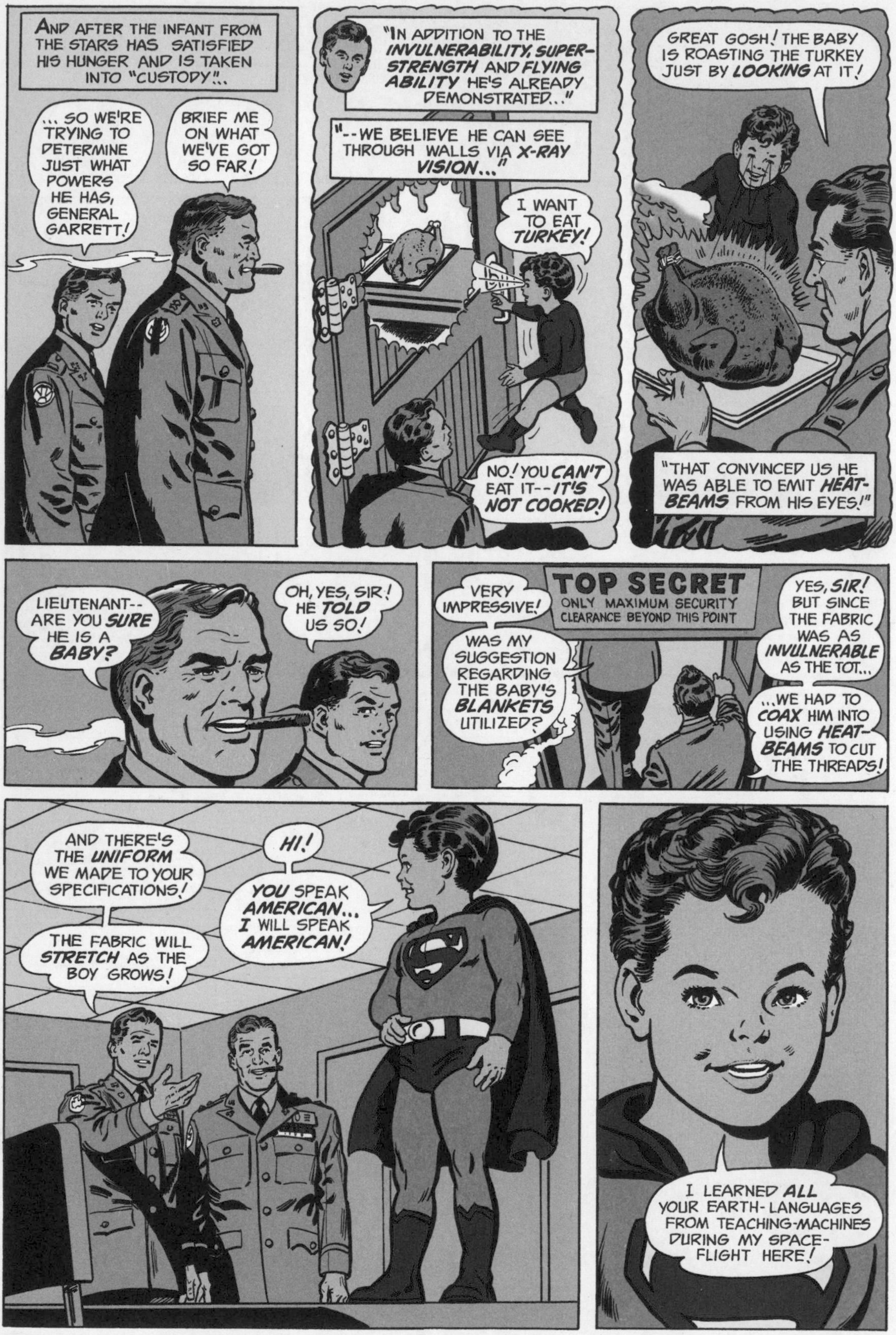

AND AFTER THE INFANT FROM THE STARS HAS SATISFIED HIS HUNGER AND IS TAKEN INTO "CUSTODY"...
...SO WE'RE TRYING TO DETERMINE JUST WHAT POWERS HE HAS, GENERAL GARRETT!
BRIEF ME ON WHAT WE'VE GOT SO FAR!
"IN ADDITION TO THE INVULNERABILITY, SUPER-STRENGTH AND FLYING ABILITY HE'S ALREADY DEMONSTRATED..."
"--WE BELIEVE HE CAN SEE THROUGH WALLS VIA X-RAY VISION..."
I WANT TO EAT TURKEY!
NO! YOU CAN'T EAT IT--IT'S NOT COOKED!
GREAT GOSH! THE BABY IS ROASTING THE TURKEY JUST BY LOOKING AT IT!
"THAT CONVINCED US HE WAS ABLE TO EMIT HEAT-BEAMS FROM HIS EYES!"
LIEUTENANT--ARE YOU SURE HE IS A BABY?
OH, YES, SIR! HE TOLD US SO!
TOP SECRET
ONLY MAXIMUM SECURITY CLEARANCE BEYOND THIS POINT
VERY IMPRESSIVE!
WAS MY SUGGESTION REGARDING THE BABY'S BLANKETS UTILIZED?
YES, SIR! BUT SINCE THE FABRIC WAS AS INVULNERABLE AS THE TOT...
...WE HAD TO COAX HIM INTO USING HEAT-BEAMS TO CUT THE THREADS!
AND THERE'S THE UNIFORM WE MADE TO YOUR SPECIFICATIONS!
THE FABRIC WILL STRETCH AS THE BOY GROWS!
HI!
YOU SPEAK AMERICAN... I WILL SPEAK AMERICAN!
I LEARNED ALL YOUR EARTH-LANGUAGES FROM TEACHING-MACHINES DURING MY SPACE-FLIGHT HERE!

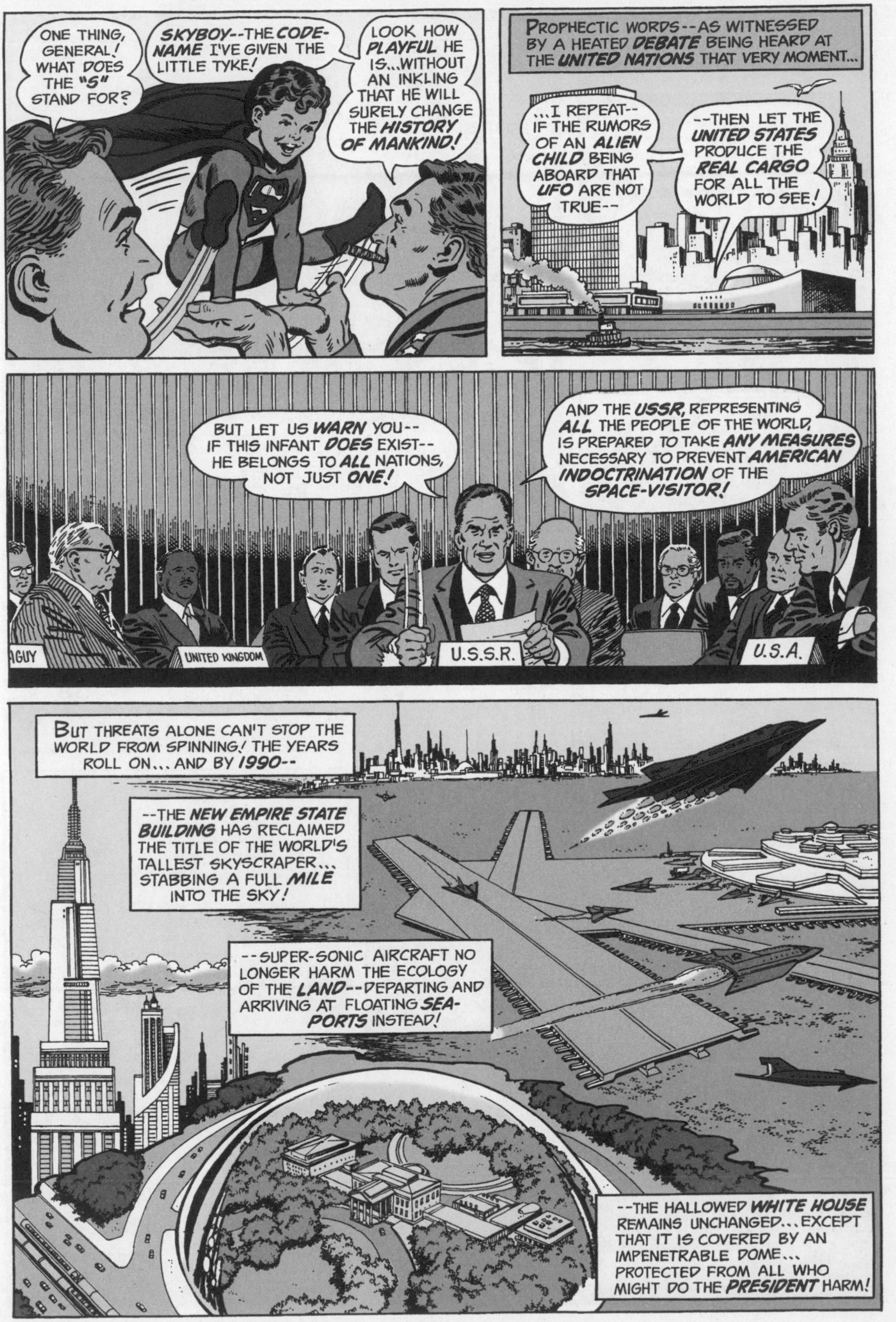
ONE THING, GENERAL! WHAT DOES THE "S" STAND FOR?
SKYBOY--THE CODE-NAME I'VE GIVEN THE LITTLE TYKE!
LOOK HOW PLAYFUL HE IS...WITHOUT AN INKLING THAT HE WILL SURELY CHANGE THE HISTORY OF MANKIND!
PROPHECTIC WORDS--AS WITNESSED BY A HEATED DEBATE BEING HEARD AT THE UNITED NATIONS THAT VERY MOMENT...
...I REPEAT--IF THE RUMORS OF AN ALIEN CHILD BEING ABOARD THAT UFO ARE NOT TRUE--
--THEN LET THE UNITED STATES PRODUCE THE REAL CARGO FOR ALL THE WORLD TO SEE!
BUT LET US WARN YOU--IF THIS INFANT DOES EXIST--HE BELONGS TO ALL NATIONS, NOT JUST ONE!
AND THE USSR, REPRESENTING ALL THE PEOPLE OF THE WORLD, IS PREPARED TO TAKE ANY MEASURES NECESSARY TO PREVENT AMERICAN INDOCTRINATION OF THE SPACE-VISITOR!
AGUY
UNITED KINGDOM
U.S.S.R.
U.S.A.
BUT THREATS ALONE CAN'T STOP THE WORLD FROM SPINNING! THE YEARS ROLL ON... AND BY 1990--
--THE NEW EMPIRE STATE BUILDING HAS RECLAIMED THE TITLE OF THE WORLD'S TALLEST SKYSCRAPER... STABBING A FULL MILE INTO THE SKY!
--SUPER-SONIC AIRCRAFT NO LONGER HARM THE ECOLOGY OF THE LAND--DEPARTING AND ARRIVING AT FLOATING SEA-PORTS INSTEAD!
--THE HALLOWED WHITE HOUSE REMAINS UNCHANGED... EXCEPT THAT IT IS COVERED BY AN IMPENETRABLE DOME... PROTECTED FROM ALL WHO MIGHT DO THE PRESIDENT HARM!

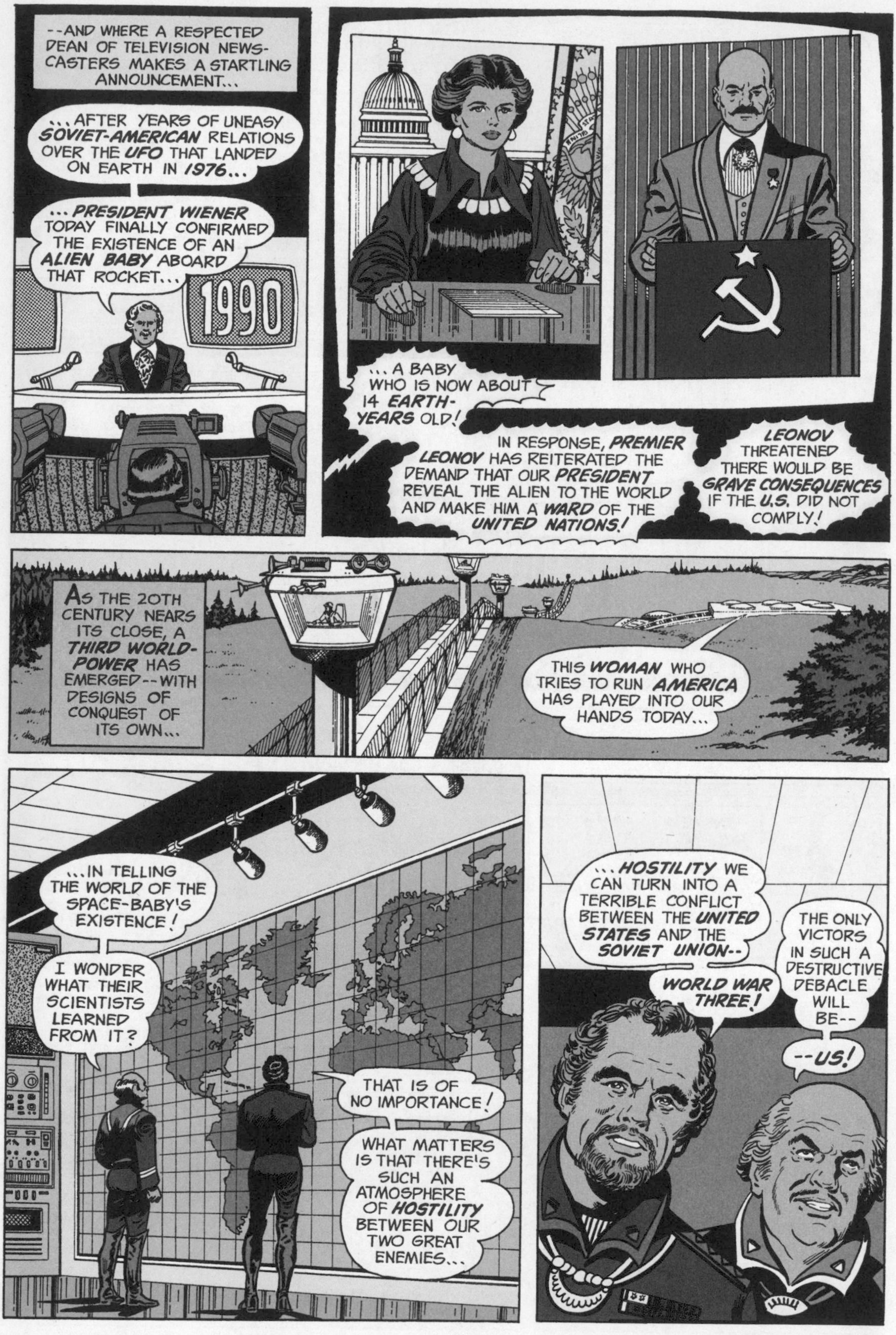
--AND WHERE A RESPECTED DEAN OF TELEVISION NEWSCASTERS MAKES A STARTLING ANNOUNCEMENT...
...AFTER YEARS OF UNEASY SOVIET-AMERICAN RELATIONS OVER THE UFO THAT LANDED ON EARTH IN 1976...
...PRESIDENT WIENER TODAY FINALLY CONFIRMED THE EXISTENCE OF AN ALIEN BABY ABOARD THAT ROCKET...
1990
...A BABY WHO IS NOW ABOUT 14 EARTH-YEARS OLD!
IN RESPONSE, PREMIER LEONOV HAS REITERATED THE DEMAND THAT OUR PRESIDENT REVEAL THE ALIEN TO THE WORLD AND MAKE HIM A WARD OF THE UNITED NATIONS!
LEONOV THREATENED THERE WOULD BE GRAVE CONSEQUENCES IF THE U.S. DID NOT COMPLY!
AS THE 20TH CENTURY NEARS ITS CLOSE, A THIRD WORLD-POWER HAS EMERGED--WITH DESIGNS OF CONQUEST OF ITS OWN...
THIS WOMAN WHO TRIES TO RUN AMERICA HAS PLAYED INTO OUR HANDS TODAY...
...IN TELLING THE WORLD OF THE SPACE-BABY'S EXISTENCE!
I WONDER WHAT THEIR SCIENTISTS LEARNED FROM IT?
THAT IS OF NO IMPORTANCE!
WHAT MATTERS IS THAT THERE'S SUCH AN ATMOSPHERE OF HOSTILITY BETWEEN OUR TWO GREAT ENEMIES...
...HOSTILITY WE CAN TURN INTO A TERRIBLE CONFLICT BETWEEN THE UNITED STATES AND THE SOVIET UNION--
WORLD WAR THREE!
THE ONLY VICTORS IN SUCH A DESTRUCTIVE DEBACLE WILL BE--
--US!

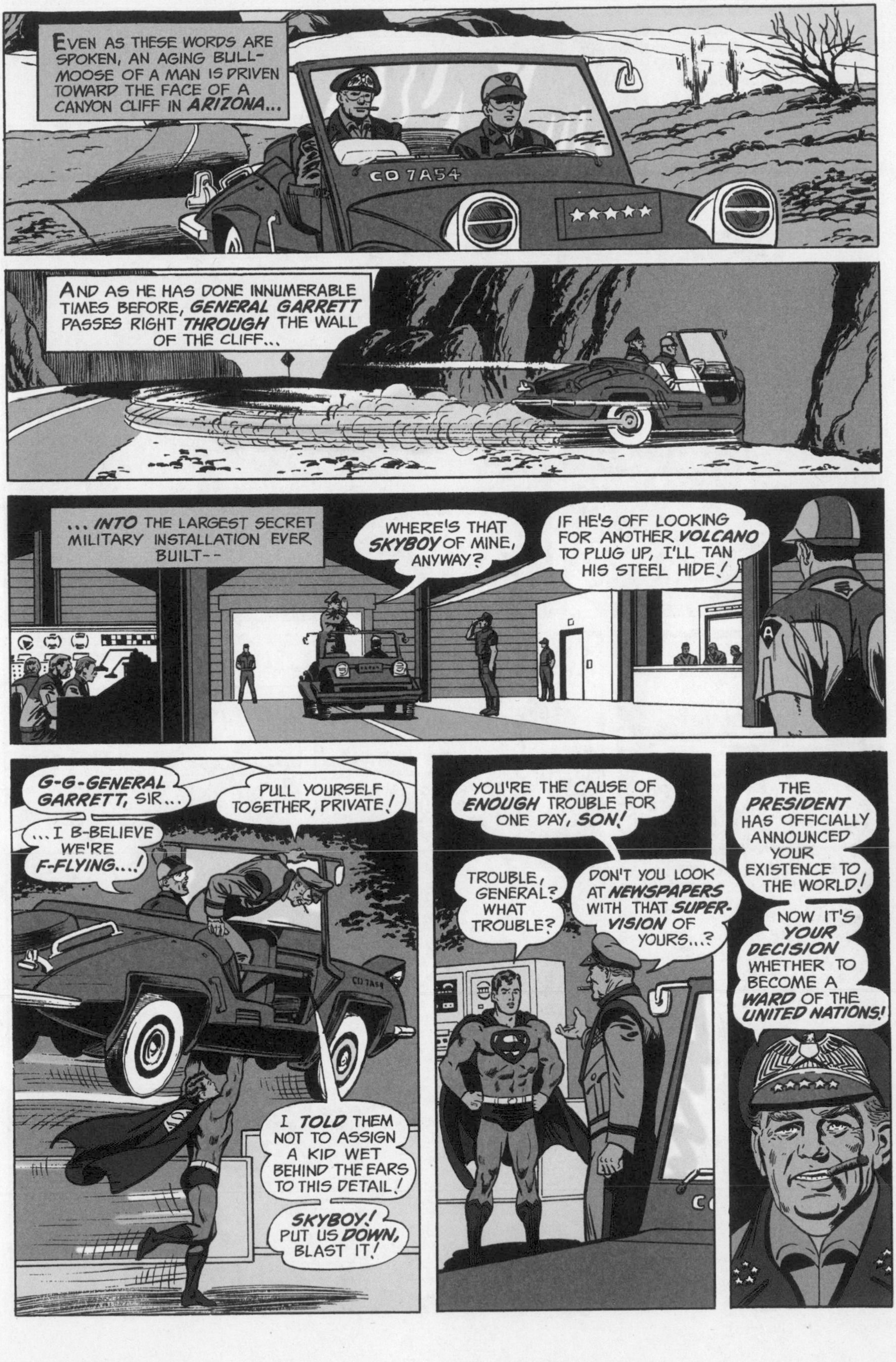
EVEN AS THESE WORDS ARE SPOKEN, AN AGING BULL-MOOSE OF A MAN IS DRIVEN TOWARD THE FACE OF A CANYON CLIFF IN ARIZONA...
CD 7A54
AND AS HE HAS DONE INNUMERABLE TIMES BEFORE, GENERAL GARRETT PASSES RIGHT THROUGH THE WALL OF THE CLIFF...
...INTO THE LARGEST SECRET MILITARY INSTALLATION EVER BUILT--
WHERE'S THAT SKYBOY OF MINE, ANYWAY?
IF HE'S OFF LOOKING FOR ANOTHER VOLCANO TO PLUG UP, I'LL TAN HIS STEEL HIDE!
G-G-GENERAL GARRETT, SIR...
PULL YOURSELF TOGETHER, PRIVATE!
...I B-BELIEVE WE'RE F-FLYING...!
I TOLD THEM NOT TO ASSIGN A KID WET BEHIND THE EARS TO THIS DETAIL!
SKYBOY! PUT US DOWN, BLAST IT!
YOU'RE THE CAUSE OF ENOUGH TROUBLE FOR ONE DAY, SON!
TROUBLE, GENERAL? WHAT TROUBLE?
DON'T YOU LOOK AT NEWSPAPERS WITH THAT SUPER-VISION OF YOURS...?
THE PRESIDENT HAS OFFICIALLY ANNOUNCED YOUR EXISTENCE TO THE WORLD!
NOW IT'S YOUR DECISION WHETHER TO BECOME A WARD OF THE UNITED NATIONS!

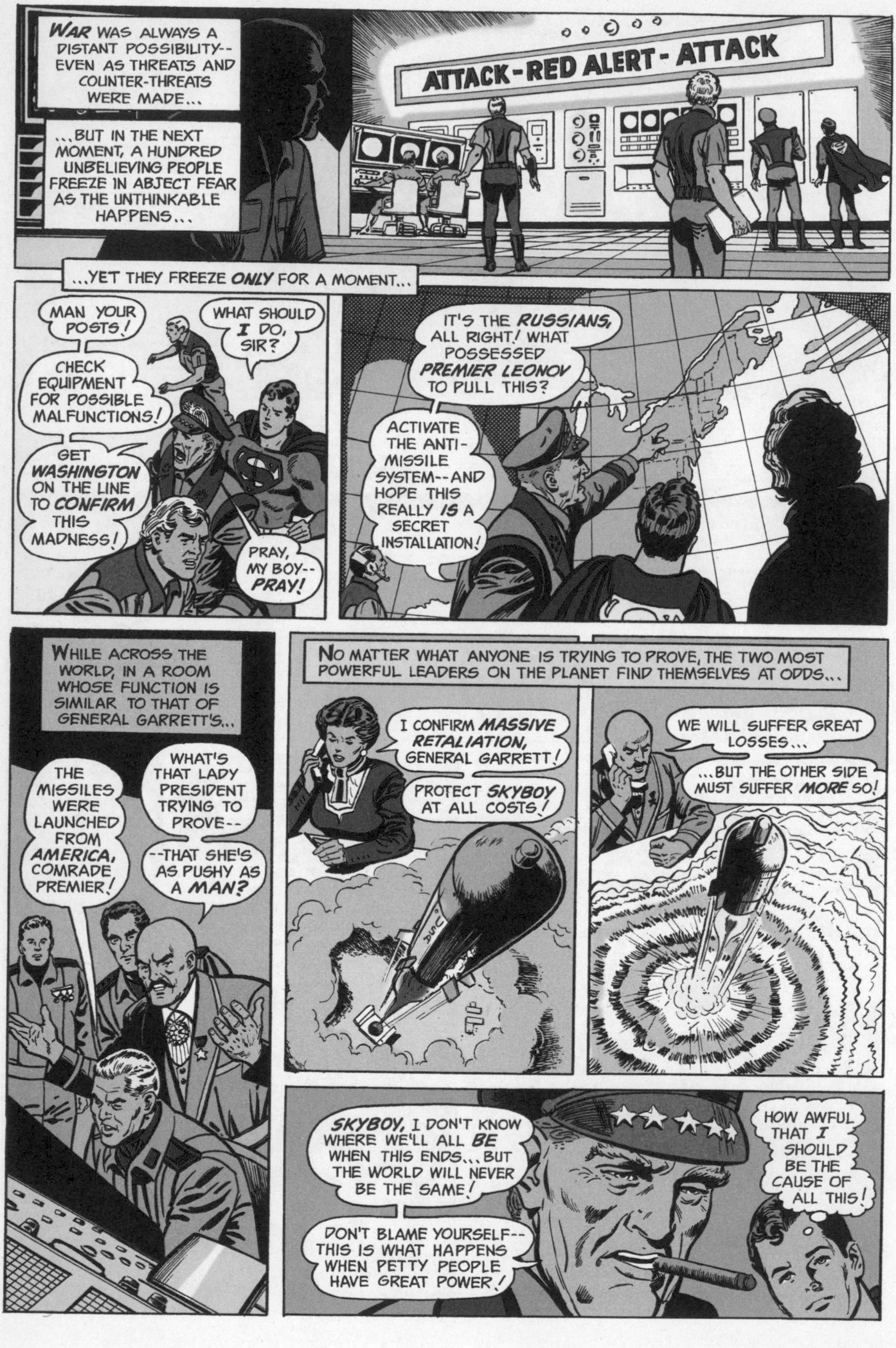
WAR WAS ALWAYS A DISTANT POSSIBILITY-- EVEN AS THREATS AND COUNTER-THREATS WERE MADE...
...BUT IN THE NEXT MOMENT, A HUNDRED UNBELIEVING PEOPLE FREEZE IN ABJECT FEAR AS THE UNTHINKABLE HAPPENS...
ATTACK - RED ALERT - ATTACK
...YET THEY FREEZE ONLY FOR A MOMENT...
MAN YOUR POSTS!
CHECK EQUIPMENT FOR POSSIBLE MALFUNCTIONS!
GET WASHINGTON ON THE LINE TO CONFIRM THIS MADNESS!
WHAT SHOULD I DO, SIR?
PRAY, MY BOY-- PRAY!
IT'S THE RUSSIANS, ALL RIGHT! WHAT POSSESSED PREMIER LEONOV TO PULL THIS?
ACTIVATE THE ANTI-MISSILE SYSTEM--AND HOPE THIS REALLY IS A SECRET INSTALLATION!
WHILE ACROSS THE WORLD, IN A ROOM WHOSE FUNCTION IS SIMILAR TO THAT OF GENERAL GARRETT'S...
THE MISSILES WERE LAUNCHED FROM AMERICA, COMRADE PREMIER!
WHAT'S THAT LADY PRESIDENT TRYING TO PROVE--
--THAT SHE'S AS PUSHY AS A MAN?
NO MATTER WHAT ANYONE IS TRYING TO PROVE, THE TWO MOST POWERFUL LEADERS ON THE PLANET FIND THEMSELVES AT ODDS...
I CONFIRM MASSIVE RETALIATION, GENERAL GARRETT!
PROTECT SKYBOY AT ALL COSTS!
WE WILL SUFFER GREAT LOSSES...
...BUT THE OTHER SIDE MUST SUFFER MORE SO!
SKYBOY, I DON'T KNOW WHERE WE'LL ALL BE WHEN THIS ENDS... BUT THE WORLD WILL NEVER BE THE SAME!
DON'T BLAME YOURSELF-- THIS IS WHAT HAPPENS WHEN PETTY PEOPLE HAVE GREAT POWER!
HOW AWFUL THAT I SHOULD BE THE CAUSE OF ALL THIS!

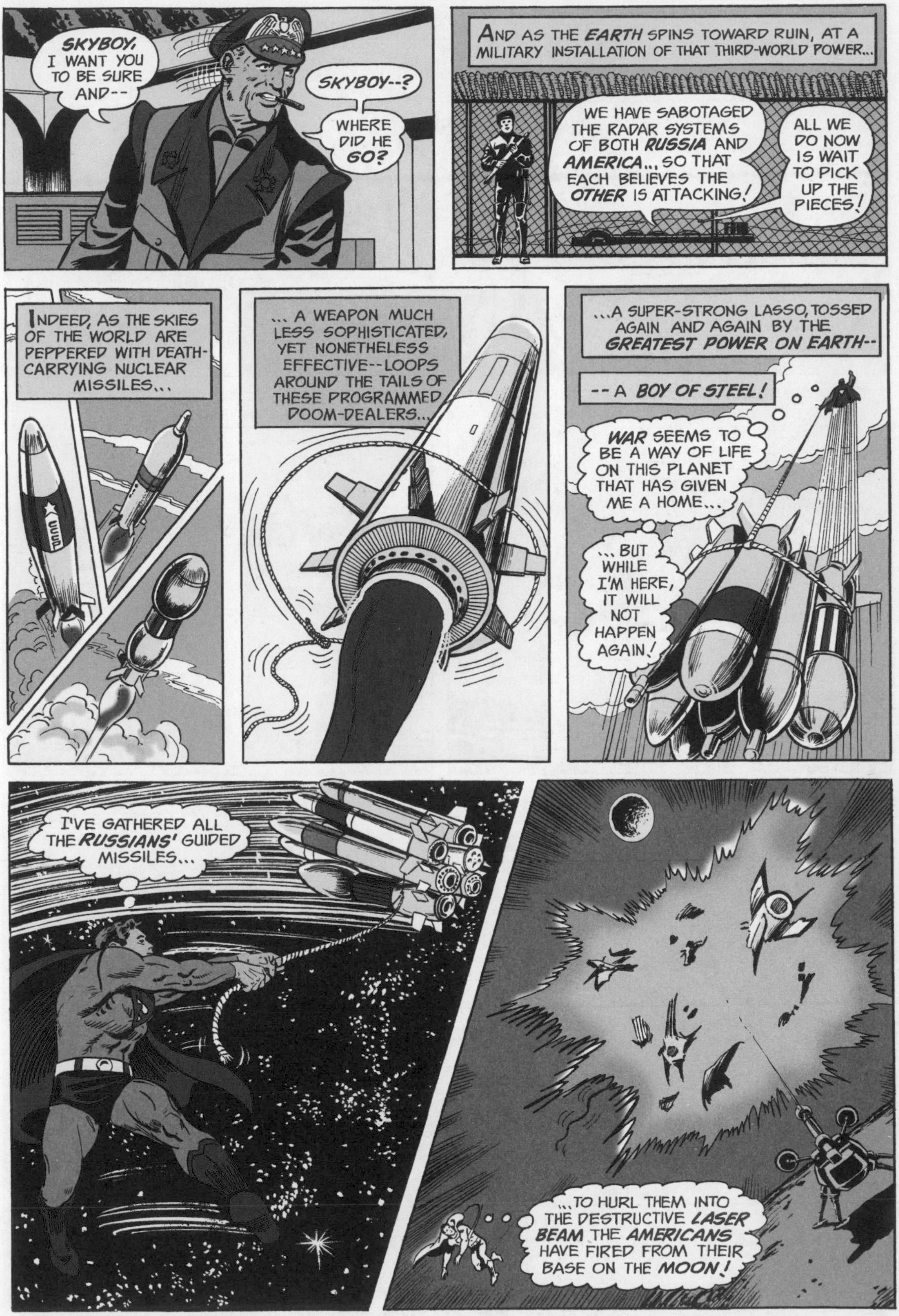

SKYBOY, I WANT YOU TO BE SURE AND--
SKYBOY--?
WHERE DID HE GO?
AND AS THE EARTH SPINS TOWARD RUIN, AT A MILITARY INSTALLATION OF THAT THIRD-WORLD POWER...
WE HAVE SABOTAGED THE RADAR SYSTEMS OF BOTH RUSSIA AND AMERICA... SO THAT EACH BELIEVES THE OTHER IS ATTACKING!
ALL WE DO NOW IS WAIT TO PICK UP THE PIECES!
INDEED, AS THE SKIES OF THE WORLD ARE PEPPERED WITH DEATH-CARRYING NUCLEAR MISSILES...
... A WEAPON MUCH LESS SOPHISTICATED, YET NONETHELESS EFFECTIVE--LOOPS AROUND THE TAILS OF THESE PROGRAMMED DOOM-DEALERS...
...A SUPER-STRONG LASSO, TOSSED AGAIN AND AGAIN BY THE GREATEST POWER ON EARTH--
-- A BOY OF STEEL!
WAR SEEMS TO BE A WAY OF LIFE ON THIS PLANET THAT HAS GIVEN ME A HOME...
...BUT WHILE I'M HERE, IT WILL NOT HAPPEN AGAIN!
I'VE GATHERED ALL THE RUSSIANS' GUIDED MISSILES...
...TO HURL THEM INTO THE DESTRUCTIVE LASER BEAM THE AMERICANS HAVE FIRED FROM THEIR BASE ON THE MOON!

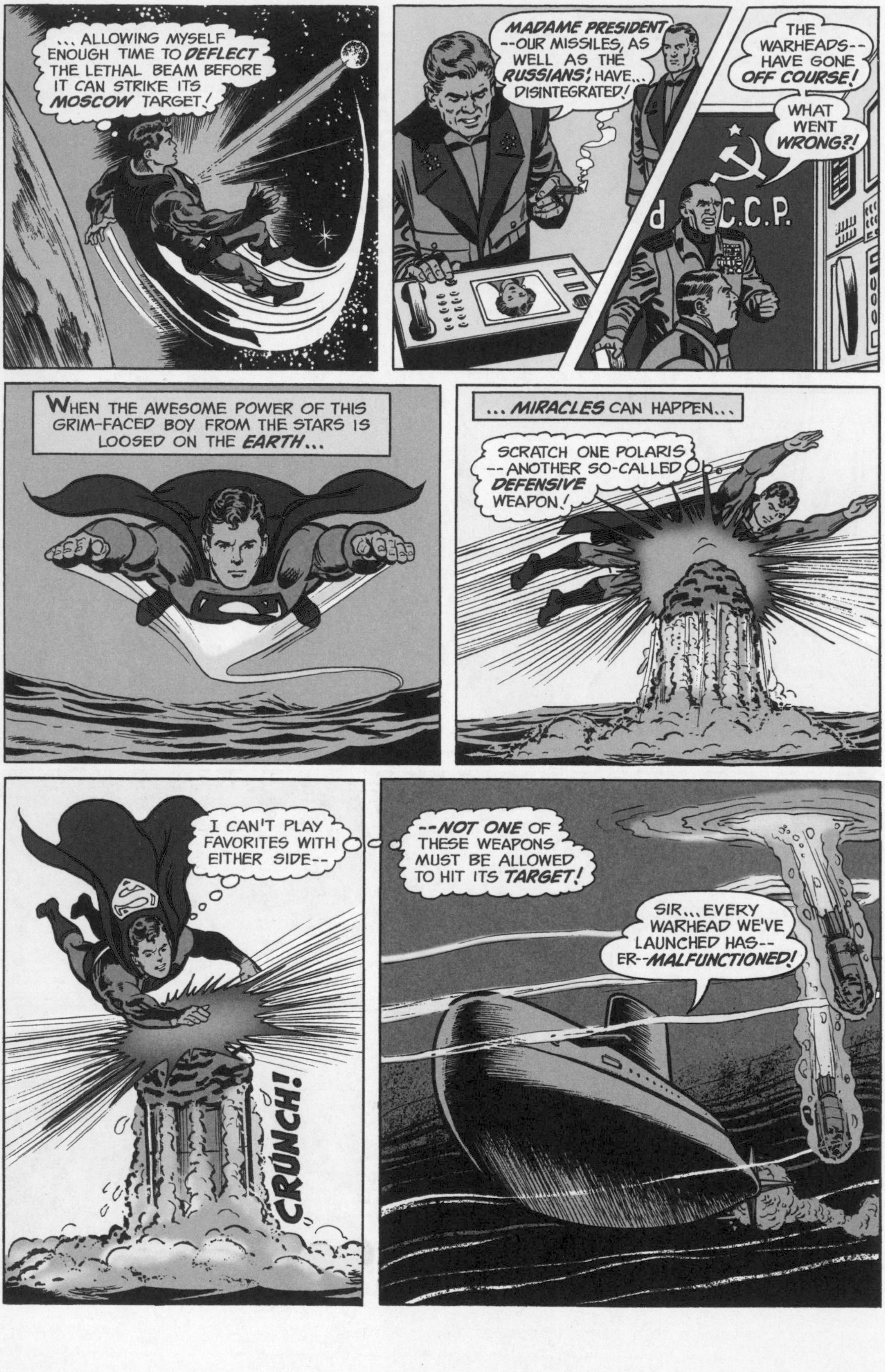

...ALLOWING MYSELF ENOUGH TIME TO DEFLECT THE LETHAL BEAM BEFORE IT CAN STRIKE ITS MOSCOW TARGET!
MADAME PRESIDENT --OUR MISSILES, AS WELL AS THE RUSSIANS; HAVE... DISINTEGRATED!
THE WARHEADS-- HAVE GONE OFF COURSE!
WHAT WENT WRONG?!
C.C.C.P.
WHEN THE AWESOME POWER OF THIS GRIM-FACED BOY FROM THE STARS IS LOOSED ON THE EARTH...
...MIRACLES CAN HAPPEN...
SCRATCH ONE POLARIS --ANOTHER SO-CALLED DEFENSIVE WEAPON!
I CAN'T PLAY FAVORITES WITH EITHER SIDE--
--NOT ONE OF THESE WEAPONS MUST BE ALLOWED TO HIT ITS TARGET!
CRUNCH!
SIR...EVERY WARHEAD WE'VE LAUNCHED HAS-- ER--MALFUNCTIONED!

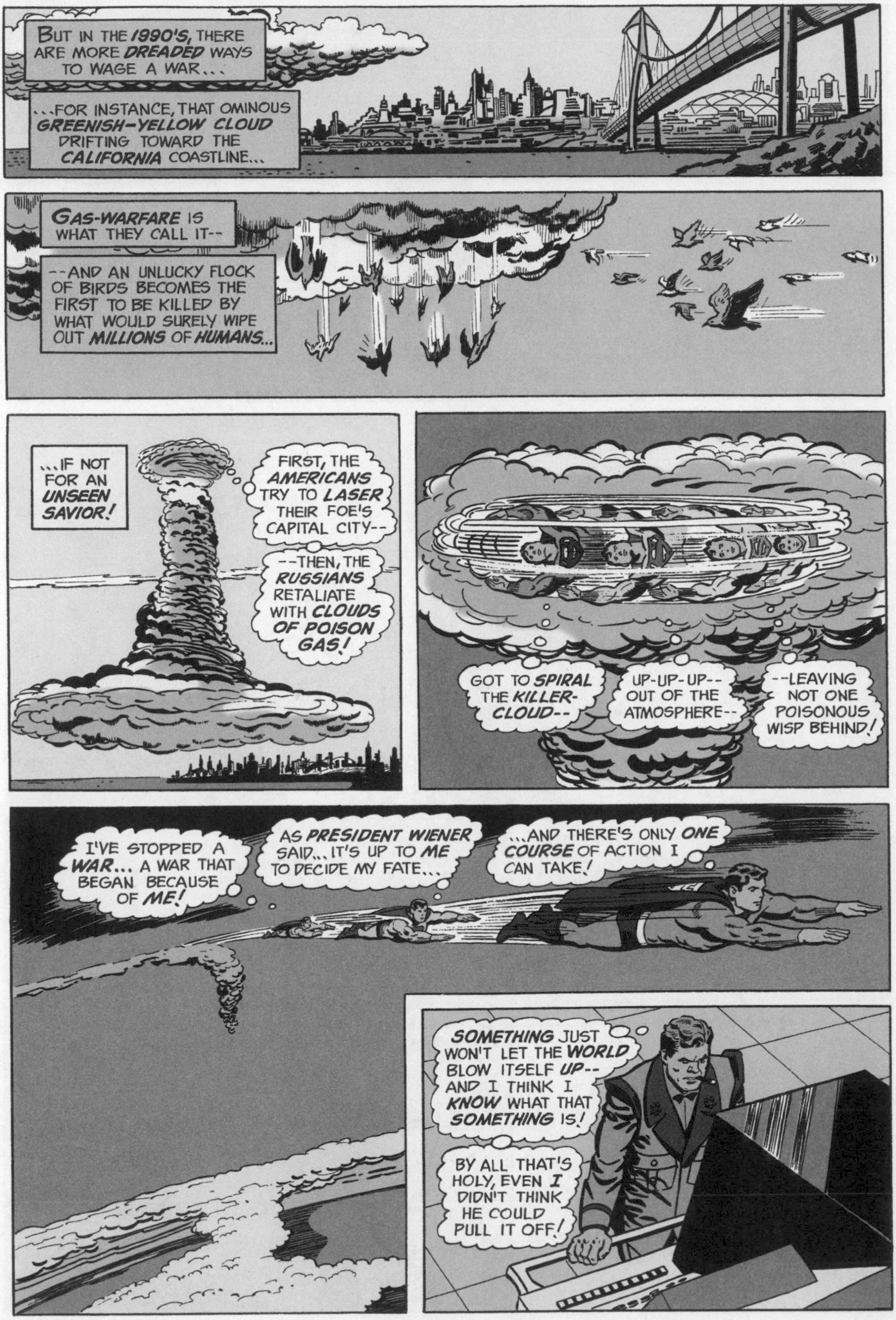
BUT IN THE 1990'S, THERE ARE MORE DREADED WAYS TO WAGE A WAR...
...FOR INSTANCE, THAT OMINOUS GREENISH-YELLOW CLOUD DRIFTING TOWARD THE CALIFORNIA COASTLINE...
GAS-WARFARE IS WHAT THEY CALL IT--
--AND AN UNLUCKY FLOCK OF BIRDS BECOMES THE FIRST TO BE KILLED BY WHAT WOULD SURELY WIPE OUT MILLIONS OF HUMANS...
...IF NOT FOR AN UNSEEN SAVIOR!
FIRST, THE AMERICANS TRY TO LASER THEIR FOE'S CAPITAL CITY--
--THEN, THE RUSSIANS RETALIATE WITH CLOUDS OF POISON GAS!
GOT TO SPIRAL THE KILLER-CLOUD--
UP-UP-UP-- OUT OF THE ATMOSPHERE--
--LEAVING NOT ONE POISONOUS WISP BEHIND!
I'VE STOPPED A WAR... A WAR THAT BEGAN BECAUSE OF ME!
AS PRESIDENT WIENER SAID... IT'S UP TO ME TO DECIDE MY FATE...
...AND THERE'S ONLY ONE COURSE OF ACTION I CAN TAKE!
SOMETHING JUST WON'T LET THE WORLD BLOW ITSELF UP-- AND I THINK I KNOW WHAT THAT SOMETHING IS!
BY ALL THAT'S HOLY, EVEN I DIDN'T THINK HE COULD PULL IT OFF!

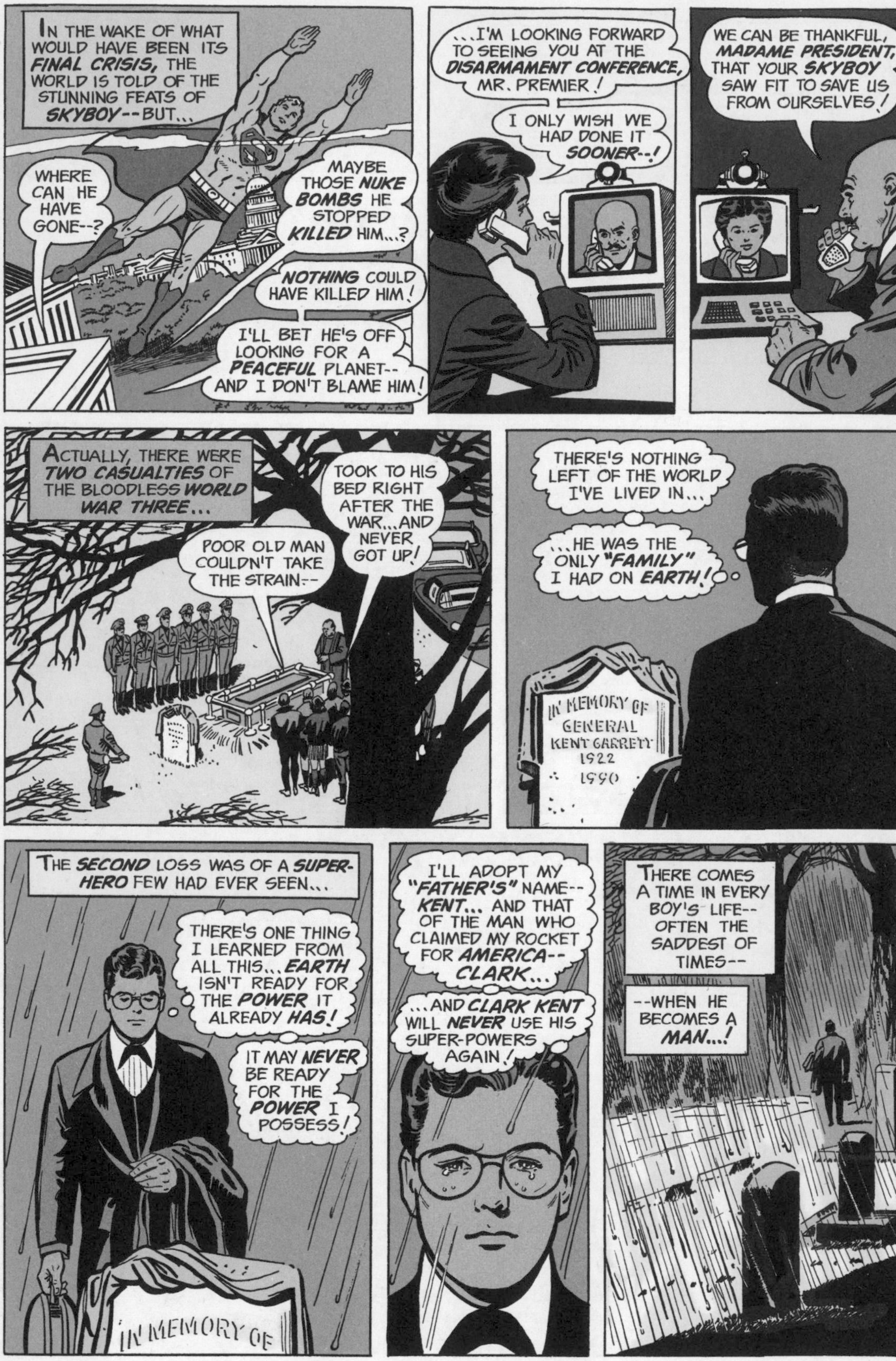
IN THE WAKE OF WHAT WOULD HAVE BEEN ITS FINAL CRISIS, THE WORLD IS TOLD OF THE STUNNING FEATS OF SKYBOY--BUT...
WHERE CAN HE HAVE GONE--?
MAYBE THOSE NUKE BOMBS HE STOPPED KILLED HIM...?
NOTHING COULD HAVE KILLED HIM!
I'LL BET HE'S OFF LOOKING FOR A PEACEFUL PLANET--AND I DON'T BLAME HIM!
...I'M LOOKING FORWARD TO SEEING YOU AT THE DISARMAMENT CONFERENCE, MR. PREMIER!
I ONLY WISH WE HAD DONE IT SOONER--!
WE CAN BE THANKFUL, MADAME PRESIDENT, THAT YOUR SKYBOY SAW FIT TO SAVE US FROM OURSELVES!
ACTUALLY, THERE WERE TWO CASUALTIES OF THE BLOODLESS WORLD WAR THREE...
POOR OLD MAN COULDN'T TAKE THE STRAIN--
TOOK TO HIS BED RIGHT AFTER THE WAR...AND NEVER GOT UP!
THERE'S NOTHING LEFT OF THE WORLD I'VE LIVED IN...
...HE WAS THE ONLY "FAMILY" I HAD ON EARTH!
IN MEMORY OF GENERAL KENT GARRETT 1922 1990
THE SECOND LOSS WAS OF A SUPER-HERO FEW HAD EVER SEEN...
THERE'S ONE THING I LEARNED FROM ALL THIS...EARTH ISN'T READY FOR THE POWER IT ALREADY HAS!
IT MAY NEVER BE READY FOR THE POWER I POSSESS!
IN MEMORY OF
I'LL ADOPT MY "FATHER'S" NAME--KENT... AND THAT OF THE MAN WHO CLAIMED MY ROCKET FOR AMERICA--CLARK...
...AND CLARK KENT WILL NEVER USE HIS SUPER-POWERS AGAIN!
THERE COMES A TIME IN EVERY BOY'S LIFE--OFTEN THE SADDEST OF TIMES--
--WHEN HE BECOMES A MAN...!

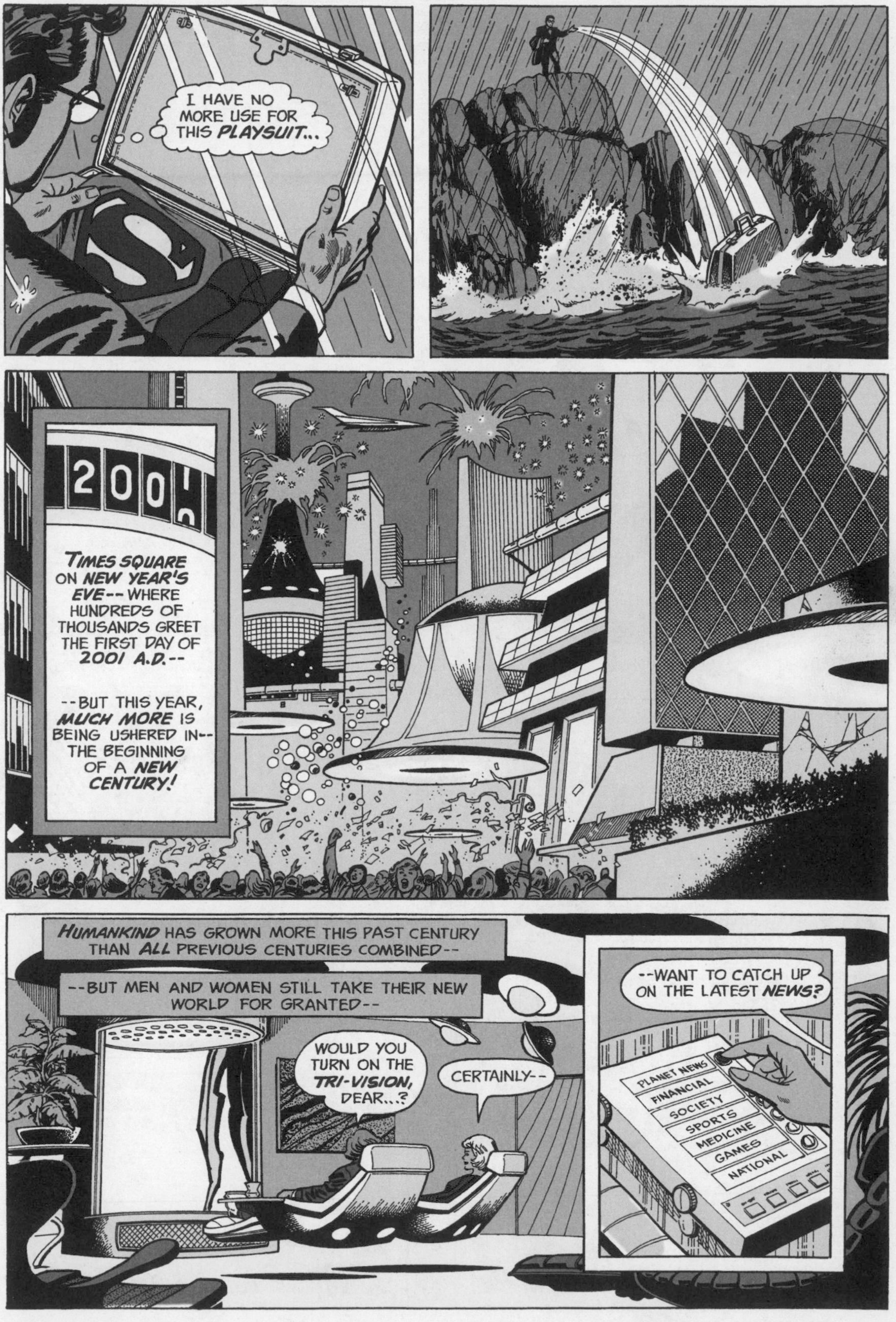
I HAVE NO MORE USE FOR THIS PLAYSUIT...
2001
TIMES SQUARE ON NEW YEAR'S EVE-- WHERE HUNDREDS OF THOUSANDS GREET THE FIRST DAY OF 2001 A.D.--
--BUT THIS YEAR, MUCH MORE IS BEING USHERED IN-- THE BEGINNING OF A NEW CENTURY!
HUMANKIND HAS GROWN MORE THIS PAST CENTURY THAN ALL PREVIOUS CENTURIES COMBINED--
--BUT MEN AND WOMEN STILL TAKE THEIR NEW WORLD FOR GRANTED--
WOULD YOU TURN ON THE TRI-VISION, DEAR...?
CERTAINLY--
--WANT TO CATCH UP ON THE LATEST NEWS?
PLANET NEWS
FINANCIAL
SOCIETY
SPORTS
MEDICINE
GAMES
NATIONAL

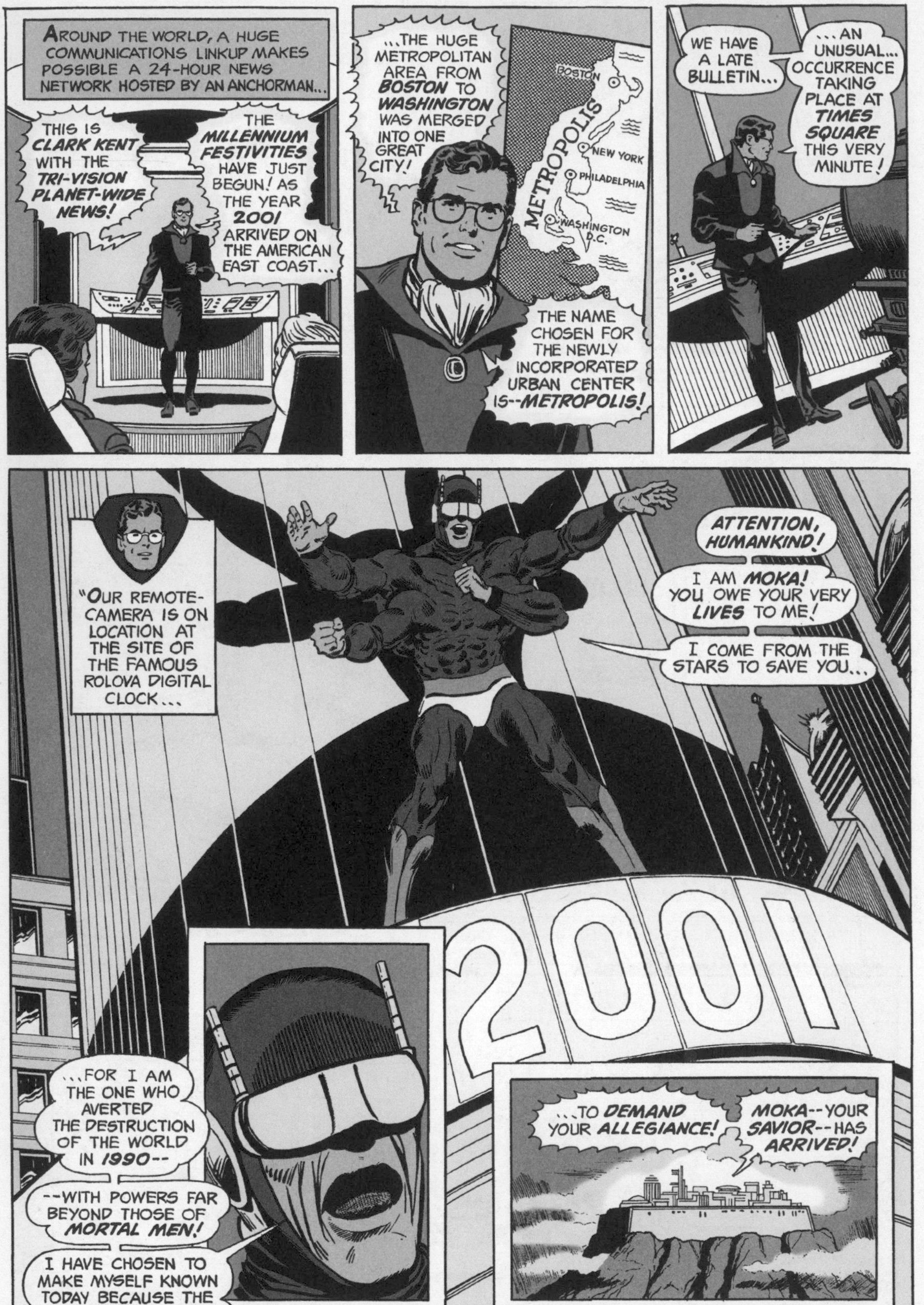

AROUND THE WORLD, A HUGE COMMUNICATIONS LINKUP MAKES POSSIBLE A 24-HOUR NEWS NETWORK HOSTED BY AN ANCHORMAN...
THIS IS CLARK KENT WITH THE TRI-VISION PLANET-WIDE NEWS!
THE MILLENNIUM FESTIVITIES HAVE JUST BEGUN! AS THE YEAR 2001 ARRIVED ON THE AMERICAN EAST COAST...
...THE HUGE METROPOLITAN AREA FROM BOSTON TO WASHINGTON WAS MERGED INTO ONE GREAT CITY!
BOSTON
METROPOLIS
NEW YORK
PHILADELPHIA
WASHINGTON D.C.
THE NAME CHOSEN FOR THE NEWLY INCORPORATED URBAN CENTER IS--METROPOLIS!
WE HAVE A LATE BULLETIN...
...AN UNUSUAL... OCCURRENCE TAKING PLACE AT TIMES SQUARE THIS VERY MINUTE!
"OUR REMOTE-CAMERA IS ON LOCATION AT THE SITE OF THE FAMOUS ROLOVA DIGITAL CLOCK...
ATTENTION, HUMANKIND!
I AM MOKA! YOU OWE YOUR VERY LIVES TO ME!
I COME FROM THE STARS TO SAVE YOU...
2001
...FOR I AM THE ONE WHO AVERTED THE DESTRUCTION OF THE WORLD IN 1990--
--WITH POWERS FAR BEYOND THOSE OF MORTAL MEN!
I HAVE CHOSEN TO MAKE MYSELF KNOWN TODAY BECAUSE THE TIME HAS COME...
...TO DEMAND YOUR ALLEGIANCE!
MOKA--YOUR SAVIOR--HAS ARRIVED!

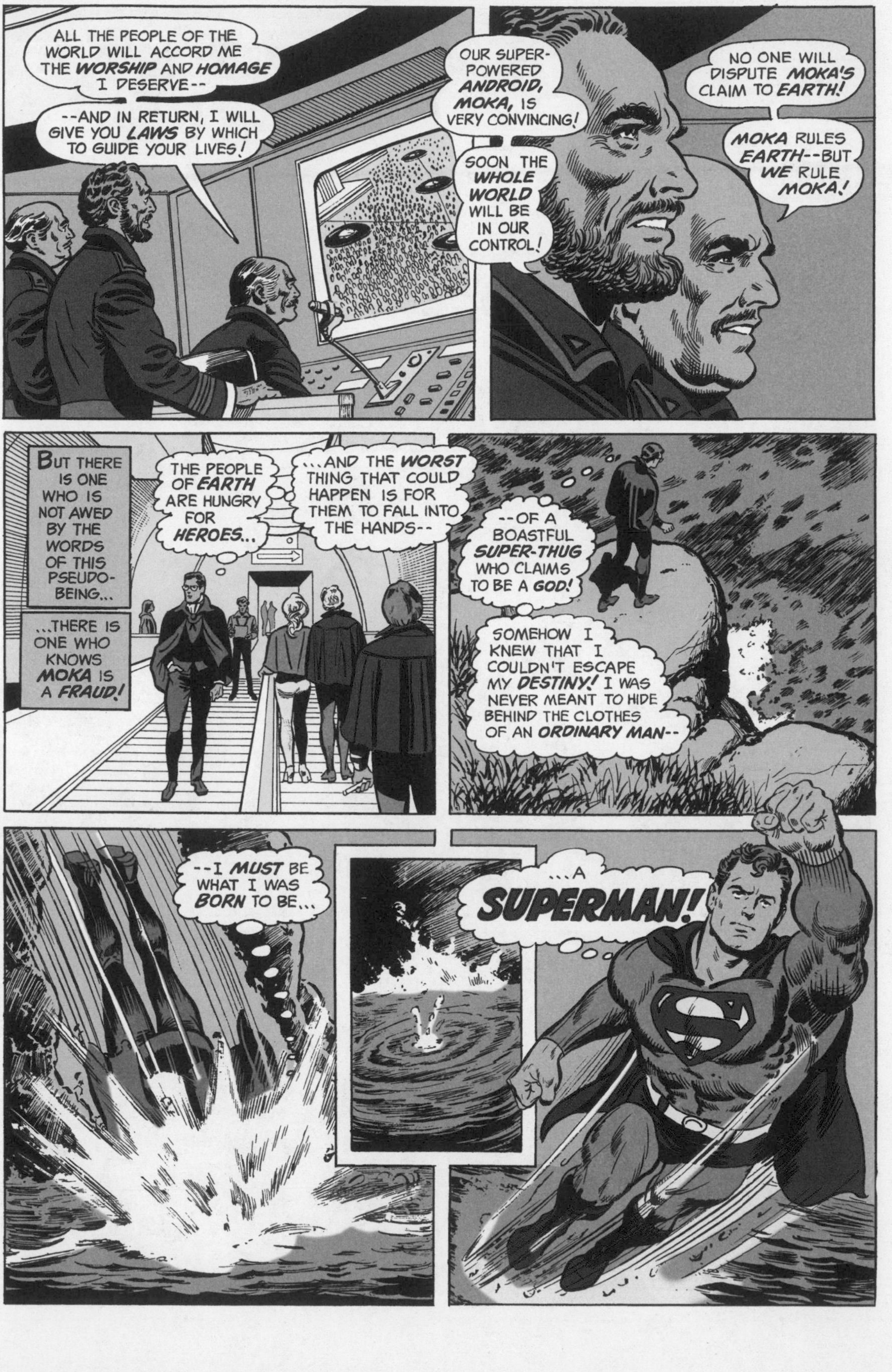
ALL THE PEOPLE OF THE WORLD WILL ACCORD ME THE WORSHIP AND HOMAGE I DESERVE--
--AND IN RETURN, I WILL GIVE YOU LAWS BY WHICH TO GUIDE YOUR LIVES!
OUR SUPER-POWERED ANDROID, MOKA, IS VERY CONVINCING!
SOON THE WHOLE WORLD WILL BE IN OUR CONTROL!
NO ONE WILL DISPUTE MOKA'S CLAIM TO EARTH!
MOKA RULES EARTH--BUT WE RULE MOKA!
BUT THERE IS ONE WHO IS NOT AWED BY THE WORDS OF THIS PSEUDO-BEING...
...THERE IS ONE WHO KNOWS MOKA IS A FRAUD!
THE PEOPLE OF EARTH ARE HUNGRY FOR HEROES...
...AND THE WORST THING THAT COULD HAPPEN IS FOR THEM TO FALL INTO THE HANDS--
--OF A BOASTFUL SUPER-THUG WHO CLAIMS TO BE A GOD!
SOMEHOW I KNEW THAT I COULDN'T ESCAPE MY DESTINY! I WAS NEVER MEANT TO HIDE BEHIND THE CLOTHES OF AN ORDINARY MAN--
--I MUST BE WHAT I WAS BORN TO BE...
...A SUPERMAN!

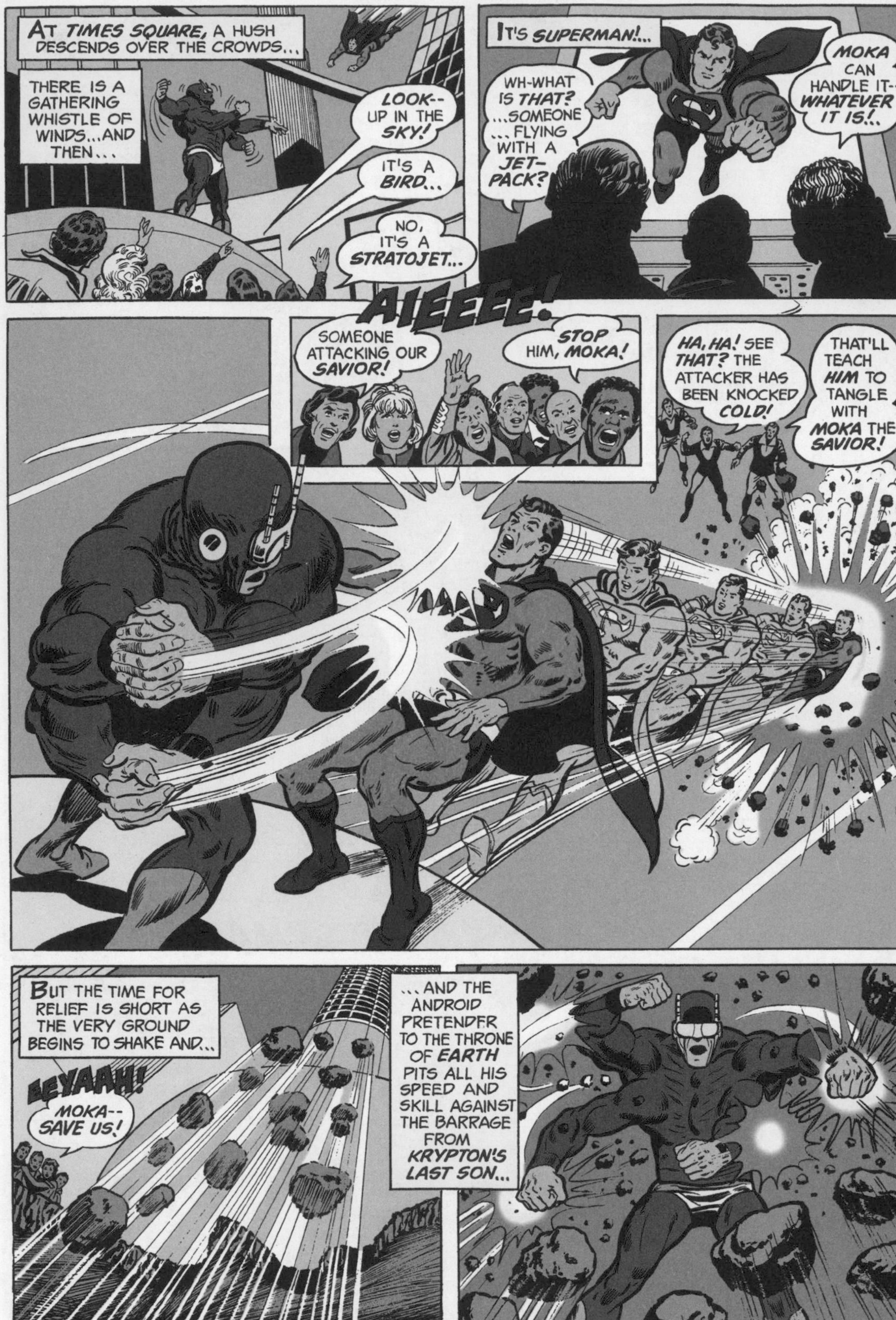

AT TIMES SQUARE, A HUSH DESCENDS OVER THE CROWDS...
THERE IS A GATHERING WHISTLE OF WINDS...AND THEN...
LOOK-- UP IN THE SKY!
IT'S A BIRD...
NO, IT'S A STRATOJET...
IT'S SUPERMAN!...
WH-WHAT IS THAT? ...SOMEONE ... FLYING WITH A JET-PACK?
MOKA CAN HANDLE IT-- WHATEVER IT IS!..
AIEEEE!
SOMEONE ATTACKING OUR SAVIOR!
STOP HIM, MOKA!
HA, HA! SEE THAT? THE ATTACKER HAS BEEN KNOCKED COLD!
THAT'LL TEACH HIM TO TANGLE WITH MOKA THE SAVIOR!
BUT THE TIME FOR RELIEF IS SHORT AS THE VERY GROUND BEGINS TO SHAKE AND...
EEYAAH!
MOKA-- SAVE US!
...AND THE ANDROID PRETENDER TO THE THRONE OF EARTH PITS ALL HIS SPEED AND SKILL AGAINST THE BARRAGE FROM KRYPTON'S LAST SON...

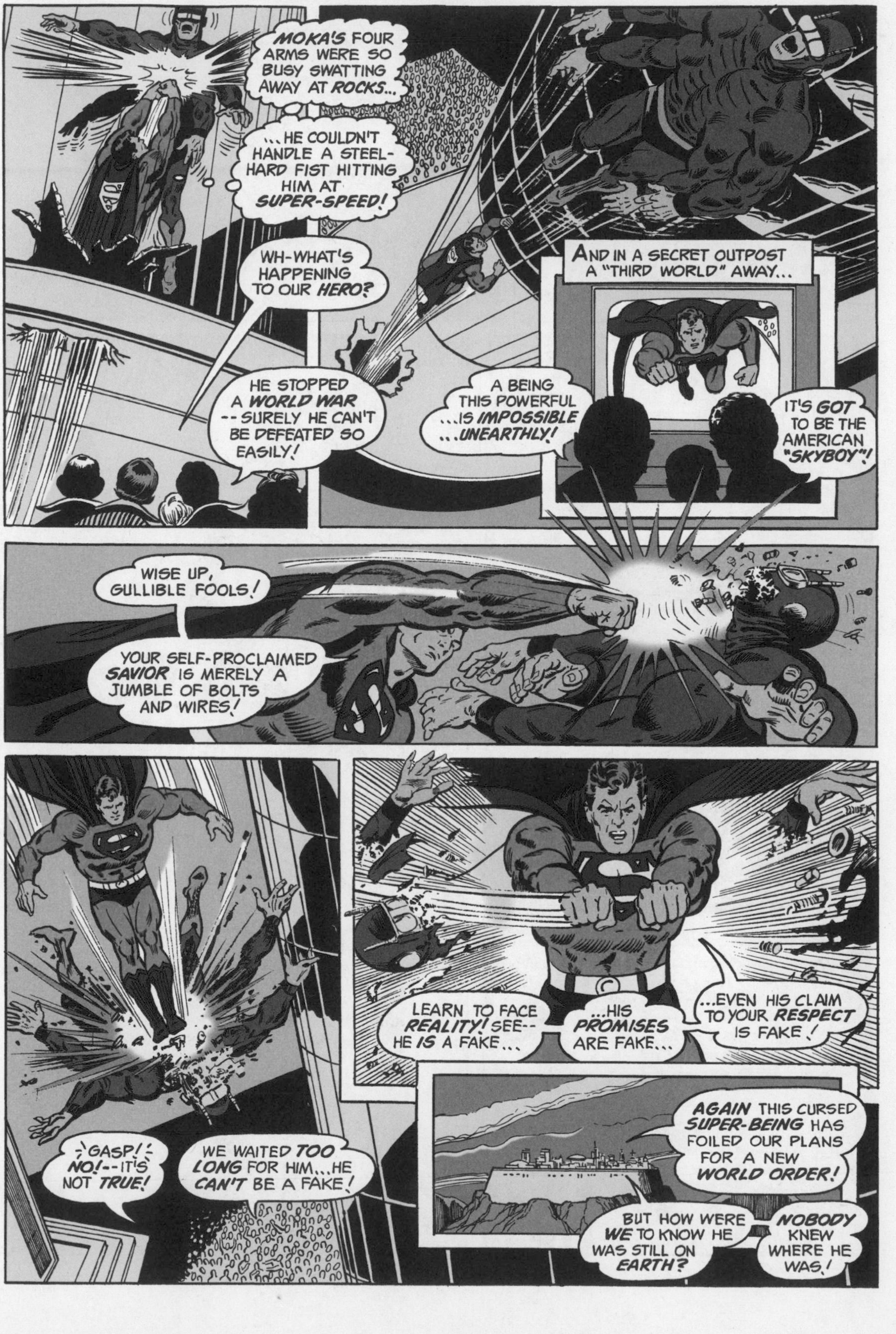
MOKA'S FOUR ARMS WERE SO BUSY SWATTING AWAY AT ROCKS...
...HE COULDN'T HANDLE A STEEL-HARD FIST HITTING HIM AT SUPER-SPEED!
WH-WHAT'S HAPPENING TO OUR HERO?
HE STOPPED A WORLD WAR -- SURELY HE CAN'T BE DEFEATED SO EASILY!
AND IN A SECRET OUTPOST A "THIRD WORLD" AWAY...
A BEING THIS POWERFUL ...IS IMPOSSIBLE ...UNEARTHLY!
IT'S GOT TO BE THE AMERICAN "SKYBOY"!
WISE UP, GULLIBLE FOOLS!
YOUR SELF-PROCLAIMED SAVIOR IS MERELY A JUMBLE OF BOLTS AND WIRES!
-GASP!- NO!--IT'S NOT TRUE!
WE WAITED TOO LONG FOR HIM...HE CAN'T BE A FAKE!
LEARN TO FACE REALITY! SEE-- HE IS A FAKE...
...HIS PROMISES ARE FAKE...
...EVEN HIS CLAIM TO YOUR RESPECT IS FAKE!
AGAIN THIS CURSED SUPER-BEING HAS FOILED OUR PLANS FOR A NEW WORLD ORDER!
BUT HOW WERE WE TO KNOW HE WAS STILL ON EARTH?
NOBODY KNEW WHERE HE WAS!

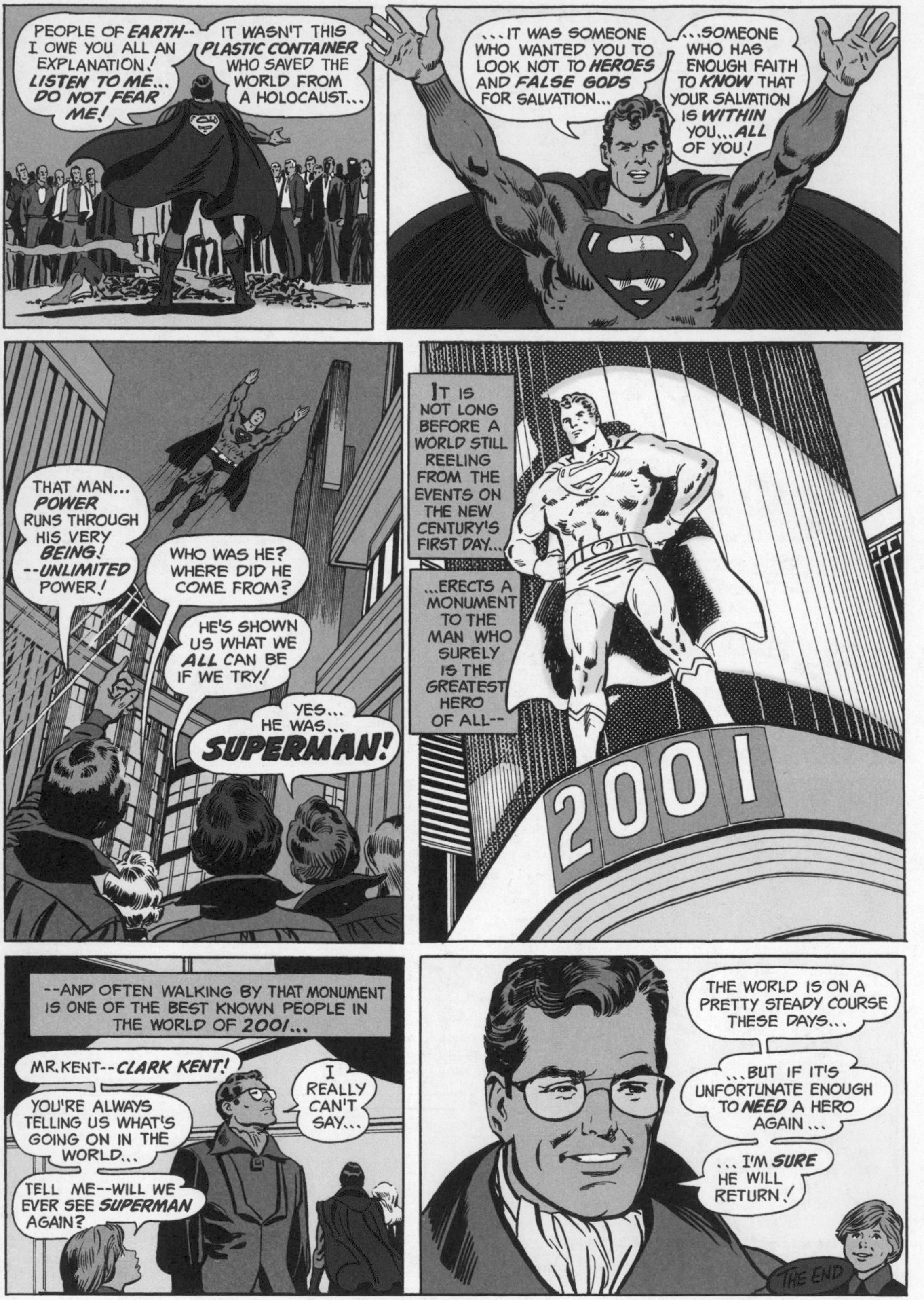
PEOPLE OF EARTH-- I OWE YOU ALL AN EXPLANATION! LISTEN TO ME... DO NOT FEAR ME!
IT WASN'T THIS PLASTIC CONTAINER WHO SAVED THE WORLD FROM A HOLOCAUST...
...IT WAS SOMEONE WHO WANTED YOU TO LOOK NOT TO HEROES AND FALSE GODS FOR SALVATION...
...SOMEONE WHO HAS ENOUGH FAITH TO KNOW THAT YOUR SALVATION IS WITHIN YOU...ALL OF YOU!
THAT MAN... POWER RUNS THROUGH HIS VERY BEING! --UNLIMITED POWER!
WHO WAS HE? WHERE DID HE COME FROM?
HE'S SHOWN US WHAT WE ALL CAN BE IF WE TRY!
YES... HE WAS... SUPERMAN!
IT IS NOT LONG BEFORE A WORLD STILL REELING FROM THE EVENTS ON THE NEW CENTURY'S FIRST DAY...
...ERECTS A MONUMENT TO THE MAN WHO SURELY IS THE GREATEST HERO OF ALL--
2001
--AND OFTEN WALKING BY THAT MONUMENT IS ONE OF THE BEST KNOWN PEOPLE IN THE WORLD OF 2001...
MR. KENT--CLARK KENT!
YOU'RE ALWAYS TELLING US WHAT'S GOING ON IN THE WORLD...
TELL ME--WILL WE EVER SEE SUPERMAN AGAIN?
I REALLY CAN'T SAY...
THE WORLD IS ON A PRETTY STEADY COURSE THESE DAYS...
...BUT IF IT'S UNFORTUNATE ENOUGH TO NEED A HERO AGAIN...
...I'M SURE HE WILL RETURN!
THE END

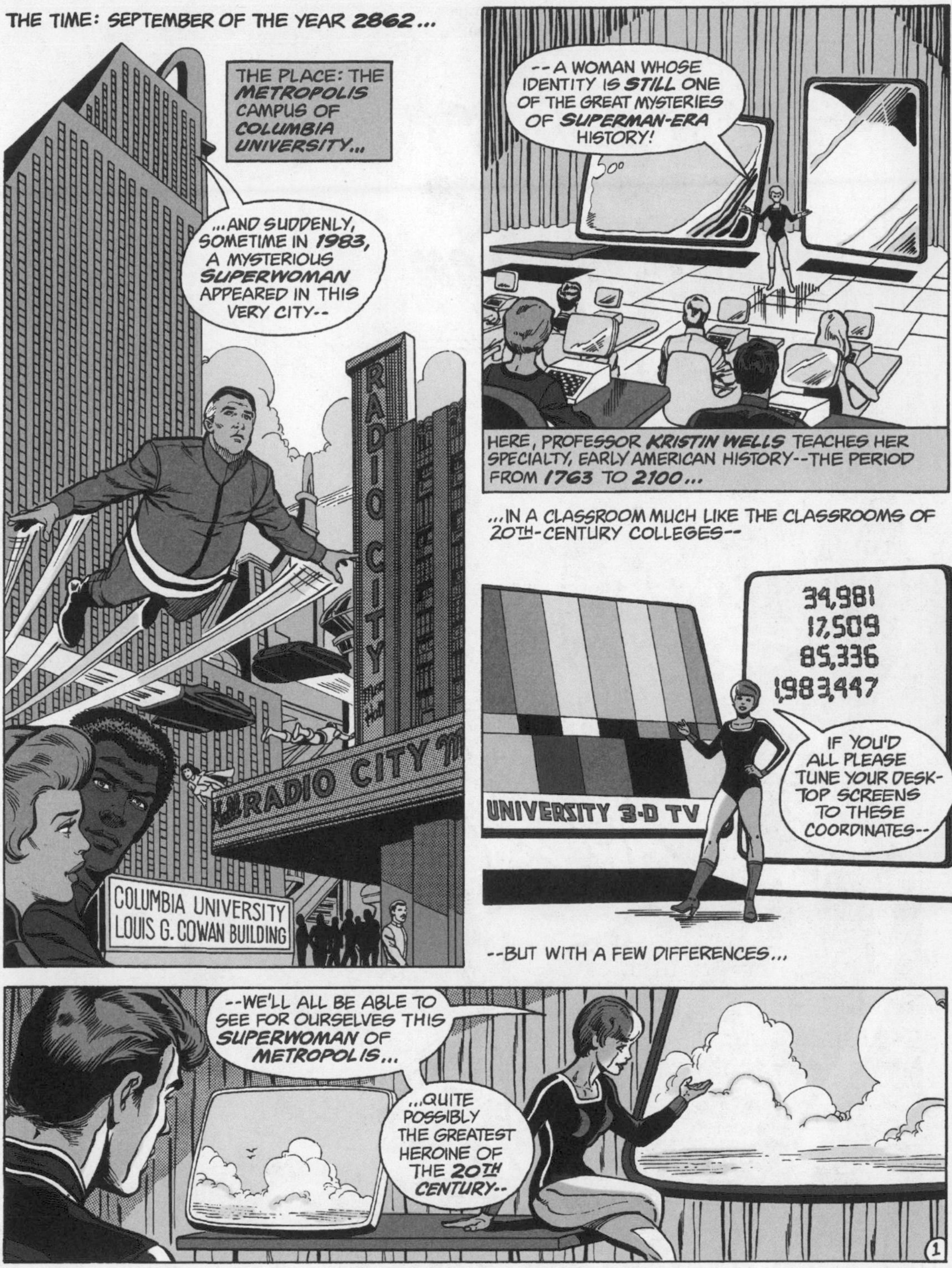
THE TIME: SEPTEMBER OF THE YEAR 2862...
THE PLACE: THE METROPOLIS CAMPUS OF COLUMBIA UNIVERSITY...
...AND SUDDENLY, SOMETIME IN 1983, A MYSTERIOUS SUPERWOMAN APPEARED IN THIS VERY CITY--
RADIO CITY
COLUMBIA UNIVERSITY
LOUIS G. COWAN BUILDING
--A WOMAN WHOSE IDENTITY IS STILL ONE OF THE GREAT MYSTERIES OF SUPERMAN-ERA HISTORY!
HERE, PROFESSOR KRISTIN WELLS TEACHES HER SPECIALTY, EARLY AMERICAN HISTORY--THE PERIOD FROM 1763 TO 2100...
...IN A CLASSROOM MUCH LIKE THE CLASSROOMS OF 20TH-CENTURY COLLEGES--
34,981
17,509
85,336
1,983,447
UNIVERSITY 3-D TV
IF YOU'D ALL PLEASE TUNE YOUR DESK-TOP SCREENS TO THESE COORDINATES--
--BUT WITH A FEW DIFFERENCES...
--WE'LL ALL BE ABLE TO SEE FOR OURSELVES THIS SUPERWOMAN OF METROPOLIS...
...QUITE POSSIBLY THE GREATEST HEROINE OF THE 20TH CENTURY--
1

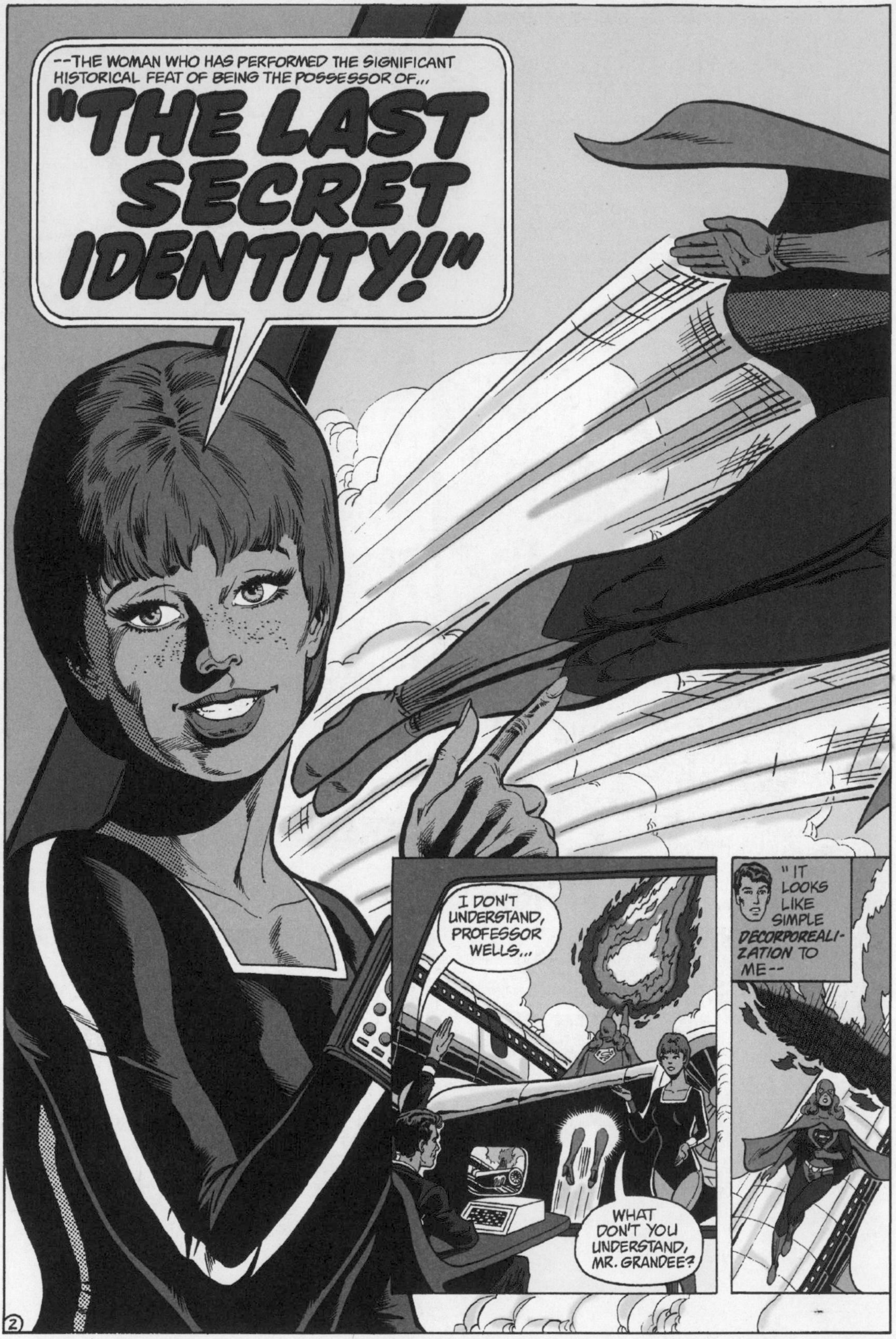
--THE WOMAN WHO HAS PERFORMED THE SIGNIFICANT HISTORICAL FEAT OF BEING THE POSSESSOR OF...
"THE LAST SECRET IDENTITY!"
I DON'T UNDERSTAND, PROFESSOR WELLS...
WHAT DON'T YOU UNDERSTAND, MR. GRANDEE?
"IT LOOKS LIKE SIMPLE DECORPOREALIZATION TO ME--
2

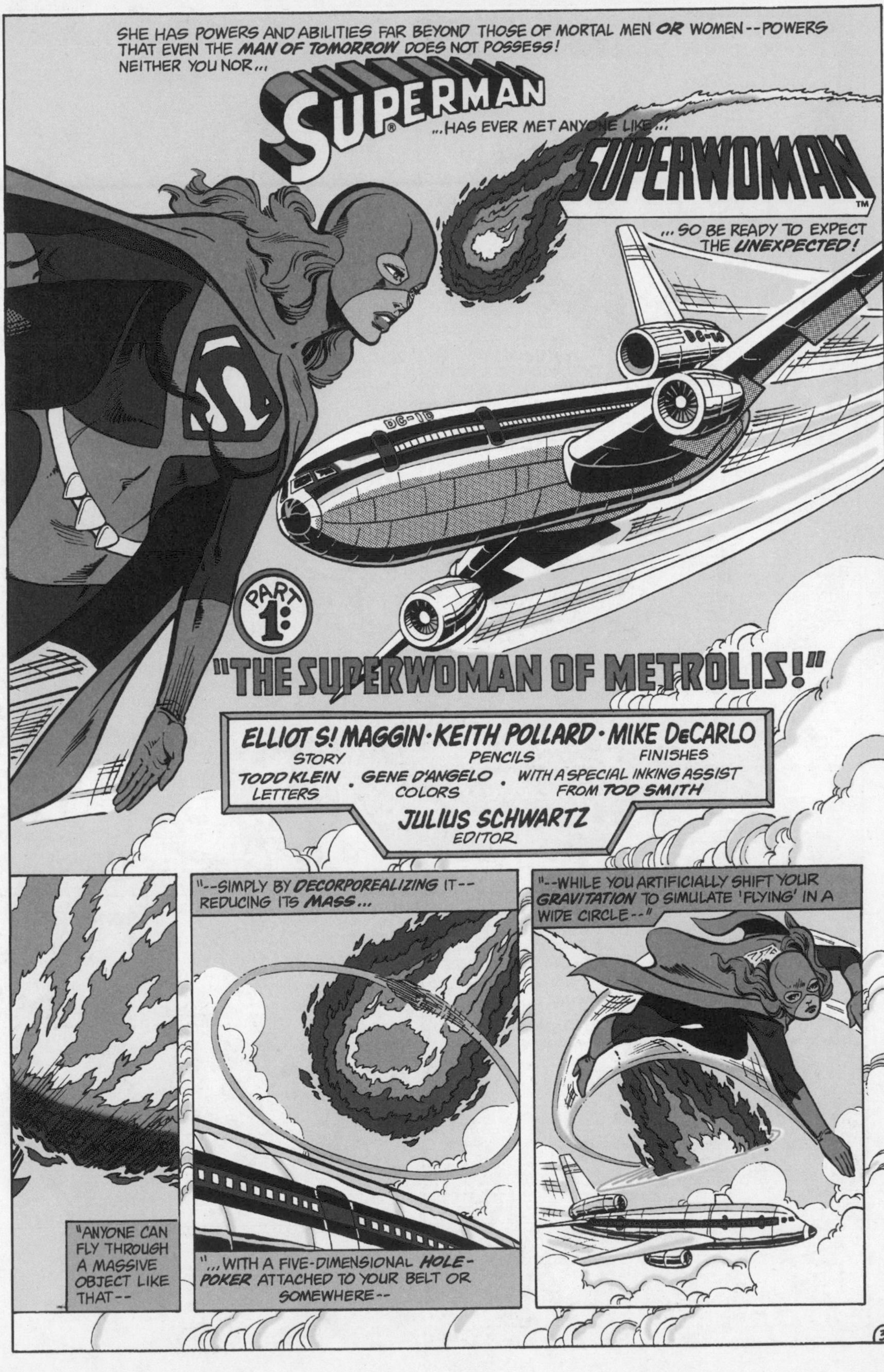
SHE HAS POWERS AND ABILITIES FAR BEYOND THOSE OF MORTAL MEN OR WOMEN--POWERS THAT EVEN THE MAN OF TOMORROW DOES NOT POSSESS! NEITHER YOU NOR...
SUPERMAN
...HAS EVER MET ANYONE LIKE...
SUPERWOMAN
...SO BE READY TO EXPECT THE UNEXPECTED!
DC-10
PART 1:
"THE SUPERWOMAN OF METROLIS!"
ELLIOT S! MAGGIN · KEITH POLLARD · MIKE DeCARLO
STORY PENCILS FINISHES
TODD KLEIN LETTERS · GENE D'ANGELO COLORS · WITH A SPECIAL INKING ASSIST FROM TOD SMITH
JULIUS SCHWARTZ EDITOR
"ANYONE CAN FLY THROUGH A MASSIVE OBJECT LIKE THAT--
"--SIMPLY BY DECORPOREALIZING IT-- REDUCING ITS MASS...
"...WITH A FIVE-DIMENSIONAL HOLE-POKER ATTACHED TO YOUR BELT OR SOMEWHERE--
"--WHILE YOU ARTIFICIALLY SHIFT YOUR GRAVITATION TO SIMULATE 'FLYING' IN A WIDE CIRCLE--"
3

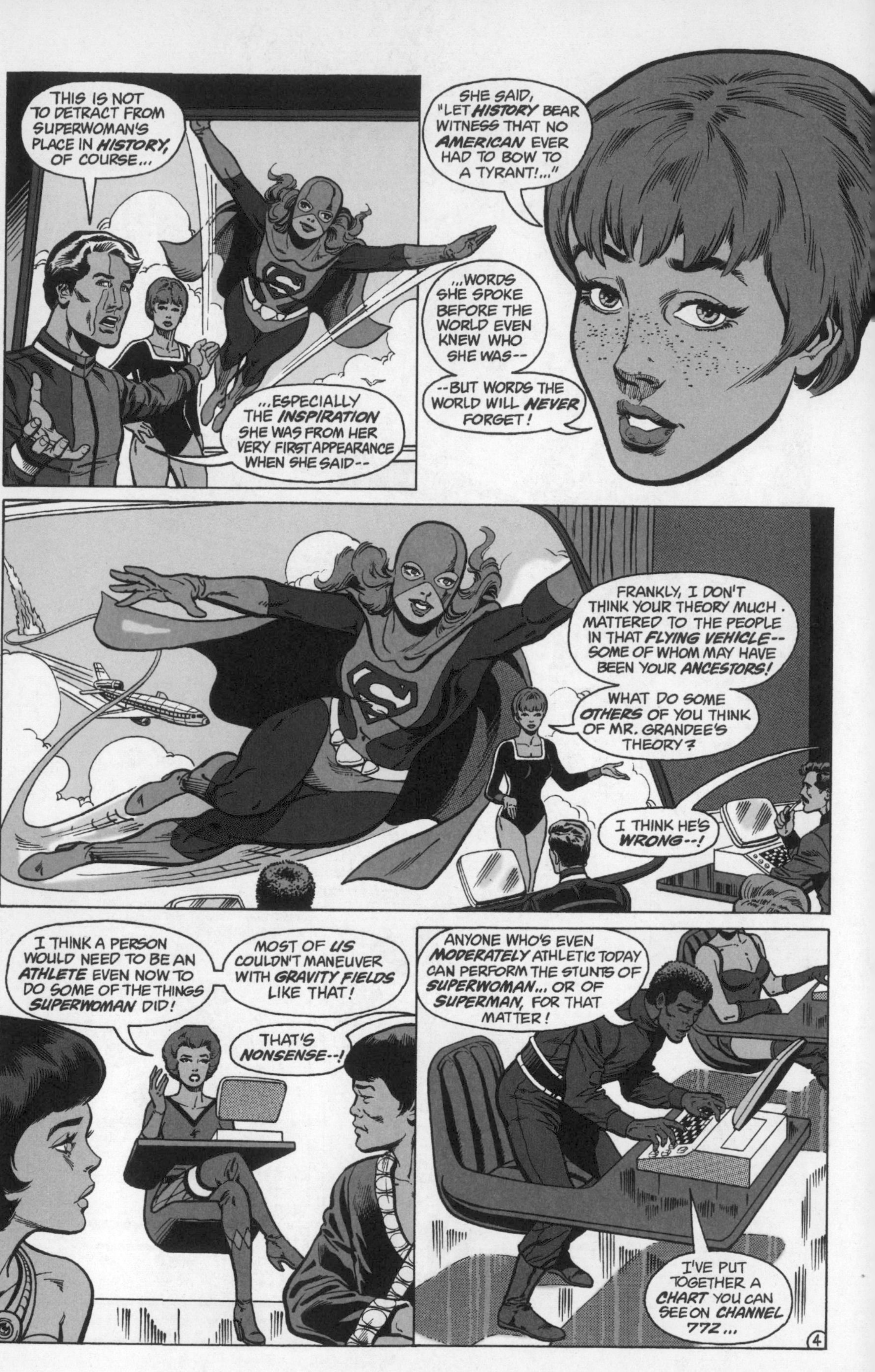
THIS IS NOT TO DETRACT FROM SUPERWOMAN'S PLACE IN HISTORY, OF COURSE...
...ESPECIALLY THE INSPIRATION SHE WAS FROM HER VERY FIRST APPEARANCE WHEN SHE SAID--
SHE SAID, "LET HISTORY BEAR WITNESS THAT NO AMERICAN EVER HAD TO BOW TO A TYRANT!..."
...WORDS SHE SPOKE BEFORE THE WORLD EVEN KNEW WHO SHE WAS--
--BUT WORDS THE WORLD WILL NEVER FORGET!
FRANKLY, I DON'T THINK YOUR THEORY MUCH MATTERED TO THE PEOPLE IN THAT FLYING VEHICLE-- SOME OF WHOM MAY HAVE BEEN YOUR ANCESTORS!
WHAT DO SOME OTHERS OF YOU THINK OF MR. GRANDEE'S THEORY?
I THINK HE'S WRONG--!
I THINK A PERSON WOULD NEED TO BE AN ATHLETE EVEN NOW TO DO SOME OF THE THINGS SUPERWOMAN DID!
MOST OF US COULDN'T MANEUVER WITH GRAVITY FIELDS LIKE THAT!
THAT'S NONSENSE--!
ANYONE WHO'S EVEN MODERATELY ATHLETIC TODAY CAN PERFORM THE STUNTS OF SUPERWOMAN... OR OF SUPERMAN, FOR THAT MATTER!
I'VE PUT TOGETHER A CHART YOU CAN SEE ON CHANNEL 772...
4

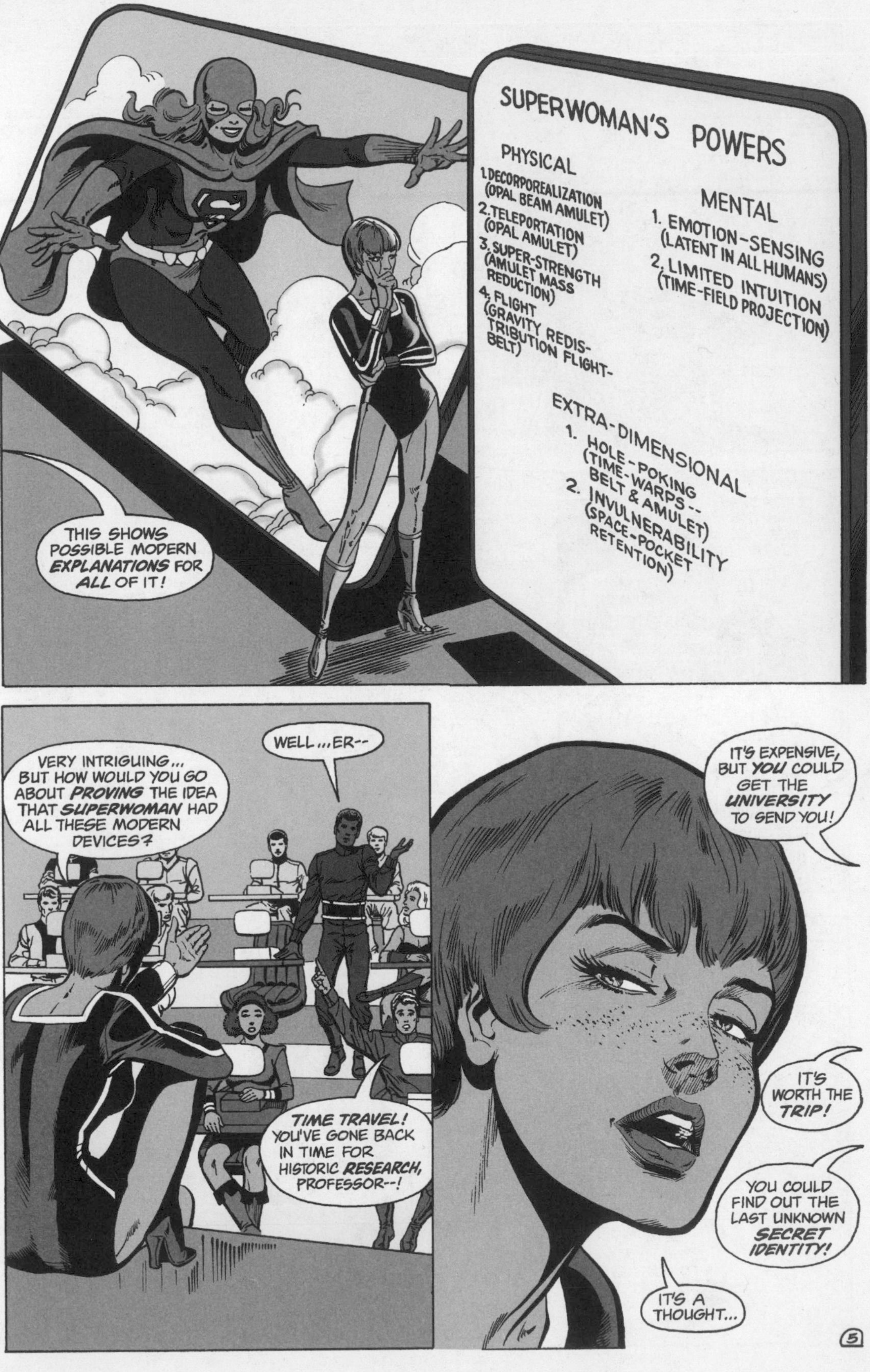
SUPERWOMAN'S POWERS
PHYSICAL
1. DECORPOREALIZATION (OPAL BEAM AMULET)
2. TELEPORTATION (OPAL AMULET)
3. SUPER-STRENGTH (AMULET MASS REDUCTION)
4. FLIGHT (GRAVITY REDIS-TRIBUTION FLIGHT-BELT)
MENTAL
1. EMOTION-SENSING (LATENT IN ALL HUMANS)
2. LIMITED INTUITION (TIME-FIELD PROJECTION)
EXTRA-DIMENSIONAL
1. HOLE-POKING (TIME-WARPS-- BELT & AMULET)
2. INVULNERABILITY (SPACE-POCKET RETENTION)
THIS SHOWS POSSIBLE MODERN EXPLANATIONS FOR ALL OF IT!
VERY INTRIGUING... BUT HOW WOULD YOU GO ABOUT PROVING THE IDEA THAT SUPERWOMAN HAD ALL THESE MODERN DEVICES?
WELL...ER--
TIME TRAVEL! YOU'VE GONE BACK IN TIME FOR HISTORIC RESEARCH, PROFESSOR--!
IT'S EXPENSIVE, BUT YOU COULD GET THE UNIVERSITY TO SEND YOU!
IT'S WORTH THE TRIP!
YOU COULD FIND OUT THE LAST UNKNOWN SECRET IDENTITY!
IT'S A THOUGHT...
5

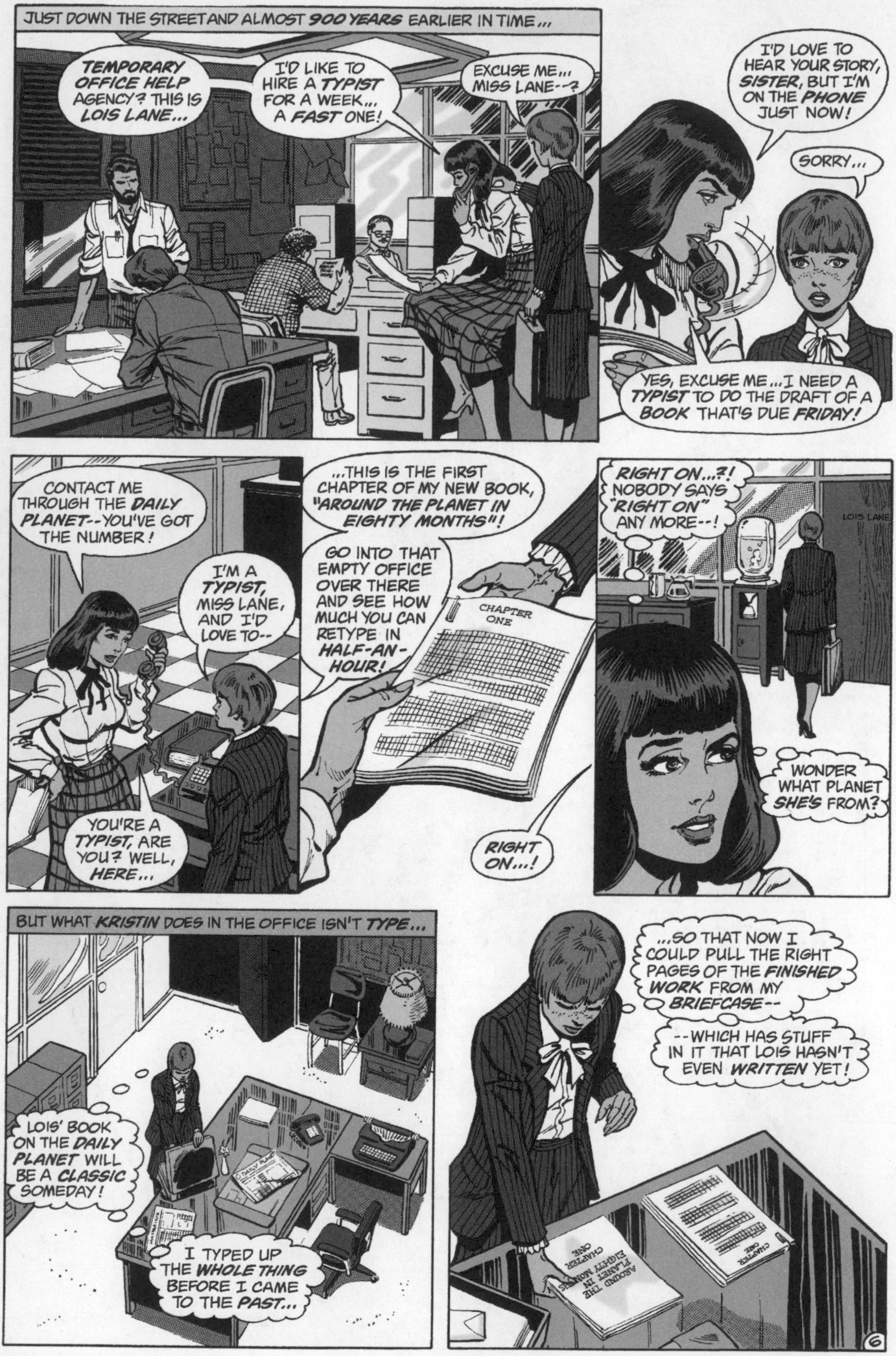
JUST DOWN THE STREET AND ALMOST 900 YEARS EARLIER IN TIME...
TEMPORARY OFFICE HELP AGENCY? THIS IS LOIS LANE...
I'D LIKE TO HIRE A TYPIST FOR A WEEK... A FAST ONE!
EXCUSE ME... MISS LANE--?
I'D LOVE TO HEAR YOUR STORY, SISTER, BUT I'M ON THE PHONE JUST NOW!
SORRY...
YES, EXCUSE ME... I NEED A TYPIST TO DO THE DRAFT OF A BOOK THAT'S DUE FRIDAY!
CONTACT ME THROUGH THE DAILY PLANET--YOU'VE GOT THE NUMBER!
I'M A TYPIST, MISS LANE, AND I'D LOVE TO--
YOU'RE A TYPIST, ARE YOU? WELL, HERE...
...THIS IS THE FIRST CHAPTER OF MY NEW BOOK, "AROUND THE PLANET IN EIGHTY MONTHS"!
GO INTO THAT EMPTY OFFICE OVER THERE AND SEE HOW MUCH YOU CAN RETYPE IN HALF-AN-HOUR!
CHAPTER ONE
RIGHT ON...!
RIGHT ON...?! NOBODY SAYS "RIGHT ON" ANY MORE--!
LOIS LANE
WONDER WHAT PLANET SHE'S FROM?
BUT WHAT KRISTIN DOES IN THE OFFICE ISN'T TYPE...
LOIS' BOOK ON THE DAILY PLANET WILL BE A CLASSIC SOMEDAY!
I TYPED UP THE WHOLE THING BEFORE I CAME TO THE PAST...
...SO THAT NOW I COULD PULL THE RIGHT PAGES OF THE FINISHED WORK FROM MY BRIEFCASE--
--WHICH HAS STUFF IN IT THAT LOIS HASN'T EVEN WRITTEN YET!
6

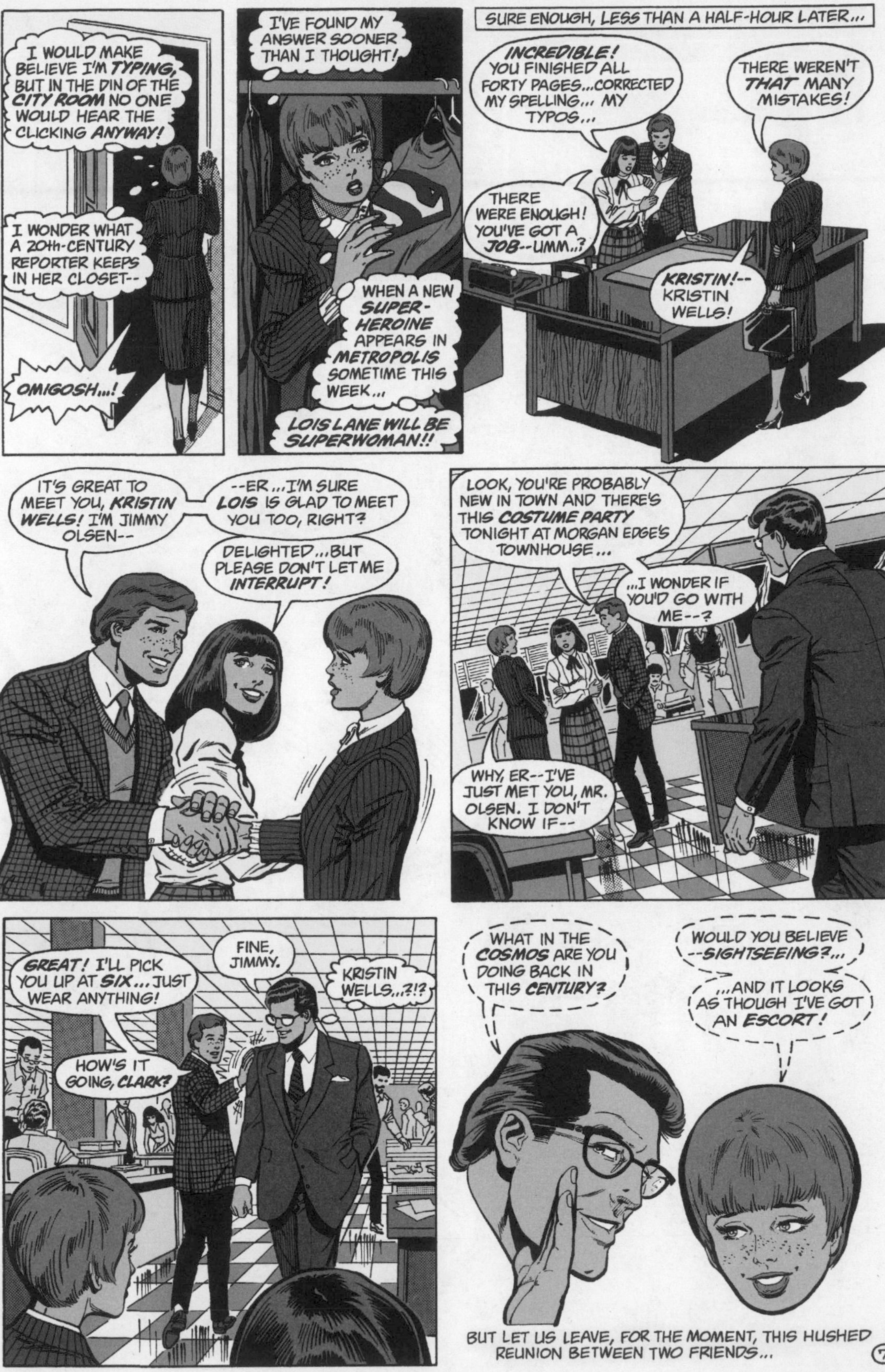
I WOULD MAKE BELIEVE I'M TYPING, BUT IN THE DIN OF THE CITY ROOM NO ONE WOULD HEAR THE CLICKING ANYWAY!
I WONDER WHAT A 20th-CENTURY REPORTER KEEPS IN HER CLOSET--
OMIGOSH...!
I'VE FOUND MY ANSWER SOONER THAN I THOUGHT!
WHEN A NEW SUPER-HEROINE APPEARS IN METROPOLIS SOMETIME THIS WEEK...
LOIS LANE WILL BE SUPERWOMAN!!
SURE ENOUGH, LESS THAN A HALF-HOUR LATER...
INCREDIBLE! YOU FINISHED ALL FORTY PAGES...CORRECTED MY SPELLING... MY TYPOS...
THERE WEREN'T THAT MANY MISTAKES!
THERE WERE ENOUGH! YOU'VE GOT A JOB--UMM..?
KRISTIN!-- KRISTIN WELLS!
IT'S GREAT TO MEET YOU, KRISTIN WELLS! I'M JIMMY OLSEN--
--ER...I'M SURE LOIS IS GLAD TO MEET YOU TOO, RIGHT?
DELIGHTED...BUT PLEASE DON'T LET ME INTERRUPT!
LOOK, YOU'RE PROBABLY NEW IN TOWN AND THERE'S THIS COSTUME PARTY TONIGHT AT MORGAN EDGE'S TOWNHOUSE...
...I WONDER IF YOU'D GO WITH ME--?
WHY, ER--I'VE JUST MET YOU, MR. OLSEN. I DON'T KNOW IF--
GREAT! I'LL PICK YOU UP AT SIX... JUST WEAR ANYTHING!
FINE, JIMMY.
KRISTIN WELLS..?!?
HOW'S IT GOING, CLARK?
WHAT IN THE COSMOS ARE YOU DOING BACK IN THIS CENTURY?
WOULD YOU BELIEVE --SIGHTSEEING?...
...AND IT LOOKS AS THOUGH I'VE GOT AN ESCORT!
BUT LET US LEAVE, FOR THE MOMENT, THIS HUSHED REUNION BETWEEN TWO FRIENDS...
7

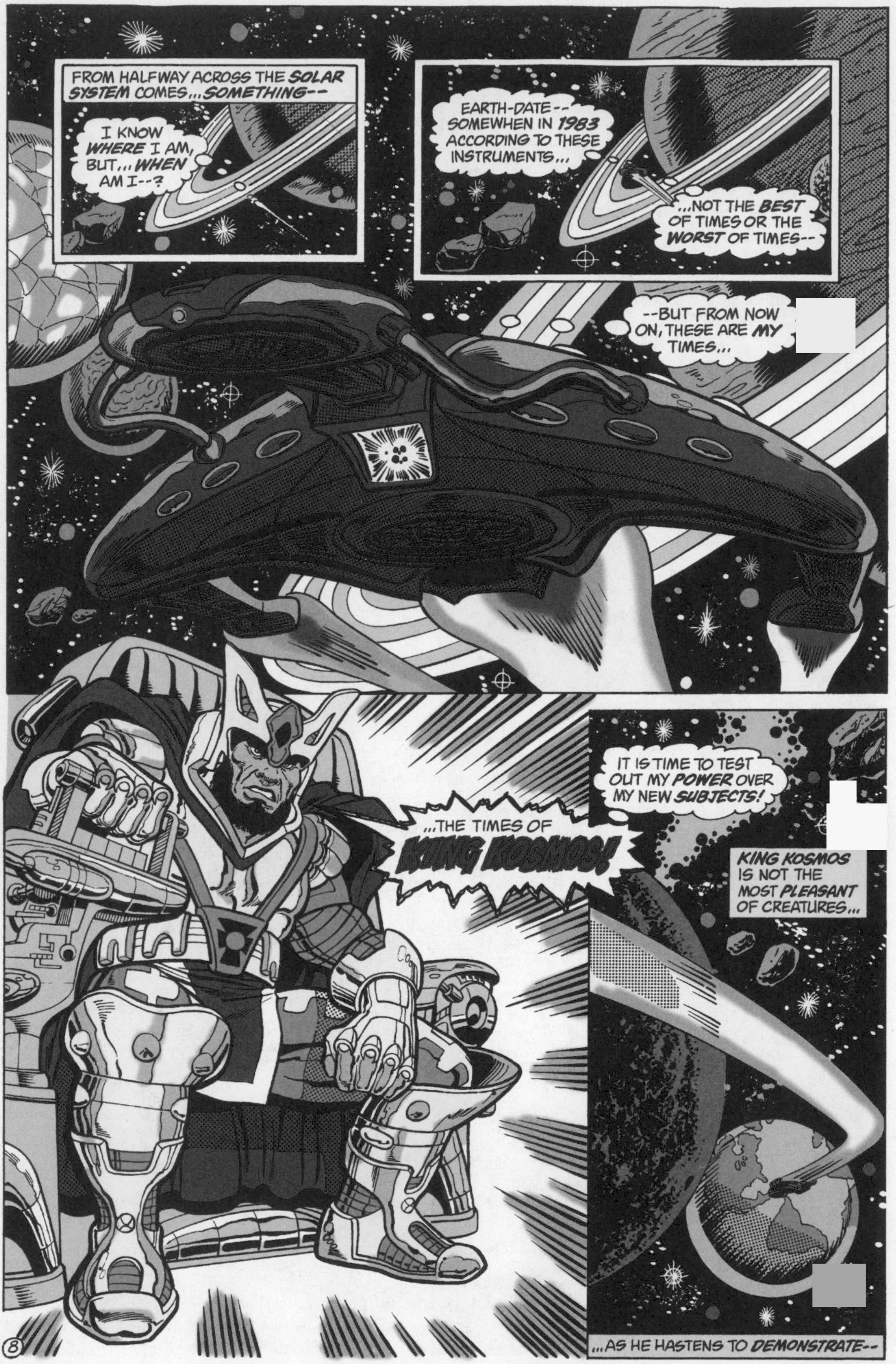
FROM HALFWAY ACROSS THE SOLAR SYSTEM COMES... SOMETHING--
I KNOW WHERE I AM, BUT... WHEN AM I--?
EARTH-DATE-- SOMEWHEN IN 1983 ACCORDING TO THESE INSTRUMENTS...
...NOT THE BEST OF TIMES OR THE WORST OF TIMES--
--BUT FROM NOW ON, THESE ARE MY TIMES...
...THE TIMES OF KING KOSMOS!
IT IS TIME TO TEST OUT MY POWER OVER MY NEW SUBJECTS!
KING KOSMOS IS NOT THE MOST PLEASANT OF CREATURES...
...AS HE HASTENS TO DEMONSTRATE--
8

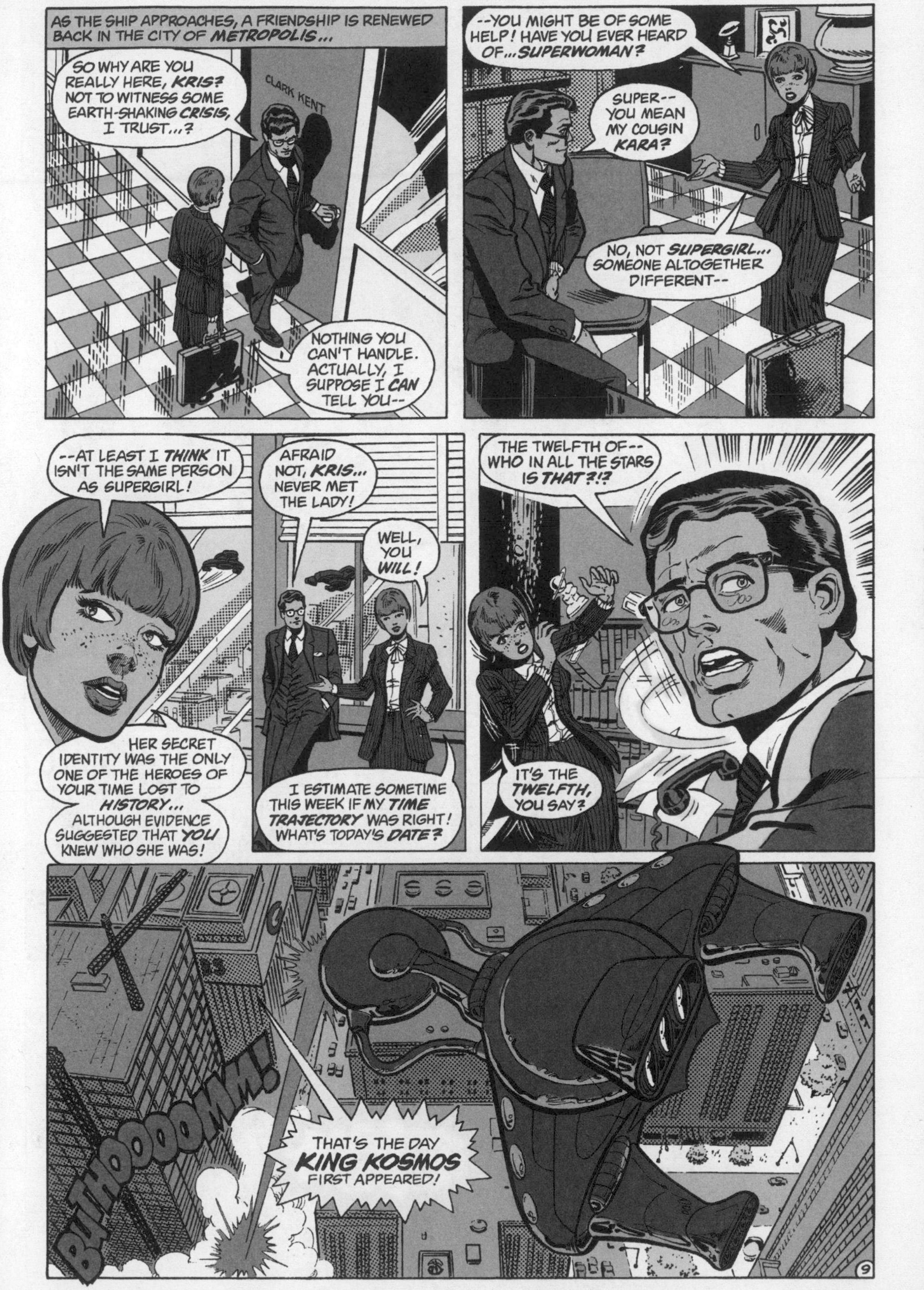
AS THE SHIP APPROACHES, A FRIENDSHIP IS RENEWED BACK IN THE CITY OF METROPOLIS...
SO WHY ARE YOU REALLY HERE, KRIS? NOT TO WITNESS SOME EARTH-SHAKING CRISIS, I TRUST...?
CLARK KENT
NOTHING YOU CAN'T HANDLE. ACTUALLY, I SUPPOSE I CAN TELL YOU--
--YOU MIGHT BE OF SOME HELP! HAVE YOU EVER HEARD OF...SUPERWOMAN?
SUPER-- YOU MEAN MY COUSIN KARA?
NO, NOT SUPERGIRL... SOMEONE ALTOGETHER DIFFERENT--
--AT LEAST I THINK IT ISN'T THE SAME PERSON AS SUPERGIRL!
HER SECRET IDENTITY WAS THE ONLY ONE OF THE HEROES OF YOUR TIME LOST TO HISTORY... ALTHOUGH EVIDENCE SUGGESTED THAT YOU KNEW WHO SHE WAS!
AFRAID NOT, KRIS... NEVER MET THE LADY!
WELL, YOU WILL!
I ESTIMATE SOMETIME THIS WEEK IF MY TIME TRAJECTORY WAS RIGHT! WHAT'S TODAY'S DATE?
IT'S THE TWELFTH, YOU SAY?
THE TWELFTH OF-- WHO IN ALL THE STARS IS THAT?!?
BUHOOOOOMM!
THAT'S THE DAY KING KOSMOS FIRST APPEARED!
9

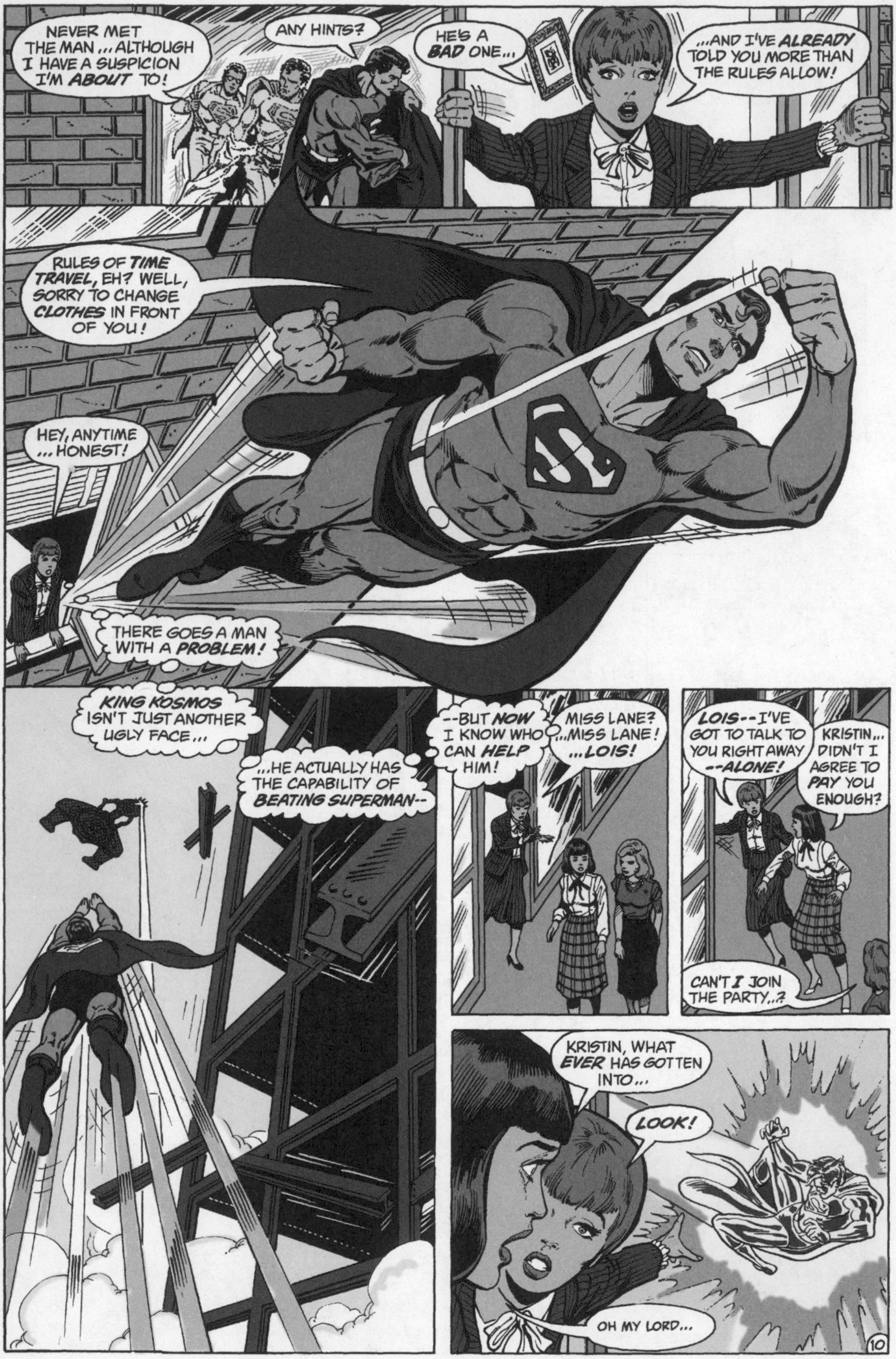
NEVER MET THE MAN ... ALTHOUGH I HAVE A SUSPICION I'M ABOUT TO!
ANY HINTS?
HE'S A BAD ONE...
...AND I'VE ALREADY TOLD YOU MORE THAN THE RULES ALLOW!
RULES OF TIME TRAVEL, EH? WELL, SORRY TO CHANGE CLOTHES IN FRONT OF YOU!
HEY, ANYTIME ...HONEST!
THERE GOES A MAN WITH A PROBLEM!
KING KOSMOS ISN'T JUST ANOTHER UGLY FACE...
...HE ACTUALLY HAS THE CAPABILITY OF BEATING SUPERMAN--
--BUT NOW I KNOW WHO CAN HELP HIM!
MISS LANE? ...MISS LANE! ...LOIS!
LOIS--I'VE GOT TO TALK TO YOU RIGHT AWAY --ALONE!
KRISTIN... DIDN'T I AGREE TO PAY YOU ENOUGH?
CAN'T I JOIN THE PARTY..?
KRISTIN, WHAT EVER HAS GOTTEN INTO...
LOOK!
OH MY LORD...
10

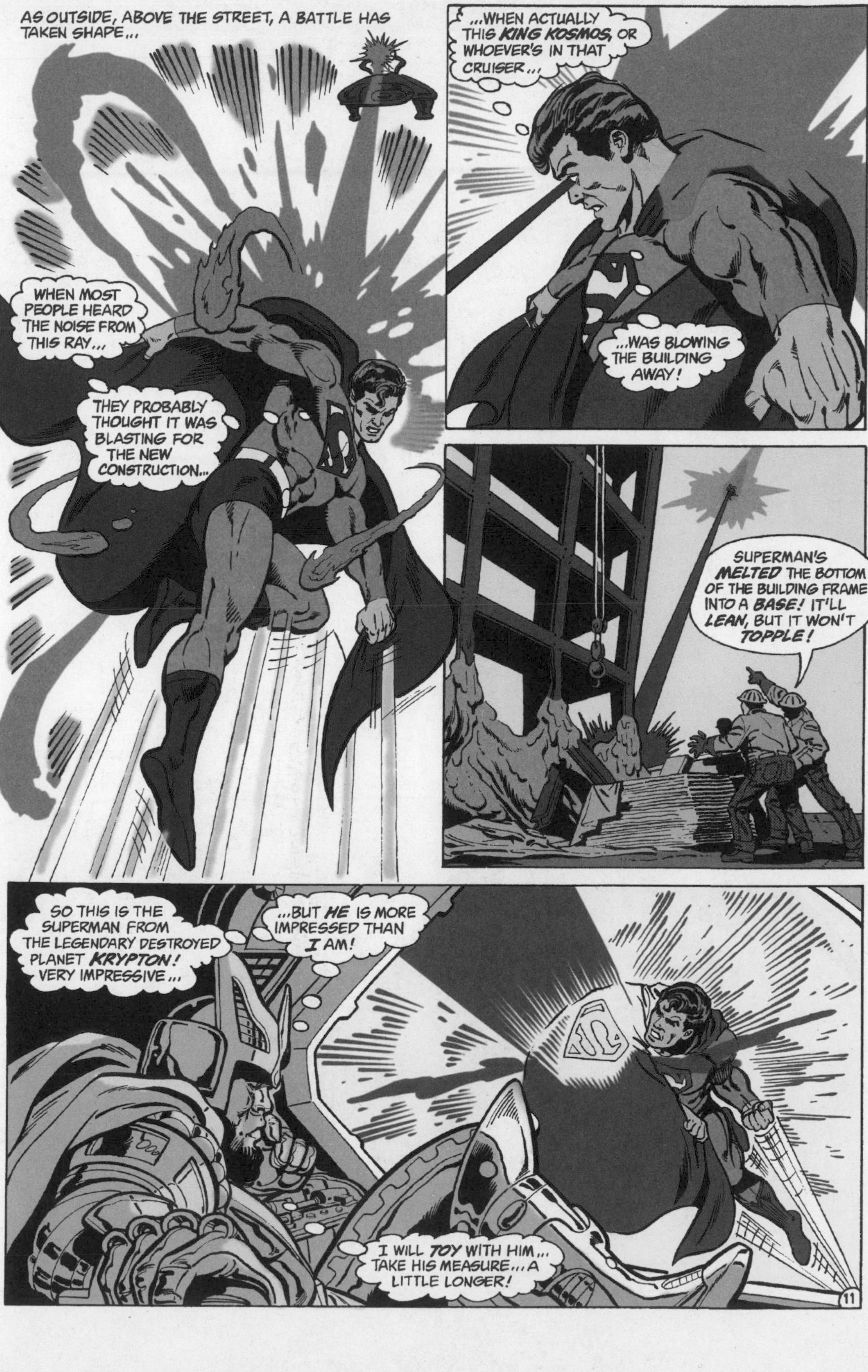

AS OUTSIDE, ABOVE THE STREET, A BATTLE HAS TAKEN SHAPE...
WHEN MOST PEOPLE HEARD THE NOISE FROM THIS RAY...
THEY PROBABLY THOUGHT IT WAS BLASTING FOR THE NEW CONSTRUCTION...
...WHEN ACTUALLY THIS KING KOSMOS, OR WHOEVER'S IN THAT CRUISER...
...WAS BLOWING THE BUILDING AWAY!
SUPERMAN'S MELTED THE BOTTOM OF THE BUILDING FRAME INTO A BASE! IT'LL LEAN, BUT IT WON'T TOPPLE!
SO THIS IS THE SUPERMAN FROM THE LEGENDARY DESTROYED PLANET KRYPTON! VERY IMPRESSIVE...
...BUT HE IS MORE IMPRESSED THAN I AM!
I WILL TOY WITH HIM... TAKE HIS MEASURE... A LITTLE LONGER!
11

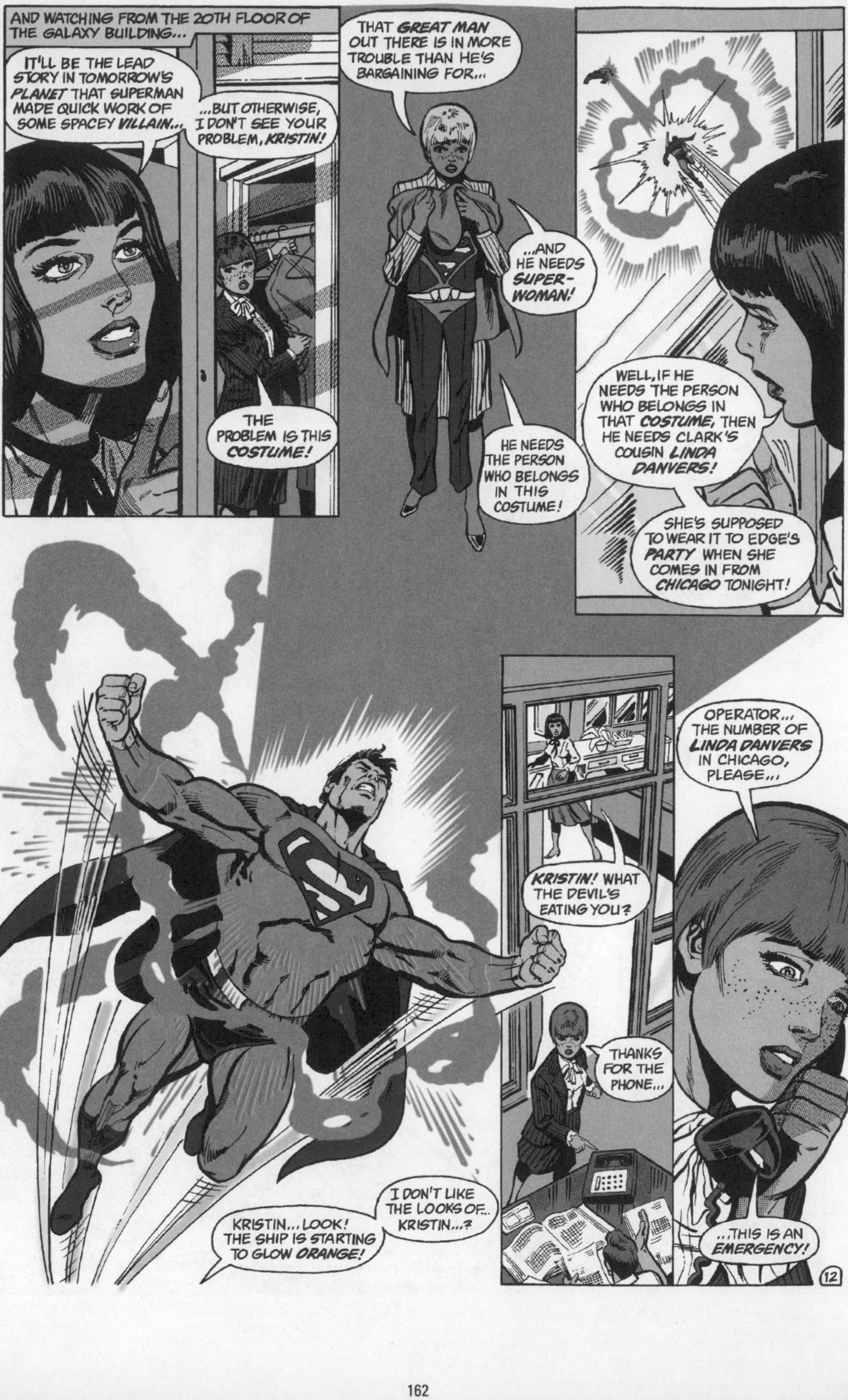
AND WATCHING FROM THE 20TH FLOOR OF THE GALAXY BUILDING...
IT'LL BE THE LEAD STORY IN TOMORROW'S PLANET THAT SUPERMAN MADE QUICK WORK OF SOME SPACEY VILLAIN...
...BUT OTHERWISE, I DON'T SEE YOUR PROBLEM, KRISTIN!
THE PROBLEM IS THIS COSTUME!
THAT GREAT MAN OUT THERE IS IN MORE TROUBLE THAN HE'S BARGAINING FOR...
...AND HE NEEDS SUPER-WOMAN!
HE NEEDS THE PERSON WHO BELONGS IN THIS COSTUME!
WELL, IF HE NEEDS THE PERSON WHO BELONGS IN THAT COSTUME, THEN HE NEEDS CLARK'S COUSIN LINDA DANVERS!
SHE'S SUPPOSED TO WEAR IT TO EDGE'S PARTY WHEN SHE COMES IN FROM CHICAGO TONIGHT!
KRISTIN... LOOK! THE SHIP IS STARTING TO GLOW ORANGE!
I DON'T LIKE THE LOOKS OF... KRISTIN...?
KRISTIN! WHAT THE DEVIL'S EATING YOU?
THANKS FOR THE PHONE...
OPERATOR... THE NUMBER OF LINDA DANVERS IN CHICAGO, PLEASE...
...THIS IS AN EMERGENCY!
12

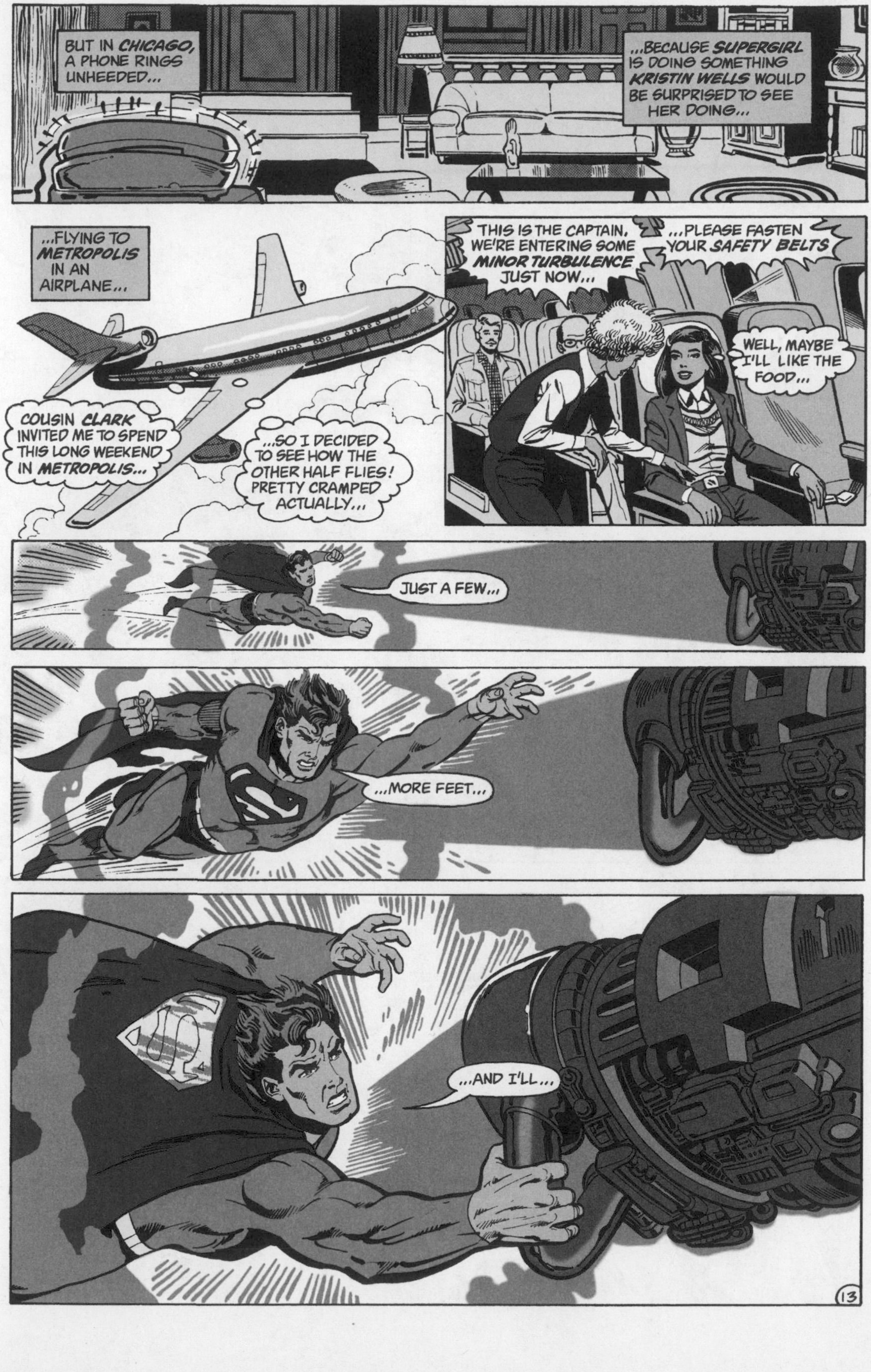
BUT IN CHICAGO, A PHONE RINGS UNHEEDED...
...BECAUSE SUPERGIRL IS DOING SOMETHING KRISTIN WELLS WOULD BE SURPRISED TO SEE HER DOING...
...FLYING TO METROPOLIS IN AN AIRPLANE...
COUSIN CLARK INVITED ME TO SPEND THIS LONG WEEKEND IN METROPOLIS...
...SO I DECIDED TO SEE HOW THE OTHER HALF FLIES! PRETTY CRAMPED ACTUALLY...
THIS IS THE CAPTAIN. WE'RE ENTERING SOME MINOR TURBULENCE JUST NOW...
...PLEASE FASTEN YOUR SAFETY BELTS
WELL, MAYBE I'LL LIKE THE FOOD...
JUST A FEW...
...MORE FEET...
...AND I'LL...
13

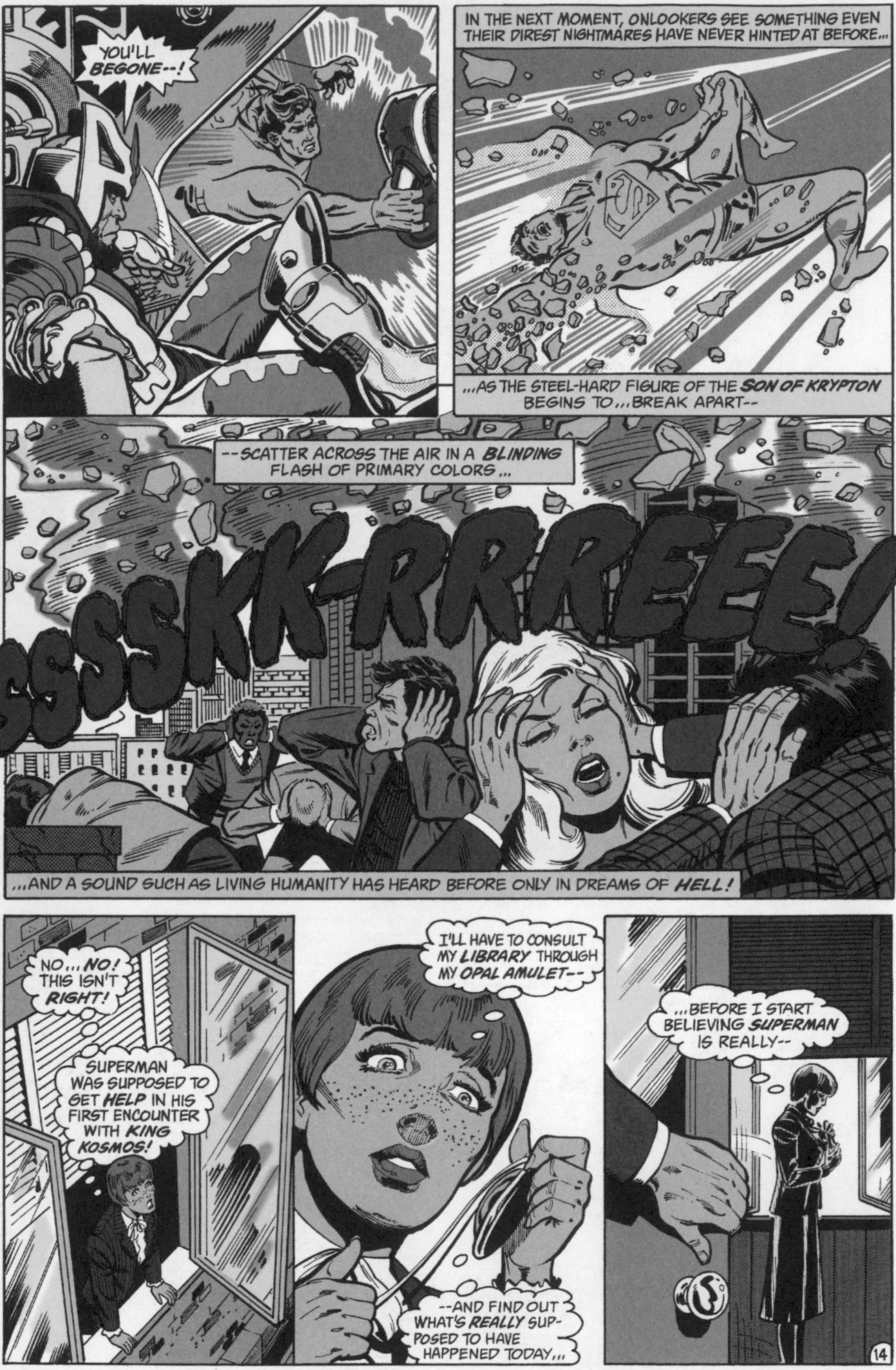
YOU'LL BEGONE--!
IN THE NEXT MOMENT, ONLOOKERS SEE SOMETHING EVEN THEIR DIREST NIGHTMARES HAVE NEVER HINTED AT BEFORE...
...AS THE STEEL-HARD FIGURE OF THE SON OF KRYPTON BEGINS TO... BREAK APART--
--SCATTER ACROSS THE AIR IN A BLINDING FLASH OF PRIMARY COLORS...
SSSSKK-RRRREEE!
...AND A SOUND SUCH AS LIVING HUMANITY HAS HEARD BEFORE ONLY IN DREAMS OF HELL!
NO... NO! THIS ISN'T RIGHT!
SUPERMAN WAS SUPPOSED TO GET HELP IN HIS FIRST ENCOUNTER WITH KING KOSMOS!
I'LL HAVE TO CONSULT MY LIBRARY THROUGH MY OPAL AMULET--
--AND FIND OUT WHAT'S REALLY SUPPOSED TO HAVE HAPPENED TODAY...
...BEFORE I START BELIEVING SUPERMAN IS REALLY--
14

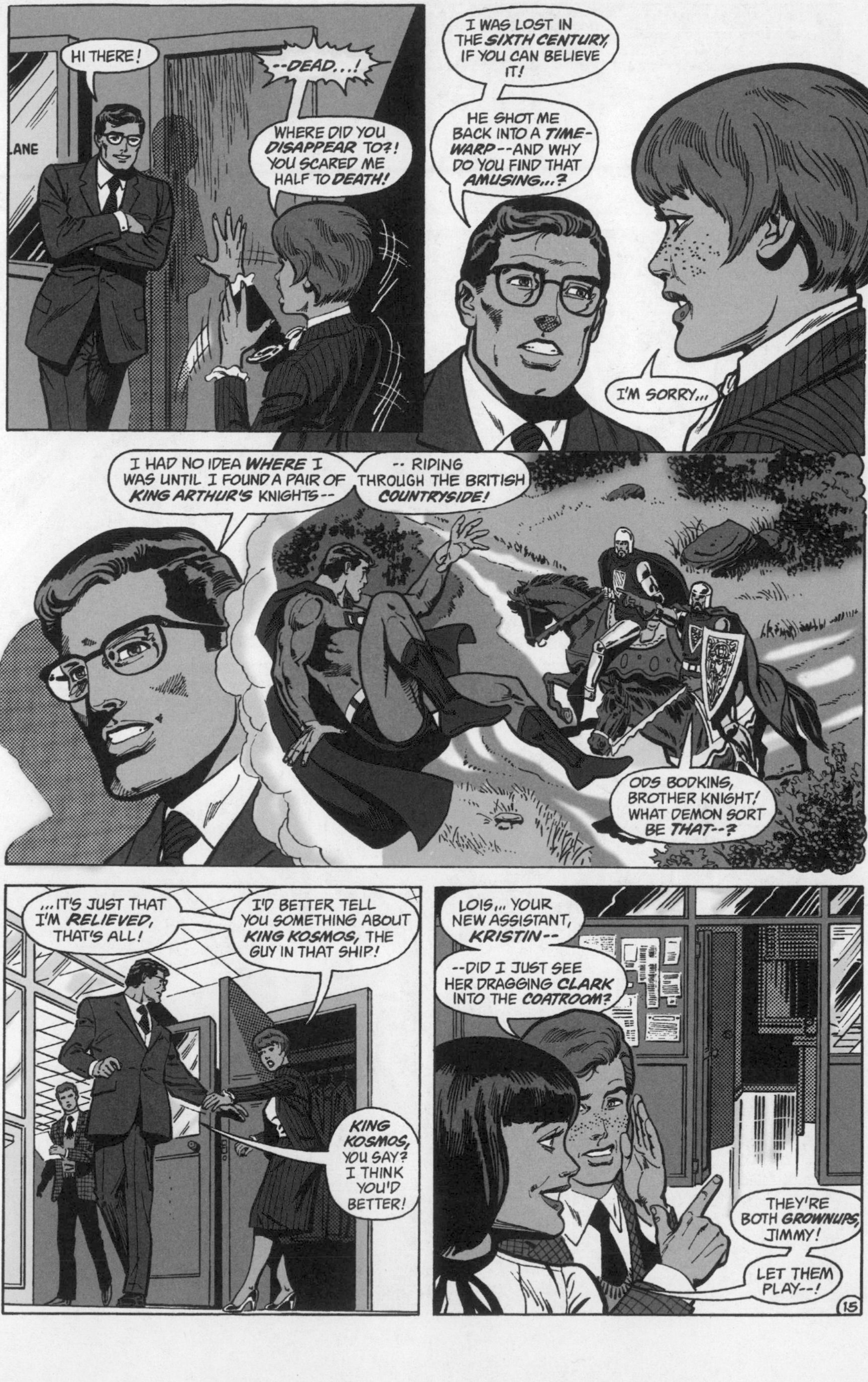
HI THERE!
--DEAD...!
WHERE DID YOU DISAPPEAR TO?! YOU SCARED ME HALF TO DEATH!
LANE
I WAS LOST IN THE SIXTH CENTURY, IF YOU CAN BELIEVE IT!
HE SHOT ME BACK INTO A TIME-WARP--AND WHY DO YOU FIND THAT AMUSING...?
I'M SORRY...
I HAD NO IDEA WHERE I WAS UNTIL I FOUND A PAIR OF KING ARTHUR'S KNIGHTS--
-- RIDING THROUGH THE BRITISH COUNTRYSIDE!
ODS BODKINS, BROTHER KNIGHT! WHAT DEMON SORT BE THAT--?
...IT'S JUST THAT I'M RELIEVED, THAT'S ALL!
I'D BETTER TELL YOU SOMETHING ABOUT KING KOSMOS, THE GUY IN THAT SHIP!
KING KOSMOS, YOU SAY? I THINK YOU'D BETTER!
LOIS... YOUR NEW ASSISTANT, KRISTIN--
--DID I JUST SEE HER DRAGGING CLARK INTO THE COATROOM?
THEY'RE BOTH GROWNUPS, JIMMY!
LET THEM PLAY--!
15

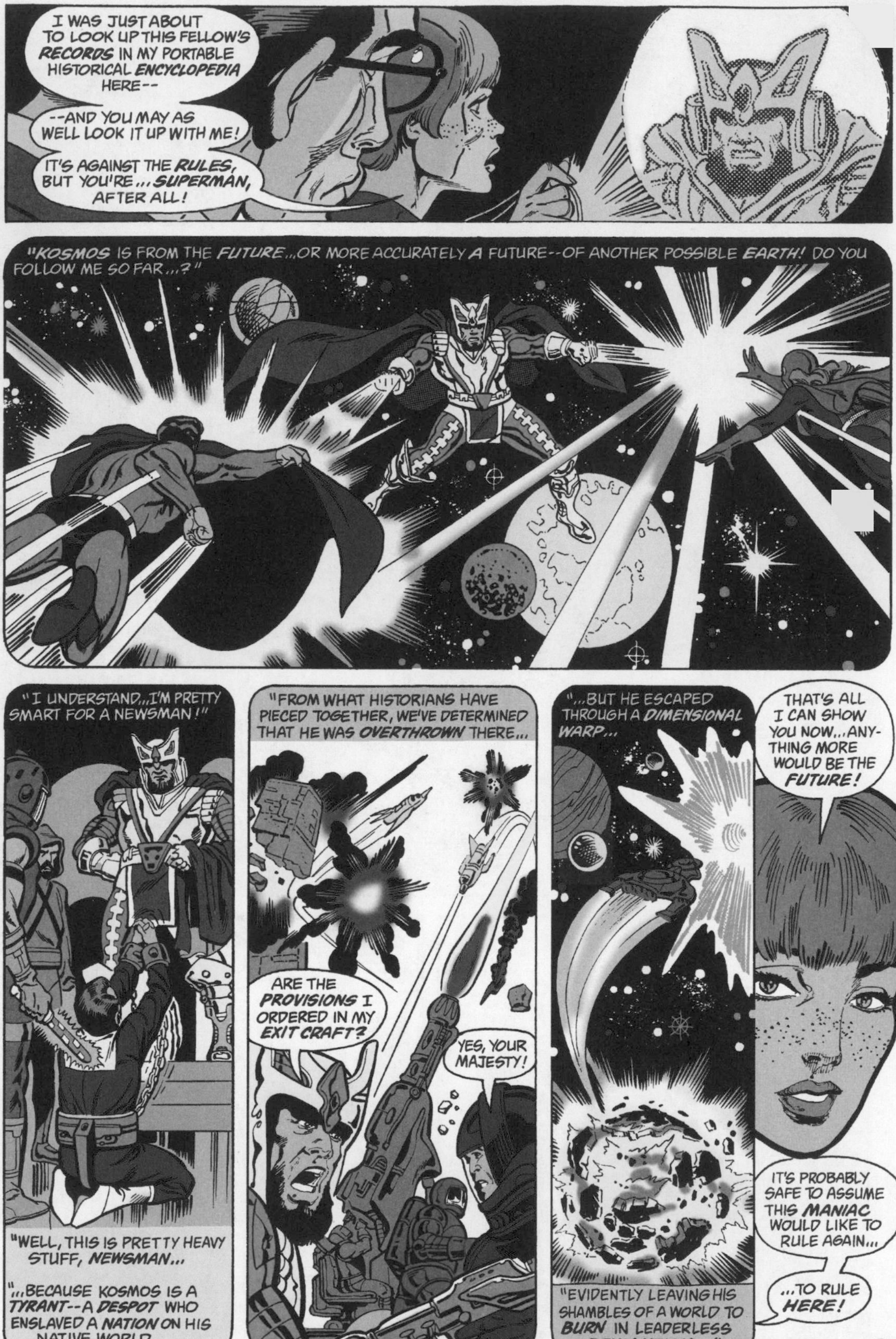
I WAS JUST ABOUT TO LOOK UP THIS FELLOW'S RECORDS IN MY PORTABLE HISTORICAL ENCYCLOPEDIA HERE--
--AND YOU MAY AS WELL LOOK IT UP WITH ME!
IT'S AGAINST THE RULES, BUT YOU'RE... SUPERMAN, AFTER ALL!
"KOSMOS IS FROM THE FUTURE... OR MORE ACCURATELY A FUTURE--OF ANOTHER POSSIBLE EARTH! DO YOU FOLLOW ME SO FAR...?"
"I UNDERSTAND... I'M PRETTY SMART FOR A NEWSMAN!"
"WELL, THIS IS PRETTY HEAVY STUFF, NEWSMAN...
"...BECAUSE KOSMOS IS A TYRANT--A DESPOT WHO ENSLAVED A NATION ON HIS NATIVE WORLD...
"FROM WHAT HISTORIANS HAVE PIECED TOGETHER, WE'VE DETERMINED THAT HE WAS OVERTHROWN THERE...
ARE THE PROVISIONS I ORDERED IN MY EXIT CRAFT?
YES, YOUR MAJESTY!
"...BUT HE ESCAPED THROUGH A DIMENSIONAL WARP...
"EVIDENTLY LEAVING HIS SHAMBLES OF A WORLD TO BURN IN LEADERLESS REVOLUTION..."
THAT'S ALL I CAN SHOW YOU NOW... ANYTHING MORE WOULD BE THE FUTURE!
IT'S PROBABLY SAFE TO ASSUME THIS MANIAC WOULD LIKE TO RULE AGAIN...
...TO RULE HERE!
16

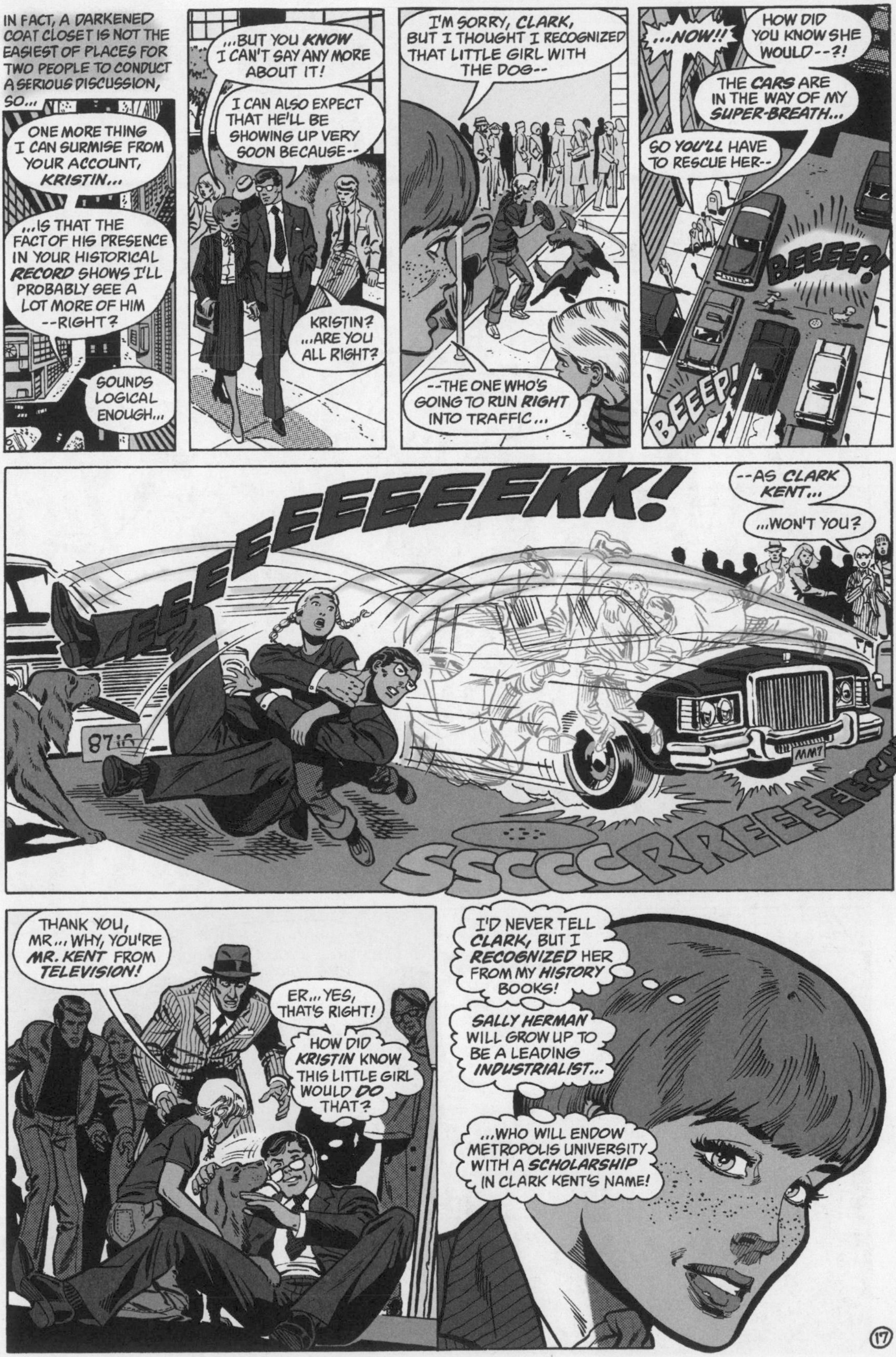
IN FACT, A DARKENED COAT CLOSET IS NOT THE EASIEST OF PLACES FOR TWO PEOPLE TO CONDUCT A SERIOUS DISCUSSION, SO...
ONE MORE THING I CAN SURMISE FROM YOUR ACCOUNT, KRISTIN...
...IS THAT THE FACT OF HIS PRESENCE IN YOUR HISTORICAL RECORD SHOWS I'LL PROBABLY SEE A LOT MORE OF HIM --RIGHT?
SOUNDS LOGICAL ENOUGH...
...BUT YOU KNOW I CAN'T SAY ANY MORE ABOUT IT!
I CAN ALSO EXPECT THAT HE'LL BE SHOWING UP VERY SOON BECAUSE--
KRISTIN? ...ARE YOU ALL RIGHT?
I'M SORRY, CLARK, BUT I THOUGHT I RECOGNIZED THAT LITTLE GIRL WITH THE DOG--
--THE ONE WHO'S GOING TO RUN RIGHT INTO TRAFFIC...
...NOW!!
HOW DID YOU KNOW SHE WOULD--?!
THE CARS ARE IN THE WAY OF MY SUPER-BREATH...
SO YOU'LL HAVE TO RESCUE HER--
BEEEEP!
BEEEP!
EEEEEEEEEEKK!
--AS CLARK KENT...
...WON'T YOU?
SSCCCRREEEEEECH!
THANK YOU, MR... WHY, YOU'RE MR. KENT FROM TELEVISION!
ER... YES, THAT'S RIGHT!
HOW DID KRISTIN KNOW THIS LITTLE GIRL WOULD DO THAT?
I'D NEVER TELL CLARK, BUT I RECOGNIZED HER FROM MY HISTORY BOOKS!
SALLY HERMAN WILL GROW UP TO BE A LEADING INDUSTRIALIST...
...WHO WILL ENDOW METROPOLIS UNIVERSITY WITH A SCHOLARSHIP IN CLARK KENT'S NAME!
17

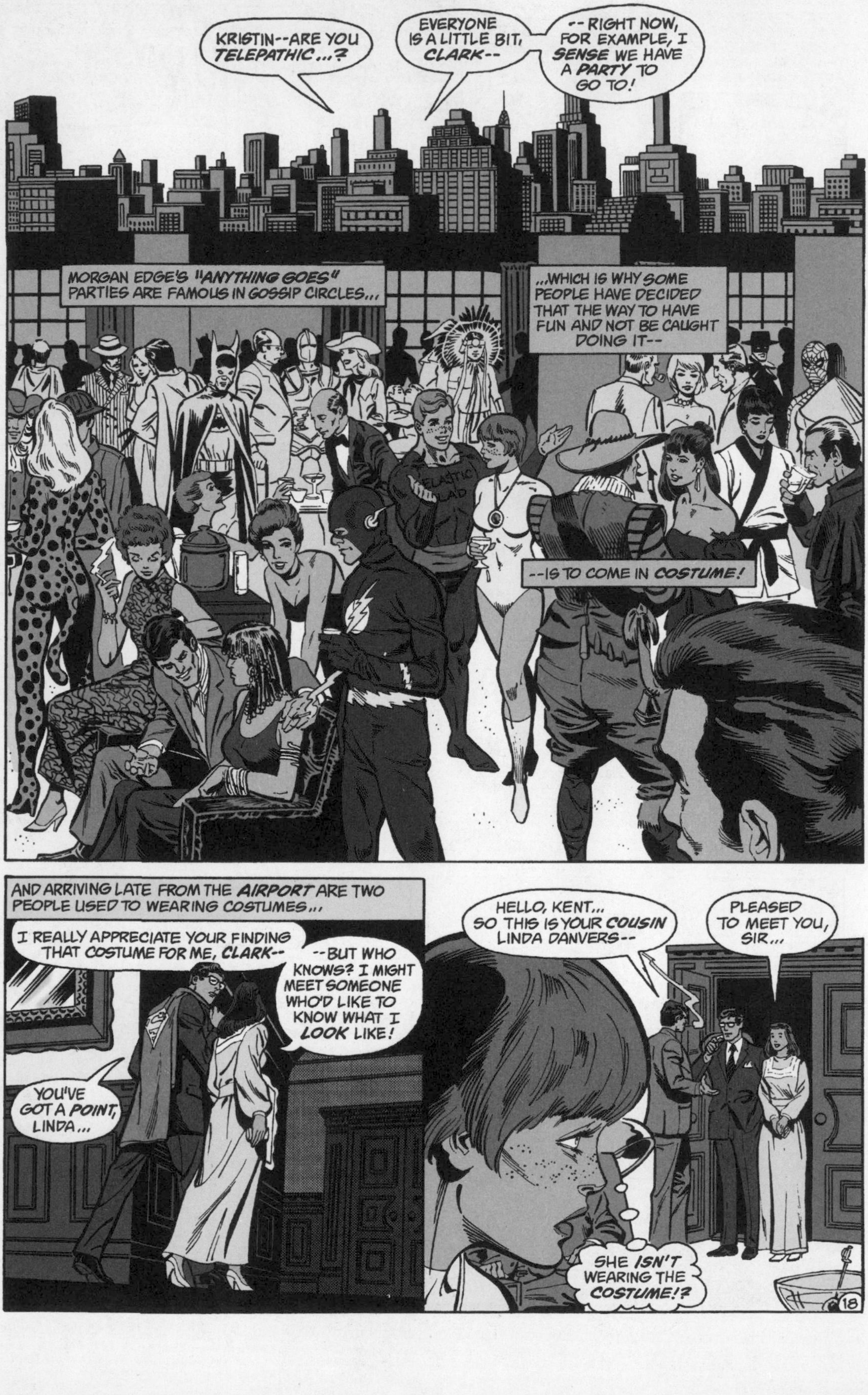
KRISTIN--ARE YOU TELEPATHIC...?
EVERYONE IS A LITTLE BIT, CLARK--
--RIGHT NOW, FOR EXAMPLE, I SENSE WE HAVE A PARTY TO GO TO!
MORGAN EDGE'S "ANYTHING GOES" PARTIES ARE FAMOUS IN GOSSIP CIRCLES...
...WHICH IS WHY SOME PEOPLE HAVE DECIDED THAT THE WAY TO HAVE FUN AND NOT BE CAUGHT DOING IT--
--IS TO COME IN COSTUME!
ELASTIC LAD
AND ARRIVING LATE FROM THE AIRPORT ARE TWO PEOPLE USED TO WEARING COSTUMES...
I REALLY APPRECIATE YOUR FINDING THAT COSTUME FOR ME, CLARK--
--BUT WHO KNOWS? I MIGHT MEET SOMEONE WHO'D LIKE TO KNOW WHAT I LOOK LIKE!
YOU'VE GOT A POINT, LINDA...
HELLO, KENT... SO THIS IS YOUR COUSIN LINDA DANVERS--
PLEASED TO MEET YOU, SIR...
SHE ISN'T WEARING THE COSTUME!?
18

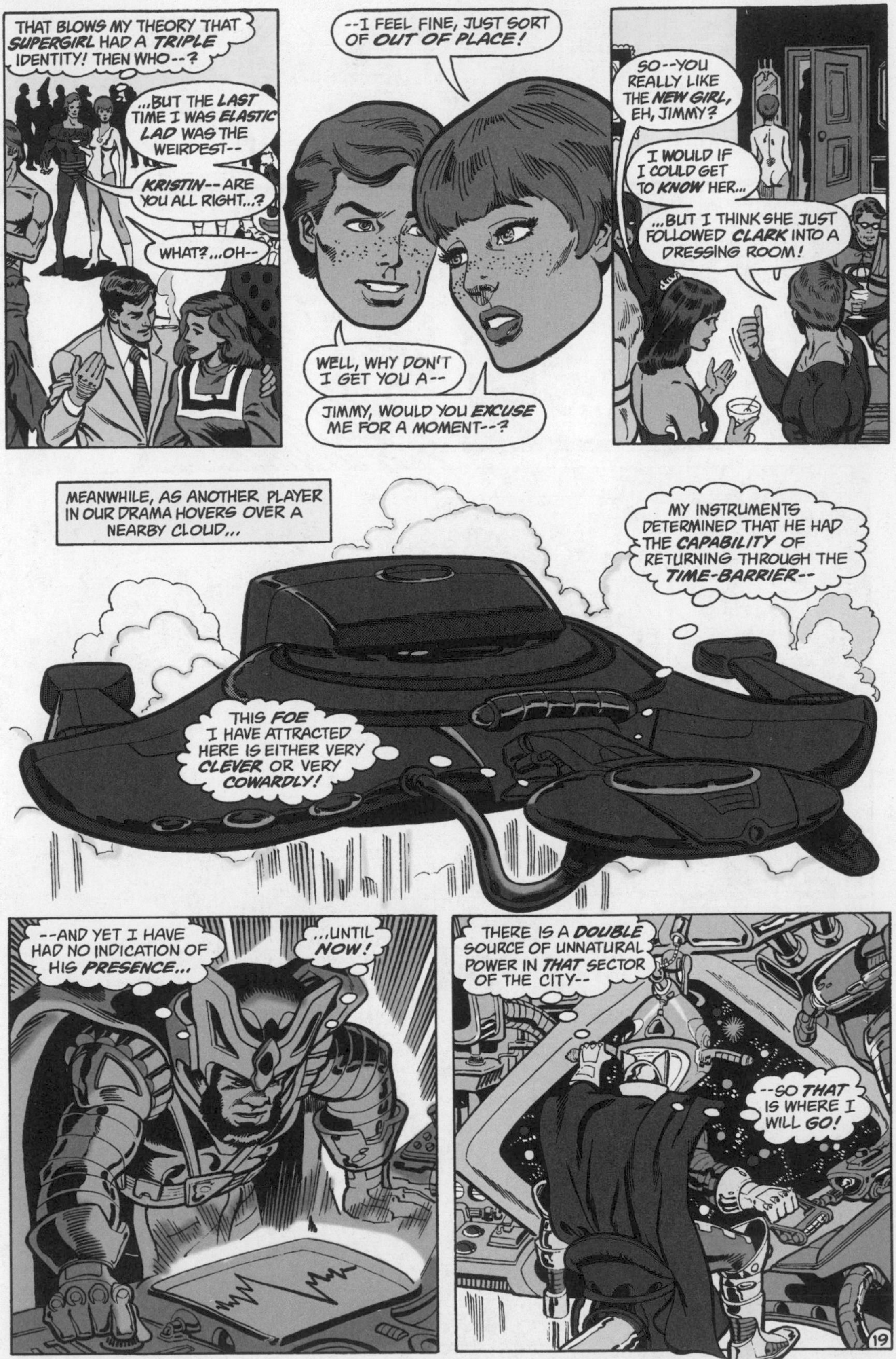
THAT BLOWS MY THEORY THAT SUPERGIRL HAD A TRIPLE IDENTITY! THEN WHO--?
...BUT THE LAST TIME I WAS ELASTIC LAD WAS THE WEIRDEST--
KRISTIN-- ARE YOU ALL RIGHT...?
WHAT?...OH--
--I FEEL FINE, JUST SORT OF OUT OF PLACE!
WELL, WHY DON'T I GET YOU A--
JIMMY, WOULD YOU EXCUSE ME FOR A MOMENT--?
SO--YOU REALLY LIKE THE NEW GIRL, EH, JIMMY?
I WOULD IF I COULD GET TO KNOW HER...
...BUT I THINK SHE JUST FOLLOWED CLARK INTO A DRESSING ROOM!
MEANWHILE, AS ANOTHER PLAYER IN OUR DRAMA HOVERS OVER A NEARBY CLOUD...
MY INSTRUMENTS DETERMINED THAT HE HAD THE CAPABILITY OF RETURNING THROUGH THE TIME-BARRIER--
THIS FOE I HAVE ATTRACTED HERE IS EITHER VERY CLEVER OR VERY COWARDLY!
--AND YET I HAVE HAD NO INDICATION OF HIS PRESENCE...
...UNTIL NOW!
THERE IS A DOUBLE SOURCE OF UNNATURAL POWER IN THAT SECTOR OF THE CITY--
--SO THAT IS WHERE I WILL GO!
19

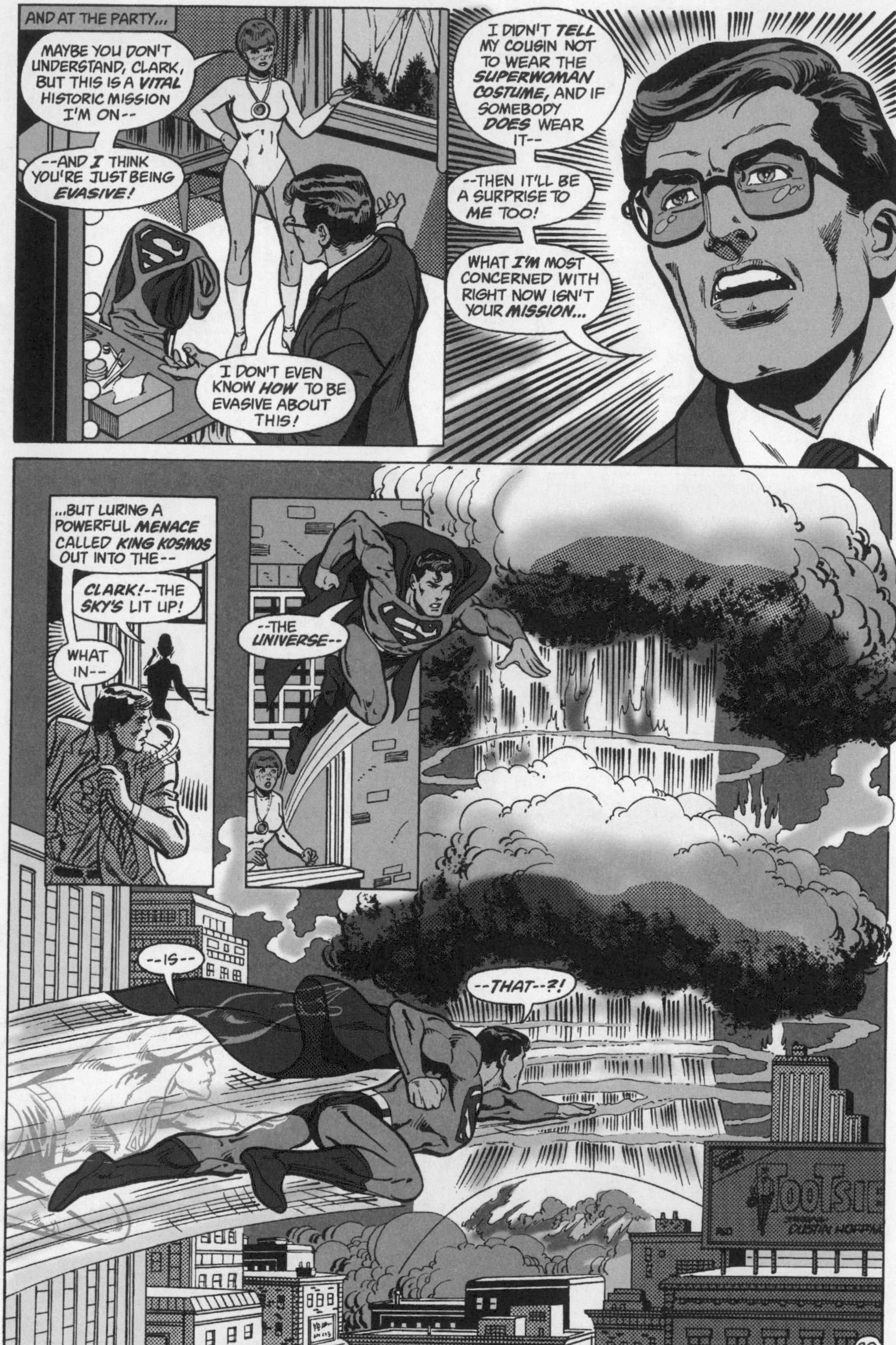
AND AT THE PARTY...
MAYBE YOU DON'T UNDERSTAND, CLARK, BUT THIS IS A VITAL HISTORIC MISSION I'M ON--
--AND I THINK YOU'RE JUST BEING EVASIVE!
I DON'T EVEN KNOW HOW TO BE EVASIVE ABOUT THIS!
I DIDN'T TELL MY COUSIN NOT TO WEAR THE SUPERWOMAN COSTUME, AND IF SOMEBODY DOES WEAR IT--
--THEN IT'LL BE A SURPRISE TO ME TOO!
WHAT I'M MOST CONCERNED WITH RIGHT NOW ISN'T YOUR MISSION...
...BUT LURING A POWERFUL MENACE CALLED KING KOSMOS OUT INTO THE--
CLARK!--THE SKY'S LIT UP!
WHAT IN--
--THE UNIVERSE--
--IS--
--THAT--?!
20

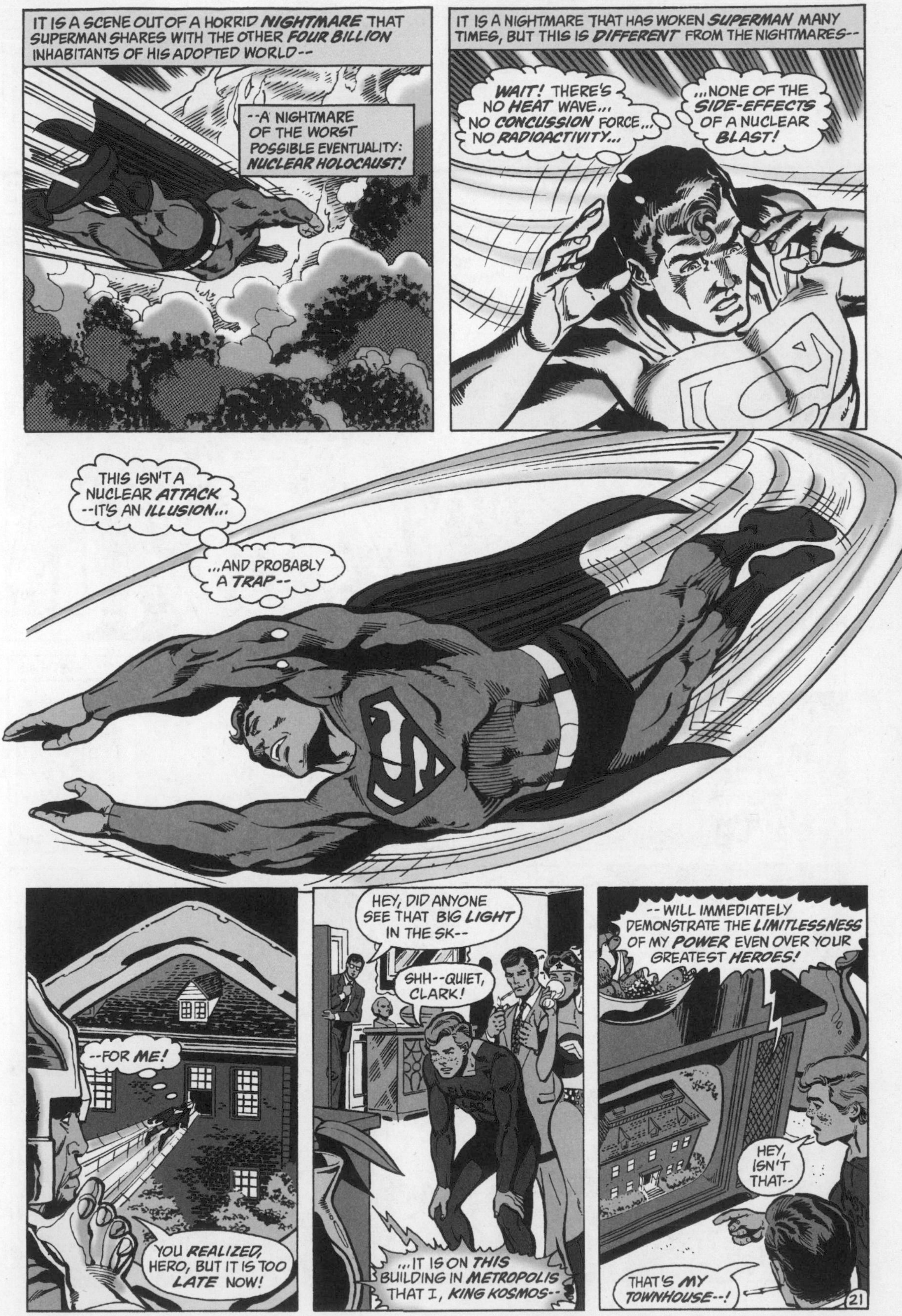
IT IS A SCENE OUT OF A HORRID NIGHTMARE THAT SUPERMAN SHARES WITH THE OTHER FOUR BILLION INHABITANTS OF HIS ADOPTED WORLD--
--A NIGHTMARE OF THE WORST POSSIBLE EVENTUALITY: NUCLEAR HOLOCAUST!
IT IS A NIGHTMARE THAT HAS WOKEN SUPERMAN MANY TIMES, BUT THIS IS DIFFERENT FROM THE NIGHTMARES--
WAIT! THERE'S NO HEAT WAVE... NO CONCUSSION FORCE... NO RADIOACTIVITY...
...NONE OF THE SIDE-EFFECTS OF A NUCLEAR BLAST!
THIS ISN'T A NUCLEAR ATTACK --IT'S AN ILLUSION...
...AND PROBABLY A TRAP--
--FOR ME!
YOU REALIZED, HERO, BUT IT IS TOO LATE NOW!
HEY, DID ANYONE SEE THAT BIG LIGHT IN THE SK--
SHH--QUIET, CLARK!
...IT IS ON THIS BUILDING IN METROPOLIS THAT I, KING KOSMOS--
--WILL IMMEDIATELY DEMONSTRATE THE LIMITLESSNESS OF MY POWER EVEN OVER YOUR GREATEST HEROES!
HEY, ISN'T THAT--
THAT'S MY TOWNHOUSE--!
21

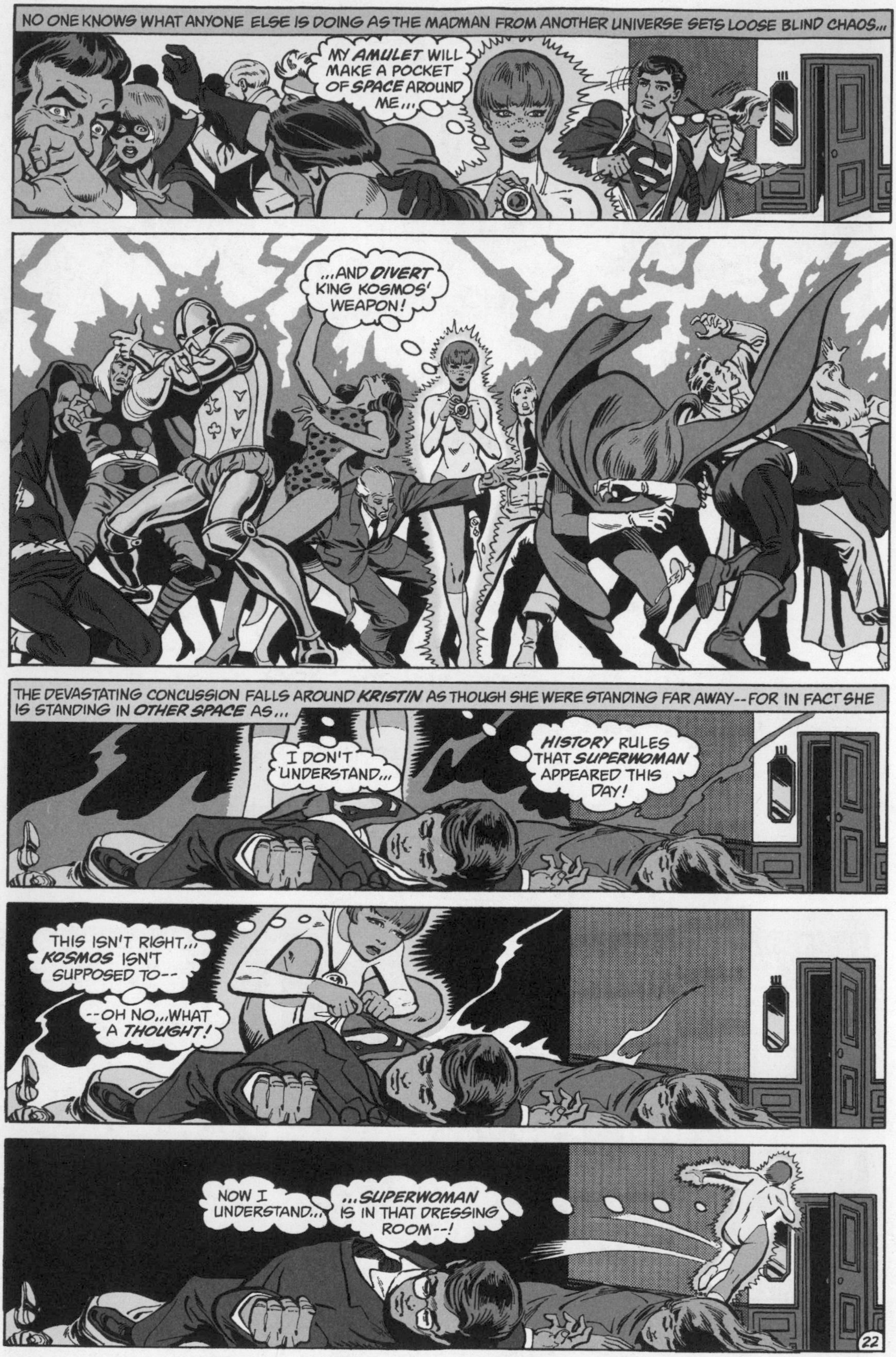
NO ONE KNOWS WHAT ANYONE ELSE IS DOING AS THE MADMAN FROM ANOTHER UNIVERSE SETS LOOSE BLIND CHAOS...
MY AMULET WILL MAKE A POCKET OF SPACE AROUND ME...
...AND DIVERT KING KOSMOS' WEAPON!
THE DEVASTATING CONCUSSION FALLS AROUND KRISTIN AS THOUGH SHE WERE STANDING FAR AWAY--FOR IN FACT SHE IS STANDING IN OTHER SPACE AS...
I DON'T UNDERSTAND...
HISTORY RULES THAT SUPERWOMAN APPEARED THIS DAY!
THIS ISN'T RIGHT... KOSMOS ISN'T SUPPOSED TO--
--OH NO...WHAT A THOUGHT!
NOW I UNDERSTAND...
...SUPERWOMAN IS IN THAT DRESSING ROOM--!
22

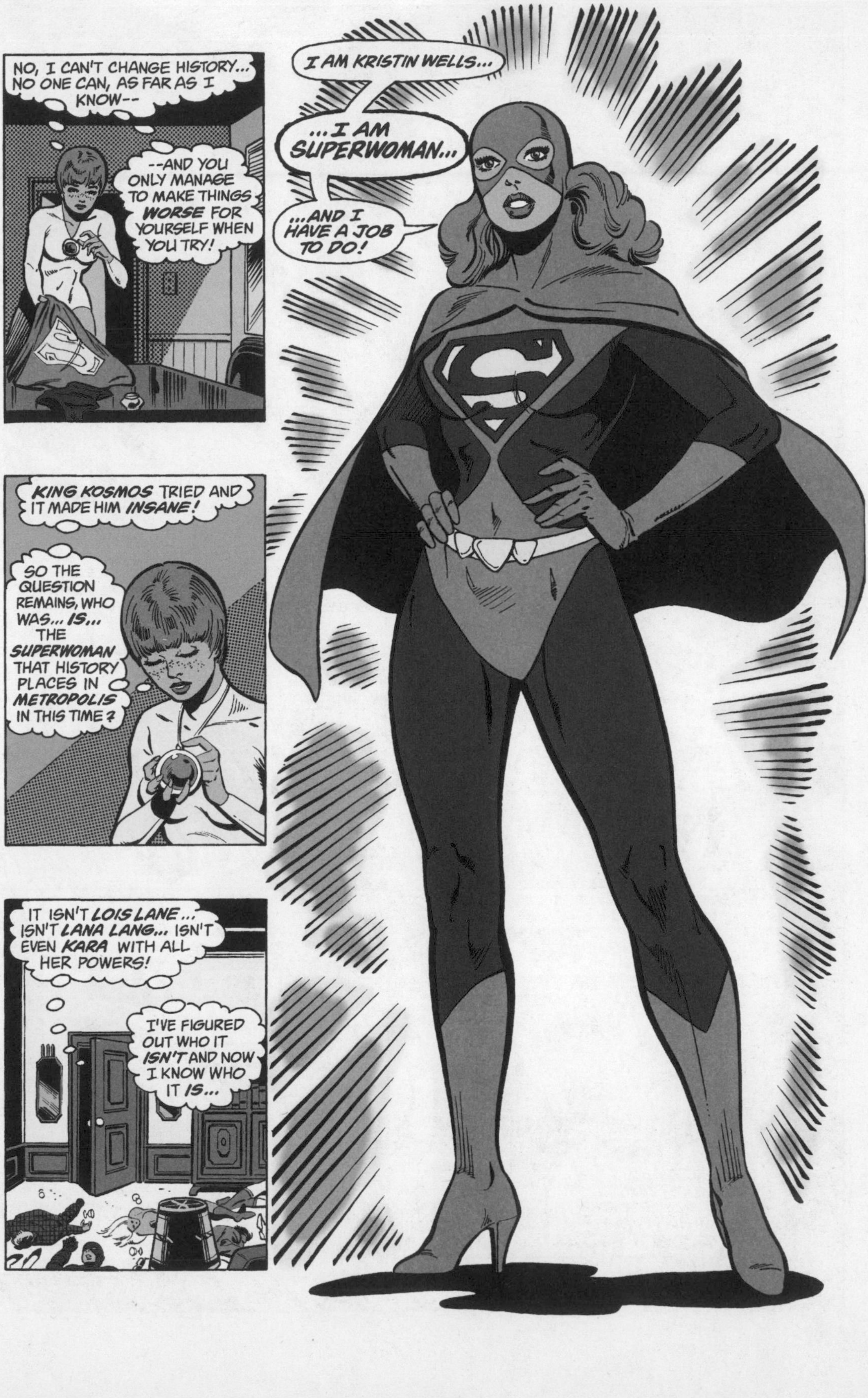
NO, I CAN'T CHANGE HISTORY... NO ONE CAN, AS FAR AS I KNOW--
--AND YOU ONLY MANAGE TO MAKE THINGS WORSE FOR YOURSELF WHEN YOU TRY!
KING KOSMOS TRIED AND IT MADE HIM INSANE!
SO THE QUESTION REMAINS, WHO WAS... IS... THE SUPERWOMAN THAT HISTORY PLACES IN METROPOLIS IN THIS TIME?
IT ISN'T LOIS LANE... ISN'T LANA LANG... ISN'T EVEN KARA WITH ALL HER POWERS!
I'VE FIGURED OUT WHO IT ISN'T AND NOW I KNOW WHO IT IS...
I AM KRISTIN WELLS...
...I AM SUPERWOMAN...
...AND I HAVE A JOB TO DO!

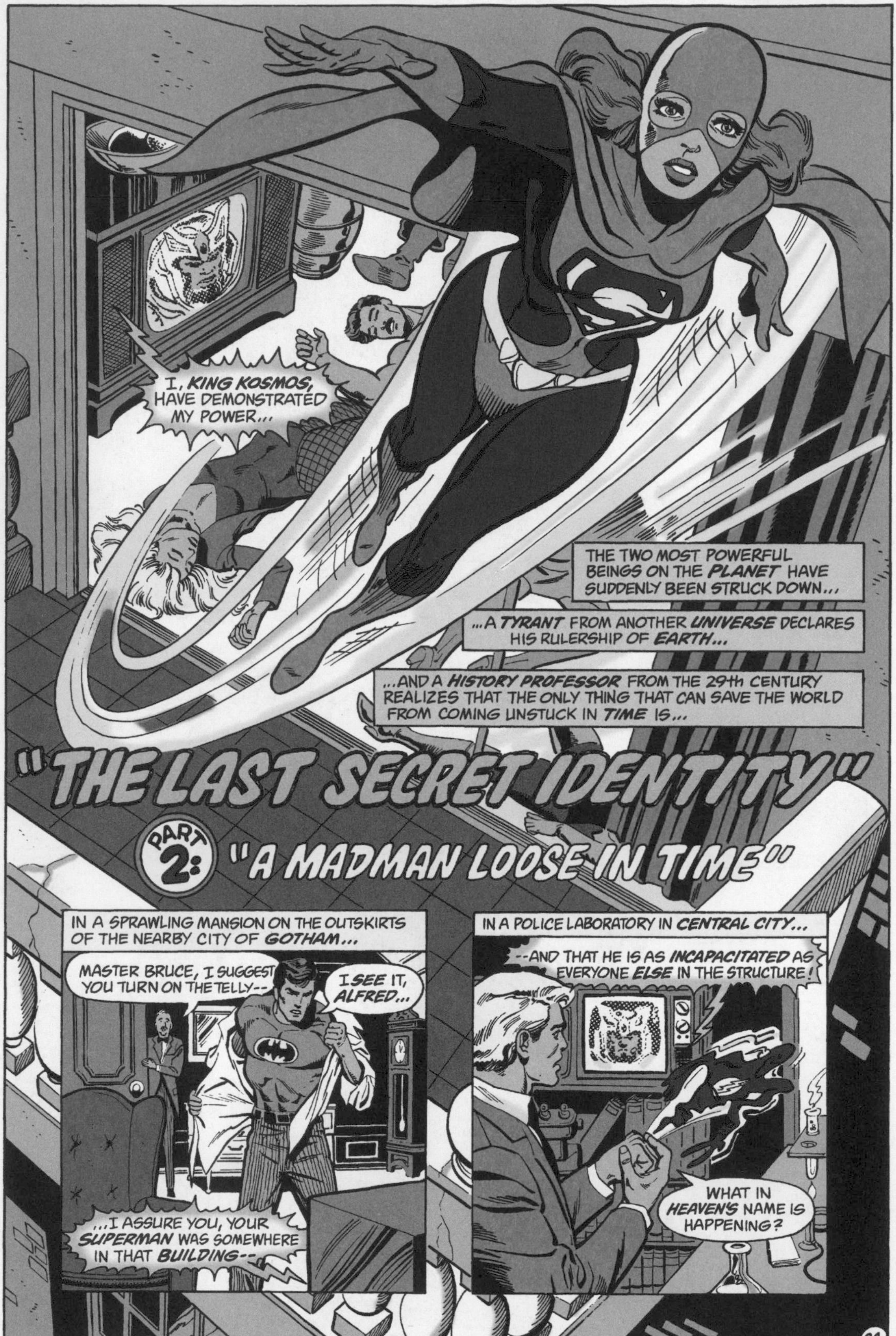
I, KING KOSMOS, HAVE DEMONSTRATED MY POWER...
THE TWO MOST POWERFUL BEINGS ON THE PLANET HAVE SUDDENLY BEEN STRUCK DOWN...
...A TYRANT FROM ANOTHER UNIVERSE DECLARES HIS RULERSHIP OF EARTH...
...AND A HISTORY PROFESSOR FROM THE 29th CENTURY REALIZES THAT THE ONLY THING THAT CAN SAVE THE WORLD FROM COMING UNSTUCK IN TIME IS...
"THE LAST SECRET IDENTITY"
PART 2: "A MADMAN LOOSE IN TIME"
IN A SPRAWLING MANSION ON THE OUTSKIRTS OF THE NEARBY CITY OF GOTHAM...
MASTER BRUCE, I SUGGEST YOU TURN ON THE TELLY--
I SEE IT, ALFRED...
...I ASSURE YOU, YOUR SUPERMAN WAS SOMEWHERE IN THAT BUILDING--
IN A POLICE LABORATORY IN CENTRAL CITY...
--AND THAT HE IS AS INCAPACITATED AS EVERYONE ELSE IN THE STRUCTURE!
WHAT IN HEAVEN'S NAME IS HAPPENING?
24

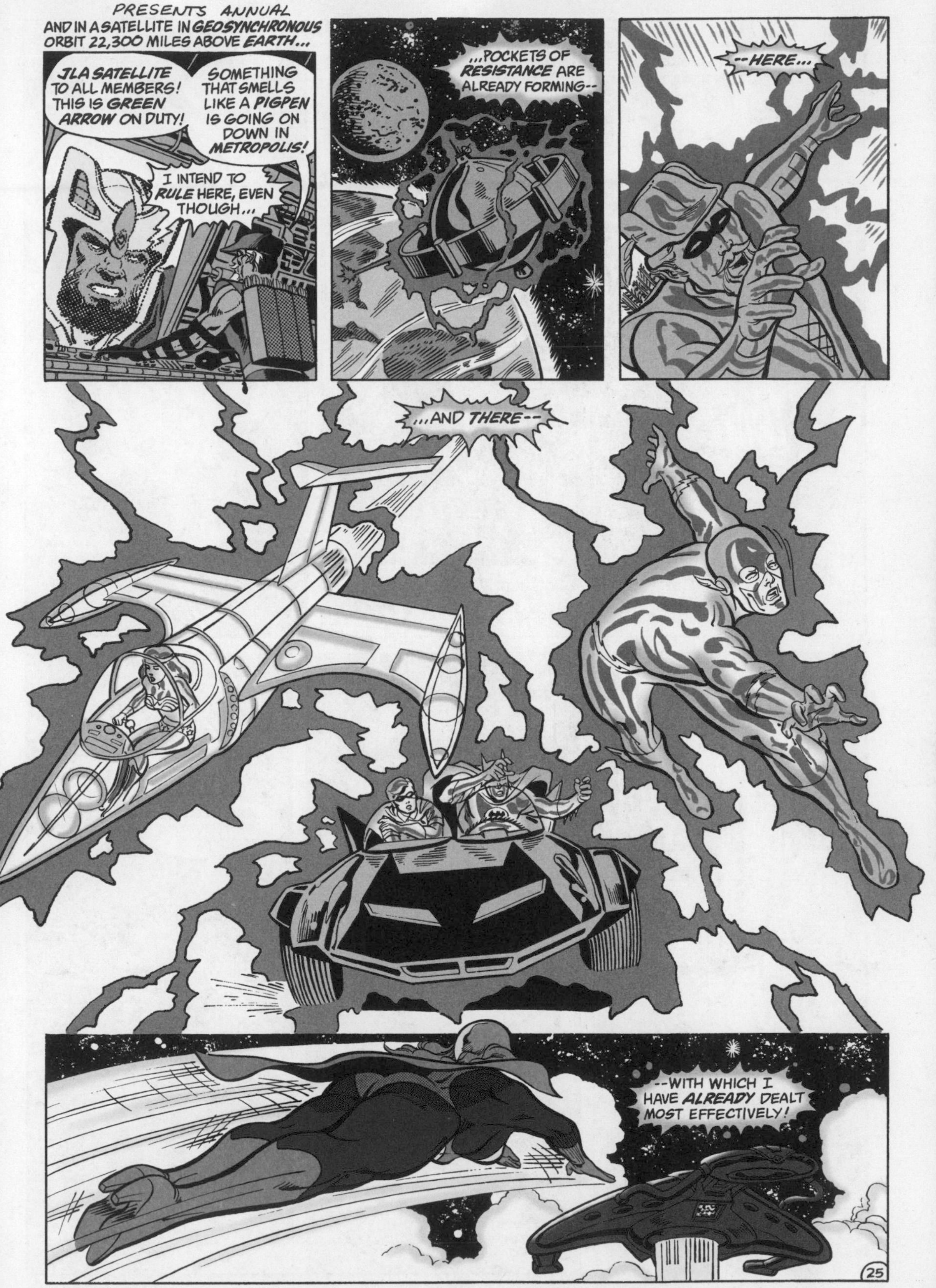
PRESENTS ANNUAL
AND IN A SATELLITE IN GEOSYNCHRONOUS ORBIT 22,300 MILES ABOVE EARTH...
JLA SATELLITE TO ALL MEMBERS! THIS IS GREEN ARROW ON DUTY!
SOMETHING THAT SMELLS LIKE A PIGPEN IS GOING ON DOWN IN METROPOLIS!
I INTEND TO RULE HERE, EVEN THOUGH...
...POCKETS OF RESISTANCE ARE ALREADY FORMING--
--HERE...
...AND THERE--
--WITH WHICH I HAVE ALREADY DEALT MOST EFFECTIVELY!
25

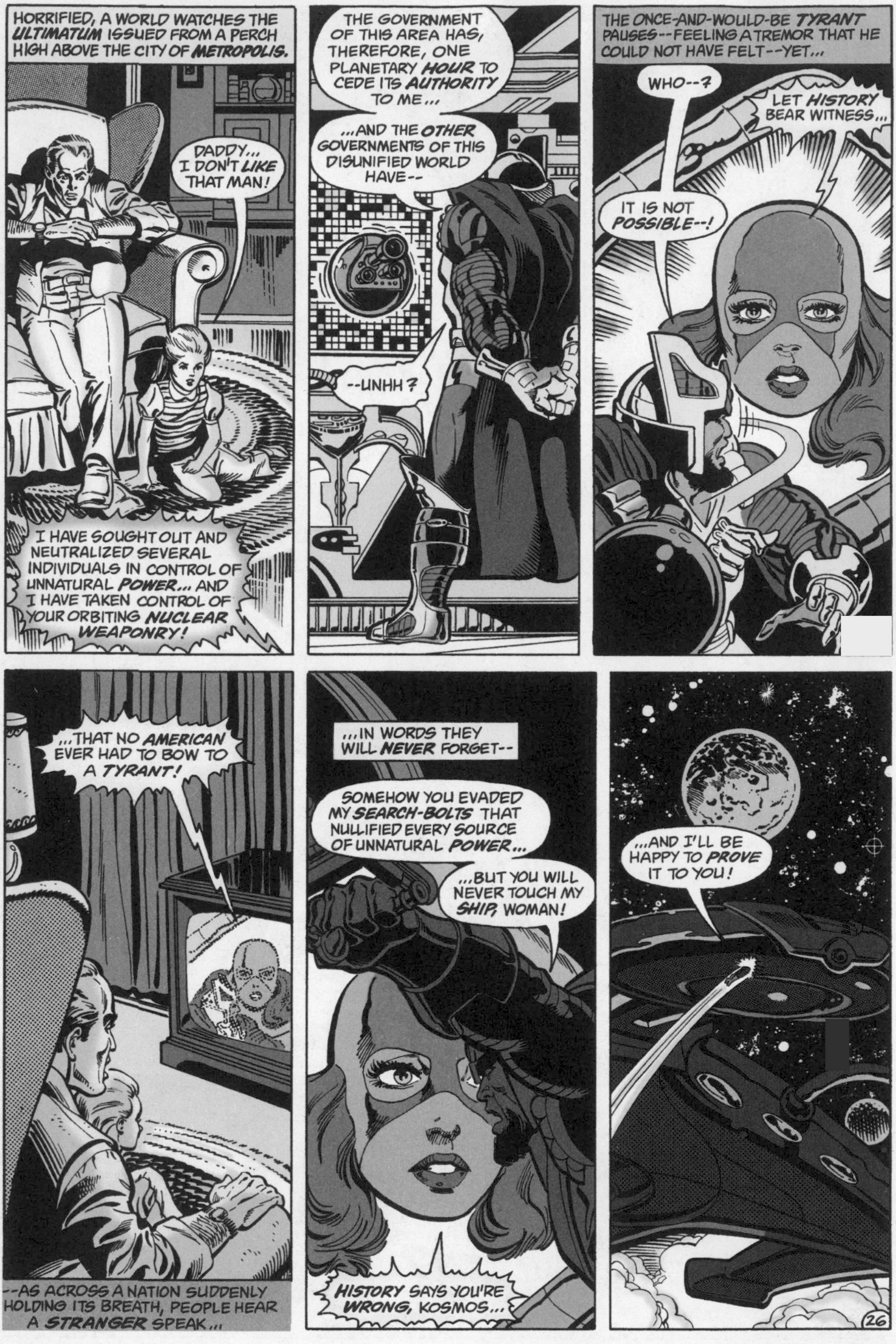
HORRIFIED, A WORLD WATCHES THE ULTIMATUM ISSUED FROM A PERCH HIGH ABOVE THE CITY OF METROPOLIS.
DADDY... I DON'T LIKE THAT MAN!
I HAVE SOUGHT OUT AND NEUTRALIZED SEVERAL INDIVIDUALS IN CONTROL OF UNNATURAL POWER... AND I HAVE TAKEN CONTROL OF YOUR ORBITING NUCLEAR WEAPONRY!
THE GOVERNMENT OF THIS AREA HAS, THEREFORE, ONE PLANETARY HOUR TO CEDE ITS AUTHORITY TO ME...
...AND THE OTHER GOVERNMENTS OF THIS DISUNIFIED WORLD HAVE--
--UNHH?
THE ONCE-AND-WOULD-BE TYRANT PAUSES--FEELING A TREMOR THAT HE COULD NOT HAVE FELT--YET...
WHO--?
LET HISTORY BEAR WITNESS...
IT IS NOT POSSIBLE--!
...THAT NO AMERICAN EVER HAD TO BOW TO A TYRANT!
--AS ACROSS A NATION SUDDENLY HOLDING ITS BREATH, PEOPLE HEAR A STRANGER SPEAK...
...IN WORDS THEY WILL NEVER FORGET--
SOMEHOW YOU EVADED MY SEARCH-BOLTS THAT NULLIFIED EVERY SOURCE OF UNNATURAL POWER...
...BUT YOU WILL NEVER TOUCH MY SHIP, WOMAN!
HISTORY SAYS YOU'RE WRONG, KOSMOS...
...AND I'LL BE HAPPY TO PROVE IT TO YOU!
26

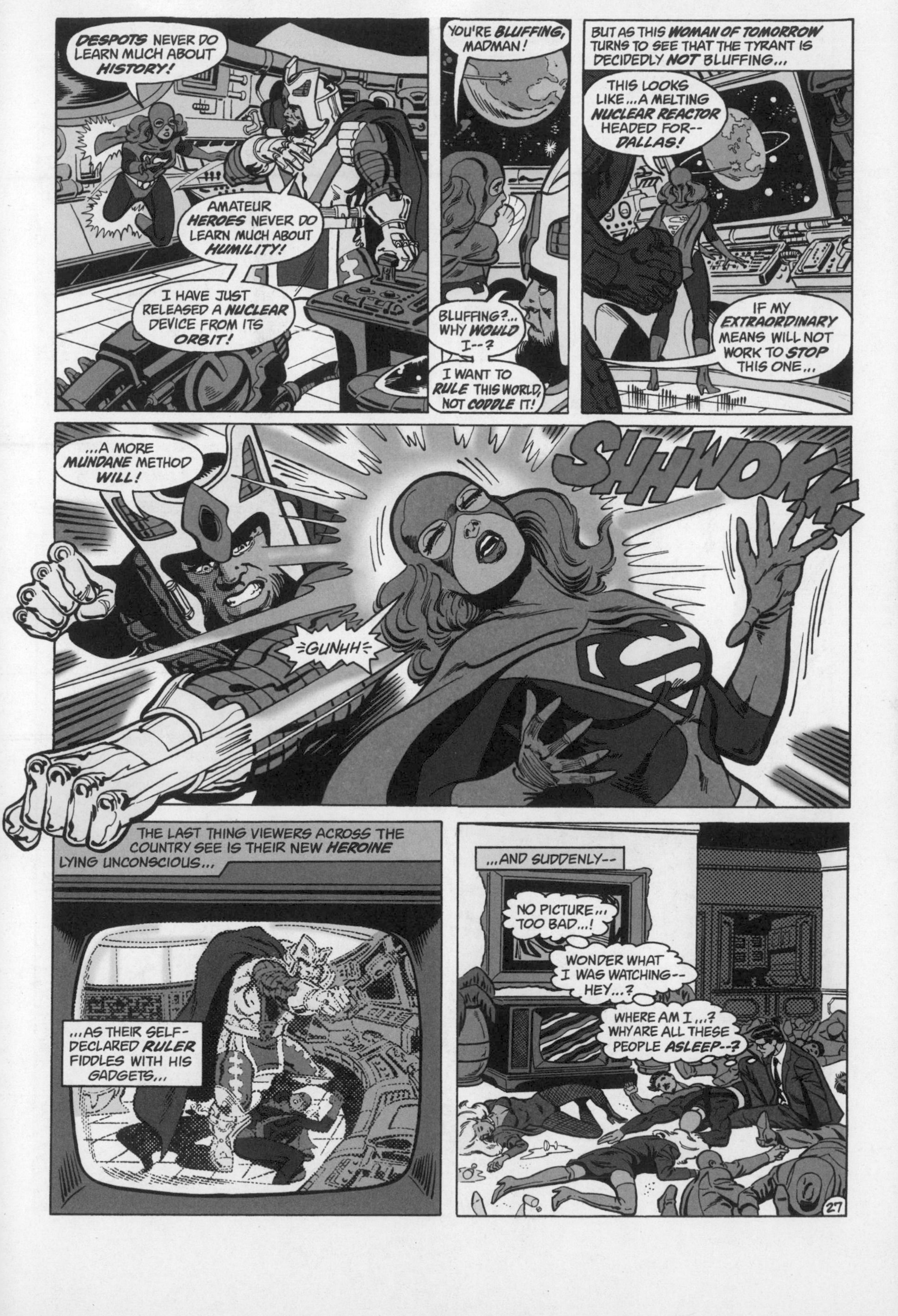
DESPOTS NEVER DO LEARN MUCH ABOUT HISTORY!
AMATEUR HEROES NEVER DO LEARN MUCH ABOUT HUMILITY!
I HAVE JUST RELEASED A NUCLEAR DEVICE FROM ITS ORBIT!
YOU'RE BLUFFING, MADMAN!
BLUFFING?... WHY WOULD I--?
I WANT TO RULE THIS WORLD, NOT CODDLE IT!
BUT AS THIS WOMAN OF TOMORROW TURNS TO SEE THAT THE TYRANT IS DECIDEDLY NOT BLUFFING...
THIS LOOKS LIKE...A MELTING NUCLEAR REACTOR HEADED FOR--DALLAS!
IF MY EXTRAORDINARY MEANS WILL NOT WORK TO STOP THIS ONE...
...A MORE MUNDANE METHOD WILL!
SHHWOKK!
GUNHH
THE LAST THING VIEWERS ACROSS THE COUNTRY SEE IS THEIR NEW HEROINE LYING UNCONSCIOUS...
...AS THEIR SELF-DECLARED RULER FIDDLES WITH HIS GADGETS...
...AND SUDDENLY--
NO PICTURE... TOO BAD...!
WONDER WHAT I WAS WATCHING--HEY...?
WHERE AM I...? WHY ARE ALL THESE PEOPLE ASLEEP--?
27

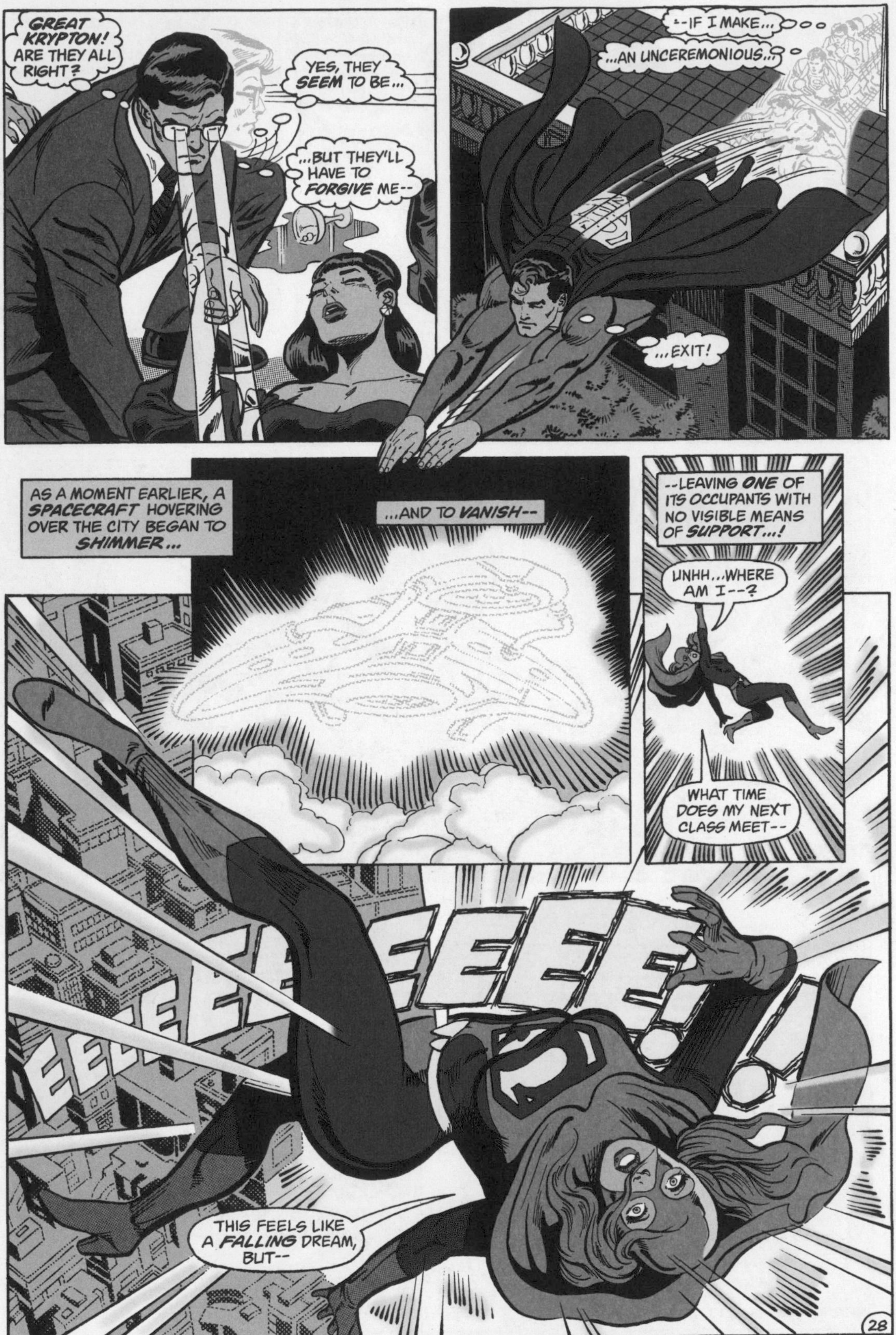
GREAT KRYPTON! ARE THEY ALL RIGHT?
YES, THEY SEEM TO BE...
...BUT THEY'LL HAVE TO FORGIVE ME--
--IF I MAKE...
...AN UNCEREMONIOUS...
...EXIT!
AS A MOMENT EARLIER, A SPACECRAFT HOVERING OVER THE CITY BEGAN TO SHIMMER...
...AND TO VANISH--
--LEAVING ONE OF ITS OCCUPANTS WITH NO VISIBLE MEANS OF SUPPORT...!
UNHH...WHERE AM I--?
WHAT TIME DOES MY NEXT CLASS MEET--
EEEEEEEE!
THIS FEELS LIKE A FALLING DREAM, BUT--
28

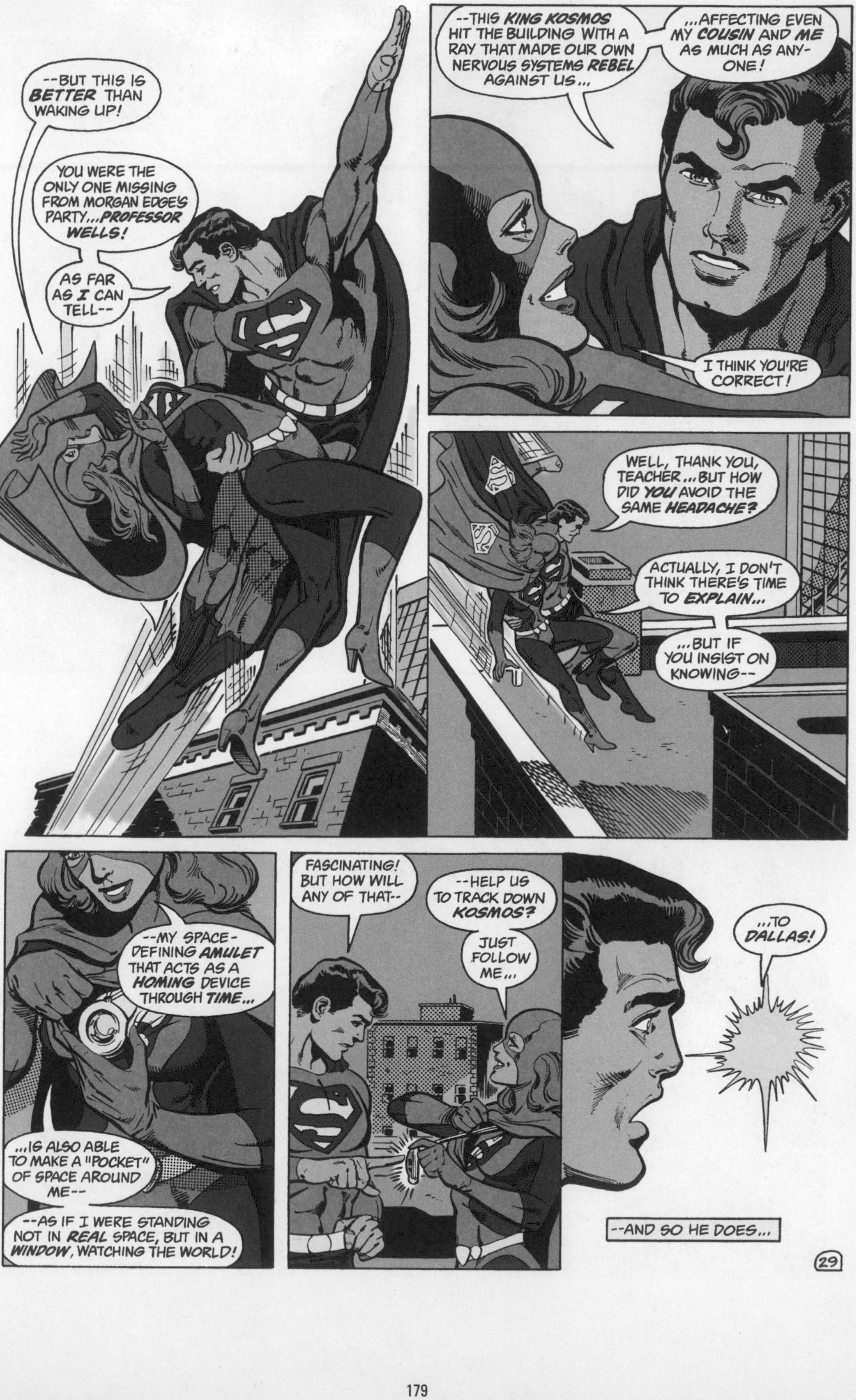
--BUT THIS IS BETTER THAN WAKING UP!
YOU WERE THE ONLY ONE MISSING FROM MORGAN EDGE'S PARTY...PROFESSOR WELLS!
AS FAR AS I CAN TELL--
--THIS KING KOSMOS HIT THE BUILDING WITH A RAY THAT MADE OUR OWN NERVOUS SYSTEMS REBEL AGAINST US...
...AFFECTING EVEN MY COUSIN AND ME AS MUCH AS ANY-ONE!
I THINK YOU'RE CORRECT!
WELL, THANK YOU, TEACHER...BUT HOW DID YOU AVOID THE SAME HEADACHE?
ACTUALLY, I DON'T THINK THERE'S TIME TO EXPLAIN...
...BUT IF YOU INSIST ON KNOWING--
--MY SPACE-DEFINING AMULET THAT ACTS AS A HOMING DEVICE THROUGH TIME...
...IS ALSO ABLE TO MAKE A "POCKET" OF SPACE AROUND ME--
--AS IF I WERE STANDING NOT IN REAL SPACE, BUT IN A WINDOW, WATCHING THE WORLD!
FASCINATING! BUT HOW WILL ANY OF THAT--
--HELP US TO TRACK DOWN KOSMOS?
JUST FOLLOW ME...
...TO DALLAS!
--AND SO HE DOES...
29

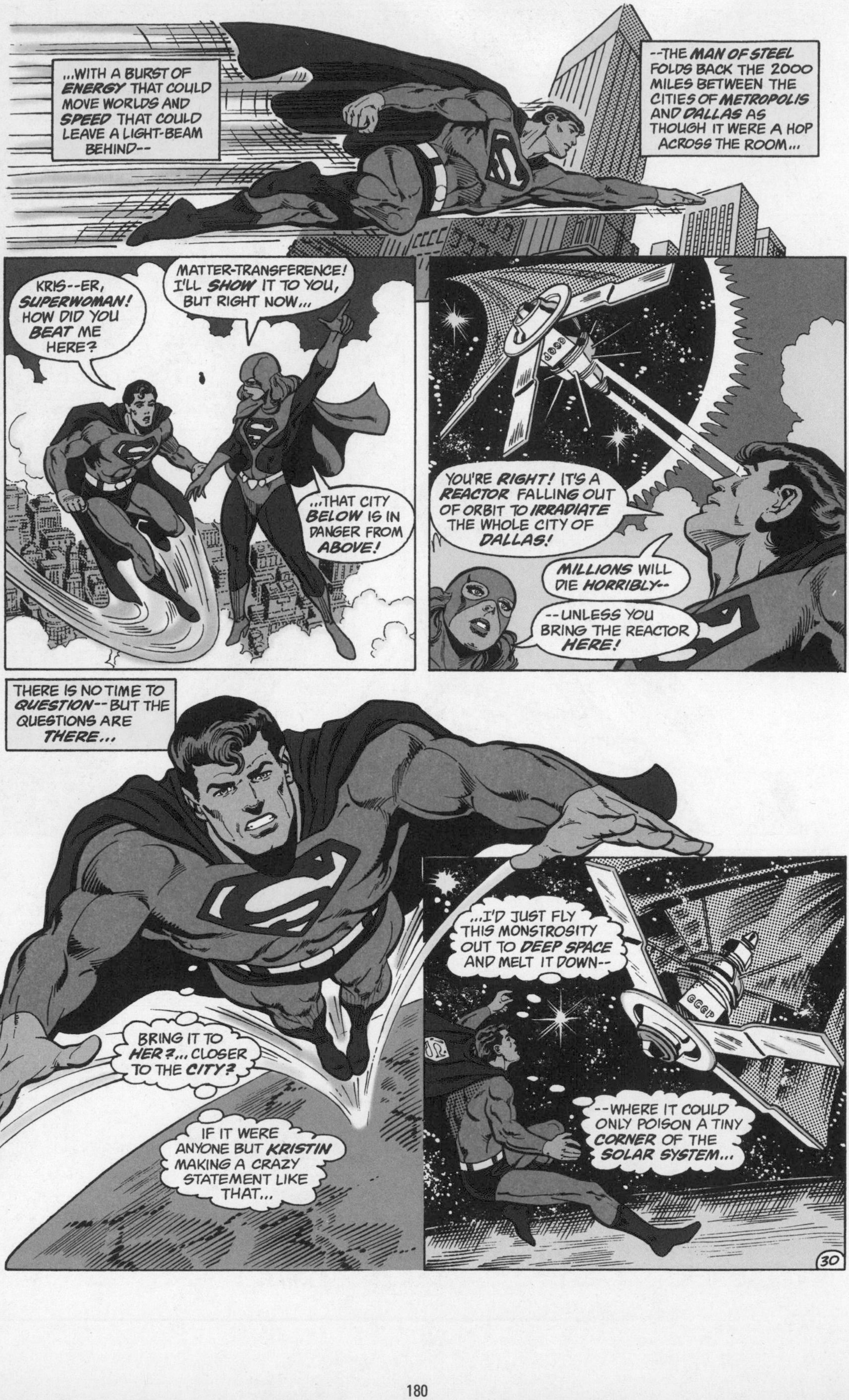
...WITH A BURST OF ENERGY THAT COULD MOVE WORLDS AND SPEED THAT COULD LEAVE A LIGHT-BEAM BEHIND--
--THE MAN OF STEEL FOLDS BACK THE 2000 MILES BETWEEN THE CITIES OF METROPOLIS AND DALLAS AS THOUGH IT WERE A HOP ACROSS THE ROOM...
KRIS--ER, SUPERWOMAN! HOW DID YOU BEAT ME HERE?
MATTER-TRANSFERENCE! I'LL SHOW IT TO YOU, BUT RIGHT NOW...
...THAT CITY BELOW IS IN DANGER FROM ABOVE!
YOU'RE RIGHT! IT'S A REACTOR FALLING OUT OF ORBIT TO IRRADIATE THE WHOLE CITY OF DALLAS!
MILLIONS WILL DIE HORRIBLY--
--UNLESS YOU BRING THE REACTOR HERE!
THERE IS NO TIME TO QUESTION-- BUT THE QUESTIONS ARE THERE...
BRING IT TO HER?... CLOSER TO THE CITY?
IF IT WERE ANYONE BUT KRISTIN MAKING A CRAZY STATEMENT LIKE THAT...
...I'D JUST FLY THIS MONSTROSITY OUT TO DEEP SPACE AND MELT IT DOWN--
--WHERE IT COULD ONLY POISON A TINY CORNER OF THE SOLAR SYSTEM...
30

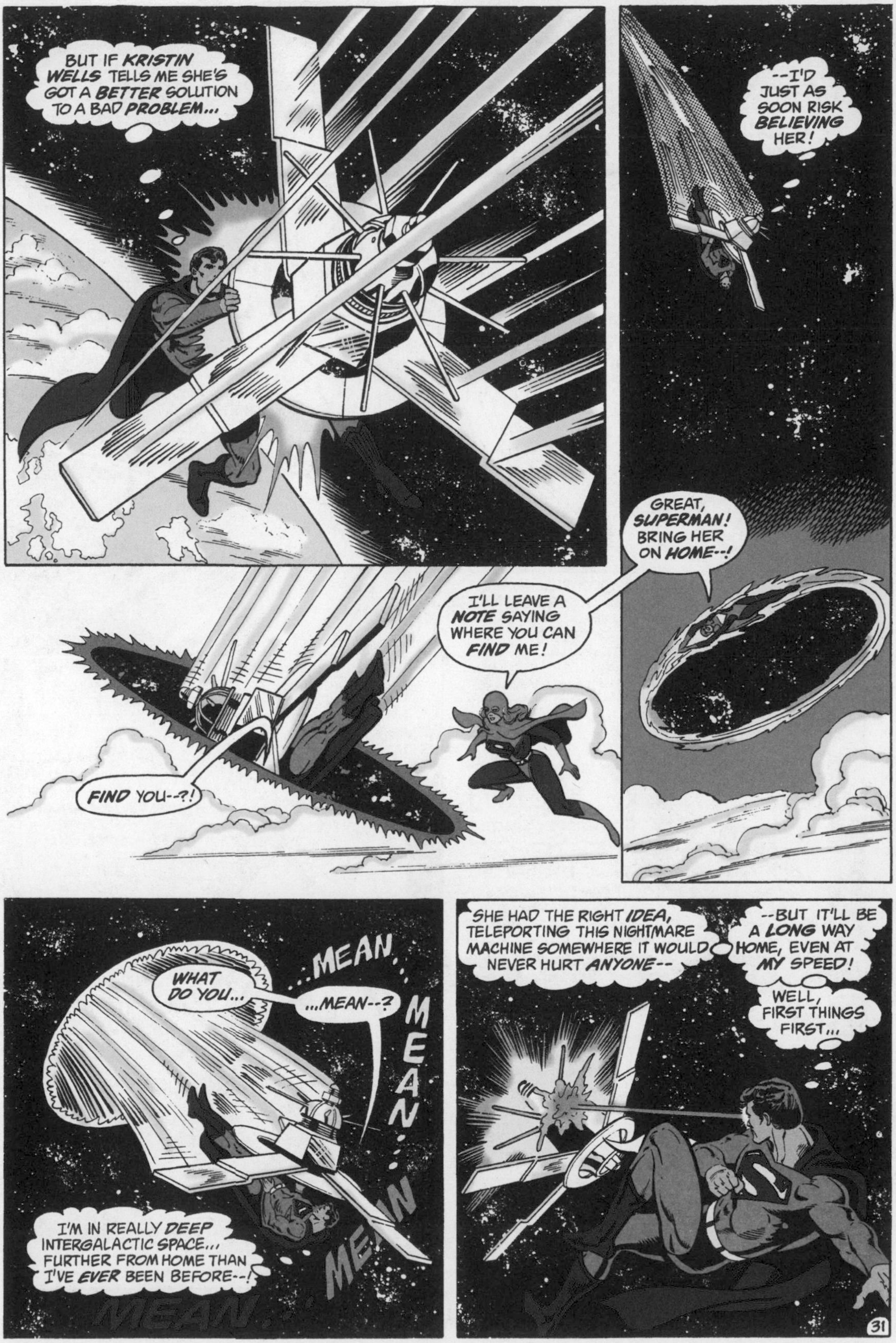
BUT IF KRISTIN WELLS TELLS ME SHE'S GOT A BETTER SOLUTION TO A BAD PROBLEM...
--I'D JUST AS SOON RISK BELIEVING HER!
I'LL LEAVE A NOTE SAYING WHERE YOU CAN FIND ME!
FIND YOU--?!
GREAT, SUPERMAN! BRING HER ON HOME--!
WHAT DO YOU...
...MEAN--?
...MEAN...
MEAN...
MEAN...
MEAN
MEAN...
I'M IN REALLY DEEP INTERGALACTIC SPACE... FURTHER FROM HOME THAN I'VE EVER BEEN BEFORE--!
SHE HAD THE RIGHT IDEA, TELEPORTING THIS NIGHTMARE MACHINE SOMEWHERE IT WOULD NEVER HURT ANYONE--
--BUT IT'LL BE A LONG WAY HOME, EVEN AT MY SPEED!
WELL, FIRST THINGS FIRST...
31

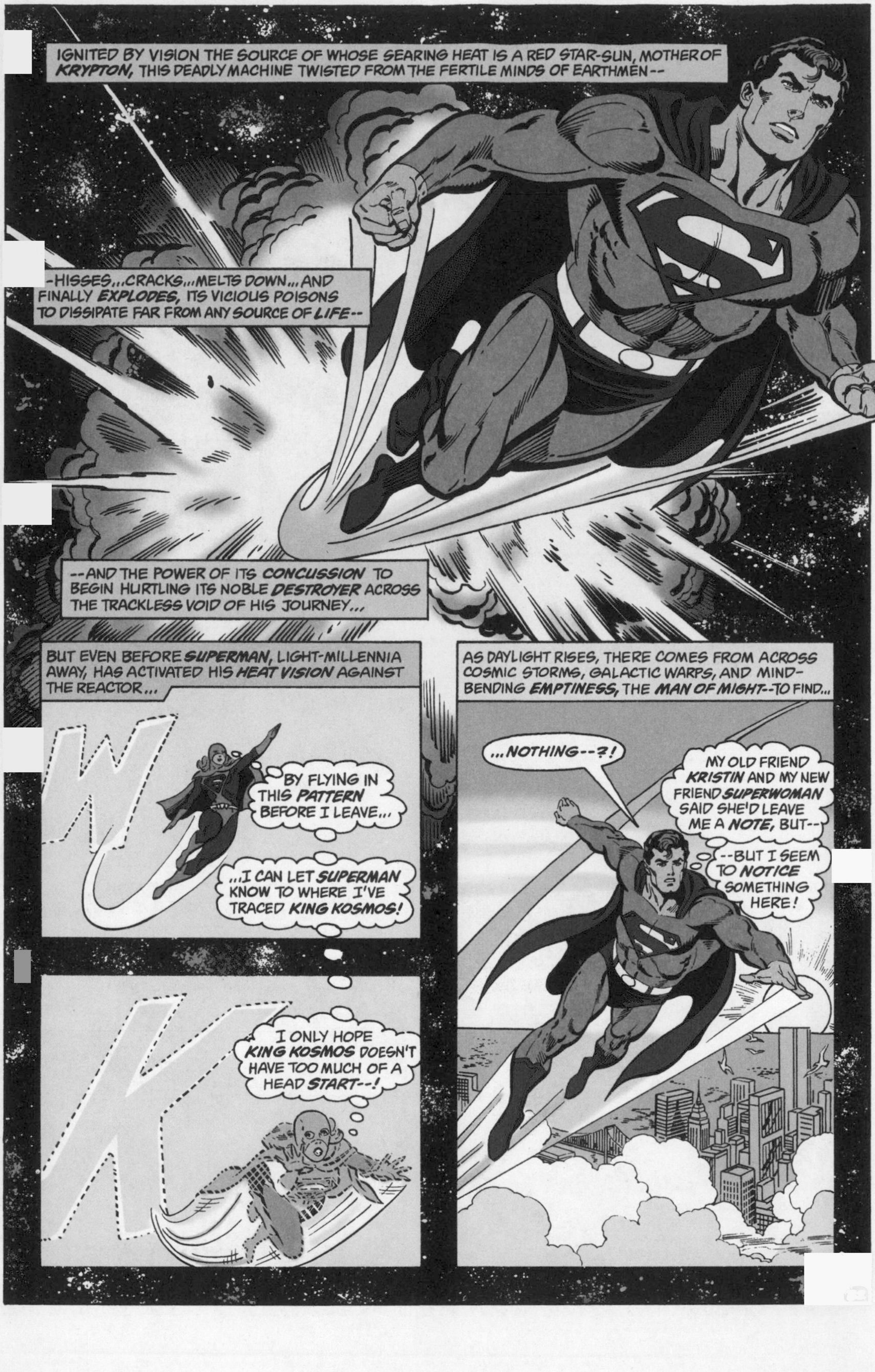
IGNITED BY VISION THE SOURCE OF WHOSE SEARING HEAT IS A RED STAR-SUN, MOTHER OF KRYPTON, THIS DEADLY MACHINE TWISTED FROM THE FERTILE MINDS OF EARTHMEN--
-HISSES...CRACKS...MELTS DOWN... AND FINALLY EXPLODES, ITS VICIOUS POISONS TO DISSIPATE FAR FROM ANY SOURCE OF LIFE--
--AND THE POWER OF ITS CONCUSSION TO BEGIN HURTLING ITS NOBLE DESTROYER ACROSS THE TRACKLESS VOID OF HIS JOURNEY...
BUT EVEN BEFORE SUPERMAN, LIGHT-MILLENNIA AWAY, HAS ACTIVATED HIS HEAT VISION AGAINST THE REACTOR...
BY FLYING IN THIS PATTERN BEFORE I LEAVE...
...I CAN LET SUPERMAN KNOW TO WHERE I'VE TRACED KING KOSMOS!
I ONLY HOPE KING KOSMOS DOESN'T HAVE TOO MUCH OF A HEAD START--!
AS DAYLIGHT RISES, THERE COMES FROM ACROSS COSMIC STORMS, GALACTIC WARPS, AND MIND-BENDING EMPTINESS, THE MAN OF MIGHT--TO FIND...
...NOTHING--?!
MY OLD FRIEND KRISTIN AND MY NEW FRIEND SUPERWOMAN SAID SHE'D LEAVE ME A NOTE, BUT--
--BUT I SEEM TO NOTICE SOMETHING HERE!

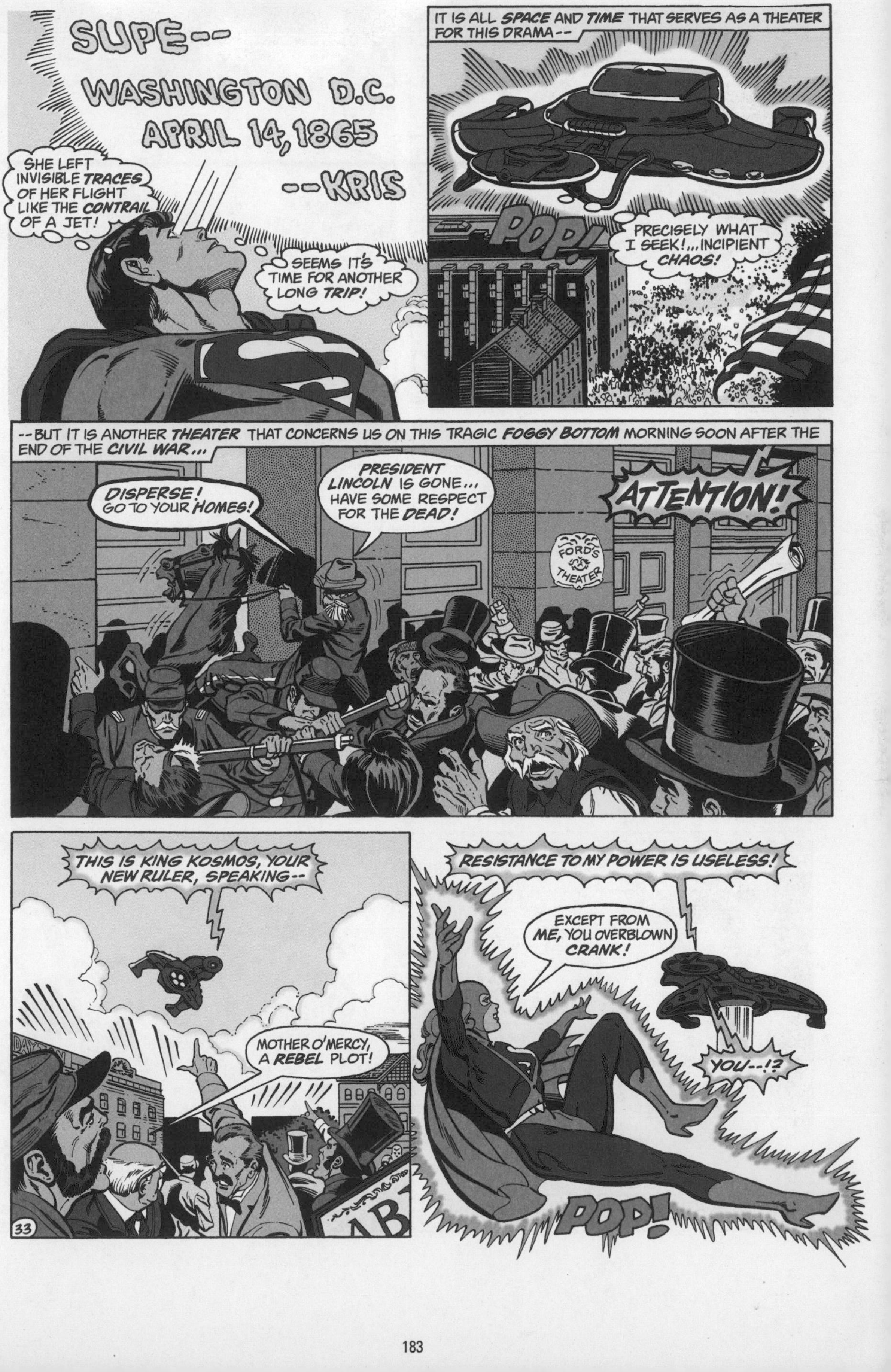
SUPE--
WASHINGTON D.C. APRIL 14, 1865 --KRIS
SHE LEFT INVISIBLE TRACES OF HER FLIGHT LIKE THE CONTRAIL OF A JET!
SEEMS IT'S TIME FOR ANOTHER LONG TRIP!
IT IS ALL SPACE AND TIME THAT SERVES AS A THEATER FOR THIS DRAMA--
POP!
PRECISELY WHAT I SEEK!... INCIPIENT CHAOS!
--BUT IT IS ANOTHER THEATER THAT CONCERNS US ON THIS TRAGIC FOGGY BOTTOM MORNING SOON AFTER THE END OF THE CIVIL WAR...
DISPERSE! GO TO YOUR HOMES!
PRESIDENT LINCOLN IS GONE... HAVE SOME RESPECT FOR THE DEAD!
ATTENTION!
FORD'S THEATER
THIS IS KING KOSMOS, YOUR NEW RULER, SPEAKING--
MOTHER O'MERCY, A REBEL PLOT!
33
RESISTANCE TO MY POWER IS USELESS!
EXCEPT FROM ME, YOU OVERBLOWN CRANK!
YOU--!?
POP!

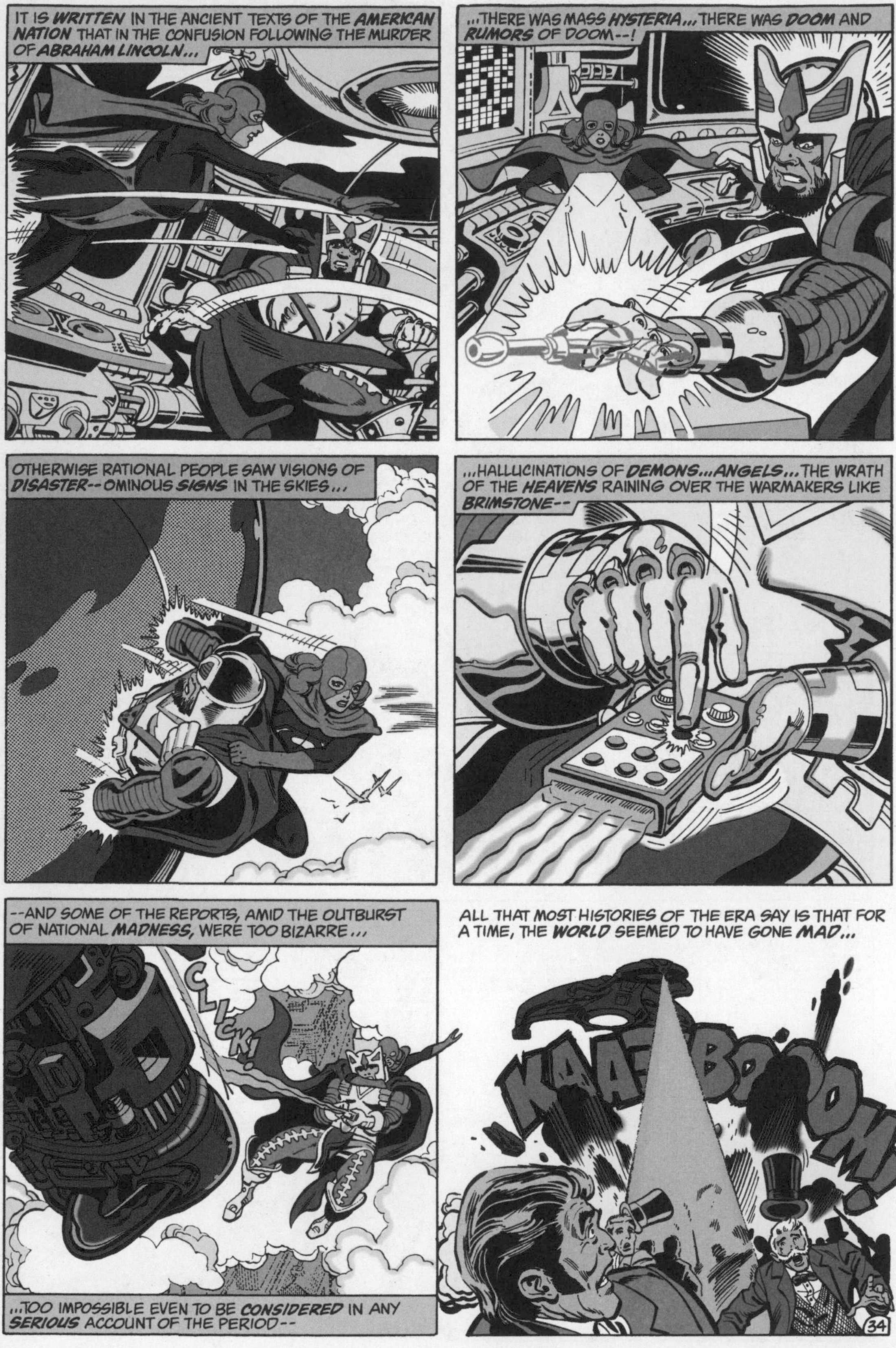
IT IS WRITTEN IN THE ANCIENT TEXTS OF THE AMERICAN NATION THAT IN THE CONFUSION FOLLOWING THE MURDER OF ABRAHAM LINCOLN...
...THERE WAS MASS HYSTERIA... THERE WAS DOOM AND RUMORS OF DOOM--!
OTHERWISE RATIONAL PEOPLE SAW VISIONS OF DISASTER--OMINOUS SIGNS IN THE SKIES...
...HALLUCINATIONS OF DEMONS... ANGELS... THE WRATH OF THE HEAVENS RAINING OVER THE WARMAKERS LIKE BRIMSTONE--
--AND SOME OF THE REPORTS, AMID THE OUTBURST OF NATIONAL MADNESS, WERE TOO BIZARRE...
CLICK!
...TOO IMPOSSIBLE EVEN TO BE CONSIDERED IN ANY SERIOUS ACCOUNT OF THE PERIOD--
ALL THAT MOST HISTORIES OF THE ERA SAY IS THAT FOR A TIME, THE WORLD SEEMED TO HAVE GONE MAD...
34

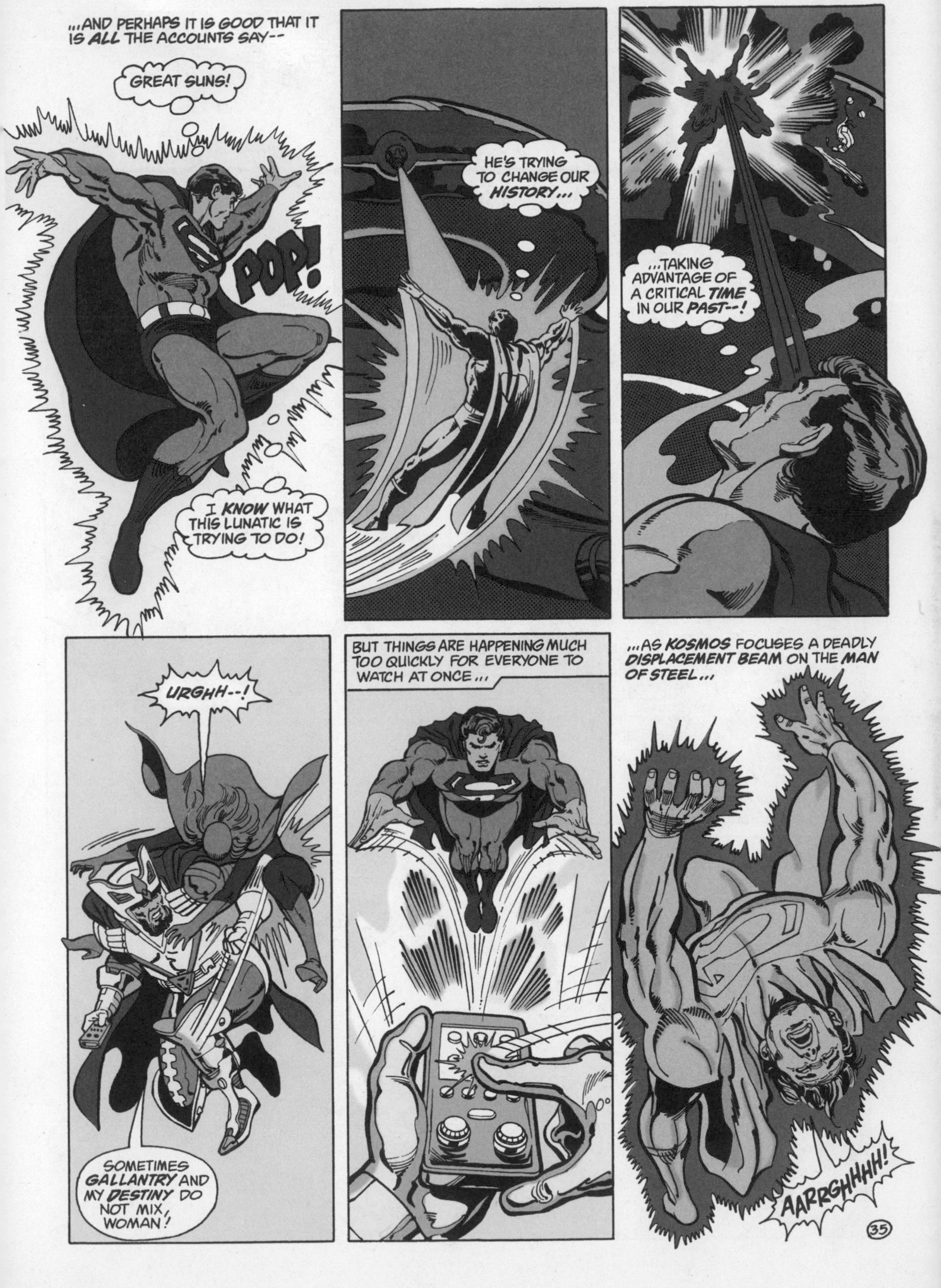
...AND PERHAPS IT IS GOOD THAT IT IS ALL THE ACCOUNTS SAY--
GREAT SUNS!
POP!
I KNOW WHAT THIS LUNATIC IS TRYING TO DO!
HE'S TRYING TO CHANGE OUR HISTORY...
...TAKING ADVANTAGE OF A CRITICAL TIME IN OUR PAST--!
URGHH--!
SOMETIMES GALLANTRY AND MY DESTINY DO NOT MIX, WOMAN!
BUT THINGS ARE HAPPENING MUCH TOO QUICKLY FOR EVERYONE TO WATCH AT ONCE...
...AS KOSMOS FOCUSES A DEADLY DISPLACEMENT BEAM ON THE MAN OF STEEL...
AARRGHHHH!
35

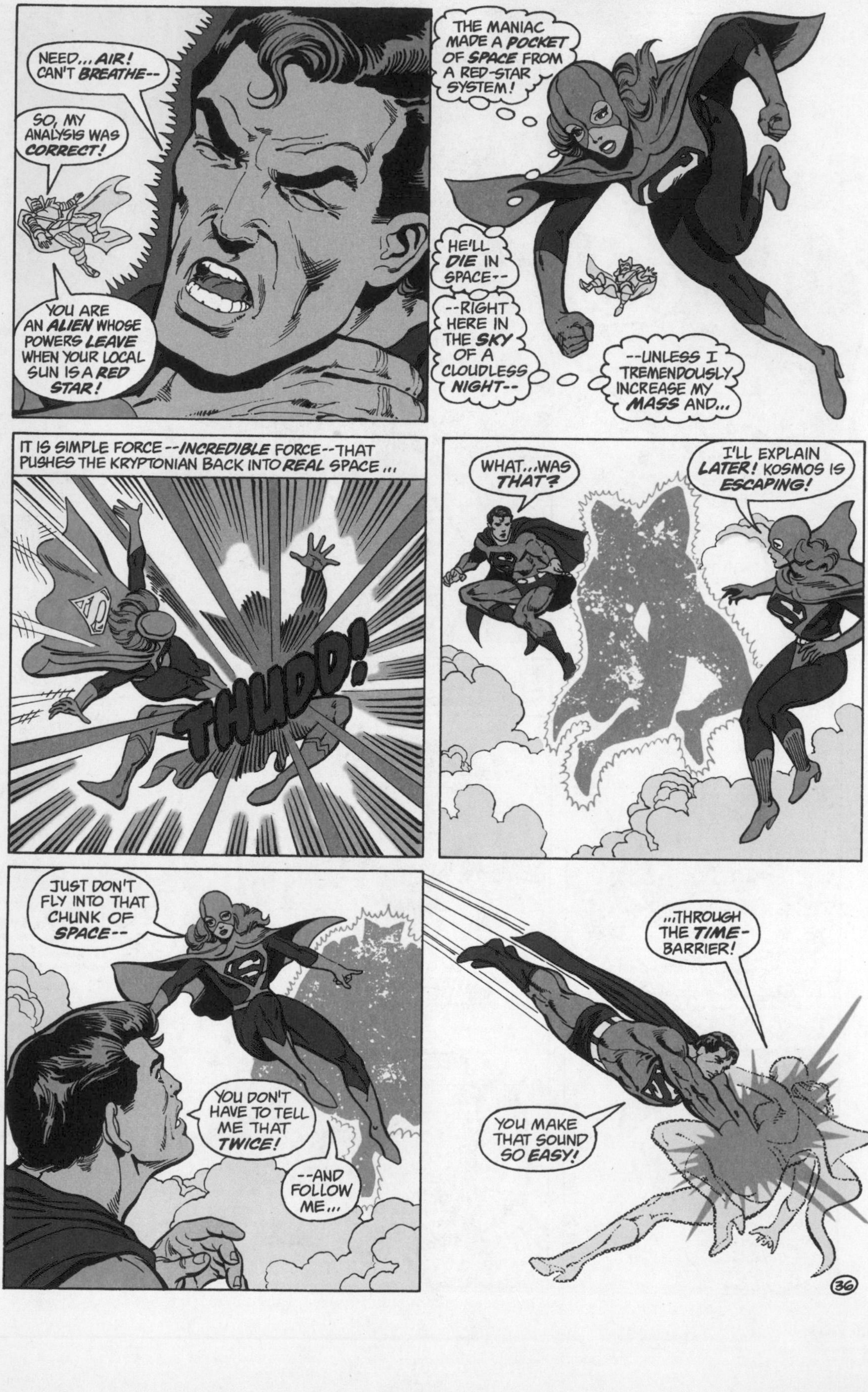
NEED... AIR! CAN'T BREATHE--
SO, MY ANALYSIS WAS CORRECT!
YOU ARE AN ALIEN WHOSE POWERS LEAVE WHEN YOUR LOCAL SUN IS A RED STAR!
THE MANIAC MADE A POCKET OF SPACE FROM A RED-STAR SYSTEM!
HE'LL DIE IN SPACE--
--RIGHT HERE IN THE SKY OF A CLOUDLESS NIGHT--
--UNLESS I TREMENDOUSLY INCREASE MY MASS AND...
IT IS SIMPLE FORCE--INCREDIBLE FORCE--THAT PUSHES THE KRYPTONIAN BACK INTO REAL SPACE...
THUDD!
WHAT...WAS THAT?
I'LL EXPLAIN LATER! KOSMOS IS ESCAPING!
JUST DON'T FLY INTO THAT CHUNK OF SPACE--
YOU DON'T HAVE TO TELL ME THAT TWICE!
--AND FOLLOW ME...
...THROUGH THE TIME-BARRIER!
YOU MAKE THAT SOUND SO EASY!
36

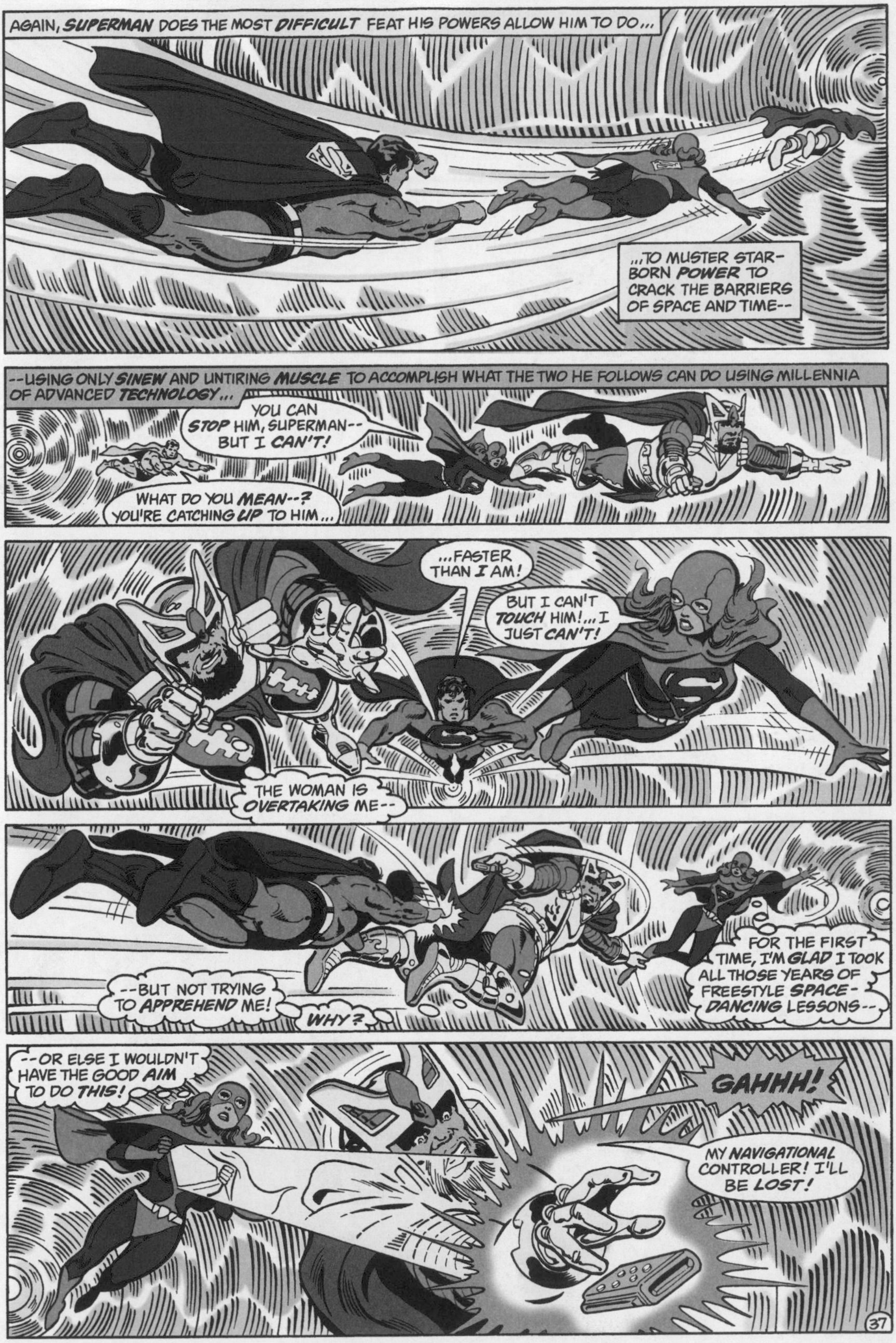

AGAIN, SUPERMAN DOES THE MOST DIFFICULT FEAT HIS POWERS ALLOW HIM TO DO...
...TO MUSTER STAR-BORN POWER TO CRACK THE BARRIERS OF SPACE AND TIME--
--USING ONLY SINEW AND UNTIRING MUSCLE TO ACCOMPLISH WHAT THE TWO HE FOLLOWS CAN DO USING MILLENNIA OF ADVANCED TECHNOLOGY...
YOU CAN STOP HIM, SUPERMAN--BUT I CAN'T!
WHAT DO YOU MEAN--? YOU'RE CATCHING UP TO HIM...
...FASTER THAN I AM!
BUT I CAN'T TOUCH HIM!... I JUST CAN'T!
THE WOMAN IS OVERTAKING ME--
--BUT NOT TRYING TO APPREHEND ME!
WHY?
FOR THE FIRST TIME, I'M GLAD I TOOK ALL THOSE YEARS OF FREESTYLE SPACE-DANCING LESSONS--
--OR ELSE I WOULDN'T HAVE THE GOOD AIM TO DO THIS!
GAHHH!
MY NAVIGATIONAL CONTROLLER! I'LL BE LOST!
37

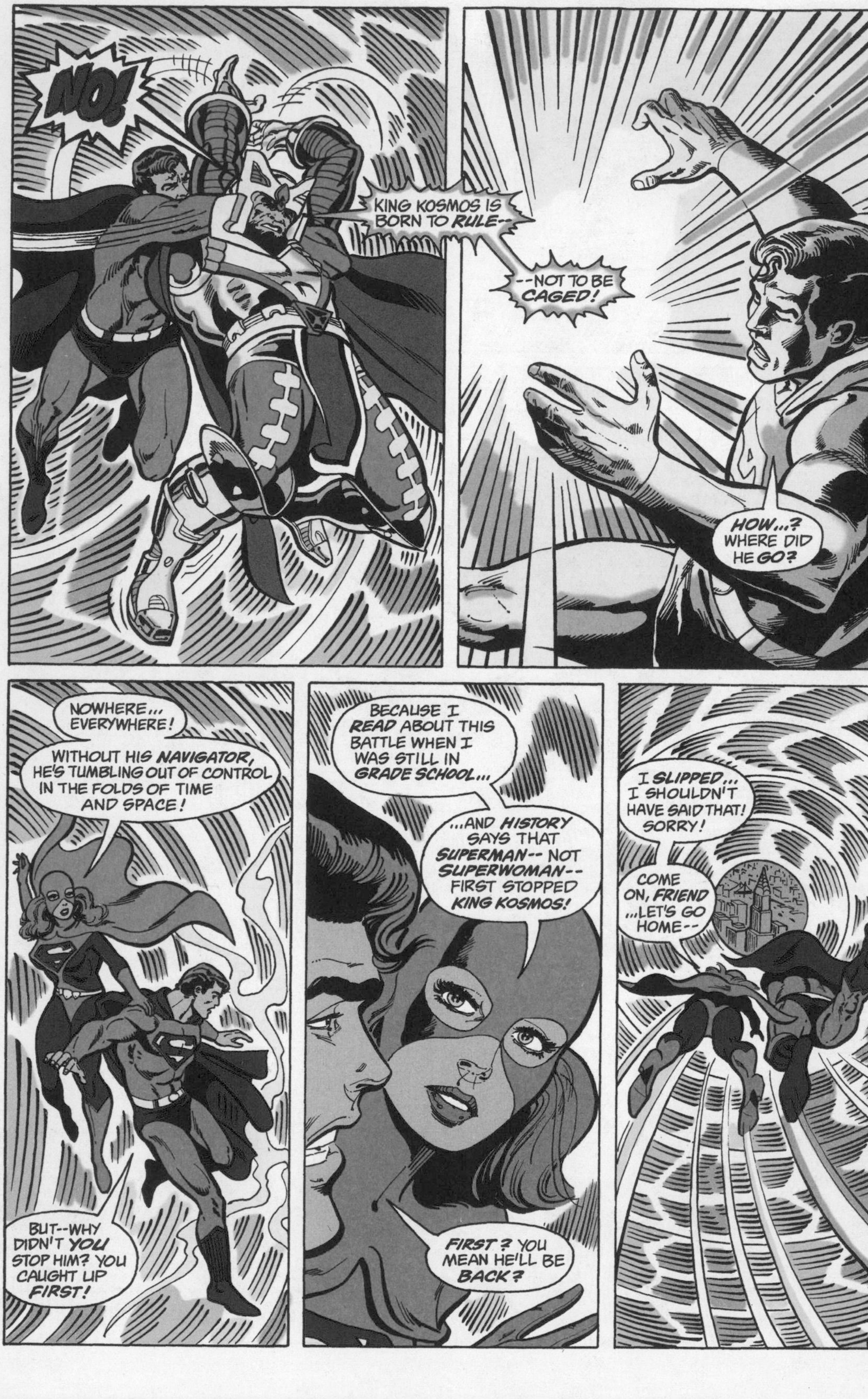
NO!
KING KOSMOS IS BORN TO RULE--
--NOT TO BE CAGED!
HOW...? WHERE DID HE GO?
NOWHERE... EVERYWHERE!
WITHOUT HIS NAVIGATOR, HE'S TUMBLING OUT OF CONTROL IN THE FOLDS OF TIME AND SPACE!
BUT--WHY DIDN'T YOU STOP HIM? YOU CAUGHT UP FIRST!
BECAUSE I READ ABOUT THIS BATTLE WHEN I WAS STILL IN GRADE SCHOOL...
...AND HISTORY SAYS THAT SUPERMAN-- NOT SUPERWOMAN-- FIRST STOPPED KING KOSMOS!
FIRST? YOU MEAN HE'LL BE BACK?
I SLIPPED... I SHOULDN'T HAVE SAID THAT! SORRY!
COME ON, FRIEND ...LET'S GO HOME--
38

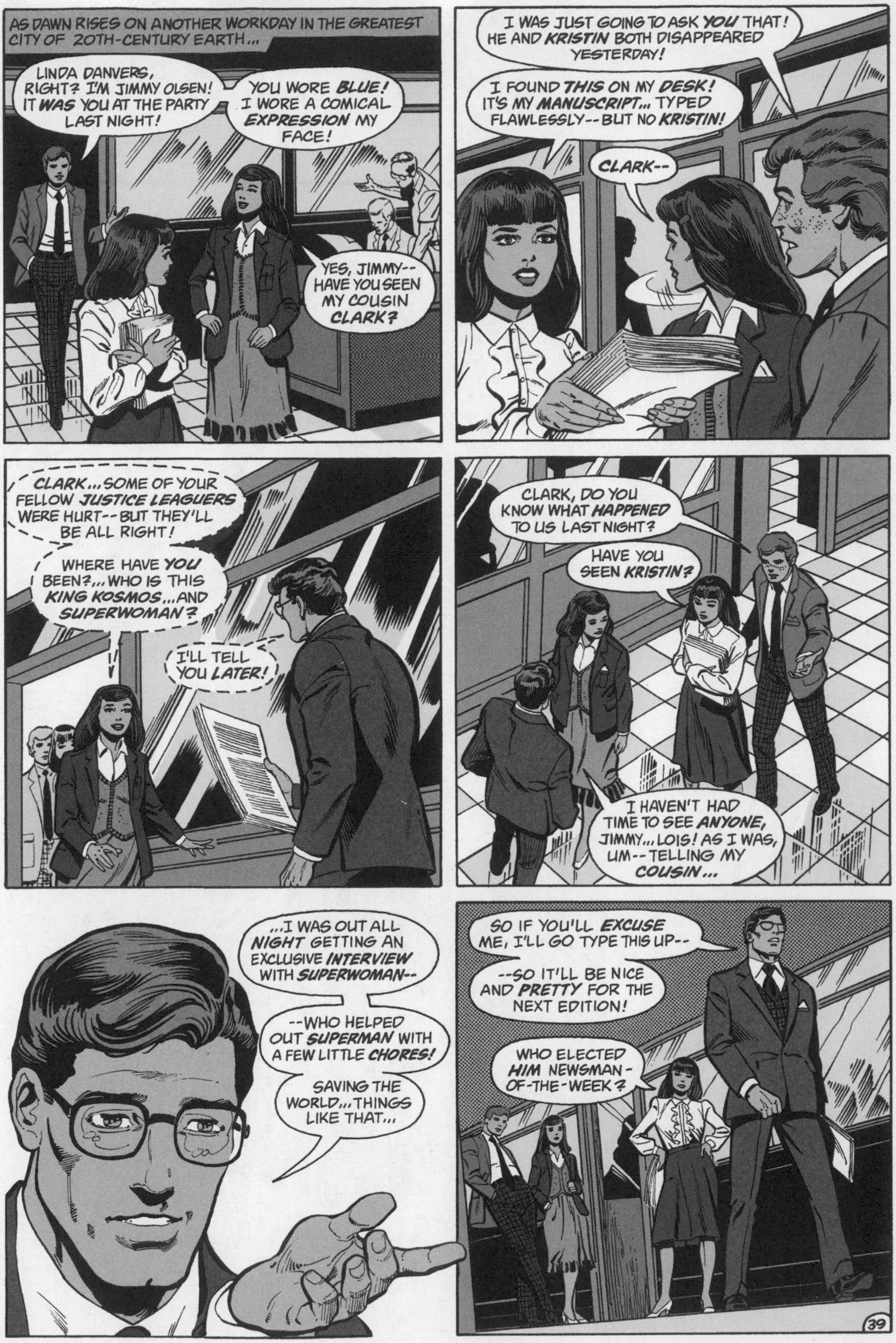
AS DAWN RISES ON ANOTHER WORKDAY IN THE GREATEST CITY OF 20TH-CENTURY EARTH...
LINDA DANVERS, RIGHT? I'M JIMMY OLSEN! IT WAS YOU AT THE PARTY LAST NIGHT!
YOU WORE BLUE! I WORE A COMICAL EXPRESSION MY FACE!
YES, JIMMY-- HAVE YOU SEEN MY COUSIN CLARK?
I WAS JUST GOING TO ASK YOU THAT! HE AND KRISTIN BOTH DISAPPEARED YESTERDAY!
I FOUND THIS ON MY DESK! IT'S MY MANUSCRIPT... TYPED FLAWLESSLY--BUT NO KRISTIN!
CLARK--
CLARK... SOME OF YOUR FELLOW JUSTICE LEAGUERS WERE HURT--BUT THEY'LL BE ALL RIGHT!
WHERE HAVE YOU BEEN?... WHO IS THIS KING KOSMOS... AND SUPERWOMAN?
I'LL TELL YOU LATER!
CLARK, DO YOU KNOW WHAT HAPPENED TO US LAST NIGHT?
HAVE YOU SEEN KRISTIN?
I HAVEN'T HAD TIME TO SEE ANYONE, JIMMY... LOIS! AS I WAS, UM--TELLING MY COUSIN...
...I WAS OUT ALL NIGHT GETTING AN EXCLUSIVE INTERVIEW WITH SUPERWOMAN--
--WHO HELPED OUT SUPERMAN WITH A FEW LITTLE CHORES!
SAVING THE WORLD... THINGS LIKE THAT...
SO IF YOU'LL EXCUSE ME, I'LL GO TYPE THIS UP--
--SO IT'LL BE NICE AND PRETTY FOR THE NEXT EDITION!
WHO ELECTED HIM NEWSMAN-OF-THE-WEEK?
39

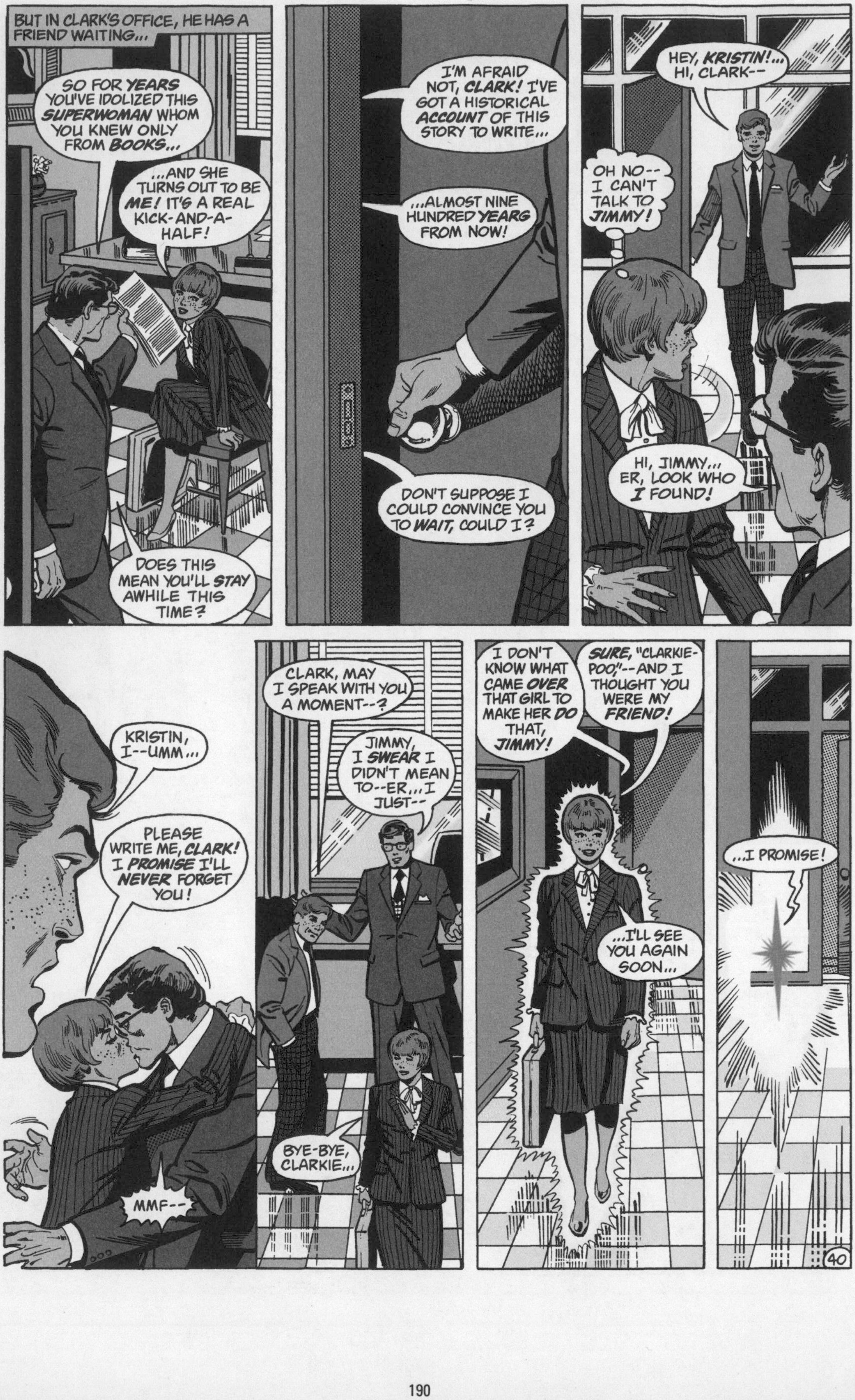
BUT IN CLARK'S OFFICE, HE HAS A FRIEND WAITING...
SO FOR YEARS YOU'VE IDOLIZED THIS SUPERWOMAN WHOM YOU KNEW ONLY FROM BOOKS...
...AND SHE TURNS OUT TO BE ME! IT'S A REAL KICK-AND-A-HALF!
DOES THIS MEAN YOU'LL STAY AWHILE THIS TIME?
I'M AFRAID NOT, CLARK! I'VE GOT A HISTORICAL ACCOUNT OF THIS STORY TO WRITE...
...ALMOST NINE HUNDRED YEARS FROM NOW!
DON'T SUPPOSE I COULD CONVINCE YOU TO WAIT, COULD I?
HEY, KRISTIN!... HI, CLARK--
OH NO-- I CAN'T TALK TO JIMMY!
HI, JIMMY... ER, LOOK WHO I FOUND!
KRISTIN, I--UMM...
PLEASE WRITE ME, CLARK! I PROMISE I'LL NEVER FORGET YOU!
MMF--
CLARK, MAY I SPEAK WITH YOU A MOMENT--?
JIMMY, I SWEAR I DIDN'T MEAN TO--ER... I JUST--
BYE-BYE, CLARKIE...
I DON'T KNOW WHAT CAME OVER THAT GIRL TO MAKE HER DO THAT, JIMMY!
SURE, "CLARKIE-POO,"--AND I THOUGHT YOU WERE MY FRIEND!
...I'LL SEE YOU AGAIN SOON...
...I PROMISE!
40

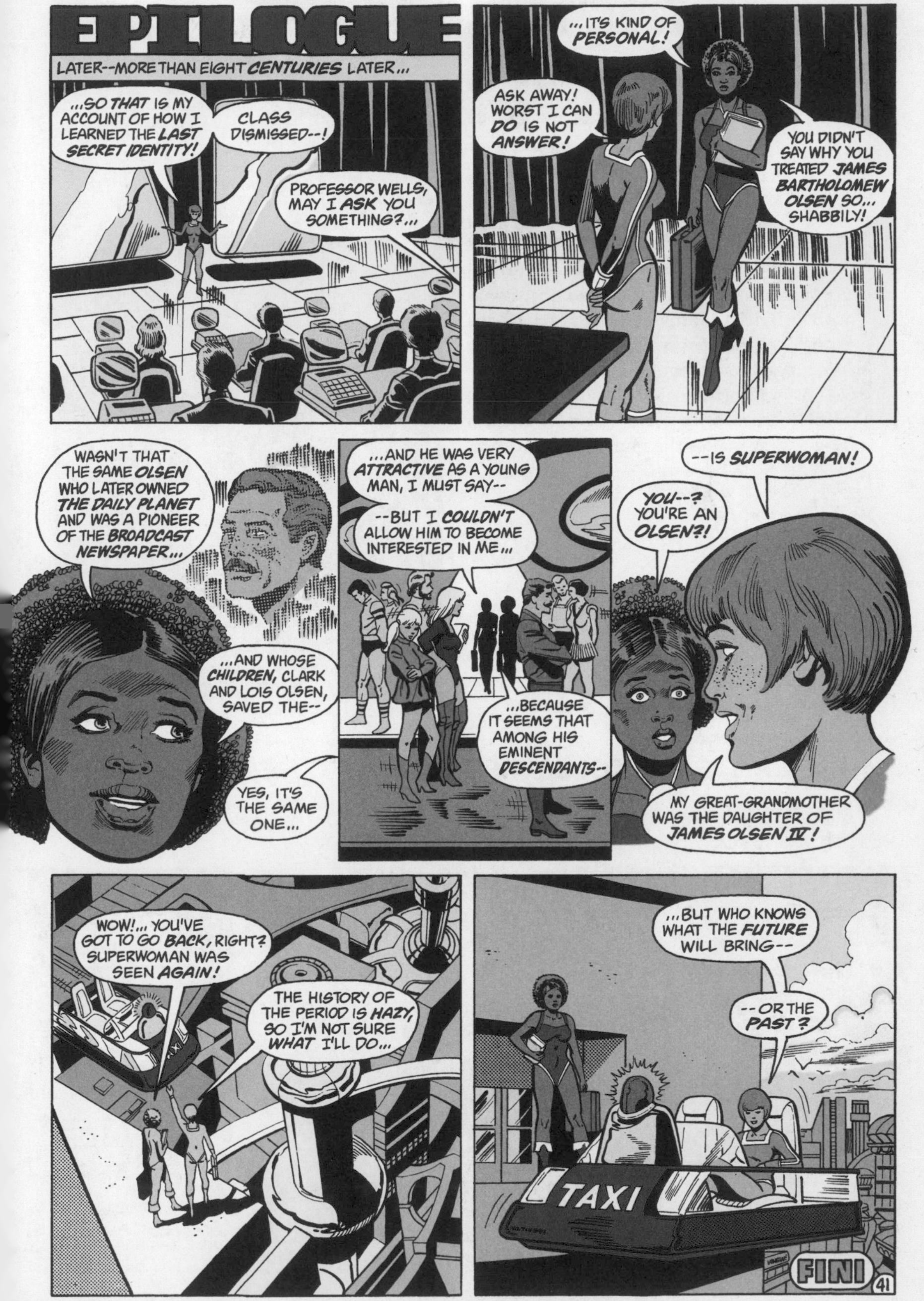
EPILOGUE
LATER--MORE THAN EIGHT CENTURIES LATER...
...SO THAT IS MY ACCOUNT OF HOW I LEARNED THE LAST SECRET IDENTITY!
CLASS DISMISSED--!
PROFESSOR WELLS, MAY I ASK YOU SOMETHING?...
...IT'S KIND OF PERSONAL!
ASK AWAY! WORST I CAN DO IS NOT ANSWER!
YOU DIDN'T SAY WHY YOU TREATED JAMES BARTHOLOMEW OLSEN SO... SHABBILY!
WASN'T THAT THE SAME OLSEN WHO LATER OWNED THE DAILY PLANET AND WAS A PIONEER OF THE BROADCAST NEWSPAPER...
...AND WHOSE CHILDREN, CLARK AND LOIS OLSEN, SAVED THE--
YES, IT'S THE SAME ONE...
...AND HE WAS VERY ATTRACTIVE AS A YOUNG MAN, I MUST SAY--
--BUT I COULDN'T ALLOW HIM TO BECOME INTERESTED IN ME...
...BECAUSE IT SEEMS THAT AMONG HIS EMINENT DESCENDANTS--
--IS SUPERWOMAN!
YOU--? YOU'RE AN OLSEN?!
MY GREAT-GRANDMOTHER WAS THE DAUGHTER OF JAMES OLSEN IV!
WOW!... YOU'VE GOT TO GO BACK, RIGHT? SUPERWOMAN WAS SEEN AGAIN!
THE HISTORY OF THE PERIOD IS HAZY, SO I'M NOT SURE WHAT I'LL DO...
...BUT WHO KNOWS WHAT THE FUTURE WILL BRING--
--OR THE PAST?
TAXI
FINI
41

**FROM THE WRITER OF
BATMAN: THE LONG HALLOWEEN**

JEPH LOEB

with TIM SALE

This coming-of-age tale is an emotional and insightful examination of Clark Kent's transformation from a powerful boy into a heroic man. Told through the course of four seasons in the Man of Steel's adolescent life, it illustrates that it is the person, not the powers, that makes the Man of Steel a hero.

MORE CRITICALLY ACCLAIMED TALES OF THE MAN OF STEEL

SUPERMAN:
FOR TOMORROW VOL. 1

SUPERMAN:
FOR TOMORROW VOL. 2

THE DEATH
OF SUPERMAN

**BRIAN AZZARELLO
JIM LEE**

**BRIAN AZZARELLO
JIM LEE**

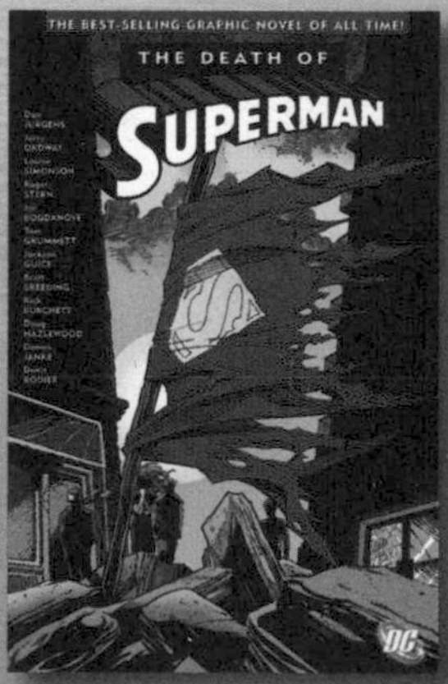

**VARIOUS
WRITERS & ARTISTS**

SEARCH THE GRAPHIC NOVELS SECTION OF
DCCOMICS.COM
FOR ART AND INFORMATION ON ALL OF OUR BOOKS!